TRAUMA BEGETS GENEALOGY

The Bible in the Modern World, 66

Series Editors
David J.A. Clines
J. Cheryl Exum

Amsterdam Studies in the Bible and Religion, 8

Series Editor
Athalya Brenner-Idan

TRAUMA BEGETS GENEALOGY

GENDER AND MEMORY IN CHRONICLES

Ingeborg Löwisch

SHEFFIELD PHOENIX PRESS

2015

Copyright © 2015 Sheffield Phoenix Press

Published by Sheffield Phoenix Press
Department of Biblical Studies, University of Sheffield
Sheffield S3 7QB

www.sheffieldphoenix.com

A CIP catalogue record for this book
is available from the British Library

Typeset by CA Typesetting Ltd
Printed on acid-free paper by Lightning Source

ISBN-13 978-1-909697-68-3
ISSN 1747-9630

Fortsetzung

Die wir uns
fortsetzen
durch Liebe

Wir geben uns hin
dem Tod
und nehmen uns
das Leben

vom Baum
der
Erkenntnis

Rose Ausländer

CONTENTS

ACKNOWLEDGEMENTS

Reconsidering the way this book—and the PhD behind it—came about, my gratitude first goes to Athalya Brenner, who developed the project with me, and taught me to trust my intuition as indispensable drive for a sound research project. Thank you for sharing your love for our field in such a generous way, which was, again and again, an extraordinary motivation for my own work. Thank you to Bob Becking who provided a paid position to manifest the project in a book and supported me with a great openness to my interdisciplinary and feminist agenda. Thank you to Julia Noordegraf, who accompanied the research from the side of media studies and who encouraged me to formulate my own conclusions rather than to stop before the end of an argument. Thank you to Anne-Mareike Wetter, Emma England, Gemma Kwantes, Martin Ruf, Nienke Pruiksma, Annette Merz, Marjo Korpel, Arian Verheij and Anne-Marie Korte, who shared with me academic daily life in Utrecht and Amsterdam as colleagues, peers, mentors and friends: The larger research would not have been possible without the many tiny but precious exchanges of ideas next to the Uithof's copying machine or at the Oude Doelenstraat's Coffee Company. Thank you to David Clines for kindly accepting the manuscript for a publication in *The Bible in the Modern World* series, and to Ailsa Parkin for your support at Sheffield Phoenix Press.

Thank you to my friends and family for providing me with the love, support, empathy and sometimes criticism I needed to make my own way and to craft such a personal piece of work: thank you to Jutta Brettschneider, who accompanied the project from initial dream to ready manuscript as a true midwife of mind; to Tino Köhler, who provided me with a bed and good meal in the Netherlands whenever necessary; to Christiane Textor, Barbara Zeitler, Sina Vogt, Christine Meier, Annette Rosenfeld, Barbara Becker, Annette Kempken, Gesa Renken and Maike Stöckmann for your friendship and commitment. Thank you to my sister Henni Löwisch for doing the bulk of the copy-editing; to my siblings Anne Löwisch and Georg Löwisch and my parents Sigrun and Manfred Löwisch. Thank you to my spouse Marianne Löwisch for the love, joy, understanding and inspiration we share. You know that without your persistent support, I would not have managed to bring the project to such a good end.

A genealogy performs the past in view of the present, but would not make sense without hope for the future. The many children and teenagers of our extended family already shape the next generation. Among them, and dearest to me Noah and Ruth: To you I dedicate this book.

Hamburg, Spring 2015

ABBREVIATIONS

AB	Anchor Bible
ABD	David Noel Freedman (ed.), *The Anchor Bible Dictionary* (New York: Doubleday, 1992)
BBB	*Bonner biblische Beiträge*
BDR	Kocku von Stuckrad (ed.), *The Brill Dictionary of Religion* (Leiden: E.J. Brill, 2007)
BE	Biblische Enzyklopädie
BEATAJ	Beiträge zur Erforschung des Alten Testaments und des antiken Judentums
BHS	K. Ellinger and W. Rudolph (eds.), *Biblia Hebraica Stuttgartensia* (Stuttgart: Deutsche Bibelgesellschaft, 1983)
BIS	Biblical Interpretation Series
BKAT	Biblischer Kommentar zum Alten Testament
BZAW	Beihefte zur Zeitschrift für die Alttestamentliche Wissenschaft
CBOTS	Coniectanea Biblica, Old Testament Series
DCH	David J.A. Clines (ed.), *The Dictionary of Classical Hebrew* (Sheffield: Sheffield Academic Press, 1996)
DCLSt	Deuterocanonical and Cognate Literature Studies
FAT	Forschungen zum Alten Testament
HAT	Handbuch zum Alten Testament
HBS	Herders biblische Studien
HThKAT	*Herders Theologischer Kommentar zum Alten Testament*
ICC	*The International Critical Commentary*
Int. Zoo Yb.	*International Zoo Yearbook*
JBL	*Journal of Biblical Literature*
JHS	*The Journal of Hebrew Scriptures* (online http://www.jhsonline.org; accessed June 6, 2013)
JPS	Jewish Publication Society
JSOT	*Journal for the Study of the Old Testament*
JSOTSup	Journal for the Study of the Old Testament, Supplement Series
JSS	*Journal of Semitic Studies*
KAT	Kommentar zum Alten Testament
LHBOTS	Library Hebrew Bible/Old Testament Studies
LXX	Septuagint
MT	Masoretic Text
NCamBC	*New Cambridge Bible Commentary*
NCB	New Century Bible

NRSV	New Revised Standard Version
OTS	Oudtestamentische Studiën, Old Testament Studies
SBLAcBib	Society of Biblical Literature, Academia Biblica
SBS	Stuttgarter Bibelstudien
SEThV	Salzburger Exegetische Theologische Vorträge
SKG.G	Schriften der Königsberger Gelehrten Gesellschaft, Geisteswissenschaftliche Klasse
SNTSMS	Society for New Testament Studies Monograph Series
SR	*Studies in Religion/Sciences Religieuses*
SSN	Studia Semitica Neerlandica
STHV	*Science, Technology & Human Values*
VHB	*Verklaring van de Hebreeuwse Bijbel*
VTSup	Vetus Testamentum, Supplement
VWGTh	Veröffentlichungen der Wissenschaftlichen Gesellschaft für Theologie
WiS	Carol Meyers, Ross Kraemer and Toni Craven (eds.), *Women in Scripture: A Dictionary of Named and Unnamed Women in the Hebrew Bible, the Apocryphal / Deuterocanonical Books and the New Testament* (Boston, MA: Houghton Mifflin Company, 2000)

INTRODUCTION

This is the list of the descendants of Adam. When God created humankind, he made them in the likeness of God. Male and female he created them, and he blessed them and named them 'Humankind' when they were created.

When Adam had lived one hundred thirty years, he became the father of a son in his likeness, according to his image, and named him Seth. The days of Adam after he became the father of Seth were eight hundred years; and he had other sons and daughters. Thus all the days that Adam lived were nine hundred thirty years; and he died.

When Seth had lived one hundred five years, he became the father of Enosh. Seth lived after the birth of Enosh eight hundred seven years, and had other sons and daughters. Thus all the days of Seth were nine hundred twelve years; and he died.

When Enosh had lived ninety years, he became the father of Kenan. Enosh lived after the birth of Kenan eight hundred fifteen years, and had other sons and daughters. Thus all the days of Enosh were nine hundred five years; and he died.

When Kenan had lived seventy years, he became the father of Mahalalel. Kenan lived after the birth of Mahalalel eight hundred and forty years, and had other sons and daughters. Thus all the days of Kenan were nine hundred and ten years; and he died.

When Mahalalel had lived sixty-five years, he became the father of Jared. Mahalalel lived after the birth of Jared eight hundred thirty years, and had other sons and daughters. Thus all the days of Mahalalel were eight hundred ninety-five years; and he died.

When Jared had lived one hundred sixty-two years he became the father of Enoch. Jared lived after the birth of Enoch eight hundred years, and had other sons and daughters. Thus all the days of Jared were nine hundred sixty-two years; and he died.

When Enoch had lived sixty-five years, he became the father of Methuselah. Enoch walked with God after the birth of Methuselah three hundred years, and had other sons and daughters. Thus all the days of Enoch were three hundred sixty-five years. Enoch walked with God; then he was no more, because God took him.

When Methuselah had lived one hundred eighty-seven years, he became the father of Lamech. Methuselah lived after the birth of Lamech seven hundred eighty-two years, and had other sons and daughters. Thus all the days of Methuselah were nine hundred sixty-nine years; and he died.

When Lamech had lived one hundred eighty-two years, he became the father of a son; he named him Noah, saying, 'Out of the ground that the LORD has cursed this one shall bring us relief from our work and from the toil of our hands'. Lamech lived after the birth of Noah five hundred ninety-five years, and had other sons and daughters. Thus all the days of Lamech were seven hundred seventy-seven years; and he died.

After Noah was five hundred years old, Noah became the father of Shem, Ham, and Japheth (Genesis 5, NRSV).

This book is about genealogies. To be precise, it is about gendered genealogies and the question of how they function in response to fractured pasts. But what exactly are genealogies? In what respect are they gendered? In what way might seemingly dry lists of names be meaningful for coping with traumatic pasts?

An ancient and somehow prototypical genealogy is the list of generations, or *toledoth*, in Genesis 5 (quoted above). The structure of the genealogy is iterative and rhythmic. Wandering down the generations, the text connects one life cycle to the next and unfolds a succession of fathers from Adam to Noah. After the disturbing narrative of the fratricide in Genesis 4, the rhythmic list comes as a relief. It reassures us that the line of life was not broken, but is still passed on from generation to generation. And indeed, the first impulse for this research originates in my memory of the Genesis *toledoth* as conveyed to me in Sunday School: music, carried on by the beat of life.[1]

But then, Genesis 5 is also a disturbing text. The lineage is completely male-centered. Genesis 5.1-2 recalls that humankind was created as masculine and feminine in the likeness of God (Gen. 1.27), but does not mention the feminine/Eve any more. Similarly, mothers are generally missing. From a female standpoint, the text is difficult to identify with.

And there are other disturbing elements. For example, Gen. 5.24 breaks with the iterative rhythmic structure: it does not round off the life cycle of Enoch, but recounts that he was taken by God. Moreover, the basic principle of succession is modified the moment it is installed: Gen. 5.3 does not list Cain, the firstborn of Adam, but Seth, the son who was given to Eve in place of her murdered son Abel.

This latter fracture, no more than a fissure, struck my interest. Here, the *toledoth*, in a tiny deviation from the principal structure, responds to the traumatic violence in the narratives of the beginnings. The text skips the firstborn, Cain, does not mention Abel, the second son, but builds the lineage on the substitute son, Seth. This moment of deviation opens a space for life to be handed down and the lineage to continue.

The ideological stance of the genealogy becomes even more apparent when looking at a second genealogy in the same narrative vicinity:

1.   For the rhythmic nature of the Genesis genealogies see Franziska Bark, 'The God Who Will Be and the Generations of Men: Time and the Torah', in *Judaism* 49 (2000), pp. 259-68 (259-60).

Cain knew his wife and she conceived and bore Enoch; and he built a city and named it Enoch after his son Enoch. To Enoch was born Irad; and Irad was the father of Mehujael and Mehujael the father of Methushael and Methushael the father of Lamech. Lamech took two wives; the name of the one was Adah and the name of the other Zillah. Adah bore Jabal; he was the ancestor of those who live in tents and have livestock. His brother's name was Jubal; he was the ancestor of all those who play the lyre and pipe. Zillah bore Tubal-cain, who made all kinds of bronze and iron tools. The sister of Tubal-cain was Naamah (Gen. 4.17-22, NRSV).

Genesis 4 recalls the descendants of Cain and his anonymous wife over seven generations. It is constructed as a segmented genealogy, much less regular in form and quite different in character from the *toledoth* in Genesis 5.[2] The line branches out by listing the mothers and co-wives Adah and Zillah and presents their sons as founders of civilization and the arts. The text also lists their daughter Naamah in a fragment that might be read as presenting her as mother of professional singers.[3]

The genealogies in Genesis 4 and 5 respond to the fracturing events of the preceding narratives in extremely different ways. Here we have a segmented list; there we have a rhythmic *toledoth*. Here we have Adah and Zillah, mothers of founders of culture, and a fragment about Zillah's daughter Naamah; there we have the absence of mothers and only a general hint about the anonymous daughters. Here we have the pursuit of the line of Cain, the firstborn; there we have the decision to trust the continuation of the line to Seth, the substitute son.

The different ways in which Gen. 4.17-22 and Genesis 5 deal with the traumatic backstory point to the deliberate, ideological and performative character of genealogies. In the case of Genesis 5, the features interfering with the smooth course of the iterative clear-cut structure are critical starting points for an understanding of the particular ways in which this genealogy performs the past. Such interfering features are variation of form, deviation from the dominant rule of succession and gender. More generally speaking, the example of Genesis 5 points to fractures and irregularities as

2. Following a broad scholarly consensus on the setup of Genesis, I assume that the genealogies in Gen. 4 and 5 derive from different sources. See Konrad Schmid, *Literaturgeschichte des Alten Testaments: Eine Einführung* (Darmstadt: Wissenschaftliche Buchgesellschaft, 2008), pp. 37-39, 153-56. Still, the final version of the book, which places the two genealogies side by side, urges us to consider the one when reading the other. So, e.g., Joseph Blenkinsopp, *Creation, Un-creation, Re-creation: A Discursive Commentary on Genesis 1–11* (Edinburgh: T. & T. Clark, 2011), pp. 82-105.

3. One possible reading of the name Naamah is 'singer'. Hence, Naamah might have been the ancestor of the vocal singers in accordance with her brothers who are listed as eponymous ancestors of different arts and crafts. See U. Cassuto, *A Commentary on the Book of Genesis* (trans. Israel Abraham; Jerusalem: Magnes Press, 1944), p. 238; and Carol Meyers, 'Naamah', in *WiS*, p. 129.

keys to understanding how genealogies function in response to traumatic pasts.

Reading Genesis 5, I formed the hypothesis that fractures and variations would serve as apt places to learn more about how genealogies function as a form of memory in the aftermath of trauma and crisis.[4] During my research, looking at the genealogies of the Hebrew Bible at large substantiated this hypothesis. It also showed that irregularity is often coupled with references to women. As a consequence, gender appeared to be a critical notion in exploring the genealogies' capacity to respond to traumatic and disturbing pasts.

In the Hebrew Bible, genealogical references to women often appear as fragments, such as the hint at Eve in Gen. 5.2, or the reference to Naamah, the singing one, in Gen. 4.22. Involving gender in my research on Hebrew Bible genealogies immediately raised the problem of how to deal with the fragmented character of female-gendered references. In order to fully understand how fractures, variation and gender interplay in the genealogies' capacity to respond to traumatic pasts, I decided to call in one extrabiblical genealogy that would feature gender in a more central place than the biblical genealogies do, hence serving as a point of comparison or control. In doing so, I went to the other extreme and settled on using female lineages as portrayed in a contemporary documentary film. This sharp contrast facilitated the carving out of the particular form and functions of the gendered fragments. In addition, the different perspectives of gendered genealogies—here gendered fragments, there an elaborated female line—established a balance that was necessary to draw more general lines and discuss gendered genealogy performance beyond the case studies.

The genealogies in the Hebrew Bible are diverse, as are female lineages in contemporary film. Still, in surveying my materials, pairs suggested themselves on the basis of particular core themes. The pair I eventually settled on was the genealogy composition in 1 Chronicles 1–9 and the 2003 post-Shoah documentary film *My Life Part 2* by Berlin filmmaker Angelika Levi.[5]

---

4. My understanding of trauma is based on Cathy Caruth's definition of trauma as 'unclaimed experience' (Cathy Caruth, *Unclaimed Experience: Trauma, Narrative and History* [Baltimore, MD: Johns Hopkins University Press, 1996]).

5. Other pairs that I considered were the genealogies of Genesis together with *Antonia's Line* (dir. Marleen Gorris, NL, 1995), a pair that would have highlighted the issues of female reproduction and its control, sexual violence and the role of outsiders; as well as the biblical fragments on Serah bat Asher and her afterlife in rabbinical literature together with the films *Mrs Dalloway* (dir. Marleen Gorris, UK/NL, 1996) and *The Hours* (dir. Stephen Daldry, US, 2001), a pair that would have highlighted the issues of female ancestors and identification and symbolic and especially literary lineages.

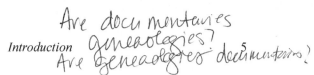

My Life Part 2 documents the life of the filmmaker's mother during National Socialism and in post-war Germany in a collage of archive materials. It addresses how the traumatic childhood of her mother impacts the life of the family and explores intersections of personal and political histories with regard to Jewish-German identities in Germany today. The composition of a female lineage that serves as anchor point for the filmmaker's appropriating her traumatic legacy and responding to it is located at the center of the film.

On a formal level, I decided to work with a documentary because the biblical genealogies and the genre of documentary film feature an intriguing overlap of central topics, e.g. the relation of fact and fiction; interconnections of past and present; the notion of framing; implications of editing; and the role of narrative.[6] Moreover, reading Bible texts alongside documentaries constitutes new ground in Biblical Studies, thus allowing me to engage in highly innovative research. On the level of content, *My Life Part 2* contributed three key aspects: first, the notion of discontinuity as part of and precondition for gendered genealogy composition in response to trauma; second, the interplay of given and imagined lineages with regard to a resource-oriented genealogy composition; and third, the notion of the archive as key to understanding genealogical memory acts in the context of traumatic pasts.

1 Chronicles 1–9 provides a heterogeneous nine-chapter-long genealogy composition. The genealogies start with Adam and end with the first returnees from Exile. Most tribes are covered, but there is a strong focus on Judah and Levi. The genealogies propose a self-conception of Israel before the real story begins (1 Chron. 10–2 Chron. 36). This self-conception responds to fracturing events of contemporaneous history.[7] It presents a strong statement in the context of controversial discourses on memory and identities, and contested claims on religious and sociopolitical authority and land in the postexilic period.[8]

The book of Chronicles is often read as a conservative, rather patriarchal account of Israel's past, which smoothes out everything that might shed a

---

6. See Bill Nichols, *Introduction to Documentary* (Bloomington, IN: Indiana University Press, 2001); and Stella Bruzzi, *New Documentary: A Critical Introduction* (London: Routledge, 2000).

7. Fracturing events concern the destruction of state and temple, deportations and exile in the early sixth century BCE, as well as the emergence of Jewish centers in the Diaspora with the parallel restoration in Judah/Yehud. For an introduction in 1 Chronicles 1–9, including discussion on its dating, see Chapter 3, below.

8. I use the terms 'political' and 'sociopolitical' not in the strict literal sense of state politics, but in a more general sense that includes sociopolitical movements and discourses.

negative light on David, Jerusalem and the temple.[9] Accordingly, the gene-alogies might be expected to be patrilinear, male-centered, pro-Davidic and keen to rule out contradictions or dead ends. This, however, does not turn out to be so. 1 Chronicles 1–9 is indeed a largely male-centered composi-tion of patrilineages. Nevertheless, it features more than fifty women, some of them in rather unexpected positions. For example, Sheerah, the daugh-ter of Ephraim, is listed as builder of three cities (1 Chron. 7.24). The gene-alogies of Judah (2.3–4.23) in particular feature a dense web of references to women. They are listed as female members of the house of David or for-eign women, eponymous ancestresses or nameless wives, female heads of houses or sisters without history. Tiny as they are, the female fragments interrupt, roughen and partly subvert the patrilinear succession.

1 Chronicles 1–9 does not comply with prevalent expectations in yet another way: its genealogies are heterogeneous, sometimes chaotic and incomplete. In the case of Judah, lineages are often fractured, endangered, or only loosely connected. The genealogies of 1 Chronicles 1–9, and espe-cially the lineages of Judah, do not run smoothly. Instead, they involve rup-tures, loose ends and gendered fragments that, in fact, make statements about Israel's past, present, and future. They provide an excellent opportu-nity to study how fractures and gender interact in a genealogy composition that responds to a traumatic past.

1 Chronicles 1–9 features gender in a most distinctive way, namely in the form of gendered fragments. This quality implies a particular angle for analysis. The second case study, the documentary *My Life Part 2*, tack-les gender in genealogy composition from an entirely different vantage point—the angle of female-centered lineage, or *gynealogy* composition, as I have decided to call it in the film analysis in Chapter 5. The additional perspective of gynealogy composition balances the perspectives on gen-dered genealogy composition and addresses the possibility of alternative or counter-present genealogy performances.

In *My Life Part 2*, Berlin filmmaker Angelika Levi documents the life of her mother Ursula Levi in the context of her Jewish-German family story during National Socialism and later on in West Germany. Building on the personal collections of her mother, the film arranges interview excerpts, audio records, home movies, photographs and memorial objects into an archive that is introduced and explained by the personal voice-over of the filmmaker. The archive is organized around a female line, the lineage of Levi women. In the film, this lineage is spelled out from the filmmaker's great-grandmother down to herself. However, this is only a piece of a larger, imagined lineage, which the filmmaker's mother, Ursula Levi, traces down

   9.   Pancratius C. Beentjes, *Tradition and Transformation in the Book of Chronicles* (SSN, 52; Leiden: E.J. Brill, 2008), pp. 1-13.

from the biblical Levi to herself. The film recalls the past, but likewise addresses the question: How can the filmmaker, as artist and as daughter, respond to her traumatic legacy? The format of an experimental documentary film allows the filmmaker to address the relevant issues in closer compliance with the genealogy genre than a family saga would. For example, the skeleton-like structure that is so characteristic of genealogies appears in a sequence of photographs of murdered family members (00:18:40). In this visual genealogy, photographs are shown in succession, while the voice-over only gives the name, date and place of the murder.

My Life Part 2 represents an increasing interest in notions of genealogy and generation in contemporary literature and film. Beyond conventional family sagas, such works explore the potential of genealogical and generational narratives that deal with family mythology and secrets, economic interdependencies, chosen genealogies, denials of the future, afterlife of the dead and the ongoing impact of memories and legacies. Such works bring still-existing links between generations as well as their fragility to the fore.[10]

Against the backdrop of this interest is a recent crisis in traditional modes of transferring memories, traditions and identities. These modes of transfer usually presuppose intact relationship models over three generations, as well as functioning social frames.[11] However, an increasing normality of migration, diasporic identities and cultural hybridity has led to substantial changes in the constitution of families and peer groups.[12] These changes shake and alienate generational bonds, rendering 'the traditional modes for transmitting cultural, ethnic and racial memory—both memories passed from parent to child and those disseminated through community life— increasingly inadequate.'[13] Moreover, traumatic histories, such as the Shoah or slavery in the USA, induce a breaking apart of relations between parents

10. So the advertisement of the *Literaturtage 2008:* 'Am Nullpunkt der Familie: Generationen und Genealogien in der Gegenwartsliteratur' and corresponding research projects at the *Zentrum für Literatur- und Kulturforschung Berlin* (http://www.zfl-berlin.org/veranstaltungen-detail/items/am-nullpunkt-der-familie-generationen-und-genealogien-in-der-geg.html, accessed June 8, 2013).

11. E.g. Paul Connerton, who, in his conceptualizing cultural memory as acts of transfer, attributes a key role to the relationship between grandparents and grandchildren. Paul Connerton, *How Societies Remember* (Cambridge: Cambridge University Press, 1989), pp. 39-40. For the idea of social frames as the basis of memory production, see Maurice Halbwachs, *Das Gedächtnis und seine sozialen Bedingungen* (ed. Heinz Maus and Friedrich Fürstenberg; trans. Lutz Geldsetzer; Berlin: Luchterhand, 1966), especially pp. 361-90.

12. See *Shooting the Family: Transnational Media and Intercultural Values* (ed. Patricia Pisters and Wim Staat; Amsterdam: Amsterdam University Press, 2005).

13. Alison Landsberg, *Prosthetic Memory: The Transformation of American Remembrance in the Age of Mass Culture* (New York: Columbia University Press, 2004), p. 2.

and children, as well as between individuals and communities, making traditional modes of transfer insufficient and/or inaccessible.[14]

Working with *My Life Part 2* and the filmmaker's struggle for an artistic expression of her legacy in the discourse on post-Shoah memory in Germany and beyond, meant throwing a spotlight on the recent crisis of modes
of transfer that forms the backdrop of this research. It is a crisis that echoes
the crisis of memory transfer which is likewise present in the biblical text.
For me, it shifted the attention from identity to memory performance. It
also showed how the study of the biblical genealogies can be important to
the present. Hence, my research feeds into the extra-biblical discussion on
modes of transfer and provides an additional historical perspective on it.

The initial drive to pair 1 Chronicles 1–9 and *My Life Part 2* was based
on their heterogeneous form: both Bible text and film assemble their genealogies from bits and pieces. In the case of 1 Chronicles 1–9, heterogeneity is often assessed negatively, or at least considered highly problematic.[15]
In the reception of *My Life Part 2*, however, heterogeneity is related to
the archival character of the documentary and assessed positively.[16] In the
course of reading *My Life Part 2* alongside 1 Chronicles 1–9, interpreting
the film's collage as an archive opened up a way of making sense of the heterogeneous character of 1 Chronicles 1–9. As I hope to show in Chapter 6,
the notion of archive can function as a shared concept for genealogy composition in response to a fractured past: it allows tracing a genealogical taxonomy, while at the same time departing from it again and again, with the
intention of accounting for breaks, fragments and loose ends in memory
performance, more often gendered than not.

While the archive notion opened the way for looking at the taxonomy of
the genealogy composition in 1 Chronicles 1–9, the sisters in the lineages of
Judah, Manasseh and Ephraim drove me to a deeper understanding of how
gender functions in the composition's response to the crisis of exile and the
postexilic reconceptualization of Jewish identities. 1 Chronicles 1–9 features a set of references to sisters. For example, 1 Chronicles 3 provides

---

14. Landsberg, *Prosthetic Memory*, p. 2. Landsberg consequently proposes 'prosthetic memories' as new/alternative modes of transfer. See my Chapter 1, below. I here
refer to the Shoah and slavery in the USA even though more recent traumatic histories could be named. Yet, they have continued impact and are still the central reference
points in the scholarly and cultural discourse on cultural memory. See, e.g., Marianne
Hirsch and Valerie Smith, 'Feminism and Cultural Memory: An Introduction', *Signs*
28.1 (2002), pp. 1-19.

15. Exemplary in this respect is Julius Wellhausen, *Prolegomena zur Geschichte
Israels* (Berlin: W. de Gruyter, 6th edn, 1927), pp. 206-17; see especially his discussion
of the genealogies of Manasseh (1 Chron. 7.14-19), p. 209.

16. Madeleine Bernstorff, 'MEIN LEBEN TEIL 2 von Angelika Levi, D 2003' (http://
www.madeleinebernstorff.de/seiten/lebentx.html, accessed June 8, 2013).

the lineage of the house of David down to the postexilic Davidites. The lineage is entirely male, with the exception of 1 Chron. 3.19, which lists two sons of Zerubbabel and adds: 'and Shelomith, their sister'. In a similar way, the genealogies of Asher in 1 Chron. 7.30-40 include the sisters Serah and Shua.

> The sons of Asher: Imnah, Ishvah, Ishvi, Beriah, and their sister Serah. The sons of Beriah: Heber and Malchiel, who was the father of Birzaith. Heber became the father of Japhlet, Shomer, Hotham, and their sister Shua. The sons of Japhlet: Pasach, Bimhal, and Ashvath. These are the sons of Japhlet (1 Chron. 7.30-33, NRSV).

References to sisters come in a particular iterative formulation and run throughout the genealogical archive. Many of the sisters are otherwise unknown. Names such as Shelomith, Shua and Hazzelelponi (1 Chron. 4.3) do not have a familiar ring. As such, the text remains utterly incomprehensible as to why they are included. Yet, they are included, and this specific form of presentation creates what I have called a 'structure of shaped gaps'.[17] Shaped gaps are gaps that do not simply become apparent between the lines, but are specifically pointed out, to bring them into focus. These gaps introduce a counter-movement: while the frequent identification of woman figures as wives and mothers of sons co-establishes the picture of a genealogical stream, recalling seemingly non-functional sisters evokes the image of coves in this stream. Centering on woman figures who remain without a story, these coves are not filled but bequeathed as particularly shaped and thus obvious gaps. Shaped gaps work in different directions. As gaps, they repress the remembrance of woman figures. As visibly shaped formations, they recall that there is more to remember than the texts actually do. Recurring again and again, they invite projection and gap-filling and suggest a potential to recall absent and marginalized groups beyond the biblical genealogies. Finally, looking at the structure of shaped gaps from the angle of archival taxonomy, they propose that still waters and absence of movement are a critical part of a genealogical memory act in response to trauma.

My Life Part 2 features a dynamic which I understood to be connected with the structure of shaped gaps only at a later stage. Watching the film again and again, what struck me most was the crack in the middle of its gynealogy. The filmmaker carefully sets up a lineage of mothers, ideologically shaped, but then, in a personal voice-over, states that she herself will not become a mother, but has decided to live with women and remain childless. The scene likewise establishes a counter-movement to the otherwise

---

17. Ingeborg Löwisch, 'Genealogies, Gender and the Politics of Memory: 1 Chronicles 1–9 and the Documentary Film "Mein Leben Teil 2"', in *Memory in Biblical Narrative and Beyond* (ed. Athalya Brenner and Frank Polak; Sheffield: Sheffield Phoenix Press, 2009), pp. 228-56 (243-44).

dominant sense of continuous succession. Paradoxical as it might be, this move is a precondition for the filmmaker's appropriation of her traumatic legacy and of making sense of the past, as I will further demonstrate in Chapter 5.

Investigating the structure of shaped gaps in 1 Chronicles 1–9 as well as the film's paradox of breaking up the carefully built lineage of mothers has had major consequences for the setup of this book. The frequent occurrence of female figures without a story in 1 Chronicles 1–9, sisters and others, brought me from an interest in identification with female ancestors, which had prevailed in the beginnings of my research, to placing emphasis on the question: how does gender work on a functional structural level within a genealogical memory act?[18] Shifting away from the focus on identification involved a whole set of new themes. Focusing on identification had bound my attention to issues of identity and to the importance of continuity in reconstructing the past, both of which are broadly accepted issues in the exegetical discussion on genealogies. Moreover, focusing on identification tied in with the mainstream of feminist exegesis, which centers on prominent female figures such as Sarah, Judith, Esther, or Lady Wisdom. Shifting the attention to fractures, gaps, and structural functions of the females listed opened the way for bringing notions of discontinuity and paradox to the fore. These are aspects which I regard as crucial to fully delving into the issue of genealogies responding to traumatic pasts. The moment of breaking up the carefully constructed line of mothers in *My Life Part 2* supported this shift, inasmuch as it confirmed my assumption that breaks and contradictions are critical drivers for genealogy performance in response to trauma.

Shifting away from identification raised yet another question. If feminist Bible criticism is not tied to a primary interest in the character and story of women, the mass of (exclusively) male-centered texts in the Hebrew Bible comes into focus, be they genealogies, legal texts, wisdom literature, or narratives. Taking this much broader text basis into view led me to ask what form feminist hermeneutics can or should take without female figures, female voices, or power relations between men and women on which to focus—and it allowed me to develop preliminary answers.[19]

18. My initial interest in identification with female ancestors is reflected in Ingeborg Löwisch, 'Frauengenealogien in Film und Hebräischer Bibel: Erinnerungsformen und politische Akte', *Schlangenbrut* 23 (2005), pp. 14-18.

19. The problematic absence of feminist criticism of 'intransigent and arid' texts such as the book of Chronicles and Ezra–Nehemiah has also been highlighted by Roland Boer. See Roland Boer, 'No Road: On the Absence of Feminist Criticism of Ezra–Nehemiah', in *Her Master's Tools?: Feminist and Postcolonial Engagements of Historical-Critical Discourse* (ed. Caroline Vander Stichele and Todd Penner; Global Perspectives on Biblical Literature, 9; Atlanta, GA: Society of Biblical Literature, 2005), pp. 233-52 (233).

Methodology

Reading a Bible text in conjunction with a film that does not recycle biblical narratives or notions, but shares a common interest with the Bible text, constitutes new ground. I therefore needed to develop a methodology which would allow bringing both genealogies together, and to make sense of them in view of my question: how do gendered genealogies function in response to traumatic and disturbing pasts? For my methodology, I built on the notion of intertextuality as proposed by Julia Kristeva,[20] but also borrowed from the field of biology and used the concept of socializing. In biology, socializing means that different species are brought to the same environment. This 'cohousing' does not only aim at coexistence, but likewise tries to create a setting that is beneficial for both parties.[21] Used as a metaphorical term, the notion of socializing describes both Bible text and film as dwelling in the same analytical space, both providing impulses for the analyses. An important aspect of socializing is to provide a frame for the analytical space. In the same way as in the natural sciences, where the environment of co-housing is crucial, the success of effectively socializing Bible text and film depends on the strength of the analytical frame. The analytical frame of this project is based on notions of cultural memory, as well as on notions of archival theory, performance theory and Gender Studies included in the broader concept of Memory Studies. It allows for analyzing Bible text and film independently, using the tools of the disciplines they belong to. At the same time, the setting allows for bringing similar questions to both texts, reading each one from the perspective, as well as to the benefit, of the other. I set up the analytical frame in Chapter 1 and explain the methodology of socializing in Chapter 2.

My research on gendered genealogies in response to trauma builds on ongoing research on the genealogies in the Hebrew Bible, especially on 1 Chronicles 1–9. Most fundamental in this respect is Robert Wilson's proposition to analyze biblical genealogies with categories derived from anthropological research into oral tribal genealogies.[22] Key categories in this approach are the notions of segmentation, depth and fluidity. Segmentation describes the branching out of genealogies. It maps—and proposes— affiliation and difference. Depth refers to the length of a given lineage, often related to claims of authority in the present, for example, claims to offices or land. Finally, fluidity describes—and acknowledges—the fact that genealogies may change, according to the actual needs of the situation in which

---

20. Julia Kristeva, *Desire in Language: A Semiotic Approach to Literature and Art* (ed. Leon S. Roudiez; trans. Thomas Gora, Alice Jardine and Leon S. Roudiez; New York: Columbia University Press, 1980). For an introduction to the concept of intertextuality, see Chapter 2, below.

21. N. Dorman and D.C. Bourne, 'Canids and ursids in mixed-species Exhibits', *Int. Zoo Yb.* 44 (2010), pp. 75-86 (76-77).

22. Robert R. Wilson, *Genealogies and History in the Biblical World* (New Haven, CT: Yale University Press, 1977).

they are performed. This implies that different genealogies that process the same data can exist side by side, both being equally true but responding to different contexts and settings.[23]

Even though comparing biblical textual genealogies with tribal oral genealogies has been critiqued,[24] Wilson's work has had a deep impact on issues central to subsequent research into the genealogies of the Hebrew Bible, such as on the issues of identity;[25] continuity and lineage bond power claims;[26] and the ideological and theological character of a given genealogy and the literary functions it fulfills.[27] A key work in this development is Thomas Hieke's synchronic reception-aesthetic study of the *toledoth* system of the book of Genesis, in which he identifies: (a) sociocultural, political and ethnic functions, among them the construction of identity; (b) literary functions; and (c) the theological message, as main targets of this set of genealogies.[28] More generally speaking, research on Hebrew Bible genealogies has started to interpret the biblical genealogies as purposefully designed entities that advance ideological worldviews and pursue theological as well as political aims in the community of their composers. As to 1 Chronicles 1–9, such an understanding of genealogies is still a relatively recent development. For example, one important result of Manfred Oeming's 1990 monograph on 1 Chronicles 1–9 is that the genealogy composition must indeed be understood as a kerygmatic text.[29] In this context, research into new collections of comparative materials, for example ancient Greek genealogical literature, has been critical for appreciating the ideological character of 1 Chronicles 1–9.[30]

23. Wilson, *Genealogies and History*, pp. 18-36.

24. E.g., Manfred Oeming, *Das wahre Israel: Die 'genealogische Vorhalle' 1 Chronik 1–9* (Stuttgart: Kohlhammer, 1990), p. 72.

25. E.g., Irmtraud Fischer, *Die Erzeltern Israels: Feministisch-theologische Studien zu Genesis* (BZAW, 222; Berlin: W. de Gruyter, 1994); Ehud Ben Zvi, *History, Literature and Theology in the Book of Chronicles* (London: Equinox, 2006); Gary N. Knoppers, 'Intermarriage, Social Complexity and Ethnic Diversity in the Genealogy of Judah', *Journal of Biblical Literature* 120 (2001), pp. 15-30.

26. E.g., Marshall D. Johnson, *The Purpose of the Biblical Genealogies with Special Reference to the Setting of the Genealogies of Jesus* (Cambridge: Cambridge University Press, 1969), pp. 42, 79.

27. E.g., Sara Japhet, *The Ideology of the Book of Chronicles and Its Place in Biblical Thought* (BEATAJ, 9; Frankfurt: Peter Lang, 1997); and Thomas Hieke, *Die Genealogien der Genesis* (HBS, 39; Freiburg: Herder, 2003).

28. Hieke, *Die Genealogien der Genesis*, pp. 343-52 (345).

29. Oeming, *Das wahre Israel*, pp. 206-207.

30. G.N. Knoppers, *1 Chronicles 1–9: A New Translation with Introduction and Commentary* (AB, 12; New York: Doubleday, 2003), pp. 254-57. See also Oeming, who discusses contemporaneous comparative materials from Greece, Egypt and Persia. Oeming, *Das wahre Israel*, pp. 22-36.

While there is growing research on Hebrew Bible genealogies, only a handful of studies thoroughly investigate the texts from a gender perspective.[31] More often than not, references to women are not carefully looked at, if at all. For example, commentaries regularly pass over references to sisters in 1 Chronicles 1–9, or read them superficially.[32] Prominent in this respect is Oeming, who does not even differentiate between the terms sister (אחות) and daughter (בת).[33] At the same time, the significance of the passages is played down. Indeed, Oeming argues that the genealogies of Judah present a succession of 'particular important males', whereas women play only negative roles in the texts, or have no roles at all.[34]

This notorious failure to meet the challenge to provide a convincing analysis of these often difficult passages is striking, for several reasons. First of all, most genealogies indeed include references to women. Secondly, a focus on gender suggests itself, given the research focus on identity and power. Finally, as a rule, the genealogies are strongly gendered: they usually attribute competence to pass on the line to the male members of the community. This rule of succession means that they have a strongly male-gendered building plan before women actually appear. As I will argue, this configuration qualifies gender to have a leading part in all functions that complicate and subvert the succession.[35] Hence, gender should be an inher-

31. E.g., Isa Breitmaier, 'Angestaute Gegenwart: Zur Zeitkonstruktion in Genealogien (Gen 5)', in *Zeit wahrnehmen: Feministisch-Theologische Perspektiven auf das Erste Testament* (ed. Hedwig-Jahnow-Forschungsprojekt; SBS, 222; Stuttgart: Katholisches Bibelwerk, 2010), pp. 66-99; Thomas Hieke, 'Genealogie als Mittel der Geschichtsdarstellung in der Tora und die Rolle der Frauen im genealogischen System', in *Hebräische Bibel—Altes Testament: Tora* (ed. Irmtraud Fischer, Mercedes Puerto Navarra, and Andrea Taschl-Erber; Die Bibel und die Frauen, 1.1; Stuttgart: W. Kohlhammer, 2009), pp. 149–85; Julie Kelso, *Oh Mother, Where Art Thou?: An Irigarayan Reading of the Book of Chronicles* (London: Equinox, 2007), pp. 115-66; Jan Willem van Henten, 'Judith as an Alternative Leader: A Rereading of Judith 7–13', in *Esther, Judith and Susanna: A Feminist Companion to the Bible* (ed. Athalya Brenner; Sheffield: Sheffield Academic Press, 1995), pp. 224-52; and Tamara C. Eskenazi, 'Out from the Shadows: Biblical Women in the Post-Exilic Era', in *A Feminist Companion to Samuel and Kings* (ed. Athalya Brenner; Sheffield: Sheffield Academic Press, 1994), pp. 252-71.

32. E.g., Shelomith (3.19) and the nameless sister of Naham (4.19) are passed over by Jacob M. Myers, *I Chronicles* (AB, 12; New York: Doubleday, 1965), pp. 20-21, 29 and by H.G.M. Williamson, *1 and 2 Chronicles* (NCB, 20; Grand Rapids, MI: Eerdmans, 1982), pp. 57-60.

33. Oeming refers to Zeruiah and Abigail as sisters (2.16-17), but refers to both Shelomith (3.19) and Hazzelelponi (4.3) as daughters. Oeming, *Das wahre Israel*, pp. 102-105.

34. Oeming, *Das wahre Israel*, p. 208.

35. Hieke formulates a comparable conclusion in his analysis of the Genesis *toledoth*. He argues that women occur when a differentiation of the lineage is necessary, when the

synchronic Reception p.14 [handwritten margin note]

ent part of any research on biblical genealogies, as well as any analysis of their capacity to respond to traumatic pasts.

Building on ongoing research, I understand biblical genealogies as purposefully designed, ideological texts that negotiate power and are directed at audiences contemporaneous with the authors. This perception of biblical genealogies—including 1 Chronicles 1–9—led to my decision to analyze the final form of the text in a synchronic reception-oriented reading. The synchronic reading is concerned with the existing text as a communicative composition rather than with the text's components, history and provenance, without, however, neglecting the latter.[36] It emphasizes that biblical texts are literary works, and that 'their authors have exercised consummate and imaginative creativity in their carefully arranged and rhetorically powerful discourse'.[37] In addition, my synchronic approach is reception-oriented inasmuch as it focuses on the communication between text and reader. In terms of Literary Studies, it is a reception-aesthetical text analysis.[38] In consequence, the synchronic reception-oriented approach does not deny that the text processes various older materials, but emphasizes that the text makes sense in its existing form.[39] It encourages a close analysis of fractures in the genealogical structure by investigating the functions of formations, variations and exceptions in their literary context. This especially qualifies the synchronic approach to investigate the functions of gender, which in 1 Chronicles 1–9 mostly appear as fragments or absence.[40]

Next, to bring an understanding of genealogies as manufactured ideological texts more explicitly into play, I decided to conceptualize genealogies as performances and acts of cultural recall. Conceptualizing genealogies as

receptiv [handwritten margin note]

---

succession needs to be slowed down and in cases in which a special initiative is needed in order to keep up the succession. Hieke, *Genealogien der Genesis*, pp. 278-98.

36. Uta Schmidt emphasizes that the synchronic analysis of texts in their final canonical form indeed involves the apprehension of the sociocultural background of the texts, e.g., by means of the close reading of the Hebrew text, which leads to perceiving the strangeness and particularity of the text in detail. Uta Schmidt, *Zentrale Randfiguren: Strukturen der Darstellung von Frauen in den Erzählungen der Königsbücher* (Gütersloh: Chr. Kaiser Verlag, 2003), p. 55.

37. Carol Meyers, *Exodus* (NCamBC; Cambridge: Cambridge University Press, 2005), p. 2.

38. Hieke, *Genealogien der Genesis*, pp. 15-17.

39. For a discussion of the implications of a synchronic reception-oriented analysis of a larger corpus of Hebrew Bible genealogies see Hieke, *Genealogien der Genesis*, pp. 13-17; and Frank Crüsemann, 'Human Solidarity and Ethnic Identity: Israel's Self-Definition in the Genealogical System of Genesis', in *Ethnicity and the Bible* (ed. Mark G. Brett; BIS, 19; Leiden: E.J. Brill, 1996), pp. 57-76 (60).

40. The synchronic approach is not usually used to analyze 1 Chron. 1–9. One of the few examples is Kelso's Irigarayan reading of the book of Chronicles, which includes a synchronic reading of the genealogies. Kelso, *Oh Mother, Where Art Thou?*, pp. 115-66.

Memory = performance //Bal (handwritten)

performances borrows from Cultural Memory Studies, where memory acts are understood as performances.[41] It ties in with the idea that they are purposefully built entities, more precisely described as art works than as biological records.[42] Moreover, it allows conceptualizing this purposeful act more precisely. For example, the concept of performance encompasses both the notion of ritual, important for analyzing the aspects of rhythm and form in genealogies, and the notion of play, important for analyzing aspects of variation and fissures. Conceptualizing genealogies as performances also takes up the notion of fluidity. It assumes that genealogies are not universally valid reflections of the past, but active creations that depend on contexts and settings, and are responsive to particular challenges and interests.

Understanding genealogies as acts of cultural recall performed during the time of their composition builds on an interest in identity, as well as on work on the ideology of particular sets of genealogies.[43] The notion of cultural memory allows for specifying the inherently political character of genealogies inasmuch as memory acts can be hegemonic or form alternative counter-present acts of recall.[44] In the same way, genealogies are a tool that can be used both for domination and for resistance. It is important that the theoretical frame is capable of acknowledging and analyzing the potential for both. Finally, the idea of memory performance is important, because it emphasizes the active process of setting up a genealogy while—at the same time—being fully aware of the importance of unconscious and repressed dynamics that can be involved.[45]

Whereas conceptualizing genealogies as memory performances ties in relatively closely with ongoing research, my focus on genealogies' responses to trauma, as well as my interest in fractures, gaps and paradoxes as a primary starting point for investigating this issue, break new ground. In order

41. For using the notion of performance in the context of cultural recall see Mieke Bal, 'Introduction', in *Acts of Memory: Cultural Recall in the Present* (ed. Mieke Bal, Jonathan Crewe and Leo Spitzer; Hanover: University Press of New England, 1999), pp. vii-xvii.

42. See Johnson, who has advocated such an understanding of genealogies in reference to André Lefèvre. He describes genealogies as art works, that could be used 'as an alternative to narrative or poetic forms of expression', which are not primarily interested in giving exact accounts of the past, but which are interested in legal, economic, socio-cultural and religious matters. Johnson, *Purpose of Genealogies*, pp. 73, 81.

43. My understanding of the notion of identity builds on Baumann and Gingrich, who conceptualize identity as interplay between identity and alterity. See *Grammars of Identity/Alterity: A Structural Approach* (ed. Gerd Baumann and Andre Gingrich; London: Berghahn, 2004). This is appropriate for work on genealogies, because they form and confirm identity in a permanent movement of defining belonging as well as demarcation.

44. For the use of the terms 'alternative' and 'counter-present' forms of recall, see Hirsch and Smith, 'Feminism and Cultural Memory', pp. 1-19.

45. See Bal, 'Introduction', p. vii.

Foucault

to orient myself on this new ground, I explored notions of genealogy out-side of Biblical Studies. Here, the notions of discontinuity and imagination revealed themselves as extremely helpful.[46]

The notion of discontinuity as a critical aspect of genealogies has been proposed by Michel Foucault.[47] In his study on genealogies, Foucault capi-talizes on emergence (*Entstehung*) and descent (*Herkunft*) in contrast to the idea of origin (*Ursprung*) as critical notions for understanding genealogies.[48] Emphasizing the importance of power dynamics that constitute the emer-gence of a phenomenon, he asks: what political processes and ideological discourses, what coincidences and events, what desires, what breaks and discontinuities, and even what moments of absence, have shaped a given genealogy, and turned a phenomenon into what it is?[49] This approach intro-duces the idea of discontinuity to the genealogical discourse: 'The purpose of history, guided by genealogy, is not to discover the roots of our identity but to commit itself to its dissipation. It does not seek to define our unique threshold of emergence, the homeland to which metaphysicians promise a return; it seeks to make visible all of those discontinuities that cross us.'[50] Understanding power as aiming to legitimate claims or offices is based on the assumption of continuity.[51] In contrast, discontinuity moves into focus when understanding power as forces that forge the emergence of a phe-nomenon. Conceptualizing discontinuity as intra-genealogical rather than anti-genealogical is crucial. It exposes genealogies as fictions, which appear smoothly and logically derived from a seemingly singular line of origin. At the same time, it suggests that fracturing events are part of the tissue of which genealogies are made—and that they bestow meaning to the genre. Even though Foucault looks at genealogies from a different angle than I do—he investigates genealogies as a way of understanding historical pro-cesses and as an alternative approach to historiography, while I look at actual ancestor trees—his plea for understanding discontinuity as a decisive

discontinuity

---

46. Beyond the issue of genealogies, important examples of how Biblical Stud-ies engages notions of trauma are Kathleen M. O'Connor, *Jeremiah: Pain and Prom-ise* (Minneapolis, MN: Fortress Press, 2012); and Meira Polliack, 'Joseph's Trauma: Memory and Resolutions', in *Performing Memory in Biblical Narrative and Beyond* (ed. Athalya Brenner and Frank H. Polak; Sheffield: Sheffield Phoenix Press, 2009), pp. 73-105.

47. Michel Foucault, 'Nietzsche, Genealogy, History', in *Language, Counter-Memory, Practice: Selected Essays and Interviews* (ed. Donald F. Bouchard; New York: Cornell University Press, 1977), pp. 139-64.

48. Foucault's use of German terms is due to his discussion of the terms Friedrich Nietzsche uses in his *Zur Genealogie der Moral: Eine Streitschrift*.

49. Foucault, 'Nietzsche, Genealogy, History', pp. 145-52, 139-40.

50. Foucault, 'Nietzsche, Genealogy, History', pp. 148, 162.

51. So e.g. Knoppers, *1 Chronicles 1–9*, pp. 250-53.

engine for the emergence of a genealogy is critical for this study. Besides continuity, discontinuity is a dynamic at the core of genealogical functions. This invites analyzing fissures in the structure, gaps, exceptions, or breakdown of form not as accidents that can be explained away by source and redaction criticism, but as features of the composition that need to be explored and interpreted. *Imaghatr*

The second notion I have borrowed from outside Biblical Studies is the notion of imagination in the process of genealogy constitution. The phenomenon of imagination occurs plainly in *My Life Part 2*. In an interview sequence, Ursula Levi, the filmmaker's mother, draws a line from biblical Levi down to herself, which is mainly based on the shared name, on the experience of concurrently belonging and being set apart, and on a fictive biological descent ('I feel it in my genes').[52] As Ursula Levi is not Jewish in the strict sense of the term (Ursula Levi's father but not her mother was Jewish, hence, according to Jewish *halakhah,* she herself is not Jewish), the fictitious lineage is critical for Ursula Levi's identity. It allows her to integrate her experiences during National Socialism and beyond into a broader story, and to make sense of the fracturing events that affected her life. I hold that such instances of imagination are not unusual in genealogies, especially not if they try to respond to trauma and loss. In order to describe this phenomenon, rather than evaluate it as fiction, I use the term *imagined lineages.* The term is inspired by Benedict Anderson's concept of 'imagined communities', inasmuch as it connotes the invention of a lineage with a sense of imagining and creation rather than with a sense of fabrication and falsity.[53] I also intentionally connote the aspect of *community*, because imagined lineages aim at establishing links and bonding in a situation in which the given ancestry has a gap or is not able to represent a position or perspective that is needed to understand, balance, bear, or appropriate a genealogy.[54]

This book integrates research on the genealogies of the Hebrew Bible into a broader discourse on genealogies, memory performance and gender, both academic and artistic. It opens new perspectives for an understanding of why genealogies are a key genre in the Hebrew Bible and how they function. Moreover, it elucidates the biblical material not only in a theological

52. *My Life Part 2*, interview sequence (00:00:56).

53. Benedict Anderson, *Imagined Communities: Reflections on the Origin and Spread of Nationalism* (New York: Verso, 2nd edn, 1991), p. 6.

54. An alternative concept would have been the concept of *invented traditions* as proposed by Eric Hobsbawm and Terence Ranger. I decided against using this terminology, because the concept focuses on traditions that are established by official authorities, which also benefit from them. It connotes institutions, rituals and functionalities underlying the process of inventing, and points in another direction than the one I am pursuing in this research. See Eric Hobsbawm and Terence Ranger (eds.), *The Invention of Tradition* (Cambridge: Cambridge University Press, 1983).

context, but also in the context of the humanities, with which Biblical Studies is now more and more incorporated. The book is structured as follows.

Chapter 1 sets the theoretical frame. It explains what it means to conceptualize gendered genealogies as cultural memory performances, and discusses notions of cultural memory that are critical for this subject. This includes reflections on cultural memory as an overall concept; on cultural memory as performance and activity in the present; on narrative memory versus traumatic recall; on counter-present memory and alternative archives; on mediation of memory and prosthetic memories; as well as on cultural memory and gender.

Chapter 2 explains the method of socializing. It reflects on the hermeneutical starting point for reading a biblical text together with a documentary film. It discusses the concept of intertextuality as theoretical backdrop for the socializing project and critically reviews ongoing research on Bible and film. Finally, the chapter proposes the method of socializing and discusses its methodological implications.

Chapter 3 prepares for the close reading of 1 Chronicles 1–9. It introduces the female-gendered passages of the genealogy composition and assesses gender perspectives in the research on 1 Chronicles 1–9. Next, it places 1 Chronicles 1–9 in the context of Chronicles scholarship, both on a literary and a sociohistorical level. Finally, it explains why the genealogies of Judah are a key text in the subsequent close readings.

Chapter 4 provides a first sample of close readings from the genealogies of Judah (1 Chron. 2.2–4.23). The chapter centers on three key issues: the patriarchal succession at risk in two embedded narratives (2.3-4 and 2.34-35); gender fluidity in genealogical key roles and formalized genealogical language on the basis of the references to Ephrathah (2.19, 50; 4.3) and Zeruiah (2.16-17); and obscured female agency and ownership through breakdowns of syntactical coherence and meaning in 2.18-19 and 4.17-18.

Chapter 5 shifts the focus to the film. It analyzes how gendered genealogies are realized in *My Life Part 2*, and which functions they have in the film's attempt to appropriate and respond to the past. In order to do so, the chapter discusses the film's location in time and space. It traces how the lineage of Levi women unfolds and analyzes this form of gynealogy composition. It analyzes the impulse of discontinuity and the answer of a gynealogical memory act, as well as the issue of mediating cultural memory and stimulating political alliances and agency. Finally, the chapter proposes a transfer of the results of the film analysis to 1 Chronicles 1–9.

In Chapter 6, I return to Chronicles to examine the gendered fragments in a more structural way. The chapter again dives into the genealogies of Judah, this time with the help of concepts from cultural studies, for example on identity and alterity, as well as with the additional angle of the film analysis. The main objective of the chapter is to understand how gendered fragments function as a structural force in the overall genealogy composition.

Finally, Chapter 7 brings the discussion back to my initial research object and concludes this book with a meta-discussion of the genealogy genre and its capacity to respond to fractured pasts.

Two appendixes provide an overview of the female-gendered passages in 1 Chronicles 1–9, as well as a scene protocol of *My Life Part 2*. All translations of the Masoretic text are mine, unless stated otherwise. For the spelling of names, I follow the NRSV.

Questions:
- How will she accomplish synchroniz reception-oriented reading?
- How much will narrative, & phigmatin play a role?
- Psych & social → balance
- Interplay of method & theory

Chapter 1

CONCEPTUALIZING GENDERED GENEALOGIES
AS CULTURAL RECALL IN THE PRESENT

Genealogies have been studied from various perspectives, including anthropological, historical, and philosophical ones.[1] In this study, I suggest the perspectives of cultural memory and gender as central analytical categories. Hence, I conceptualize genealogies as cultural recall in the time of their composition and define them as performances of cultural memory. This conceptualization allows me to bring into focus the ideas that genealogy composition involves negotiation and contest; performs the past in view of the present and the future; and results from collective agency rather than from historical necessity. Gender as a second, complementary approach allows me to focus on fractures and contradictions, as well as on counter-present dynamics in genealogy performances. By doing so, the gender perspective significantly adds to the investigating of the potential of genealogies to respond to fractured and disturbing pasts.

Cultural memory significantly differs from the perspective of history. Historiography focuses on the past. It seeks to explain events by reconstructing their contexts and associating them with larger sociohistorical patterns. In contrast, an interpretative framework based on the perspective of cultural memory is concerned with the present. It studies how agents in the present appropriate and (re)interpret the past for the sake of the present and future.[2] A decisive turning point in the development of the memory concept in Cultural Studies was World War I. Here, the traumatic experience of the

1. E.g., the anthropological studies by Terry Prewitt and Irma McClaurin and the philosophical reflection by Michel Foucault. Terry J. Prewitt, 'Kinship Structures and the Genesis Genealogies', *Journal of Near Eastern Studies* 40.2 (1981), pp. 87-98; *Black Feminist Anthropology: Theory, Politics, Praxis and Poetics* (ed. Irma McClaurin; New Brunswick, NJ: Rutgers University Press: 2001), especially pp. 1-48; Michel Foucault, 'Nietzsche, Genealogy, History', in *Language, Counter-Memory, Practice: Selected Essays and Interviews* (ed. Donald F. Bouchard; New York: Cornell University Press, 1977), pp. 139-64.

2. Aleida Assmann, 'Gedächtnis als Leitbegriff der Kulturwissenschaft', in *Kulturwissenschaften: Forschung-Praxis-Positionen* (ed. Lutz Musner *et al.*; Freiburg: Rombach, 2003), pp. 27-47 (45).

war disrupted the capability to communicate about experiences and to narrate the past:

> The most important changes in attitudes towards the past were brought about by World War I, which created the 1914 generation's new ideas and perception of temporality as well as a new memory of war. For Walter Benjamin, the war experience was a decisive moment in a longer-term trend, typified by a decline of storytelling that left people without the possibility to tell their tales and without communicable experiences to tell.[3]

In this context, memory rather than history became a workable concept to address the experience of trauma and speechlessness.

Cathy Caruth has defined trauma as 'unclaimed experience'.[4] A trauma is a wound inflicted on the mind (and often also on the body), which is so extreme that it cannot be experienced in the moment of its taking place. Instead, it imposes itself again, belatedly, in traumatic flashbacks or repetitive actions of the survivor.[5] Between the past, in which the trauma was not fully experienced, and the present, in which traumatic flashbacks and re-enactments are not fully understood, a traumatic experience is a history that has no place and is not claimed by the one who survived it.[6] As a consequence, trauma 'does not simply serve as record of the past but precisely registers the force of an experience that is not yet fully owned'.[7] With reference to Shoshana Felman, Caruth points out that the difficulty in accessing traumatic experiences reaches beyond the individual and indicates a 'larger, more profound, less definable crisis of truth...proceeding from contemporary trauma'.[8] This crisis 'urgently demands historical awareness and yet denies our usual modes of access to it'.[9] Here, again, the notion of trauma emphasizes the priority of the memory perspective and especially to memory practices that try to respond to collective traumata.

After World War I, memory practices that tried to respond to collective traumata were dominated by national memory and centralized memorial practices, for example in the form of war memorials, which directed

---

3. Barbara A. Misztal, *Theories of Social Remembering* (Theorizing Society Series, 2; Maidenhead: Open University Press, 2003), p. 45.

4. Cathy Caruth, *Unclaimed Experience: Trauma, Narrative and History* (Baltimore, MD: Johns Hopkins University Press, 1996), p. 6.

5. Caruth, *Unclaimed Experience*, pp. 3-4.

6. Cathy Caruth, 'Introduction II', in *Trauma: Explorations in Memory, Part II: Recapturing the Past* (ed. Cathy Caruth; Baltimore, MD: Johns Hopkins University Press, 1995), pp. 151-57 (153).

7. Caruth, 'Introduction II', p. 151.

8. Cathy Caruth, 'Introduction I', in *Trauma: Explorations in Memory, Part I: Trauma and Experience* (ed. Cathy Caruth; Baltimore, MD: Johns Hopkins University Press, 1995), pp. 3-12 (6).

9. Caruth, 'Introduction II', p. 151.

and subsumed personal and family memories.[10] After World War II and the Holocaust, additional forms of recall and commemoration became important. Memory practices spread until they comprised complex and varied strategies, practices and agents. In conclusion, the challenge to deal with collective traumata created a strong impulse toward the institution of memory as a fundamental concept within politics and Cultural Studies—as distinct from history/historiography—in the twentieth and twenty-first centuries CE. Today, memory has become a broad concept that encompasses diverse media, practices and structures. It has an 'umbrella quality' that helps 'to see (sometimes functional, sometimes analogical, sometimes metaphorical) relationships' between highly disparate phenomena and enables varied disciplines to engage in stimulating dialogue.[11]

Exploring gendered genealogies in response to fractured pasts from the perspective of memory has major advantages. The memory perspective's focus on how past events are transferred into something that is meaningful in the present highlights the fact that genealogies are constituted in the present and result from a complex process of narrating, negotiating, adapting, rejecting and contesting the past. Furthermore, as the memory perspective is concerned with how cultural recall in the present may respond to fragmentation and trauma in the past, it contributes scholarly experience and expertise to the process of analyzing genealogies in relation to fractured pasts. Specifically, studies on cultural memory and gender advance our understanding of the role of gender in genealogy performance in response to fractured pasts. Additionally, the umbrella quality of cultural memory is helpful in relating case studies that contribute different historical contexts, different memory practices, different media and different disciplines. Finally, defining genealogies as gendered memory performances connects my project to the wider academic debate on cultural recall. It also sets up a common theoretical framework in which the case studies can be analyzed independently as well as in relation to each other.

1. *Cultural Memory as Overall Concept of Memory*

Throughout this book, I conceptualize gendered genealogies as a form of *cultural memory*. By doing so, I accept Mieke Bal's claim that within Cultural Studies, the notion of *cultural memory* has displaced and subsumed notions of individual, collective, communicative and cultural memory.[12]

---

10. Misztal, *Theories of Social Remembering*, p. 45.

11. Astrid Erll, 'Cultural Memory Studies: An Introduction', in *Cultural Memory Studies: An International and Interdisciplinary Handbook* (ed. Astrid Erll and Ansgar Nünning; Berlin: W. de Gruyter, 2008), pp. 1-15 (2).

12. Mieke Bal, 'Introduction', in *Acts of Memory: Cultural Recall in the Present* (ed.

This claim is not without controversy in the memory debate. Jan Assmann, for example, has proposed a model that differentiates between the inner (neuronal), the social and the cultural aspects of memory, and differentiates between 'communicative memory' and 'cultural memory' (henceforth *kulturelles Gedächtnis*).[13] Communicative memory refers to the living memory of three or four interacting generations. It is concerned with history in the framework of autobiographical memory. In contrast, the notion of *kulturelles Gedächtnis* refers to the mythical history of the absolute past (more than three thousand years ago), which is communicated through highly formalized, often ceremonial recall.[14] Assmann's position is in contrast to recent approaches that, like Bal, use the concept of cultural memory alone, albeit with a much broader scope. Astrid Erll, for instance, works from an umbrella concept of cultural memory, which comprises different dimensions, levels and modes.[15] *Dimensions* of memory refers to a three-dimensional framework of culture, which comprises social aspects (people, social relations, institutions), material aspects (artifacts, media) and mental aspects (culturally defined ways of thinking, mentalities).[16] *Levels* of cultural memory refers to the level of personal memory, on the one hand, and the level of collective or cultural memory, on the other. Personal memory belongs to an individual, but is nevertheless inherently shaped by public contexts. Collective or cultural memory refers to the symbolic order, the media, institutions and practices by which social groups construct a shared past.[17] Finally, *modes* of memory refers to the question of how acts of memory are actually shaped. It encompasses, among others, memory modes such as myth, political history, trauma, family remembrance and generational memory.[18]

For the purpose of my research, I have adopted the wider notion of cultural memory as suggested by Bal and Erll. Genealogies are a mode of memory that usually involve family or group lineages in the present and the recent past. At the same time, however, they may involve mythological, literary, or public figures that connote wider cultural discourses and cover remote time frames. For example, the genealogies in 1 Chronicles 1–9 place side by side mythological figures such as the first human, Adam, and names that may have been linked to historical persons and families in the more

Mieke Bal, Jonathan Crewe, and Leo Spitzer; Hanover: University Press of New England, 1999), pp. vii-xvii (vii).

13. Jan Assmann, *Das kulturelle Gedächtnis: Schrift, Erinnerung und politische Identität der frühen Hochkulturen* (Munich: Beck, 1999); and more recently Jan Assmann, 'Communicative and Cultural Memory', in *Cultural Memory Studies*, pp. 109-18.

14. J. Assmann, 'Communicative and Cultural Memory', p. 117.

15. Erll, 'Cultural Memory Studies', pp. 3-7.

16. Erll, 'Cultural Memory Studies', p. 4.

17. Erll, 'Cultural Memory Studies', p. 5.

18. Erll, 'Cultural Memory Studies', p. 7.

recent past. Probably they also include imagined segments of lineages. It is precisely the combination of myth, history and literature that makes these genealogies interesting in terms of identity performances at the time of their composition and beyond. Through the wider notion of cultural memory, this complex conflation can serve as a starting point, while the layers of myth, history and imagination can be analyzed in a suitable way on their own as well as in their interaction.

The broader frame of cultural memory is also suitable for conceptualizing the relationship between private and public memory, which is critical for understanding the gendered genealogies of *My Life Part 2*. The differentiation between private and public memory goes beyond the categories of individual memory, collective or communicative memory and *kulturelles Gedächtnis* inasmuch as it is less concerned with demarcations of content, form, and time frames. Instead, it is concerned with intersections of private and public articulations of past and present in terms of political and social impacts of memory acts. *My Life Part 2*, for example, combines home movies of the filmmaker's family with television footage concerning core debates of the memory culture in post-Shoah Germany. Through the intersection of private and public memory established in this way, the film is able to open a debate on contemporary German-Jewish identity that involves and challenges the audience within as well as beyond the perspective of a family story. The wider notion of cultural memory thus provides an appropriate frame to discuss how the interplay of public and private memory influences genealogy composition in *My Life Part 2* against the backdrop of fractured pasts and beyond.

2. *Cultural Memory and Gender*

In the introduction, I have made a case that fissures and irregularities are critical entry points for analyzing the capability of genealogies to respond to fractured pasts. Moreover, I have claimed that the genealogy genre is inherently gendered. Consequently, fissures and irregularities are regularly linked to issues of gender. Following Rosemarie Buikema and Iris van der Tuin, I adopt an approach to gender that is based on the 'social-constructivist insight brought home by Simone de Beauvoir that we are not born as women (or as men) but that we are made women in a society characterized by patriarchal gender relations'.[19] Hence, I am not interested in predefined essentialist notions of gender. Instead, I am interested in how notions of gender are constituted in and through my research object, as well

19. Rosemarie Buikema and Iris van der Tuin, 'Introduction', in *Doing Gender in Media, Arts and Culture* (ed. Rosemarie Buikema and Iris van der Tuin; New York: Routledge, 2009), pp. 1-4 (2).

as in the impact of this specific constitution of gender on the production and transmission of knowledge on memory acts and the formation of identities, and on claims to sociopolitical and religious power.[20]

Gender research has two major centers of attention. On the one hand, it aims at analyzing power relations 'at an individual, institutional, national and geopolitical level'.[21] On the other hand, it is concerned with feminist utopias and feminist strategies for political change.[22] The twofold focus of gender theory—tracing power relations 'between men and women and also *within* men and women',[23] as well as implementing feminist visions and political change—is an effective starting point for directing gender theory back to notions of cultural memory.

In their introduction to *Feminism and Cultural Memory*, Marianne Hirsch and Valerie Smith apply the focus on power relations to analyzing dynamics of power in the work of cultural memory, for example concerning dynamics of gender, class and race.[24] Accordingly, they build on Paul Connerton's definition of social memory as 'acts of transfer' in which knowledge as well as symbolic frames of reference are handed down and reinterpreted from generation to generation, with negotiation and contest at the basis of such acts of transfer.[25]

> [Cultural memory is] an act in the present by which individuals and groups constitute their identities by recalling a shared past on the basis of common, and therefore often contested, norms, conventions and practices.[26]

This focus on negotiation and contest underscores the necessity to explore how agents of cultural memory, and the memory acts they enable, are influenced by gender, as well as by additional categories such as race, nation, generation and sexual orientation. This perspective emphasizes specific contexts of cultural memory rather than monolithic and essentialist categories of remembering.[27]

---

20. Christina von Braun and Inge Stephan, 'Einleitung', in *Gender-Studies: Eine Einführung* (ed. Christina von Braun and Inge Stephan; Stuttgart: Metzler, 2nd edn, 2006), pp. 3-9 (3).

21. Buikema and van der Tuin, 'Introduction', p. 2.

22. Buikema and van der Tuin, 'Introduction', p. 2.

23. Buikema and van der Tuin, 'Introduction', p. 2, emphasis original.

24. Marianne Hirsch and Valerie Smith, 'Feminism and Cultural Memory: An Introduction', *Signs* 28.1 (2002), pp. 1-19 (6).

25. Paul Connerton, *How Societies Remember* (Cambridge: Cambridge University Press, 1989), p. 39.

26. Hirsch and Smith, 'Feminism and Cultural Memory', p. 5.

27. Hirsch and Smith, 'Feminism and Cultural Memory', p. 6.

The second focus of Gender Studies advances feminist utopias and imaginations and 'recommendations to implement change'.[28] In the context of cultural memory, this pertains to notions of activist listening and counter-present memory performances. Again, Hirsch and Smith emphasize that combining the perspectives of gender and cultural memory makes claims on contested discursive space. Here, alternative archives such as visual images, material and popular culture, oral history, or even silence, as well as alternative reading strategies, have become the center of analysis.[29] Such focus revises hegemonic cultural memory, but also aims at de-familiarizing and irritating traditional forms of remembering with a view towards re-envisioning modes of knowing the past.[30]

Both foci of gender theory, tracing power relations and envisioning political change, highlight the location of cultural memory in the present. And it is here that I will take up the discussion of cultural memory.

3. *Cultural Memory: Performance and Activity in the Present*

Location in the Present

The contents of cultural memory concern the past, but the process of making the past tangible and shareable is anchored in the present. Cultural memory is located in the present; from here it links and relates the past to the present and the future. The location of memory in the present implies that the past does not emanate memory in logically consistent and predictable ways. Instead, cultural memory results from collective agency in the present.[31] It is an activity or performance, as Bal puts it in reference to the scope of the volume *Acts of Memory*:

> This volume grew out of the authors' conviction that cultural recall is not merely something of which you happen to be a bearer but something that you actually *perform*, even if, in many instances, such acts are not consciously and wilfully contrived.[32]

As an activity or performance in the present, cultural recall does not only produce memory, but likewise shapes, alters and appropriates the past. As Aleida Assmann puts it:

> As a rule, remembering proceeds by reconstruction, always coming from the present, thereby inevitably leading to shifts, distortion, disfiguration, re-evaluation, renewal of what is recollected at the time of its recollection. During the interval of latency, remembrance is not stored as in a safe

28. Buikema and van der Tuin, 'Introduction', p. 2.
29. Hirsch and Smith, 'Feminism and Cultural Memory', p. 12.
30. Hirsch and Smith, 'Feminism and Cultural Memory', p. 11.
31. Bal, 'Introduction', p. vii.
32. Bal, 'Introduction', p. vii, emphasis original.

depot but is exposed to a process of transformation... The act of remembering takes place in time, which actively partakes in this process. It is an essential part of the psychomotorics of remembering that remembering and forgetting always interlock inseparably, one enabling the other. We may even say: forgetting is the opponent of storing, yet it is the accomplice of remembering.[33]

Stressing the location of cultural memory in the present may render cultural memory into something random and detached from the past. However, as the recognition of 'the historical genesis and the construct-character of cultural tradition does not lead to its suspension but enters it as a self-reflexive moment', the recognition of the emergence of cultural memory in the present has not led to randomness but rather to enhanced cultural self-reflection.[34] Moreover, it does not restrict the possibility of and need for critical verification and ethical responsibility in the production of cultural memory.[35]

Gendered genealogy

Gendered genealogy composition as a specific form of cultural recall is likewise located in the present. Genealogies do not automatically emerge from the past, but result from collective agency in the time of their composition. This agency involves negotiating, selecting, privileging and repressing names and related traditions, stories and claims. It is a cornerstone of the political character of genealogies and allows for conceptualizing genealogies as responses to fractured pasts in the first place.

Understanding genealogies as cultural recall at the time of their composition also puts emphasis on the notion of fluidity. The 'fluidity' of genealogies describes the phenomenon of genealogies that refer to the same lineage and time frame, but significantly differ in content. Such fluidity does not mean that one of the genealogies is less historical. Instead, it foregrounds the possibility of and need for actualization. Actualization is crucial for the relevance of a genealogy. If genealogies are not reinterpreted, re-evaluated

fluidity

33. Aleida Assmann, *Erinnerungsräume: Formen und Wandlungen des kulturellen Gedächtnisses* (Munich: Beck, 1999), pp. 29-30. 'Das Erinnern verfährt grundsätzlich rekonstruktiv; es geht stets von der Gegenwart aus, und damit kommt es unweigerlich zu einer Verschiebung, Verformung, Entstellung, Umwertung, Erneuerung des Erinnerten zum Zeitpunkt seiner Rückrufung. Im Intervall der Latenz ruht die Erinnerung also nicht wie in einem sicheren Depot, sondern ist einem Transformationsprozess ausgesetzt... Der Akt des Erinnerns geschieht in der Zeit, die aktiv an dem Prozess mitwirkt. Zur Psychomotorik des Erinnerns gehört insbesondere, dass Erinnern und Vergessen stets untrennbar ineinandergreifen. Das eine ist die Ermöglichung des Anderen. Wir können auch sagen: Das Vergessen ist der Gegner des Speicherns, aber der Komplize des Erinnerns'. Translation Christine Meier and Marianne Löwisch.

34. Assmann, 'Gedächtnis als Leitbegriff der Kulturwissenschaft', p. 29, my translation.

35. Assmann, 'Gedächtnis als Leitbegriff der Kulturwissenschaft', p. 30.

But genealogies are actually scripted, structured, so the fluidity exist in form.

and transformed in view of the present situation of their performers, they become detached from the present and, only then, develop into anachronistic remnants of the past. However, this does not make genealogies arbitrary. Without actually correlating the past to present and future, genealogies would lose their meaning, especially in response to fractured histories.

Composing and actualizing a genealogy takes place at the time of its composition, but likewise involves the time of its reception. For example, 1 Chronicles 1–9 is a text that presents the past with a certain claim. As readers, we are confronted with this claim, and by way of interpreting the text confirm, challenge, or alter it. As a consequence, conceptualizing 1 Chronicles 1–9 as cultural recall in the present involves both the time of its writing and the time of its reception by a reader who actualizes a given genealogy composition in their time.

Performative Quality

Locating cultural memory in the present stresses its active character and performative quality. By doing so, it introduces concepts of performance and performativity as discussed in Performance Studies. In the narrowest sense, a performance refers to 'a tangible, bounded event that involves the presentation of rehearsed artistic actions', for example, a theatre play.[36] More broadly speaking, a performance is an activity that presents precast sequences of words or actions ('restored behavior'); takes place as (inter) action and relationship; and enacts power relations.[37]

While the notion of performance is closely linked to actual bodily, artistic, and/or ritual practices, the notion of performativity, as coined by J.L. Austin in the 1950s, refers to assumptions about the nature and potential of language.[38] According to Austin, the performative pertains to speech acts that effect an action. In contrast to utterances that are merely statements, the performative speech act refers to the possibility that 'to say something is to do something',[39] in other words, it refers to the fact that speech acts sometimes constitute reality.[40]

---

36. Henry Bial, 'What is Performance?', in *The Performance Studies Reader* (ed. Henry Bial; London: Routledge, 2007), pp. 59-60 (59).

37. Richard Schechner, *Performance Studies: An Introduction* (London: Routledge, 2002), p. 24.

38. Henry Bial, 'Performativity', in *The Performance Studies Reader*, pp. 175-76 (175).

39. J.L. Austin, *How to Do Things with Words: The William James Lectures delivered in Harvard University in 1955* (ed. J.O. Urmson and Marina Sbisà; Oxford: Oxford University Press, 2nd edn, 1975), p. 12.

40. Working with the Chronicles genealogies raises the question whether recent (social) reading of genealogies can be understood as a performative act. In my view, (social) reading of a genealogy can indeed be understood as a performance inasmuch

My understanding of performance builds on Austin, but then follows Judith Butler, who takes the concept of performativity further by integrating it with the concept of artistic performance.[41] Her theme is the performance and enactment of gender, but her argument is crucial for the performance of memory and genealogy, as well. Butler synthesizes the philosophical and theatrical dimensions of performances. On the one hand, she builds on the phenomenological assumption that social agents have the potency to constitute sociopolitical realities through language, gestures and symbolic signs. On the other hand, she argues that gender is constituted through performative acts, thereby involving the contingent and temporal qualities of performance as understood in theatre or anthropology. Both arguments come together in her claim that performative acts, for example acts that constitute gender, are not primarily expressive of reality but constitute reality through performative bodily and, to a large extent, stereotyped acts.[42]

Performative acts are stereotyped acts inasmuch as they take place according to given scripts. For example, performative acts that constitute gender follow culturally predefined stereotypes of how girls and boys, women and men, dress, move and behave. On the other hand, stereotyped behavior and conventions are performed by individual agents. Only this individual agency actualizes them and reproduces them as reality.[43] Performative acts are, then, understood as a 'kind of acting in concert and acting in accord' in which collective cultural scripts and roles merge with the distinct ways in which an individual puts them into action.[44] With regards to gender, Butler argues that:

> The act that gender is, the act that embodied agents *are* inasmuch as they dramatically and actively embody and, indeed, *wear* certain cultural significations, is clearly not one's act alone. Surely, there are nuanced and individual ways of *doing* one's gender, but *that* one does it, and that one does it *in accord with* certain sanctions and proscriptions, is clearly not a fully individual matter... The complex components that go into an act must be distinguished in order to understand the kind of acting in concert and acting in accord which acting one's gender invariably is.[45]

as it potentially confirms, enforces, or alters the reality constituted by the initial performative act. However, my focus is on claiming the performative character of genealogies at the moment of their composition: I propose to understand composing and uttering a genealogy, such as 1 Chron. 1–9, in oral or written form as a performative act that then had the potential to constitute reality at the time of its composition.

41. Judith Butler, 'Performative Acts and Gender Constitution: An Essay in Phenomenology and Feminist Theory (1988)', in *The Performance Studies Reader*, pp. 187-99.

42. Bial, 'Performativity', p. 176.

43. Butler, 'Performative Acts and Gender Constitution', p. 193.

44. Butler, 'Performative Acts and Gender Constitution', p. 193.

45. Butler, 'Performative Acts and Gender Constitution', p. 193, emphasis original.

Finally, Butler argues that the interplay of predefined scripts and collective roles on the one hand and individuals bringing them into action on the other hand marks the space for political action. Variation, deviation and subversion of given scripts provide an effective tool for political change.[46] In this respect, performative acts that constitute gender can serve as a strategy for the cultural transformation of gender norms.[47]

With reference to Butler, understanding memory as performance characterizes memory acts as performative bodily acts—including speech acts—that constitute reality while being contingent and temporal. Memory performances take place in the framework of established memory practices, for example national commemoration days and religious mourning rituals. However, conventions of recall need to be put into action by individual agents in particular contexts. Actualization then marks the space in which memory performances enforce, alter, and subvert predefined memory practices.

Qualifying the production of cultural memory as performative ties in with the broader development in Cultural Studies which claims and studies the performativity of culture.[48] In this context, performativity refers to processes of 'staging, participating, experiencing, interacting, negotiating and exchanging between actual agents' that are active in the constitution and definition of culture in general and cultural memory in particular.[49] This development feeds back into Memory Studies, and it therefore seems reasonable to speak about performances of memory.[50] Given this consensus, Assmann stresses that the processuality and performativity of cultural memory is only one pole in the production of cultural memory. A second pole is the textuality and monumentality of cultural memory, with productive tension existing between the two aspects.[51]

In my research, I conceptualize gendered genealogies in response to fractured pasts as acts of transfer and memory performances. Conceptualizing genealogies as transfer acts involves the question of which ideologies, structures and forms constitute the genealogical transfer, and how they shape and gender it. For example, the notion of patrilinear succession is a central concept of transfer in the genealogies of 1 Chronicles 1–9 and beyond them.

Conceptualizing genealogies as performances highlights the impact of collective agency and contest in the sociocultural context, in which one

---

46. Butler, 'Performative Acts and Gender Constitution', p. 193.

47. Bial, 'Performativity', p. 176.

48. Assmann, 'Gedächtnis als Leitbegriff der Kulturwissenschaft', pp. 30-31.

49. Assmann, 'Gedächtnis als Leitbegriff der Kulturwissenschaft', p. 31.

50. See e.g. Astrid Erll and Ann Rigney, 'Introduction: Cultural Memory and its Dynamic', in *Mediation, Remediation and the Dynamics of Cultural Memory* (ed. Astrid Erll and Ann Rigney; Berlin: W. de Gruyter, 2009), pp. 1-11, especially p. 2.

51. Assmann, 'Gedächtnis als Leitbegriff der Kulturwissenschaft', p. 32.

or several agents perform a genealogy. Next, it stresses that genealogies emerge in a complex interplay of predefined patterns of form and meaning on the one hand, and are realized in individual memory acts, on the other. Genealogy performance takes place in predefined forms and rules of succession. However, the moment of actualizing predefined forms and rules of succession marks the space in which genealogy performances are able to modify these predefined patterns, and in which the political, possibly counter-present potential of an actual genealogy performance can unfold. Performance in the sense of actualizing predefined patterns of memory practices involves the aspects of artfulness, staging and play.[52] These notions (for example repetition, variation, and fluidity) are especially important, because the genre is strongly characterized by formal language, repetitive structures and hierarchical rules of succession. How this repertoire of the genre is configured is critical in terms of creating genealogies that are meaningful.

Conceptualizing genealogies as memory performances underlines the processual and performative aspect of genealogy composition. However, this aspect needs to be complemented by the monumentality of genealogies. Even though they require actualization, genealogies also need static moments of closure. Their potential is also inherent in the bare and condensed form of a genealogy that is no longer open to all possibilities. The form mirrors a point in time when the work of constructing, negotiating and deciding ends and is completed—even though this moment must likewise be a new starting point for renegotiation and change. I understand the genealogies of 1 Chronicles 1–9 and *My Life Part 2* as mirrors of a moment of completion of a given genealogy. At the same time, however, the unresolved and open ends of both genealogy compositions make the genealogies accessible for negotiating and actualizing their meaning from the time and perspective of the reader/viewer who actualizes the genealogy in the process of reading/viewing.

4. *Narrative Memory versus Traumatic Recall*

The memory concept in Cultural Studies has developed in close relation to the study of trauma. Traumatic histories easily fall outside both personal reference systems and common sociocultural frames of reference. The attempt to prevent traumatic histories from slipping into oblivion through active remembering in the form of narrating/testifying and witnessing/confirming the past renders the practice and analysis of cultural memory into a form of political activism in its own right.[53]

52. Henry Bial, 'Play', in *The Performance Studies Reader*, pp. 135-36 (135).
53. Hirsch and Smith, 'Feminism and Cultural Memory', p. 13. See also Caruth, 'Introduction I', pp. 10-11.

Accordingly, Bal defines cultural memory as narrative memory in contrast to traumatic recall.[54] Narratable memories provide accents, benchmarks and atmospheres. They engage in a productive interplay of remembering and forgetting. And, most importantly, they are narratable in present cultural frames where others may confirm and respond to them.[55] In contrast, traumatic recall is characterized by dissociations and repressions, which interplay with the painful resurfacing of events of a traumatic nature. In reference to the work of Shoshana Felman and Dori Laub, Bal argues that the subject who suffered the traumatizing event in the past is isolated; his or her traumatic memories need to be 'legitimized and narratively integrated' before they can lose their power.[56]

Bal's methodological decision to conceptualize cultural memory through engaging the tension of narrative memory and cultural recall is undertaken from the perspective of post-Shoah memory, in which traumatic memories, the need for narrative and witnessing, and the function of social frames and mediation play a crucial role.[57] The focus on post-Shoah memory as a central reference point reflects the more general emphasis on the memory of the Shoah and the memory of slavery in the USA as critical reference points of Cultural Memory Studies in the twentieth and twenty-first century: 'The unspeakable victimization of the Holocaust, like the dehumanization of slavery, has come to shape much recent thinking about trauma, memory, memorialization and transmission.'[58] Still, other examples of disenfranchisement and genocide are likewise central for reflecting on cultural memory, trauma and transmission, for example the Armenian genocide during World War I, or, more recently, the civil war in Rwanda, during which Tutsi and moderate Hutus were also the victims of genocide.

Conceptualizing cultural memory as narrative memory hints at the social and cultural condition of memory. Narrative and memory occur in sociocultural frames, a generally accepted fact in Memory Studies which is owed to the legacy of French theorist Maurice Halbwachs. Halbwachs argued

54. Bal, 'Introduction', p. viii. So also Judith Herman, who describes 'normal memory' as the act of storytelling, which is in contrast to 'traumatic memory' that is 'wordless and static'. Judith L. Herman, *Trauma and Recovery* (New York: Basic Books, 1992), p. 175.

55. Bal, 'Introduction', p. x.

56. Bal, 'Introduction', p. viii. For the narrative integration of the traumatic events see also Caruth, 'Introduction II', p. 153; and Herman, *Trauma and Recovery*, pp. 176-81.

57. Bal, 'Introduction', p. xi.

58. Hirsch and Smith, 'Feminism and Cultural Memory', p. 4. See also Landsberg who develops the notion of prosthetic memories in reference to the history and memory of the Holocaust and the institution of slavery in the USA. Alison Landsberg, *Prosthetic Memory: The Transformation of American Remembrance in the Age of Mass Culture* (New York: Columbia University Press, 2004).

that remembering is only possible within social frames of reference.[59] Halbwachs's argument comprises both individual and collective memory. Individual memory emerges in direct communication; groups share 'publicly articulated images of collective pasts (mythology, tradition, heritage, long-term symbolic patterns)' that are starting points for the production of cultural memory.[60] The social condition of memory as proposed by Halbwachs has become a basic premise in Memory Studies. However, his more particular concept of the character of social frames has been challenged. For example, Alison Landsberg argues that Halbwachs's concept of social frames has its limitations in appropriately describing the scope of social frames produced by the technologies of mass culture in the twentieth and twenty-first centuries CE. Social frames in Halbwachs's terms would imply a 'geographically bounded community with a shared set of beliefs and a sense of "natural" connection among its members'.[61] In contrast, mass culture would have the potential to create 'shared social frameworks for people who inhabit, literally and figuratively, different social spaces, practices and beliefs'.[62]

Beyond the general notion of social memory, the context of post-Shoah memory provokes a focus on the roles of first personhood (giving testimony and narrating) and second personhood (witnessing and confirming) in the constitution of memory. The same distinction is referred to by Hirsch and Smith, who argue that the second personhood of witnessing and confirming memory implies an active choice for 'active and activist listening, empathic identification and solidarity required to imagine the experiences of the other, and therefore of the past'.[63] At the same time, active second personhood includes the conscious granting of 'the pastness and the irretrievability of the past, the irreducibility of the other and the untranslatability of the story of trauma'.[64]

The concept of narrative memory is concerned with active and primarily conscious memory acts. This corresponds with the major part of memory

---

59. Maurice Halbwachs, *Das Gedächtnis und seine sozialen Bedingungen* (ed. Heinz Maus and Friedrich Fürstenberg; trans. Lutz Geldsetzer; Berlin: Luchterhand, 1966). Halbwachs develops his argument from the differentiation between dreams and memories to discussing it with respect to the collective memory of families (Chapter 5), social groups (Chapter 6) and social classes and their traditions (Chapter 7). For a summary of his argument see his conclusion, pp. 361-90.

60. Jeffrey K. Olick, 'From Collective Memory to the Sociology of Mnemonic Practices and Products', in *Cultural Memory Studies*, pp. 151-61 (157).

61. Landsberg, *Prosthetic Memory*, p. 8.

62. Landsberg, *Prosthetic Memory*, p. 8. Landsberg focuses on the formation of social frames in the era of mass culture. Still, already in the context of Chronicles, there might have been broader social frames, e.g. as a result of migration and the Jewish Diaspora.

63. Hirsch and Smith, 'Feminism and Cultural Memory', p. 12.

64. Hirsch and Smith, 'Feminism and Cultural Memory', p. 13.

research that addresses 'those ways of making sense of the past which are intentional and performed through narrative, and which go hand in hand with the construction of identities'.[65] The target of my own research, which is also located in the nexus of narrative-performance-identity, covers a similar scope. However, the notion of cultural memory also remains open for the study of unintentional and implicit ways of cultural remembering and inherently non-narrative forms of memory, for example visual or bodily forms.[66]

At first glance, qualifying genealogies as narrative memory may seem unlikely. Genealogies are characterized by their bare skeleton-like structure, which results from the genre's restriction to names and linking elements, as well as their regular use of repetitive syntactical patterns and formalized language. Narratives only occur in the form of tiny embedded notes and comments. Yet I hold that genealogies indeed belong to the category of narrative memory, especially if opposed to traumatic recall. Genealogies feature dramaturgies and atmospheres. They alternate recalling and forgetting, and are meaningful in social frames. Genealogies are not narratives in the strict sense of the word. However, they tell a story of the past in their own way. In the context of contrasting narrative memory and traumatic recall, the reduced and somewhat bare character of genealogical storytelling has an important aspect. It may provide a mode of expression where it would not (yet) be possible to relate a fuller narrative.

The case studies for this project are concerned with traumatic pasts in different ways. *My Life Part 2* is located in the midst of the debate on post-Shoah memory. In the title sequence, the filmmaker states, in a voice-over, that she made the film in order to understand how a trauma she has not experienced herself was passed on to her and how it has influenced her perception. Here, the film seems to provide an artistic translation of Marianne Hirsch's concept of postmemory.[67] The notion of postmemory refers to the memory of survivors' children in relation to the traumatic events in the lives of their parents, which they did not experience themselves but which nevertheless shape their emotional and bodily lives. The 'stories and images with which they grew up...are so powerful, so monumental, as to constitute memory in their own right'.[68] Beyond this specific notion, *My Life Part 2* shares its more general sociocultural context with the analytical discourse on cultural memory. In pursuing her leading

65. Erll, 'Cultural Memory Studies', p. 2.
66. Erll, 'Cultural Memory Studies', p. 2.
67. Marianne Hirsch, 'Projected Memory: Holocaust Photographs in Personal and Public Fantasy', in *Acts of Memory: Cultural Recall in the Present*, pp. 3-23.
68. Hirsch, 'Projected Memory', p. 8. For a critical discussion of the concept of postmemory see Ernst J. van Alphen, 'Second Generation Testimony, the Transmission of Trauma and Postmemory', *Psychoanalyse im Widerspruch* 33 (2005), pp. 87-102.

question, Angelika Levi addresses, among other things, the transfer from traumatic recall to narrative memory; the dividing line between empathy and appropriation in the position of second personhood; and the act of counter-present memory as source of resistance.

1 Chronicles 1–9 is situated in the very different historical and cultural context of the late fourth century BCE.[69] It thus dates back to a period of the history of Israel that is often referred to as postexilic. The notion of a postexilic period has different reference points. On the one hand, it refers to the actual history of siege warfare against Judah and the destruction of state and temple, as well as deportations and exile of a part of the population of Judah in the early sixth century BCE.[70] In other words, it refers to the traumatic history that co-constitutes the sociocultural context to which 1 Chronicles 1–9 belongs. On the other hand, the notion of the postexilic period refers to the political and theological discourse on exile and return in the Second Temple period. In this discourse, the exile appears as a major reference point for the identities of postexilic Judaism. Recent research has highlighted the rhetorical and ideological character of this discourse, and has consequently suggested reconsidering biblical accounts of the exile in view of the interest of particular groups to suggest their specific experiences as a general blueprint for the identity of Israel and emerging Judaism.[71] In my view, both aspects of the debate are important. I follow Kathleen O'Connor and others in assessing the events referred to in postexilic literature as traumatic historical events.[72] However, I also think it critical to bear in mind that references to exile and return are part of a rhetorical and ideological discourse that is interested in moving these events to the centre, even though such centrality might not have been representative of the concerns of many Jewish communities at the time, for example not for the inhabitants of rural Judah who had remained in the land, or for the communities of the Diaspora.[73] Accordingly, the genealogies in 1 Chronicles 1–9 need to be investigated both in view of their response to the actual traumatic past, and in

---

69. See Chapter 3, below.

70. See Kathleen M. O'Connor, *Jeremiah: Pain and Promise* (Minneapolis, MN: Fortress Press, 2012), pp. 7-17; and Rainer Albertz, *Israel in Exile: The History and Literature of the Sixth Century B.C.E.* (trans. David Green; Studies in Biblical Literature, 3; Atlanta, GA: Society of Biblical Literature, 2003).

71. Lester L. Grabbe (ed.), *Leading Captivity Captive: 'The Exile' as History and Ideology* (JSOTSup, 278; Sheffield: Sheffield Academic Press, 1998).

72. O'Connor, *Pain and Promise*, pp. 3-17, especially pp. 4-6. See also Ruth Poser, *Das Ezechielbuch als Trauma-Literatur* (Leiden: E.J. Brill, 2012), pp. 121-248.

73. See Robert Carroll, 'Exile! What Exile? Deportation and the Discourse of Diaspora (In Memoriam Ferdinand Deist)', in *Leading Captivity Captive*, pp. 62-79 (67, 78); and Philip R. Davies, 'Exile? What Exile? Whose Exile?', in *Leading Captivity Captive*, pp. 128-38 (136-37).

view of their position in the ideological discourse about exile and return, memory, legitimacy, tradition and identity at the time.

5. *Counter-Present Memories and Alternative Archives*

Counter-Present Memory

The choice to adopt the second personhood of memory as well as to engage in active and activist listening contributes to counter-present performances of memory. Assmann defines counter-present memory as memory acts that recall persons and events at the margins of common sociocultural frames of reference and, that read publicly articulated images of collective pasts against the grain.[74] This aspect of the memory debate is crucial inasmuch as it links memory to political and ethical perspectives. Taking up Butler's notion of performativity, acts of counter-present memory are memory performances that actualize predefined memory practices in a way that alters, subverts and politicizes them.

Acts of counter-present memory and forms of activist remembering have the potential to give justice to disenfranchised individuals and groups against a 'historiography of the winners'.[75] By calling for political and cultural solidarity with traumatized and disenfranchised parties, counter-present memory acts can be integrating and healing.[76] Finally, counter-present memory acts can be a source of resistance and engagement, which may arise from the memory of the suppressed ancestors.[77] However, the political potential of memory acts can also be used by reactionary groups, as Ann Burlain has shown with the example of the international Christian Right radio ministry.[78] Counter-present memory exposes the political and ethical dimension of cultural memory. At the same time it demonstrates that the memory concept can be appropriated by different political groups and interests.

74. Aleida Assmann, 'Memory', *BDR* III, pp. 1212-18.

75. Paul Ricoeur, 'Gedächtnis–Vergessen–Geschichte', in *Historische Sinnbildung: Problemstellungen, Zeitkonzepte, Wahrnehmungshorizonte, Darstellungsstrategien* (ed. Klaus E. Müller and Jörn Rüsen; Reinbek: Rowohlt, 1997), pp. 433-54 (449-50).

76. Bal, 'Introduction', p. x.

77. See Benjamin's 'Zwölfte Geschichtsphilosophische These', in Walter Benjamin, *Zur Kritik der Gewalt und andere Aufsätze* (Edition Suhrkamp, 103; Frankfurt: Suhrkamp, 1965), p. 88.

78. Ann Burlein analyzes the international Christian Right radio ministry and shows the reactionary implications of its counter-present recall of highly selective biblical traditions and family values. Ann Burlein, 'Countermemory on the Right', in *Acts of Memory: Cultural Recall in the Present*, pp. 209-17.

Alternative Archives

The discussion of counter-present memory is a fundamental concern in relation to the claim to and the contest for discursive space in the work of cultural memory. Hirsch and Smith stress that research in cultural memory and gender has criticized public media and official archives as tools designed to commemorate the experiences and interests of the powerful and 'those who control hegemonic discursive spaces'.[79] At the same time, alternative archives (e.g. visual images, material and popular culture, oral history, silence) and alternative reading strategies have become the center of analysis. This shift in focus revises hegemonic cultural memory, but also aims at de-familiarizing and interrupting traditional forms of remembering in favour of re-envisioning alternative modes of knowing the past.[80]

Engaging the notion of (alternative) archives in the context of activist and counter-present memory corresponds with recent conceptualizations of the archive. In recent archival theory, archives are understood as sites of knowledge production rather than sites of knowledge retrieval and storage.[81] They are 'cross-sections of contested knowledge',[82] in which notions of power and control are key categories.[83] Such an understanding of archives suggests a focus on power dynamics, for example of gender, involved in the knowledge production of a given archive. This comes with a focus on the taxonomy of a given archive, in which power configurations are established and maintained. As Stoler puts it, it is necessary to read an archive 'for its regularities, for its logic of recall, for its densities and distributions, for its consistencies of misinformation, omission and mistake' and to detect the specific production of knowledge through these principles.[84] In addition, archives need to be read for their tacit narratives, which are not formalized or codified but are silently active in and across dominant principles of knowledge production.[85]

The notion of archives as sites of contested knowledge production refers to different dimensions of the archive concept. On the one hand, it refers to archives in terms of collections of documents, often in the context of institutions, that are characterized by contextualizing single records in a framework of validation and classification with regard to establishing repositories

---

79. Hirsch and Smith, 'Feminism and Cultural Memory', p. 12.

80. Hirsch and Smith, 'Feminism and Cultural Memory', pp. 11-12.

81. Ann L. Stoler, 'Colonial Archives and the Arts of Governance', *Archival Science* 2 (2002), pp. 87-109 (90).

82. Stoler, 'Colonial Archives', p. 87.

83. Stoler, 'Colonial Archives', p. 97.

84. Stoler, 'Colonial Archives', p. 100.

85. Eric Ketelaar, 'Tacit Narratives: The Meaning of Archives', *Archival Science* 1 (2001), pp. 131-41 (132).

of knowledge that are useful for ensuing ages.[86] On the other hand, it refers to a re-conceptualization of the notion by Jacques Derrida, who—in addition to emphasizing the relation of archives to power and institutions—described archiving as a fundamental psychological drive and cultural impulse. This drive involves the contradictory desire to remember and hold fast on the one hand, and to forget, repress, and erase the material traces of the past on the other.[87] In this context, the archive is 'a metaphor for wider processes of remembering and forgetting, both on an individual and a collective level'.[88] The two dimensions of the archive notion intersect. For example, Derrida's emphasis on the importance of the location of an archive in an exterior place encompasses both the archive as institution and the archive in a more metaphorical sense. In both cases, the consigning of the archival contents to an exterior place assures 'the possibility of memorization, of repetition, of reproduction, or of reimpression' and is a critical starting point for the circulation and future uses of the contents.[89] As Stoler puts it, the notion of the archive refers to 'something in between a set of documents, their institutions, and a repository of memory—both a place and a cultural space that encompasses official documents but is not confined to them'.[90]

In both case studies, genealogy composition is bound to the formation of an archive. 1 Chronicles 1–9 collects earlier genealogies, military census lists, snippets of narratives and other inner-biblical intertexts in a literary archive of genealogies that documents as much as constructs the descent, identity and legacy of Israel. The film *My Life Part 2* forms an archive of the filmmaker's family lineage and the related political history through assembling home movies, photographs, objects, audio records, and television footage. In both cases, collecting, classifying and presenting archival contents points to the possibilty of future uses of the literary and cinematic archive, for example through interpretation by their readers and viewers.[91]

---

86. Julia Noordegraaf, 'Audiovisual Archives and Knowledge', in *Performing the Archive: Tracing Audiovisual Heritage in the Digital Age* (forthcoming).

87. Jacques Derrida, *Archive Fever: A Freudian Impression* (trans. E. Prenowitz; Chicago, IL: University of Chicago Press, 1996), pp. 9-16, 25-32.

88. Noordegraaf, 'Audiovisual Archives and Knowledge'.

89. Derrida, *Archive Fever*, pp. 11, 16-17. See also Aleida Assmann, who distinguishes between political archives and historical archives. The former are important tools of power; the latter are stores of information without immediate use. Still, having momentarily lost their *Sitz im Leben*, they can be re-contextualized in a 'second life'. Aleida Assmann, 'Canon and Archive', in *Cultural Memory Studies*, pp. 97-107 (103).

90. Ann L. Stoler, *Along the Archival Grain: Epistemic Anxieties and Colonial Common Sense* (Princeton, NJ: Princeton University Press, 2009), p. 49.

91. For the aim of archives to create records for the purpose of using them in the future, rather than merely preserving them, see Derrida, *Archive Fever*, pp. 11-17.

Moreover, employing the archive concept hints at the link between gendered genealogies, counter-present memory and contested discursive space.

6. *Mediation of Memory*

Mediation

Memory acts that refer to traumatic memories and/or alternative archives such as visual images or silence require mediation between the subject who experienced the trauma and the present reader or viewer.[92] Mediation implies an active choice for the second personhood in the memory act. Artists or critical readers bear witness and facilitate memory, and as second persons create artworks, photographs, or published texts that function as mediators between 'the parties to the traumatizing scene and between these and the reader or viewer'.[93] Such mediation takes place within sociocultural reference frames and constitutes acts of memory that may generate meaningful narratives; call 'for political and cultural solidarity in recognizing the traumatized party's predicament'; and, by doing so, may be 'potentially healing'.[94]

The function of mediators highlights the role of media in performing cultural memory. Actual memory performances may take the form of art works, installations, poetry and prose, school curricula, museum collections, theory, historiography, to name a few. Cultural memory is therefore open to different media. In turn, different media shape (and gender) cultural memory.

Both *My Life Part 2* and 1 Chronicles 1–9 hold two different mediation positions, namely internal (inner-filmic and inner-textual) mediation, and external mediation through the viewer and reader.

In *My Life Part 2*, the issue of mediation is characterized by the autobiographical character of the film. The film mediates between Levi's mother and other participants of the traumatizing scene of the Holocaust, and the viewer. Narrating the past takes place in audio records and interview footage, in which Levi's mother and grandmother tell their stories. But only when these narratives are taken up in Levi's cinematic memory performance are they mediated to the contemporary viewer. At the same time, the film narrates the story of the filmmaker herself. As an artist who creates an autobiographical work, Levi takes on the double role of the subject of the traumatizing scene through postmemory, and the mediator who witnesses and facilitates memory. Against this backdrop, Angelika Levi's

92. Bal, 'Introduction', p. x.
93. Bal, 'Introduction', p. x.
94. Bal, 'Introduction', p. x.

decision to inhabit second personhood in the memory act comes to the fore as her response to the traumatic past she has inherited.

In 1 Chronicles 1–9, the issue of mediation is characterized by 1 Chronicles 1–9 being a religious canonical text. This implies a third position of mediation in addition to the internal mediation of the text and the external mediation of the reader. This third position is based on its mediation through processes of transmission and interpretation, as well as liturgical performance.[95] 1 Chronicles 1–9 is at the margins of the reception and liturgical performance of biblical literature. But it nevertheless constitutes part of it and participates in this third position of mediation.

Prosthetic Memory

An important approach that explicitly takes into consideration the role of mass culture in mediating memory is Alison Landsberg's concept of prosthetic memories. In contrast to the viewpoints of Bal, Hirsch, and Smith, the concept of mediation significantly changes in Landsberg's approach. Here, testimonies are replaced by mediated representations of traumatic historical narratives in the context of 'experiential sites' such as the cinema or museums. A person's encounters with such mediated representations forge memories that are prosthetic, but nevertheless essential to the production and articulation of a person's subjectivity.[96] Landsberg's approach gives up notions of natural ownership and authenticity of memories.[97] Instead, experiential sites offer spectators from different backgrounds and ancestries the possibility of inhabiting subject positions and pasts to which they have no original connection and adding them to their own body of experiences.[98] According to Landsberg, prosthetic memories, as sensual engagements with the past, have the political potential to produce empathy and social responsibility and to provide impulses for political alliances across boundaries of ethnicity/race, class, gender and nationality.[99]

95. The book of Chronicles in general and its nine chapters of genealogies in particular have only come to the center of scholarly attention in the last 10–20 years (see Pancratius C. Beentjes, *Tradition and Transformation in the Book of Chronicles* [SSN, 52; Leiden: E.J. Brill, 2008], pp. 1-13). Likewise, they have a marginal place in the pericopes that are read in the liturgical church year.

96. Landsberg, *Prosthetic Memory*, p. 20.

97. Landsberg, *Prosthetic Memory*, p. 2.

98. Landsberg, *Prosthetic Memory*, p. 14.

99. Landsberg, *Prosthetic Memory*, p. 2. See also Caruth, who argues that '[i]n a catastrophic age, that is, trauma itself may provide the very link between cultures: not as a simple understanding of the past of others but rather, within the traumas of contemporary history, as our ability to listen through the departures we have all taken from ourselves'. Caruth, 'Introduction I', p. 11.

The shift in perspective as implied in the notion of prosthetic memory becomes apparent when comparing two well-known films on the Holocaust, namely *Schindler's List* (Steven Spielberg, USA, 1993) and Claude Lanzmann's *Shoah* (France, 1985).[100] While *Schindler's List* plainly represents events from the German camps, *Shoah* works solely with interviews with survivors and shots of the present-day sites of the camps. *Shoah* reflects the argument that consciously granting 'the pastness and irretrievability of the past, the irreducibility of the other and the untranslatability of the story of trauma' is a critical aspect of activist listening and counter-present memory acts.[101] From this perspective, the argument that (prosthetic) memories of the Holocaust may be acquired through a sensory encounter with a film such as *Schindler's List* may seem to allow for inadequate appropriations. On the other hand, *Schindler's List* is a typical example of a mass media representation of the Holocaust, which may forge prosthetic memories that induce political alliances across given social frames.[102]

The notion of prosthetic memories can be transferred to the issue of genealogy composition, thereby highlighting the function of including ancestors who transcend primarily given heritages, as well as imagined ancestors. Adding such 'externals' to a genealogy assumes that ancestors may serve as a prism for historical narratives beyond the biological or historical-cultural community to which they pertain in the first place. Taking in 'externals' risks inadequate appropriations. However, such 'prosthetic ancestors' may fulfil the role of representing voids; of actively engaging otherwise unrepresented experiences; or of claiming—or rejecting—political positions linked to the inheritance. This may add to a genealogy's potential to clarify identities in the present and to tap into the healing potential of the genealogical memory act. Moreover, it may serve as a starting point for new political alliances in the present. Cultural memory in general and the notion of prosthetic memories in particular point to the location of genealogies between arranging and appropriating the past on the one hand, and giving impetus for engaging descent and legacies with a view to political alliances and commitments on the other.

Genealogies hold potential for counter-present memory acts and are potentially healing—and here is the focus of my book. However, genealogies also hold potential for harmful memory acts, for example in the

---

100. See also Thomas Elsaesser on this controversy; Thomas Elsaesser, 'Subject Positions, Speaking Positions: From *Holocaust, Our Hitler*, and *Heimat* to *Shoah* and *Schindler's List*', in *The Persistence of History: Cinema, Television and the Modern Event* (ed. Vivian Sobchack; New York: Routledge, 1996), pp. 145-81.

101. Hirsch and Smith, 'Feminism and Cultural Memory', p. 13.

102. See my discussion of Elsaesser's analysis of the capacity of *Schindler's List* to provoke feelings of concern in Chapter 5, below.

constitution of 'pure' genealogies and in providing a tool for exclusion. For instance, this harmful potential of genealogies comes to the fore in the fascist ideology of the Nazis. Here, the construction of 'pure' genealogies and specifically the ancestral proof were used as tools of anti-Semitic politics and disenfranchisement.[103]

In this chapter, I have discussed the notions of cultural memory that I think are critical for conceptualizing genealogies as memory performances, especially in view of their capacity to respond to fractured pasts. Conceptualizing gendered genealogies as cultural recall in the present provides an essential basis for the subsequent close readings of the case studies. Moreover, explaining my understanding of cultural memory has established the analytical frame in which socializing the two case studies will take place. In the Introduction, I only briefly indicated what the concept of socializing implies. Therefore, after having set the analytical frame, I move further to methodology. The next chapter will address how to bring the analytical frame and the case studies into a productive dialogue; in other words, it will introduce the methodology of socializing.

---

103. See Eric Ehrenreich, *The Nazi Ancestral Proof: Genealogy, Racial Science and the Final Solution* (Bloomington, IN: Indiana University Press, 2007).

Chapter 2

Socializing Bible Texts and Films: Methodological Considerations

In the previous chapter, I have conceptualized gendered genealogy composition in response to fractured pasts as a form of cultural memory performance, and thereby set the analytical framework in which I will investigate my actual case studies. These case studies, 1 Chronicles 1–9 and *My Life Part 2*, perform gendered genealogies in extremely different ways. Therefore, before diving into the actual close reading, I will explain what I expect from choosing such contrasting cases, and on which methodological grounds I will read them together.

In order to do so, I will first outline the hermeneutical context for reading a Bible text in conjunction with a cultural object such as a film. This includes a brief review of previous research on the Bible and film. Next, I will introduce the notion of intertextuality as the basis for reading my case studies together. By doing so, I will also show the limits of the concept of intertextuality for reading together sources as disparate as I am engaging here. As a consequence, and as the final step of the chapter, I will propose an alternative reading strategy, namely the strategy of *socializing*, as a productive methodology for investigating gendered genealogy performance in response to fractured pasts across a Bible text and a documentary film.

Throughout the chapter, I will use the terms 'film text' and 'close reading' with regard to the film analysis. This is somewhat reductionistic, as the medium of film also includes sound and images, as well as the context of seeing, the *dispositif*.[1] However, having its basis in literary analysis, film analysis often refers to the film as appearing on the screen as 'film text', and describes its analysis as 'close reading'. My analysis will include the

---

1. See Jean-Louis Baudry's conceptualization of the screening situation in terms of the *dispositif*, as well as Frank Kessler for a current interpretation of it. Jean-Louis Baudry, 'Le Dispositif: approches métapsychologiques de l'impression de réalité', in *Communications* 23 (1975), pp. 56-72; Frank Kessler, 'The Cinema of Attractions as *Dispositif*', in *The Cinema of Attractions Reloaded* (ed. Wanda Strauven; Amsterdam: Amsterdam University Press, 2006), pp. 57-69.

audio-visual dimensions of the film, but for the sake of clarity, I stick to the terms 'film text' and 'close reading'.[2]

1. *Hermeneutical Starting Points*

This research is rooted in my broad understanding of key challenges recent Bible studies have to face: first, the challenge to determine the role and status of the Bible alongside, rather than before, other elements that have a share in the formation of religious and sociocultural identities; and second, the challenge to deal with a plurality of interpretative strategies.

The role and status of the Bible with regard to the formation of religious and sociocultural identities can easily be determined negatively: the Bible has long ago lost the status of absolute authority. However, it is not as easy to interpret it positively.[3] In (post-)secular societies, individuals and communities need to negotiate a plurality of subject and inheritance positions together with the biblical inheritance in order to perform their (religious) identities. Hence, the importance of the Bible needs to be determined alongside and in dialogue with—rather than before—other elements that have a share in the formation of religious and sociocultural identities.

The challenge to determine the status of the Bible as a participating rather than primary element of sociocultural discourses is intensified by the recent interpretative situation of biblical texts. While the first half of the twentieth century was characterized by a broad, historical-critical consensus of biblical scholarship, 'the postmodern interpretative situation' was instituted by a major 'unsettlement' of interpretative strategies and contexts.[4] In the face of a plurality of methods and reading contexts, the need to stay in dialogue about exegetical methods and interpretative strategies has taken

2.   For a discussion of the notion of text in Cinema Studies, see Astrid Söderbergh Widding, 'From Grammar to Graphics: The Concept of Text in Cinema Studies', in *Travelling Concepts: Text, Subjectivity, Hybridity* (ed. Joyce Goggin and Sonja Neef; Amsterdam: ASCA Press, 2001), pp. 67-77.

3.   In my view, the recent marginalization of Biblical Studies at Dutch universities is an indicator of the difficulty Biblical Studies has in positively determining the role of the Bible in recent academic and sociopolitical discourses on societal ethics, traditions and identities.

4.   Walter Brueggemann, *Theology of the Old Testament: Testimony, Dispute, Advocacy* (Minneapolis, MN: Fortress Press, 1997), p. xv. More specifically, Brueggemann discusses the new postmodern interpretative situation in reference to 'the end of a cultural period that was dominated by objective positivism that made a thin kind of historical scholarship possible and that granted interpretative privilege to certain advantaged perspectives'. Brueggemann, *Theology of the Old Testament*, p. 61.

centre stage. This center has displaced the aim of setting up a new authoritative canon of methods.[5]

At the basis of this book is the contention that the change in the Bible's status and the plurality of its interpreters' strategies and contexts is a deeply positive development. It is positive inasmuch as it challenges us to actively negotiate the role of the Bible on both a personal and a sociopolitical level, and to develop alternative reading strategies that are able to disclose the relevance of biblical texts in interaction with other religious, cultural and political utterances. Accordingly, the reading strategy I am suggesting here aims at meeting these challenges. Proceeding from a view of the status of the Bible as alongside rather than before other cultural and religious utterances, I propose to read biblical texts together with cultural objects that are independent from the text and do not directly relate to particular biblical notions. Examples of such cultural objects are art works, museum collections, or films. Building on the notion of intertextuality, I suggest reading a biblical text (1 Chronicles 1–9) and a cultural object (the documentary *My Life Part 2*) in conjunction, on the basis of a theme both objects have in common (gendered genealogies in response to trauma), as well as within a shared analytical frame (notions of cultural memory). Shared theme and analytical frame allow for reading the disparate objects in view of each other while maintaining their difference. Reading Bible texts and independent cultural objects together in this setting—*socializing* them, as I have called it—creates an intellectual and emotional space in which secular, cultural and biblical notions can meet. It provides the basis for developing new horizons of understanding for the respective biblical texts and cultural objects, which would otherwise remain uncovered.[6] This setting likewise aims at meeting the hybrid reality of many Bible scholars who have to integrate various subject and inheritance positions in the formation of their scholarly, religious and cultural identities. Taking up the idea of intellectual spaces, I envision creating a space in which scholars who focus on biblical

---

5. Eep Talstra, *Oude en Nieuwe Lezers: Een inleiding in de methoden van uitleg van het Oude Testament* (Kampen: Kok, 2002), p. 111.

6. The aim of creating a new interpretative space for reading biblical texts builds on George Aichele and Richard Walsh, who argue that the intertextual reading of scripture and popular film is a process that opens up a space in which new questions, ideas and associations are possible. George Aichele and Richard Walsh, 'Introduction: Scripture as Precursor', in *Screening Scripture: Intertextual Connections between Scripture and Film* (ed. George Aichele and Richard Walsh; Harrisburg, PA: Trinity Press International, 2002), pp. vii-xvi (xiii). For the potential of intertextual readings to create a space for interplay and dialogue, see also Jonathan Z. Smith, 'In Comparison a Magic Dwells', in *Imagining Religion: From Babylon to Jonestown* (ed. Jonathan Z. Smith; Chicago Studies in the History of Judaism; Chicago, IL: University of Chicago Press, 1982), pp. 19-35.

texts and other informed readers may dwell in order to wrestle with their Bibles in reference to other aspects that make up their hybrid identities.[7]

As my second cultural object besides the Bible text, I employ film. Film is an audio-visual medium and allows access to the priority of image and sound in modern and postmodern societies. The audio-visual aspect is important in the context of cultural memory, because cultural memory acts strongly involve the affective qualities of (moving) images and sound, for example in museum exhibitions, art works and commemoration practices. More specifically, the audio-visual aspect is central for genealogy composition. Recent genealogies have a strong basis in photographs, be it in the form of collections of private family photographs in the living room, or in the form of photography-based genealogies in public spaces.

An example of a public photography-based genealogy is the design of the windows of the Church of the Apostles (*Apostelkirche*) in the city center of Hamburg. After a fire in 1977, the previous stained glass windows were rebuilt with clear glass, on which three columns of black and white filmstrip run with photographs of six men and six women of different denominations in the twentieth century. These persons are presented as modern apostles on the basis of their personality and lifework.[8] The design of the church windows actualizes a segment of the sociopolitical as well as spiritual genealogy of the churches in a mainly visual way. The use of photographs engages the fact that we identify differently with text on the one hand, and with images, sound and moving pictures on the other. It is easier for us to identify with the human form, which functions as a nuanced mirror. Looking at this mirror provokes a process of differentiated affective identification.[9] On this basis, the visual genealogy of the church windows invites identification and initiates a process of recognizing the well-known persons on the one hand, and enquiring about the less-known ones on the other. This process invites reflection on ethics, resistance and agency in the history and recent self-conception of the churches.

Utilizing in a film, and especially a documentary film, as a second cultural object allows for exploring the role of audio-visual genres for the

7. For the concept of postmodern hybrid identities see Homi Bhabha, *The Location of Culture* (London: Routledge, 1994).

8. The three columns of filmstrip show photographs of Sophie Scholl, Hermann Stöhr, Martin Luther King and Dietrich Bonhoeffer; Simone Weil, Ernst Barlach, Albert Schweitzer and Mathilda Wrede; and Arnulfo Romero, Anna Paulsen, Elise Averdieck and Dorthee Day. http://www.kirche.eimsbuettel.de/kg.root/kg.1123301410.22/kg.1123 301410.22.2/index.html (accessed June 8 2013).

9. For the discussion of Media Studies' reception of neuroscientific research on mirror neurons, which play an important role in developing 'affective relations', see Julia Noordegraaf, 'Iterating Archival Footage and the Memory of War', in *The Archive: XVIII International Film Studies Conference* (ed. Alessandro Bordina, Sonia Campanini and Andrea Mariani; Udine: Forum, 2012), pp. 265-72 (267-68).

[handwritten annotations: "doing narrative work, not historical", "important to memory", "things"]

formation of cultural memory in general and genealogy performance in particular. Moreover, choosing a film as a second cultural object alongside the Bible text allows me to build on ongoing research on the Bible and film. This ongoing research marks the central area of recent research in which the Bible and cultural objects are engaged beyond reception history.

Research on the Bible and Film

To date, Bible scholars have primarily investigated films that either retell and actualize biblical texts, for example *The Ten Commandments* (Cecil B. DeMille, USA, 1956) and *The Passion of the Christ* (Mel Gibson, USA, 2004), or engage biblical themes, motives, or characters, consciously or unconsciously, for example *Magnolia* (Paul Thomas Anderson, USA, 1999) and *The Matrix* (Andrew and Lana Wachowski, USA, 1999).[10] Alongside these main foci, a third group of studies on the Bible and film has joined the field. These studies do not concentrate on films that are directly linked to the Bible in one way or the other. Instead, they focus on films that share key themes with selected Bible texts. For example, George Aichele reads together the Gospel of Mark and the film *Minority Report* (Steven Spielberg, USA, 2002), on the basis of the shared guiding theme of the paradox of blindness and seeing/insight.[11] In this third group of studies that are as exceptional as they are innovative, the shared guiding theme serves as a prism for reading together a Bible text and a film text that have no other obvious connections. Searching for more obvious connections would miss the point of these readings, because their originality is based precisely on the absence of an obvious connection between Bible text and film text.

My own research is clearly located in this third group of studies. Reading the documentary film *My Life Part 2* together with the genealogies in 1 Chronicles 1–9 is grounded in their sharing the theme of gendered

---

10. The former approach is predominant in, e.g., J. Cheryl Exum, *Plotted, Shot and Painted: Cultural Representations of Biblical Women* (JSOTSup, 215; Gender, Culture, Theory, 3; Sheffield: Sheffield Academic Press, 1996); Adele Reinhartz, *Scripture on the Silver Screen* (Louisville, KY: Westminster/John Knox Press, 2003); and Freek L. Bakker, *Jezus in beeld: Een studie naar zijn verschijnen op het witte doek* (Utrecht: Uitgeverij Van Gruting, 2011). For the latter approach see, e.g., Larry J. Kreitzer, *The Old Testament in Fiction and Film: On Reversing the Hermeneutical Flow* (Sheffield: Sheffield Academic Press, 1994); Melanie J. Wright, *Moses in America: The Cultural Uses of Biblical Narrative* (Oxford: Oxford University Press, 2002); and Francoise Mirguet, 'Implicit Biblical Motifs in Almodovar's *Hable Con Ella* and *Volver*: The Bible as Intertext', *Journal of Religion and Popular Culture* 23.1 (2011), pp. 27-39. The setup of the anthology *The Bible in Film—The Bible and Film* confirms the twofold research focus. See *The Bible in Film—The Bible and Film* (ed. J. Cheryl Exum; Leiden: E.J. Brill, 2006).

11. George Aichele, 'The Possibility of Error: Minority Report and the Gospel of Mark', in *The Bible in Film-The Bible and Film*, pp. 144-57.

genealogy performance which they both engage in order to address disturbing memories and a fractured past.[12]

Engaging films from the angle of Biblical Studies involves the question of how films are selected and on what basis they are read together. Aichele and Walsh highlight the intuitive component of choosing to pair off a Bible text and a film text. They claim that the starting point for an actual 'intertextual' reading is the scholar: 'The "real" (material) justification for any connection between Scripture and film is the scholar whose specific experience and interpretative reading alone supplies the connection.'[13] As a consequence, they conclude that the selection of cinematic intertexts cannot be more or less correct, but only more or less interesting and provocative.[14] I agree with Aichele and Walsh's emphasis on intuitive and experimental impulses at the origin of reading a Bible text and a film text together, especially if the latter does not directly relate to the former. Still, I follow Athalya Brenner in her insisting that a critical reflection on the initial impulse for the choice of case studies is possible and in order.[15] Let me therefore briefly summarize why I decided to work with the documentary *My Life Part 2*.

The first impulse for engaging *My Life Part 2* was based on the film's additional perspectives on the issues of gender and fractures in relation to genealogy composition. While 1 Chronicles 1–9 features gendered fragments, *My Life Part 2* centers on a female lineage and engages in a project of gynealogy composition. The film also provides additional perspectives on the issue of fractures in genealogy performances. While 1 Chronicles 1–9

---

12. Reading together a Bible text and a film on the basis of a shared theme constitutes closeness to the field of theology and film. Here, the film analysis likewise embarks from a theme, albeit without bringing it back to the interpretation of a specific Bible text. An important monograph that, independently from my research, proposes a comparable setting of analysis is Ulrike Vollmer's *Seeing Film and Reading Feminist Theology: A Dialogue*. Vollmer starts out with a question ('what does it mean to see and to be seen?'). She pursues this question in philosophical discourses on seeing, in feminist theologies of relatedness and in a detailed analysis of three films. Finally, she engages these three components in a dialogue that allows her to develop her own theology of seeing. See Ulrike Vollmer, *Seeing Film and Reading Feminist Theology: A Dialogue* (New York: Palgrave Macmillan, 2007). For further literature on theology and film, see *Explorations in Theology and Film: Movies and Meaning* (ed. Clive Marsh and Gaye Ortiz; Oxford: Blackwell, 1998); and the book series 'Film und Theology' by the international research group *Film and Theology*, e.g. *Blick über den Tod hinaus / Seeing Beyond Death: Bilder vom Leben nach dem Tod in Theologie und Film / Images of Afterlife in Theology and Film* (ed. Christopher Deacy and Ulrike Vollmer; Film und Theologie, 18; Marburg: Schüren-Verlag, 2011).

13. Aichele and Walsh, 'Introduction: Scripture as Precursor', p. xi.

14. Aichele and Walsh, 'Introduction: Scripture as Precursor', p. xi.

15. Athalya Brenner, 'Foreword', in *Culture, Entertainment and the Bible* (ed. George Aichele, Sheffield: Sheffield Academic Press, 2000), pp. 7-12 (8-9).

provides a multilayered network in which fissures occur, are then restricted, and resurface again, *My Life Part 2* addresses the break of its central lineage in a straightforward way and clearly engages the notion of discontinuity in its genealogy performance. In both cases, gender as well as fractures, the additional perspectives of the film provided important impulses for broadening the matrix with which I analyze gendered genealogy performance in response to fractured pasts. Hence, the initial impulse to engage *My Life Part 2* paid off throughout the research.   Genre

In this context, the genre of documentary film likewise played a central role. The genre of documentary film features characteristics that significantly add to the theme of my research. Most important in this respect is the need for documentaries to negotiate and make productive the dialectic relation between reality on the one hand, and image, interpretation, bias and representation on the other.[16] The same challenge is at the core of genealogy composition. In fact, finding a balance between recounting the past to one's best knowledge on the one hand, and creative appropriation of the past in a performance that makes sense for the present on the other, is for me the most fascinating challenge of genealogy composition in response to trauma. Hence, this feature of documentary film, as well as others, contributes to the core of the research project.[17]   Archive

The next important argument in favour of *My Life Part 2* was that the film contributes the notion of the archive and relates it to the theme of gendered genealogy performance in response to traumatic pasts. With the archive concept come issues of alternative archives and counter-present genealogies, appropriating a traumatic legacy, as well as contested knowledge production and power as active in genealogy composition. The film's engagement of the archive concept interlocks with the heterogeneous character of 1 Chronicles 1–9, which can likewise be described as an archive. Hence, *My Life Part 2* contributed a notion that is not only rich in itself, but also provided a key for an understanding of how the genealogy performance in 1 Chronicles 1–9 is meaningful in response to its fracturing past. The film's performing of an archive intrigued me for yet another reason. *My Life Part 2* builds its central lineage using photographs, documents, audiotapes and other memorial objects such as ancient herbaria of the filmmaker's mother, laundry labeled with the name of her grandmother, and a silver goblet that was handed down

---

16. Stella Bruzzi, *New Documentary: A Critical Introduction* (London: Routledge, 2000), p. 6.

17. Other aspects of the genre of documentary film that contribute to the analysis of gendered genealogies in response to trauma are the relation between past and present; the notion of framing; the role of editing; the role of the narrative and voice-over; and the performative character of documentary film. See Bruzzi, *New Documentary*; and Bill Nichols, *Introduction to Documentary* (Bloomington, IN: Indiana University Press, 2001).

in the family.[18] This takes the idea of genealogies beyond the medium of the text and points to the possibilities of both audio-visual and three-dimensional genealogy performances.

Finally, *My Life Part 2* contributes themes to the research that I think are crucial for understanding the explosive force of the genealogy genre today. Primarily, the location of the film's genealogy performance at the intersection of personal and public memory and the connected issues of mediation and agency in performing genealogical memory acts were important arguments in favour of this specific film.

Beyond intuitive and experimental impulses at the basis of partnering a Bible text and a film, the selection of *My Life Part 2* is in line with a more general research interest: I am mainly interested in alternative films over mainstream cinema, whereas 'alternative' refers to the sociopolitical contexts and perspectives of both filmmaker and the film's protagonists and contents; the economical condition of the production; and the aesthetics of the film. This interest runs parallel to my interest in alternative perspectives in and on the Bible. As Matthew Rindge puts it, it is crucial to consider international, independent and older films for the selection of films, rather than merely focusing on (Hollywood) films which are overwhelmingly 'made by white males and for white audiences'.[19] From his North American perspective, he argues that '[p]airing biblical texts solely with Anglo films has the same effect as reading biblical texts solely through the lens of white, American male interpreters. The method in each case is inherently limited'.[20]

My Life Part 2 matches this interest throughout. *My Life Part 2* is a European low-budget film made by a female filmmaker. Filmmaker and protagonists bring to the fore experiences that are at the fringe of self-conceptions in post-war Germany. Moreover, their experiences in and memories about Nazi Germany and the Holocaust have a marginal position in the discourse on post-Shoah memory in Germany and beyond it. My interest in alternative films continues in my choice of genre, a documentary film. Working with a Bible text and a documentary film is pioneering work. It significantly enlarges the scope of studies on the Bible and film toward films that engage alternative perspectives and feature experimental aesthetics.[21]

18. For the notion of memorial objects see Marianne Hirsch and Leo Spitzer, 'Testimonial Objects: Memory, Gender, Transmission', *Poetics Today* 27.2 (2006), pp. 137-63.

19. Matthew S. Rindge, Erin Runions and Richard S. Ascough, 'Teaching the Bible and Film: Pedagogical Promises, Pitfalls and Proposals', in *Teaching Theology & Religion* 13.2 (2010), pp. 140-55 (144). (The article consists of a text by Rindge and two responses by Runions and Ascough.)

20. Rindge, Runions and Ascough, 'Teaching the Bible and Film', p. 145.

21. Erin Runions's reading of the documentary *Paris is Burning* (Jennie Livingston, USA, 1990), a chronicle of the drag queen ball culture in New York City, together with

Next to the selection of films, the question of on what basis film text and Bible text are read together is crucial. In line with other studies in the field of the Bible and film, my research is based on notions of intertextuality. Therefore, in a next step, I will discuss different aspects of the concept of intertextuality in order to access its productivity as well as its limits for the actual research.

2. *Intertextuality: Potential and Limits of a Key Concept*

The notion of intertextuality refers to the general understanding of texts as part of a broad web of texts and sociopolitical discourses. Moreover, in the context of Biblical Studies, intertextuality refers to a particular method of reading.[22] In this book, the two aspects of intertextuality serve different functions. Intertextuality as an indicator of the location of texts in a broad web of texts and discourses is important for the methodological setup of the book. Intertextuality as a particular (exegetical) method of reading is important for the close reading of the biblical genealogies, especially because it brings to the fore their being embedded into the broader context of biblical literature. In this section, I first discuss intertextuality as a reading strategy within Biblical Studies and point to its relevance for the close reading of 1 Chronicles 1–9, as well as for the close reading of *My Life Part 2*. In a second step, I introduce the broader notion of intertextuality and discuss its contribution and limits with regard to reading a Bible text and a film text together.

Intertextuality as Particular Method of Reading
Intertextuality, understood as an actual reading strategy, constitutes part of the canon of exegetical methods. It describes a reading strategy which reads Bible texts as embedded into the broader context of biblical literature, and factors in the many references and dependencies within this corpus of texts.[23]

---

the book of Micah, is one of the few other examples that engage biblical literature and documentary film and works in a similar direction. See Erin Runions, *How Hysterical: Identification and Resistance in the Bible and Film* (New York: Macmillan, 2003), pp. 93-114.

22. Ellen van Wolde, 'Intertextuality: Ruth in Dialogue with Tamar', in *A Feminist Companion to the Bible: Approaches, Methods and Strategies* (ed. Athalya Brenner and Carole Fontaine; Sheffield: Sheffield Academic Press, 2nd edn, 1997), pp. 426-51 (426-32).

23. Van Wolde, 'Intertextuality: Ruth in Dialogue with Tamar', pp. 426-51. See also *Intertextuality and the Bible* (ed. George Aichele and Gary A. Phillips; Semeia, 69/70; Atlanta, GA: Scholars Press, 1995); Manfred Pfister and Ulrich Broich, *Intertextualität: Formen, Funktionen, Anglistische Fallstudien* (Tübingen: Max Niemeyer, 1985); Michael Fishbane, *Biblical Interpretation in Ancient Israel* (Oxford: Cleardon

As Michael Fishbane puts it, a canon such as the corpus of biblical literature 'presupposes the possibility of correlations among its parts, such that new texts may imbed, reuse, or otherwise allude to precursor materials—both as a strategy of meaning-making and for establishing the authority of a given innovation'.[24] References between texts produce meaning in the reading process, whereas stylistic devices of the text (e.g. theme words, motifs, or genres), as well as external, comparative issues from the larger cultural context, help readers to perceive 'latent networks of intra-and intertextual meaning'.[25] Intertextuality as an exegetical reading strategy focuses on the biblical textual community and its 'inner-community conversation'.[26] Here, the interaction of texts is understood as a process that generates 'a realm of discourse, dialogue and imagination that provides a world in which to live in'.[27]

1 Chronicles 1–9 involves a dense web of intertextual references, as I will explain in the introduction to 1 Chronicles 1–9 in Chapter 3. Here, intertextuality concerns, among other things, the use of earlier biblical genealogies as *Vorlage* of particular genealogies of 1 Chronicles 1–9, as well as references to biblical narratives, such as the reference to Genesis 38 at the beginning of the genealogies of Judah (2.3-4).[28] These intertextual connections weave the genealogies into the intertextual fabric of the Hebrew Bible, feed into their meaning and are crucial clues to understanding them. As a consequence, intertextuality as a method of reading will have a place in the research when it comes to the close reading of the Bible text and its complex references to and modifications of inner-biblical intertexts, especially in Chapters 4 and 6.

Intertextuality also plays a role in the analysis of *My Life Part 2*. On the one hand, the film establishes intertextual connections within the film: its characteristic assembling and presenting of materials leads to layers of meaning in which images, motifs, or sounds reoccur, for example the reoccurring motif of family photographs taken at the beach of the Baltic resort

---

Press, 1985); and Yair Zakovitch, 'Inner-Biblical Interpretation', in *Reading Genesis: Ten Methods* (ed. Ronald Hendel; Cambridge: Cambridge University Press, 2010), pp. 92-118.

24. Michael Fishbane, 'Types of Biblical Intertextuality', in *Congress Volume: Oslo 1998* (ed. André Lemaire and Magne Sæbø; VTSup, 80; Leiden: E.J. Brill, 2000), pp. 39-44 (39).

25. Michael Fishbane, *Text and Texture: Close Readings of Selected Biblical Texts* (New York: Schocken Books, 1979), pp. XI-XII.

26. Brueggemann, *Theology of the Old Testament*, p. 76.

27. Brueggemann, *Theology of the Old Testament*, p. 76.

28. For the use of earlier genealogies in 1 Chron. 1–9 see Martin Noth, *Überlieferungsgeschichtliche Studien 1: Die sammelnden und bearbeitenden Geschichtswerke im Alten Testament* (SKG.G, 18.2; Halle: Niemeyer, 2nd edn, 1943), pp. 116-22.

Boltenhagen. On the other hand, *My Life Part 2* engages external intertexts, such as television footage on central instances of the German debate
on post-Shoah memory. These external intertexts link the film to particular
cultural and political discourses and help to illustrate its political standpoint
(see Chapter 5).

In conclusion, in both case studies, the strength of intertextuality as an
actual reading strategy is based on reflections of concrete interconnections
and modifications of texts whose literary and sociohistorical contexts overlap. Here, intertextuality pertains to the individual close readings of the case
studies in their respective contexts. Things change if it comes to reading
together the two case studies. The literary and sociohistorical contexts of 1
Chronicles 1–9 and *My Life Part 2* are extremely different. Hence, intertextuality as an actual reading strategy is much less effective for reading them
together. If it comes to reading together a Bible text and a film text, a broad
notion of intertextuality as general indicator of the location of texts as part
of a broad web of texts and sociopolitical discourses is at stake. In order to
show the importance and limits of such a broader notion of intertextuality
for the book, I will shortly sketch the development of the concept and discuss some of its key notions.

Intertextuality as Indicator for the Location of Texts in a Broad Web of Texts and Sociopolitical Discourses

The concept of intertextuality is based on the work of Russian theorist
Mikhail Bakhtin (1895–1975). Bakhtin understands text as part of a structure that presses beyond single voice accounts, toward both internal dialogue and the participation in social dialogue.[29] This conceptualization of
text as an essentially dialogical structure provides important ideas for my
research. First, Bakhtin argues that text is inclined to inhabit multiple positions without losing its main focus.[30] This argument is an important basis for
confronting a Bible text and a film text with a dialogical process in which
different aspects of the texts will be addressed in order to tease out their
complex meanings. Next, Bakhtin assumes that text performs inner dia-
logues.[31] This assumption provides an important starting point for external dialogue with a second text or cultural object. Third, Bakhtin highlights
the text's capacity for complex interaction with its rhetorical contexts, as
well as its active participation in social dialogue.[32] This capacity allows

29. Mikhail M. Bakhtin, 'Discourse in the Novel', in *The Dialogic Imagination: Four
Essays by M.M. Bakhtin* (ed. Michael Holquist; Austin, TX: University of Texas Press,
1981), pp. 259-422.

30. Bakhtin, 'Discourse in the Novel', p. 276.

31. Bakhtin, 'Discourse in the Novel', pp. 273-74.

32. Bakhtin, 'Discourse in the Novel', pp. 272-74. See also Graham Allan, *Intertextuality: The New Critical Idiom* (London: Routledge, 2000), p. 21.

for confronting a Bible text and a film text with themes of their respective rhetorical contexts, as well as with the rhetorical contexts of their recent readers. Finally, Bakhtin's insistence on the sociopolitical location of literary communication suggests that the more the sociopolitical context of the texts is brought into play, the more radical and effective the reading together of very different materials may become.

Bakhtin's propositions have been taken up by the French-Bulgarian theorist Julia Kristeva. Kristeva engaged Bakhtin's propositions in the French academic context and coined the term *intertextuality*.[33] Building on Bakhtin's argument that literary structures do not simply exist, but are generated in relation to other structures, Kristeva describes the literary word as an 'intersection of textual surfaces' and a dialogue between the writer, the addressee and the cultural context (which she describes as the exterior text) rather than a static point with a fixed meaning.[34] This dialogue takes place on a horizontal axis between subject and addressee, as well as on an intersecting vertical axis between text and context. As a consequence, each text intersects with other texts. It is constructed as a mosaic of quotations and always absorbs and transforms other texts.[35] Understanding texts as intersections of subject and addressee, as well as text and context, locates texts in a broad semiotic texture, which she calls the cultural-historical text. This texture includes the readers as well as other texts.[36]

Of Kristeva's rich theory of intertextuality, two aspects especially are central to this book, namely her insistence on the productive rather than descriptive character of intertextuality, and her related claim that the meaning of texts primarily emerges in intertextual perspective. Kristeva emphasizes that intertextuality does not end with describing a series of relationships within texts. Instead, the space of a given text is a space in which utterances taken from other texts intersect.[37] The investment of the text in discourses contributes utterances to it that are different from the one of the author. This provokes a shift from a discursive to a textual level of utterances, as well as from an informational and communicative level to a level of productivity.[38]

---

33. Julia Kristeva, *Desire in Language: A Semiotic Approach to Literature and Art* (ed. Leon S. Roudiez; trans. Thomas Gora, Alice Jardine and Leon S. Roudiez; New York: Columbia University Press, 1980).

34. Julia Kristeva, 'Word, Dialogue and Novel', in *Desire in Language*, pp. 64-91 (64-65). See also Kirsten Nielsen, 'Intertextuality and Hebrew Bible', in *Congress Volume: Oslo 1998*, pp. 17-31 (17).

35. Kristeva, 'Word, Dialogue and Novel', p. 65.

36. Julia Kristeva, 'The Bounded Text', in *Desire in Language*, pp. 36-63 (36).

37. Kristeva, 'The Bounded Text', p. 36.

38. Kristeva, 'The Bounded Text', p. 46. See also Daniela C. Caselli, *Beckett's Dantes: Intertextuality in the Fiction and Criticism* (Manchester: Manchester University Press, 2005), pp. 1-9.

With regard to my research, Kristeva's insistence on the productive character of intertextuality highlights that intertextuality does not end with comparing texts and cannot be grasped simply in terms of sources, influences, backgrounds and contexts. In the same way, the intent of reading together gendered genealogy performance in 1 Chronicles 1–9 and in *My Life Part 2* is not primarily descriptive. Instead, the intention is production, transformation and creation of knowledge. Here, the notion of intertextuality points to the production of meaning, and by doing so, to a movement which has the potential to alter its constituents.

Kristeva takes her argument on the productivity of intertextuality one step further with her claim that the meaning of a text primarily emerges in intertextual perspective. She argues that history and morality, which she sees as central factors in the production of the meaning of a text, can thus only be disclosed through 'a practice of a signifying structure in relation or opposition to another structure'.[39] As a consequence, no extra-textual reality exists that may provide reference points for understanding the meaning of a text. Texts only exist in the mesh of the general social-historical texture, and 'meaning and reference are possible only in relation to this network, as functions of intertextuality'.[40] With regard to this book, the claim that the meaning of texts is only possible in reference to the broader network of texts anticipates the expectation that reading 1 Chronicles 1–9 and *My Life Part 2* together holds the potential to generate an understanding of gendered genealogies in response to trauma that would otherwise remain hidden.

In conclusion, notions of intertextuality are at the basis of this research. They enable it, point to its aims, and indicate its promising potential. In particular, the idea of an overreaching texture (the social-historical text) enables placing texts side by side that differ in terms of genre, theme and

39. Kristeva, 'Word, Dialogue and Novel', p. 65.
40. Bible & Culture Collective (eds.), *The Postmodern Bible* (New Haven, CT: Yale University Press, 1997), p. 130. The idea that the meaning of texts (only) emerges in intertextual perspective as well as in the context of an overall semiotic texture was taken up by Roland Barthes (1915–1980). Barthes proposed that literary works are not containers of fixed meaning, but spaces in which never ending numbers of potential relations coalesce. In the center of this process is the reader, who initiates interferences of a text with other texts. However, in this role, the reader (as well as the author, who is conceptualized by Barthes as a context-bound reader) is not an autonomous subject but is constituted as a plurality of texts. See Roland Barthes, 'From Work to Text', in *The Rustle of Language* (trans. Richard Howard; Berkeley, CA: California Press, 1989), pp. 56-64 (59-60); Roland Barthes, 'The Death of the Author', in *The Rustle of Language*, pp. 49-55 (53); Roland Barthes, *S/Z* (trans. Jürgen Hoch; Frankfurt: Suhrkamp, 1976), especially p. 14; and Ellen van Wolde, 'Trendy Intertextuality?', in *Intertextuality in Biblical Writings: Essays in Honour of Bas van Iersel* (ed. Sipke Draisma; Kampen: Kok, 1989), pp. 43-49 (47).

cultural-historical context. It effectively widens 'the thinking- and living environment of (biblical) texts',[41] and works toward projects as proposed here.

At the same time, the idea of an overreaching texture marks the limits of the use of the broad concept of intertextuality for this research. In particular, Kristeva and Roland Barthes' argument that a text is 'not a stable, self-identical, enduring object but a place of intersection in a network of signification' is problematic.[42] Defining 1 Chronicles 1–9 and *My Life Part 2* as intersections in a network of signification may too easily lead to dissolving the actual texts into a homogeneous notion of textuality. Given how extremely disparate the texts are in terms of medium, genre and sociohistorical background, it seems important to conceptualize their relation to each other in a way that keeps their differences in focus. As a consequence, methodologically I begin with the notion of intertextuality, but in a next step propose the concept of socializing to generate an analytical setting that is stronger in meeting the distinctiveness of my case studies.

3. *Socializing Bible Texts and Films*

The notion of *socializing* a Bible text and a film text relates to reading together two disparate constituents that share a guiding theme, within a shared theoretical framework. The term 'socializing' is used in order to indicate that the two disparate constituents are read in close association and, in the process of reading, mutually accompany each other.

The term *socializing* or *co-housing* in English, *vergesellschaften* in German, derives from biology where it refers to *co-housing* animals or plants that have no natural close coexistence.[43] In the natural sciences, socializing animals or plants is a concern of applied community ecology, as well as Zoo Studies. In the former case, it concerns the management of altered or reconstructed communities, for example the biomanipulation of water quality or the management of multispecies fisheries.[44] A central concern of socializing animals or plants is whether the different parties will continue to do well under the new artificial conditions (will they continue to eat, breed, socialize and stay healthy, or will they develop problematic behaviors such as [auto]aggression, illness, or depression?).[45] An additional challenge in

41. Wolde, 'Trendy Intertextuality?', p. 45.
42. Bible & Culture Collective, *The Postmodern Bible*, p. 130.
43. David. C. Wareham, *Elsevier's Dictionary of Herpetological and Related Terminology* (Amsterdam: Elsevier, 2005), p. 44.
44. Peter J. Morin, *Community Ecology* (Malden, MA: Blackwell Science, 1999), pp. 366-75 (340-48).
45. N. Dorman and D.C. Bourne, 'Canids and Ursids in Mixed-species Exhibits', *Int. Zoo Yb.* 44 (2010), pp. 75-86 (77).

co-housing animals or plants is to enable the parties to change in reference to each other and, by doing so, to foreground characteristics and develop strategies to benefit from the new situation.[46] Beyond the natural sciences, socializing also connotes coming together for communication, networking and enjoyment, as well as the image of society as a location that potentially provides space for different parties.

Borrowing the term *socializing* from the natural sciences and using it metaphorically for reading a Bible text and a film together foregrounds the following aspects. First, the notion of socializing points to the artificial setting of bringing together a Bible text and a film text, two objects that have no 'natural' coexistence beyond their existence in the same cultural environment. Next, the term emphasizes the concern for doing justice to the objects involved. Both Bible text and film text need to be analyzed adequately and according to the requirements of the disciplines they belong to in order to successfully socialize them. Next, bringing the disparate constituents of the research together in a process of socializing is done in anticipation of insights into their character and meaning that would otherwise remain hidden. Finally, the idea of socializing expresses the wish to provide an analysis that is enjoyable to researcher and reader.

Elements of Socializing

The process of socializing a Bible text and a film text comprises five central elements: shared theme, analytical frame, case studies, the process of socializing and finally the presentation of its results. Each element contributes differently to starting a process of enabling, pursuing and abandoning questions, ideas and insights, in a back and forth between the elements involved. Each element contributes differently to guide this process consciously and to make it communicable and transparent. Finally, each element contributes differently to doing justice to the integrity and difference of the case studies involved.

1. The shared guiding theme: The starting point for socializing is a particular theme rather than a specific Bible text. This guiding theme should have a basis in biblical literature as well as in recent sociocultural discourses. For example, gendered genealogies in response to fractured pasts is a traditional biblical theme from the primaeval narratives in Genesis 1–11 to the New Testament genealogies of Jesus. At the same time, gendered genealogies in response to fractured pasts are part of recent discourses on changing family conceptions, migration processes, diasporic identities and cultural hybridity. They are located at the centre of recent sociocultural discourses.

In this book, the shared guiding theme likewise involves a shared genre, namely the genealogy genre. Sharing a genre, thus 'a compositional type

46. Dorman and Bourne, 'Canids and Ursids in Mixed-species Exhibits', pp. 76-77.

conforming to a given pattern and serving a specific function', strongly accelerates the process of socializing.[47] Even though the case studies realize the genealogy genre in quite different ways, referring the actual genealogy performances back to the genre with its distinct forms and functions, as well as to the question of how it functions in response to traumatic pasts, helps to guide the process and to make it transparent.

2. The analytical frame: Socializing takes place in a particular analytical space, which is set up by the analytical frame. In this book, the analytical frame has been set by notions of cultural memory. The analytical frame conceptualizes the guiding theme in reference to the wider academic debate and keeps the analysis focused. It provides a framework in which the guiding theme as well as the Bible text and the film are analyzed both independently and in relation to each other. By means of indicating reference points for focusing the individual constituents on the same issues, questions and hypotheses, the analytical frame supports the integrity of each text, while at the same time stimulating a dialogue between them. Next, the analytical frame guides and limits the process of socializing. Defining gendered genealogies as memory performances relegates other possible roads of enquiry to the back benches. For example, anthropological or historical approaches to genealogies are apprehended but not fully played out in the actual close readings. In conclusion, clearly conceptualizing my object of research from the outset, and thereby establishing an analytical frame, aids significantly in keeping socializing transparent and communicable.

3. The case studies: The case studies are selected in view of their expected contributions to understanding the guiding theme. Moreover, they need to provide sufficient common ground to serve as a starting point for reading them together, as well as enough differences that can serve to rub surfaces for a promising reading. The film may take up biblical motives or passages. However, the presence of the Bible in the film is not the criteria for socializing the two. Instead, Bible text and film text are linked through the shared theme and analytical frame.

Socializing is concerned with perceiving both film text and Bible text as communicative and literary units, and with analyzing them on their own terms. Therefore, the case studies are analyzed according to the requirements of their respective disciplines, that is, Biblical Studies and Media Studies. In the field of Bible and film, the concern for respecting the integrity of the film is often linked to the concept of a dialogue between Bible text and film text. Here, the dialogue concept functions, among other things, as a mechanism helping to take a film seriously rather than using it only

47. William W. Hallo, 'Compare and Contrast: the Contextual Approach to Biblical Literature', in *The Bible in the Light of Cuneiform Literature* (ed. William W. Hallo, Bruce William Jones and Gerald L. Mattingly; New York: The Edwin Mellen Press, 1990), pp. 1-30 (8).

illustratively.[48] In this context, 'understanding a film in its own aesthetic integrity and thereby discerning a film's unique voice, texture and potential meanings' is understood as precondition for entering into an effective dialogue with it.[49] In addition to the focus on doing justice to the film, Runions emphasizes the equal need to read the Bible text on its own terms. In concrete terms, she advocates reading the Bible text in its textual context, in order to understand 'how and why the film might be molding or manipulating that text to its own ends'.[50] I clearly share the concern with perceiving both film text and Bible text as integral wholes and with analyzing them on their own terms. However, rather than focusing on the dialogue between the two texts, I anticipate that the elements of a shared guiding theme (and genre) and a shared analytical frame will establish a setting that works toward granting the integrity of the film, as well as toward a transparent process of reading them together.

4. The actual process of socializing: Socializing as an actual process of reading together the case studies in view of a guiding theme and in reference to the analytical frame takes place in a spiral movement. This movement runs through phases of theoretical reflection on the guiding theme and the analytical frame; through phases of separate analyses of the case studies; and through phases of synthetic interpretations of the constituents of the process in view of each other. In the latter phase, one text is read from the perspective of the other, which, in turn, sets the interpretative horizon of the other. The process of socializing involves scheduled confrontations between the respective constituents as well as their informal interaction in the course of the process. Both formal and informal socializing entails moments of highlighting, as well as repressing themes. The actual process of reading together the case studies is close to an intertextual reading. Yet I understand intertextual readings as readings that engage connections between texts in a more direct way. While the intertextual reading pursues links, quotes and shared locations between the texts, the metaphor of socializing assumes more indirect connections that are conveyed by the shared theme and analytical frame.

5. Presentation: As a last step, socializing comprises a shift from going back and forth between guiding theme and case studies to presenting its results in compact blocks of analysis. Presenting the analyses in compact chapters is another important element in keeping the socializing transparent. Throughout the research, I do not take the reader into the spiral movement from one round

---

48. E.g., Ulrike Vollmer, 'Sprechen, Hören, und dann? Film und Theologie im Dialog', *Medienheft (07.04.2003)*, pp. 1-10; Vollmer, *Seeing Film and Reading Feminist Theology*, pp. 4-6; and Rindge, Runions and Ascough, 'Teaching the Bible and Film', pp. 142-46.

49. Rindge, Runions and Ascough, 'Teaching the Bible and Film', p. 145.

50. Rindge, Runions and Ascough, 'Teaching the Bible and Film', p. 150.

of analysis to the next one, which might easily become unclear and confusing. Instead, I provide the reader with compact analyses of the individual cases against the backdrop of the process of socializing. The film analysis in particular is presented in one coherent chapter. This presentation not only provides the reader with a condensed and concise analysis; it also supports the balance between independently analyzing the individual cases and reading them in close relation to each other. Such balance works toward a sound analysis of each genealogy performance against the backdrop of the perspectives opened up by the theoretical frame and the process of socializing. It functions as anchor in the socializing process and supports its transparency.

In conclusion, the model of socializing is based on a broad understanding of intertextuality, as proposed by Kristeva, but differs from it in critical aspects. Most central in this respect are the shared guiding theme and the analytical frame as necessary additional building blocks for the setup of socializing. The whole endeavour is broader than an intertextual reading and eventually targeted at gaining insight into a theme, rather than into a specific text. The theme is a biblical theme, but also reaches beyond the Bible. As a consequence, socializing requires actual close readings and adds to the analysis of the texts under consideration, but it neither begins nor ends there. A second important difference is the quality of the assumed connections between Bible text and film text. While intertextuality implies more direct links between the two texts, socializing emphasizes the discontinuity between the case studies, as well as the artificial setting in which they are brought together. This does not mean that the analysis neglects any direct connection between the texts, but in general, it engages links in reference to shared theme and analytical frame, which provides the analytical categories to qualify and assess the texts' similarities and differences.

I anticipate that the methodology of socializing will result in a deeper understanding of the genre of genealogy, how it functions in response to fractured pasts, and what role gender plays in this. Specifically, I anticipate contributing a historical perspective on the use of gendered genealogies in the context of a recent crisis of memory transfers, especially in view of traumatic pasts. Moreover, I anticipate gaining a deeper understanding as to why genealogies are such a common genre in the Bible, and what functions gender has in this context. I also anticipate contributing to the reception of *My Life Part 2* through the presentation of the film in film-series and at film festivals, as well as in academic publications.[51] Here, the genealogy perspective is critical for appreciating the importance of the film.

---

51. E.g. Hilde Hoffmann, '*Mein Leben Teil 2–My Life Part 2* (2003): Reflections about Recent Autobiographical Documentaries', in *Gendered Memories: Transgressions in German and Israeli Film and Theatre* (ed. Vera Apfelthaler and Julia B. Köhne; Vienna: Turia & Kant, 2007), pp. 128-43.

Chapter 3

1 CHRONICLES 1–9 AND ITS GENDERED FRAGMENTS

In the previous chapter on the methodology of socializing, I emphasized that socializing aims, among other things, to recognize the characteristics of and differences between Bible text and film text. Partly, this helps to understand the case studies in their sociohistorical contexts and to analyze them according to the standards of their disciplines. Accordingly, this chapter aims to contextualize the gendered fragments of 1 Chronicles 1–9 within their literary and sociohistorical context, and to bring into focus the key issues of the exegetical debate relating to them.

There are three main issues involved in contextualizing the gendered fragments of 1 Chronicles 1–9. First, the placement of the composition at the beginning of a retold story that has already been recounted in Samuel–Kings. Second, the sociopolitical location of Chronicles in the late Persian province Yehud, with the then-predominant discourses on exile and return, as well as on mixed marriages. Third, the challenge to meet the heterogeneous character of the genealogies which is in strong contrast to their conceptual coherence, and to make sense of this tension. A challenge that I propose to meet with a synchronic reception-oriented reading and by means of conceptualizing 1 Chronicles 1–9 as an archive.

Prior to discussing these main issues, the question of which passages of 1 Chronicles 1–9 indeed contain female-gendered references needs to be addressed. My criterion for considering a passage as containing a female-gendered reference is the occurrence of a female figure, identified as such either through a female name, a female verb form and/or a relational term such as 'wife' or 'daughter'. This criterion results in thirty eight text passages that refer to approximately sixty individual women and five female groups.[1]

---

1. 1 Chron. 1.5-6, 32-33, 36, 39, 50, 51b-54; 2.3-4, 16-17, 18-19, 21, 24, 26, 29, 34-35, 46-49a, 49b, 50b; 3.1-9, 19; 4.3, 4, 5-7, 9, 17-18, 19, 27; 5.29a; 7.4, 8, 13, 14-19, 23, 24, 30, 32; 8.8-11, 29; 9.35. A survey of the references to women in 1 Chron. 1–9 is given in *Appendix 1*. In her five page long entry on 1 and 2 Chronicles in 'The Women's Bible Commentary', Alice Laffey takes the time to list all the women that occur in 1 Chronicles 1–9 by name and to indicate relational terms, intertextual references,

However, the criterion of a female name in particular turns these numbers into round figures rather than unambiguous numbers. As Marie-Theres Wacker has pointed out in one of the earliest interpretations of 1 Chronicles 1–9 from a gender perspective, names in ancient Israel were less clearly linked to gender than they are today.[2] As a consequence, Chronicles provides many gender-ambiguous names such as Shelomith or Abijah, which are attested for both males and females.[3] In many cases, the textual context allows the reader to determine the gender of a character. For example, Shelomith is listed as sister in 3.19, and Abijah is introduced as wife in 2.24. Other cases are less clear. They are open to the reader's gender projections and require interpretation.

An example of a gender-ambiguous reference is the reference to Oholibamah among the town chiefs of Edom (1.52). Oholibamah is known from the Genesis genealogies, where she is listed as one of the wives of Esau (Gen. 36.2, 14, 18, 25). This identification of Oholibamah as a female name is supported by the emphasized final ה, which often points to a female form. The same Genesis genealogy lists Oholibamah as one of the town chiefs of Edom (Gen. 36.41). In the context of 1 Chronicles, the name is gender-ambiguous. 1 Chronicles 1–9 does not include Esau's wives. But it adapts the list of town chiefs including Oholibamah and Timna, presumably another female name in the list (1 Chron. 1.51-54). Should Oholibamah be considered a female name and the list of town chiefs counted among the passages that provide references to women? Answers vary. For example, in the Anchor Bible Dictionary, Ulrich Hübner identifies Oholibamah as female in accordance with the literary context and grammar.[4] In contrast, Martin Noth identifies Oholibamah as a male name, a decision that is based on the argument that a woman could not fulfill the role of a town chief, hence, on a particular interpretation of the sociohistorical background of the text.[5]

---

indication of descendants and/or specific activities. This list is most impressive even though it 'only' includes 42 women. Alice L. Laffey, '1 and 2 Chronicles', in *The Women's Bible Commentary: Expanded Edition with Apocrypha* (ed. Carol Ann Newsom and Sharon H. Ringe; Louisville, KY: Westminster/John Knox Press, 1998), pp. 110-15 (112-13).

2.   Marie-Theres Wacker, 'Die Bücher der Chronik: Im Vorhof der Frauen', in *Kompendium Feministische Bibelauslegung* (ed. Marie-Theres Wacker and Luise Schottroff; Gütersloher Verlagshaus: Gütersloh, 3rd edn, 2007), pp. 146-55 (148). For a survey of Hebrew female names see J.J. Stamm, 'Hebräische Frauennamen', in *Hebräische Wortforschung: Festschrift zum 80. Geburtstag von Walter Baumgartner* (ed. G.W. Anderson *et al.*; VTSup, 16; Leiden: E.J. Brill, 1967), pp. 301-39.

3.   Shelomith is male in 26.25 and female in 3.19; Abijah is male in 2 Chron. 13.1-23 and female in 2.24.

4.   Ulrich Hübner, 'Oholibamah (Person)', *ABD* V, p. 10.

5.   Martin Noth, *Die israelitischen Personennamen im Rahmen der gemeinsemitischen Namengebung* (Stuttgart: Kohlhammer, 1928), pp. 158-59.

Undertaking a conscious counter-reading of exegetical politics and traditions, I suggest a reading praxis that, for a start, takes names that are clearly
identified as female at one point of the text as indeed female ones. This
presupposition will then have to be carefully checked in each respective
case. Such reading practice is especially reasonable for the text unit in question. 1 Chronicles 1–9 lists women in positions that may easily collide with
readers' gender expectations: Sheerah builds three cities (7.24), Sheshan's
daughter continues the family line in a problematic situation (2.34-35),[6]
and Zeruiah 'fulfils the role of a (male) head of her section of the family'.[7]
In these instances, the literary context makes clear that we are dealing with
women. Other passages may refer to women as clan chiefs or 'sons' without making it explicit.[8] Of course, this practice does not lead to unambiguous data. Additional women might be listed 'undercover' and only surface
in the reading process. Others might become male again.[9]

Next to the identification of female names, female-gendered passages
are characterized by female verb forms and female relational terms. An
excellent overview in this respect has been provided by Antje Labahn and
Ehud Ben Zvi. Labahn and Ben Zvi describe their article as 'preliminary,
basic observations' about the references to women in the genealogies of 1
Chronicles 1–9.[10] In fact, however, they present not only a thorough, but
to date also the only comprehensive survey that includes a short analysis
of each of the more than fifty passages under consideration. Labahn and
Ben Zvi organize their survey by categorization qua role models and dis-
tinguish between traditional family roles, such as mother–wife, mother–
divorcee and the identity as daughter or sister and lineage roles that are
usually attributed to mature males, for example, women as heads of the
family and women building cities. They argue that women in 1 Chronicles
1–9 are construed as fulfilling a variety of roles in society and conclude
that even though the text 'reflects a patriarchal point of view, it contains

---

6. See Antje Labahn and Ehud Ben Zvi, 'Observations on Women in the Genealogies of 1 Chronicles 1–9', *Biblica* 84 (2003), pp. 457-78 (465-66).

7. Labahn and Ben Zvi, 'Observations on Women', p. 473.

8. E.g., 1 Chron. 4.17-18 lists a certain Miriam among the 'sons' of Bithiah daughter of Pharaoh.

9. Examples that go further than my own survey of female figures in the text are
Japhet, who suggests that 1 Chron. 2.49 might list Shaaph as another concubine of
Caleb due to the related feminine verb form (Sarah Japhet, *I&II Chronicles: A Com-
mentary* [London: SCM Press, 1993], p. 87); and Curtis, who discusses whether Achlai,
the 'son' of Sheshan should be understood as a female name (2.31), because 2.34 states
that Sheshan had no sons but only daughters (Edward Lewis Curtis and Albert Alonzo
Madsen, *A Critical and Exegetical Commentary on the Books of Chronicles* [ICC, 11;
Edinburgh: T. & T. Clark, 1952], p. 82).

10. Labahn and Ben Zvi, 'Observations on Women', p. 457.

references that indicated to the early readers of the book that ideologically-construed gender expectations may and have been transgressed in the past and with good results'.[11]

Labahn and Ben Zvi's article is effective in showing the abundance and complexity of the references to women in 1 Chronicles 1–9. However, it requires further elaboration concerning an assessment of the findings. In my view, Labahn and Ben Zvi suggest a clearer patriarchal point of view than the texts actually advance. As a consequence, their survey has the tendency to domesticate the subversive potential of the female-gendered passages by means of reinscribing an unquestioned patriarchal perspective on the text, and defining text-inherent interferences with this perspective as exceptional transgressions only. Still, this does not invalidate the important foundation that Labahn and Ben Zvi have laid for any further work on women in 1 Chronicles 1–9.

For the purpose of contextualizing the gendered fragments of 1 Chronicles 1–9 in their literary and sociohistorical contexts, as well as to delineate the main exegetical debates, I will not (again) itemize categories of names, role models, verbal forms, or intertexts. Instead, I will discuss key issues such as eponymous names of wives or female involvement in formulaic language in relation to the introductory issues the chapter addresses.

To sketch some main threads: discussing the placement of the composition at the beginning of a retold story will take account of the absence of many biblical women in 1 Chronicles 1–9. Next, locating Chronicles in the late Persian province Yehud, with the predominant discourses on exile and return as well as on mixed marriages, will comprise the occurrence and function of foreign wives and wives with eponymous names, as well as the issue of female inheritance. Finally, conceptualizing the heterogeneous yet conceptually coherent genealogy composition as an archive will include an analysis of formations and formulaic language as means of labelling, structuring, and framing archival contents and the involvement of female-gendered passages in this process.

Part of contextualizing the gendered fragments in the exegetical debate is discussing the (few) studies that approach 1 Chronicles 1–9 from an explicit gender perspective. At the end of the chapter is an assessment of these studies and the conclusions I draw for the subsequent close reading.

1. Genealogy Composition at the Beginning of a Retold Story

Chronicles' Creative Engagement with the Literary Tradition
1 Chronicles 1–9 stands at the beginning of a retold story: the book of Chronicles recounts the history of Israel's monarchy, a well-known story

11. Labahn and Ben Zvi, 'Observations on Women', p. 457.

that has already been narrated in the books of Samuel and Kings.[12] In doing so, Chronicles does not merely copy the earlier account, but in 'creative literary involvement'[13] and as 'an integral part of a larger pattern of interpreting and applying older texts to a new context and literary setting',[14] reworks and recontextualizes passages to add new perspectives and settle distinct priorities. Intertwining intertextual references to older (authoritative) texts and critical subject matters of its own time allows the text to establish its own ideological agenda.[15] In the process of telling anew, Chronicles appears as a voice that is highly knowledgeable in reading, assessing and relating to other authoritative books such as Samuel–Kings, Genesis, Leviticus, Deuteronomy, and Jeremiah.[16]

In contrast to the narrative parts of Chronicles, the initial genealogy composition has no predecessor in Samuel–Kings.[17] Instead, the genealogies engage biblical intertexts, supposed extra-biblical sources, the own literary imagination to create a new composition.[18] The genealogies anchor

---

12. After the genealogies in 1 Chron. 1–9, the book recounts the history of Israel under David and Solomon (1 Chron. 10–2 Chron. 9) as well as the history of the kingdom of Judah from the separation of the northern tribes (2 Chron. 10–36). Chronicles ends with the Cyrus edict that consented to the return of groups of deportees to Judah and rebuilding Jerusalem and the Second Temple (2 Chron. 36.22-23).

13. Isaac Kalimi, *The Reshaping of Israelite History in Chronicles* (Winona Lake, IN: Eisenbrauns, 2005), p. 405.

14. Gary N. Knoppers, 'Comments', in *Chronicles and the Chronicler: A Response to I. Kalimi, An Ancient Israelite Historian: Studies in the Chronicler, His Time, Place and Writing*, in *JHS* 6.2 [2006]), pp. 26-35 [28]).

15. See e.g. Yairah Amit, 'Araunah's Threshing-floor: A Lesson in Shaping Historical Memory', in *Performing Memory in Biblical Narrative and Beyond* (ed. Athalya Brenner and Frank H. Polak; Sheffield: Sheffield Phoenix Press, 2009), pp. 13-23.

16. Ehud Ben Zvi, 'The Book of Chronicles: Another Look', *SR* 31 (2002), pp. 261-81 (269).

17. In rabbinical tradition, the exceptional genealogy composition earned the book the designation 'the book of genealogies' alongside the common Hebrew name 'the events/words of the day'. Japhet, *I&II Chronicles*, p. 1.

18. Potential biblical sources for 1 Chron. 1–9 are genealogies (and narratives) from Genesis and Numbers, as well as from Exodus, Joshua, Samuel–Kings, Ezra–Nehemiah and Ruth. Chronicles' genealogies have a greater affinity with the Genesis materials than with the contemporary materials of Ezra–Nehemiah. E.g., genealogies in Chronicles and Genesis are typically segmented and advance the idea of 'all Israel', while Ezra–Nehemiah provides linear lineages and restricts Israel to Judah, Levi and Benjamin. Tamara C. Eskenazi, *In an Age of Prose: A Literary Approach to Ezra–Nehemiah* (Atlanta, GA: Scholars Press, 1988), pp. 24-25. The importance of Numbers as source for 1 Chron. 1–9 has been rightly highlighted by Martin Noth. Basically, Noth understands Num. 26 as blueprint for 1 Chron. 1–9. Martin Noth, *Überlieferungsgeschichtliche Studien 1: Die sammelnden und bearbeitenden Geschichtswerke im Alten Testament* (SKG.G, 18,2; Halle: Niemeyer, 2nd edn, 1943), pp. 116-22.

the subsequent narrative in the broader history of Israel and prepare for some of its key themes. Without explicitly discussing the details of the history of Israel, the genealogies run through many of its key moments. For example, they stretch back to creation and ancestral time (1.1–2.2). They refer to the leading figures of the Exodus and the time in the wilderness (5.29). They unfold the history of the twelve tribes in the land (2.3–9.2). They reflect on the emergence of monarchy and cult (3.1-24 and 5.27–6.38). And they follow the lineages through exile and return (9.1-34). By doing so, the genealogy composition situates the subsequent story of the monarchy in a broader historical frame and anchors it 'in the social organization and composition of Israel'.[19] Moreover, 1 Chronicles 1–9 introduces basic concerns of the subsequent narrative, most importantly the priority of Judah, the Davidic monarchy, and Jerusalem,[20] as well as the emphasis on 'all Israel'.[21] In conclusion, I assume that the genealogies belong to the book of Chronicles from the beginning.[22] They rework, assess, and recontextualize biblical intertexts as skillfully as Chronicles' narrative sections do and engage both literary and oral traditions in a new systematic genealogy composition.[23] For example, the genealogy of the nations (1.1–2.2) reworks and condenses large parts of the Genesis genealogies in a way that highlights the continuous succession from Adam to Israel and establishes the ancestral period as an authoritative starting point for the subsequent lineages.[24]

19. Ben Zvi, 'Another Look', p. 270.

20. Manfred Oeming, *Das wahre Israel: Die 'genealogische Vorhalle' 1 Chronik 1–9* (Stuttgart: Kohlhammer, 1990), pp. 115-16. (The term 'Genealogische Vorhalle' goes back to J. Wilhelm Rothstein and Johannes Hänel, *Das erste Buch der Chronik übersetzt und erklärt* [KAT, 18.2; Leipzig: Deichert, 1927]; and Wilhelm Rudolph, *Chronikbücher* (HAT, 21; Tübingen: Mohr Siebeck, 1955].)

21. Sara Japhet, *The Ideology of the Book of Chronicles and Its Place in Biblical Thought* (BEATAJ, 9; Frankfurt: Peter Lang, 1997), pp. 267-351 (278-85).

22. So also Willi, who describes 1 Chron. 1–9 (10) as sum, basis and fundament of the book of Chronicles (Willi, *1 Chr 1–10*, p. 9); as well as H.G.M. Williamson, *1 and 2 Chronicles* (NCB, 20; Grand Rapids, MI: Eerdmans, 1982), p. 39; and Japhet, *I&II Chronicles*, pp. 8-9.

23. Willi, *1 Chr 1–10*, p. 72. Accordingly, Willi suggests explaining contradictions in the composition with reference to the attitude of the author toward the tradition rather than differences between redactor and sources.

24. In general, lineages are traced from their eponymous ancestor, thereby referring to and putting emphasis on the ancestral period; Gary N. Knoppers, *1 Chronicles 1–9: A New Translation with Introduction and Commentary* (AB, 12; New York: Doubleday, 2003), p. 261. For a general introduction to the role of scribes in the transmission of biblical literature see Michael Fishbane, *Biblical Interpretation in Ancient Israel* (Oxford: Clarendon Press, 1985), pp. 23-43.

The Absence of Biblical Women in 1 Chronicles 1–9

Analyzing how the genealogies refer to earlier texts is practicable and reasonable. Things become more difficult when it comes to the lack of references. When reading 1 Chronicles 1–9 for its references to women, it is striking that many female figures known to the informed reader from the Pentateuch and beyond are missing. For example, Sarah and the other Genesis matriarchs are passed over, as are the women of the priestly lineages, Jochebed, Elisheba and the daughter of Putiel (Exod. 6.14-25). It is more than likely that the author(s) of Chronicles knew a version of Genesis that included the matriarchs. Here, their 'creative literary involvement' with the literary tradition meant to actively leave out this material. Passing over many women of the ancestral period is especially striking because the reference to the ancestral period plays an important role in 1 Chronicles 1–9. Hence, reflecting on absence and silence is an important part of analyzing how Chronicles' genealogies interact with familiar texts and critical subject matters of its own time create its own account of Israel's history and identity. Moreover, the few references to female figures from the Pentateuch need to be looked at with special attention. This concerns the references to Keturah (1.32-33), to Bath-shua and Tamar (2.3-4), to Achsah (2.49), Miriam (5.29), Bilhah (7.13) and to the daughters of Zelophehad (7.15).

Rather than listing the 'great women' of the tradition, the genealogies *minor women* include several minor characters from the Pentateuch, for example Abraham's secondary wife Keturah (1.32-33), as well as a significant number of women from Samuel–Kings, for example Zeruiah and Abigail (2.16-17), Tamar (3.9), Bathsheba (3.5), Ahinoam the Jezreelite and Abigail the Carmelite (3.1).[25] In addition, the text features a large number of women that are otherwise unknown in biblical literature: 1 Chronicles 1–9 lists twenty nine women and three female groups that are distinct to this genealogy composition.

In a short article from 2011, Willien van Wieringen discusses the question of why some women were included while others were left out, especially in reference to the wives of Abraham and David. Van Wieringen argues that those women were included who played 'productive roles in the continuation of their lineages'.[26] In the genealogical context, having (many) children rather than profession, social status, religious status, or mention in intertexts

---

25. Pancratius C. Beentjes, *1 Kronieken* (Verklaring van de Hebreeuwse Bijbel; Kampen: Kok, 2002), p. 24. Many but by no means all women from Samuel–Kings are listed. E.g., Saul's wife Michal is absent; see Willien van Wieringen, 'Why Some Women Were Included in the Genealogies of 1 Chronicles 1–9', in *Rewriting Biblical History: Essays on Chronicles and Ben Sira in Honour of Pancratius C. Beentjes* (ed. Jeremy Corley and Harm van Grol; DCLSt, 7; Berlin: W. de Gruyter, 2011), pp. 291-300 (299).

26. Van Wieringen, 'Why Some Women Were Included', p. 299.

would have been relevant. This would have been supported by the genre's interest in a mainly historical account of the past, rather than in narratives. Van Wieringen concludes that women such as Sarah and Hagar, who feature in narrative intertexts but do not have many children, were of little relevance for the text, while Abraham's secondary wife Keturah, a mother of several descendants, was indeed at the center of attention.[27]

In my view, Van Wieringen unnecessarily narrows down the functions of gendered references in 1 Chronicles 1–9, rather than appreciating their complexity. She does so by means of highlighting the role of mothers, which is not justified because of the complexity of the fragments in general and the multilayered descriptions of wives and mothers in particular. Moreover, women of the tradition who indeed have many children, such as Leah, are likewise left out. The narrowness of her interpretation continues in her understanding of genealogies as mainly historical accounts, thereby sidestepping the ideological and performative character of the genealogies.

Against Van Wieringen's analysis, my own focus is on the function of the intertextual references to women, which 1 Chronicles 1–9 indeed includes, as well as on the question of what functions women fulfill in the genealogies that can be better, or even only achieved by women who have no pre- or afterlife in biblical literature. Important functions in this respect are the functions of wives to identify, distribute and other descendants through segmentation, as well as to explicitly negotiate geopolitical claims as I will demonstrate in Chapter 6.

The Place of 1 Chronicles 1–9 at the End of the Hebrew Bible Canon
The character of Chronicles as a rewritten story is reflected in its placement within the last part of the Hebrew canon, the Writings.[28] The location within the Writings points to yet another alternative perspective on the text. In her analysis of intertextual connections between the books of Ruth, Esther, the Song of Songs and Ecclesiastes on the one hand, and the book of Genesis on the other, Klara Butting has proposed that the Writings comprise a selection of books that, often from a rather late date of composition, spin webs of intertextual references from the first and second sections of the Hebrew canon, Torah and Prophets and develop meaning in close

27. Van Wieringen, 'Why Some Women Were Included', pp. 296-99.
28. Another reason why Chronicles was situated among the Writings might have been the non-prophetic character of the book, which distinguished it from the Former Prophets. Within the Writings, Chronicles had a somewhat fluid position until the book finally settled at the end of the section, where it concludes the Hebrew canon (Georg Steins, *Die Chronik als kanonisches Abschlußphänomen: Studien zur Entstehung und Theologie von 1/2 Chronik* [BBB, 93; Weinheim: Beltz Athenäum, 1995], p. 80.) The Septuagint and the Vulgate locate Chronicles among the historical books after Kings, a tradition that has been adopted in Christian canons (Japhet, *I & II Chronicles*, p. 2).

[handwritten marginalia: "intertextual referenzen / inter biblical"]

reference to earlier authoritative literature.[29] Butting concludes that the tripartite structure of the Hebrew Bible enables a pattern of (critical) inner-biblical communication. In this pattern, texts from the canonical fringe take *[handwritten mark]* up and thereby interfere with main lines of biblical traditions, for example concerning power and gender.[30]

Butting's convincing approach draws attention to the genealogical frame of the Hebrew Bible. With Genesis at the beginning and Chronicles at the *[handwritten: bookends]* end, the Hebrew Bible is framed by two books in which genealogies stand central. This frame highlights the significance of the elaborate genealogy composition at the beginning of Chronicles, specifically the relevance of the genre of genealogy for the formation and utterance of memory and identity. In addition, Butting's approach emphasizes both directions in which 1 Chronicles 1–9, as a small but powerful element of the Writings, operates. On the one hand, the composition is in dialogue with earlier texts by means of reworking their lineages and narratives in the compacted form of genealogies. On the other hand, the composition responds to actual socio-political and religious discourses and related power claims of its sociohistorical context, a process that is linked to the intertextual dialogue but does not end with it.

An example of a dialogue between 1 Chronicles 1–9 on the one hand and Torah and Prophets on the other is found in the intertextual references to Genesis 38, 2 Samuel 11 and 2 Samuel 13 in the genealogies of Judah. The Chronicles passages refer to Tamar and Bath-shua in a short embedded narrative (2.3-4), and list Tamar and Bathsheba, who here is also called Bath-shua, as members of the Davidic house (3.5-9). My analysis of the latter references in Chapter 6 proposes that the process of composing already-known lineages and related narratives anew allows the genealogies to relate the three intertexts to each other and to comment on them in view of the respective other.

2. *The Late Persian Period Context*

The Discourse on Exile and Return

I have suggested understanding genealogies as performances of memory and identity that involve negotiations of contested knowledge and power. Such contests are necessarily linked to specific sociohistorical contexts and their ideological, political and religious discourses. Hence, it is necessary to ask how central discourses from the time of Chronicles may have impacted and gendered 1 Chronicles 1–9 in general and its gendered fragments in

29. Klara Butting, *Die Buchstaben werden sich noch wundern: Innerbiblische Kritik als Wegweisung feministischer Hermeneutik* (Wittingen: Erev Rav, 2nd edn, 1998).

30. Butting, *Buchstaben*, pp. 13, 163.

particular, as well as how the genealogies themselves may have functioned as active agents in these discourses. In line with Rüdiger Lux, I understand genealogy as a genre that is accessible to a heterogeneous audience that can access the contents of a genealogy composition for different levels of information and complexity. Hence, even though the composers of the genealogies are probably to be located in the scribal context of the Second Temple in Jerusalem, they did not produce 'insider-literature'.[31] On the contrary, the genealogy genre appears 'as an open form of speech, which, due to its high level of formalization, is able to integrate an audience that is pluralistic in terms of cultural and social difference, as well as concerning its level of education'.[32] This formal capacity of the genealogy genre to integrate a pluralistic audience qualifies 1 Chronicles 1–9 to function as active agent in the discourses at the time.

Chronicles is to be situated in the first half of the Second Temple period, probably in the late Persian period in the Persian province Yehud.[33] At the time, the Levant belonged to the Trans-Euphrates satrapy, with governors

31. Rüdiger Lux, 'Die Genealogie als Strukturprinzip des Pluralismus im Alten Testament', in *Pluralismus und Identität* (ed. J. Mehlhausen; VWGT, 8; Gütersloh: Gütersloher Verlagshaus, 1995), pp. 242-58 (247-49).

For the identification of the composers of the genealogies as scribes of the Jerusalem elite see Oeming, *Das Wahre Israel*, p. 206; and Jonathan E. Dyck, *The Theocratic Ideology of the Chronicler* (Leiden: E.J. Brill, 1998), pp. 162-64. Against Yigal Levin, who claims that the *Sitz im Leben* of 1 Chronicles 1–9 would be the 'tribal, village society' at the time, rather than the urban Jerusalem elite. Yigal Levin, 'Who was the Chronicler's Audience?: A Hint from His Genealogies', in *JBL* 122.2 (2003), pp. 229-45 (245). See also Isaac Kalimi for a discussion of whether the author(s) of Chronicles should be identified as Midrashist, exegete, theologian, or historian—Kalimi opts for the latter. In my view, the important result of Kalimi's discussion is that the author has to be seen as a 'creative artist' with 'sophisticated writing methods at his disposal', howsoever he is labeled. I use the terms 'scribe' or 'scribal context' as open references to a context in which literature was perceived, discussed and produced in such a creative and knowledgeable atmosphere. Isaac Kalimi, 'Was the Chronicler a Historian?', in *The Chronicler as Historian* (ed. M. Patrick Graham, Kenneth G. Hoglund and Steven L. McKenzie; JSOTSup, 238; Sheffield: Sheffield Academic Press, 1997), pp. 73-89.

32. Lux, 'Die Genealogie als Strukturprinzip des Pluralismus', pp. 248-49 (my translation).

33. For this date, I follow Knoppers and Japhet. Knoppers sets a time frame from late fifth to mid-third century BCE. Within this frame he argues for a rather late date. Knoppers, *I Chronicles 1–9*, pp. 101-17. Japhet likewise argues for a late date at the end of the Persian or beginning of the Hellenistic period; Japhet, *I&II Chronicles*, p. 28. This is against earlier dates, e.g. the last decade of the fifth century as proposed by Bob Becking, 'Zedekiah, Josephus and the Dating of Chronicles', *SJOT* 25.2 (2011), pp. 217-33 (231) and later dates, e.g. during the Hasmonean rule in the second half of the second century BCE as proposed by Israel Finkelstein, 'The Historical Reality behind the Genealogical Lists in 1 Chronicles', in *JBL* 131.1 (2012), pp. 65-83 (83). For an introduction

in the provinces of Yehud and Samaria. In the provinces, the elders as well as priests and temple administrators were two groups with significant influence.[34] While the political framework was set, the questions of which groups claimed political and religious offices and authority as well as related land claims were subject to continuous contest. Large parts of the population, who had remained in the territory of Judah in spite of deportations and the destruction of Jerusalem, faced groups of returnees from Babylonia who were now formative for the Jerusalem elite. At the same time, Samaria formed a parallel political and religious center. Last but not least, emigrants and deportees who remained in Babylonia or Egypt developed great diasporic centers.[35] Contests between these groups concerned the constitution of Israel and its religious, political, and territorial identities. For these concerns, the discourses on exile, return and restoration were central.

In Biblical Studies, the notion of 'the exile' serves as an umbrella term for a group of events at the beginning of the sixth century BCE that included Babylonian siege warfare against Judah and the destruction of state and temple, as well as deportations to and exile in Babylonia for a part of the population of Judah. As I have explained in Chapter 1, I refer to these events when I discuss 1 Chronicles 1–9 as a genealogy performance in response to a fractured and traumatic past. The notion of the exile refers to historical events on the one hand, but also to a contemporaneous discourse about these events on the other.[36] At this point in my argument, my focus is on the notion of exile and return as a discourse at the time, moreover as a discourse of a highly ideological character. The ideological character of the discourse arises from the idea that a normative pre-exilic Israel could be reconstructed, and that a legitimate inheritance of this normative Israel could serve as a basis for actual religious, political, territorial and economical claims and related conceptions of identity.

to the historical context of the Persian period see Erhard S. Gerstenberger, *Israel in der Perserzeit: 5. und 4. Jahrhundert v. Chr.* (BE, 8; Stuttgart: Kohlhammer, 2005).

34. Rainer Kessler, *Sozialgeschichte des alten Israel: Eine Einführung* (Darmstadt: Wissenschaftliche Buchgesellschaft, 2008), pp. 139-40.

35. Kessler, *Sozialgeschichte*, p. 139. For competing sociopolitical groups in the Persian period see also Lester L. Grabbe, 'Introduction', in *Leading Captivity Captive*, p. 14; and Philip Davies, 'Exile? What Exile? Whose Exile?', in *Leading Captivity Captive*, p. 135.

36. Historical events and contemporaneous biblical discourses may differ. For example, the return of exiles from Babylon is usually depicted as a uniform mass return, whereas it probably took place in waves that lasted for over a century. See Bob Becking, 'In Babylon: The Exile in Historical (Re)construction', in *From Babylon to Eternity: The Exile Remembered and Constructed in Text and Tradition* (ed. Bob Becking, Alex Cannegieter, Wilfred van de Poll and Anne-Mareike Wetter; London: Equinox, 2009), pp. 4-33 (30-31).

In concrete terms, groups that identified as returnees from Babylonian exile claimed to be the legitimate successors of the monarchic pre-exilic Israel and consequently gave ideological priority to the notion of exile and return. The book of Chronicles contributes to this effort. For example, it emphasizes the exile as a watershed by means of ending its history with the prospect of the return (rather than with an account of the historical situation in which the text was probably written).

In fact, the impact of exile and return on the majority of Jewish communities probably stood in sharp contrast to this ideological priority. The exile as ideological construct represents the successful claim to authoritative memory and identity made by and on behalf of particular groups within Judah. As Philip Davies puts it:

> 'Exile' is not an episode in the 'history of Israel'; it is an ideological claim on behalf of a certain population element in the province of Judah during the Persian period... This group has successfully achieved its claim. They produced literature that has been canonized in Christianity and Judaism and have thus gained a historical authority they do not deserve in the first place... The uniqueness of the event is not based on the historical events, but on the successful claim of a group to be exiles and their self-definition as continuation of monarchic Judah (and Israel).[37]

Highlighting the ideological character of the discourse on exile and return is especially important for understanding the genealogy composition in 1 Chronicles 1–9. Key issues of the discourse are the role of the Davidic dynasty and the status of Jerusalem, priestly traditions and cult, as well as the role of extended family and tribes; issues that play a central role in 1 Chronicles 1–9, where they are linked to notions of inheritance, continuity and identity.[38] In this context, the book of Chronicles and its genealogies may be understood as an important agent in negotiating identity conceptions and religious-political claims within the first half of the Second Temple period. Jonathan Dyck uses the convincing picture of Chronicles as an important 'window' to its time, which may be understood 'not as an opening on a reality lying beyond, but as an element which makes up that reality'.[39] Constructing Chronicles as such an agent or window acknowledges that its account of pre-exilic Israel is in dialogue with other texts/voices of the time. Moreover, the genealogies are especially qualified to negotiate ideological identity claims that were then central. As a form of memory, genealogies recall the roots of a community; they address intergenerational transfers

37. Davies, 'Exile? What Exile? Whose Exile?', pp. 136-37.
38. See Lester Grabbe for a discussion of the link between claims of continuity and notions of ethnicity; Lester L. Grabbe, 'Reflections on the Discussion', in *Leading Captivity Captive*, pp. 146-56 (148).
39. Dyck, *The Theocratic Ideology of the Chronicler*, p. 3.

of traditions, knowledge, and subjectivity. Genealogies map continuity and aim to negotiate territorial, cultural, and religious claims in the present and future. They are thus apt means of creating a normative past; legitimizing authority claims based on continuity and inheritance; and conceptualizing collective identity with a focus on defining the self and the other, insiders and outsiders. It is thus expedient that Chronicles so heavily employs the genre of genealogy and uses it in order to make a strong initial statement on the issues indicated above before dealing with the subsequent history of the monarchy.

1 Chronicles 1–9 in the Discourse on Mixed Marriages

A second central discourse during the ST period was the discourse on mixed marriages, which likewise concerns authoritative claims on identity. 1 Chronicles 1–9 does not address the issue as directly as, for example, Ezra–Nehemiah does in its straightforward attack on mixed marriages and on foreign women and children (Ezra 9–10; Nehemiah 13).[40] However, the discourse forms an important background to the inclusion of numerous wives, as well as the frequent ethnic and territorial identifications of women, for example, by means of eponymous names. Moreover, it concerns the issues of the continuation of the jeopardized lineage, and of female inheritance, which in 1 Chronicles 1–9 is linked to the role of daughters.

Eponymous Names, Foreign Wives and Foreign Mothers of Sons. The most basic means of identifying the women in 1 Chronicles 1–9 is by their names. At the same time, names are a major source for identifying the ethnic and territorial descent of women, and especially wives. The significance of the generally intelligible names in the Hebrew Bible is debated. On the one hand, names are understood as the essence of the name-bearer and her identity.[41] On the other hand, it is claimed that one can only speak of a general 'sensitivity to the *appropriateness* of the names of persons', while 'in many cases the relation between the name and specific features of the person named may have

---

40. For a discussion of mixed marriages in Ezra–Nehemiah see Katherine Southwood, *Ethnicity and the Mixed Marriage Crisis in Ezra 9–10: An Anthropological Approach* (Oxford Theological Monograph Series; Oxford: Oxford University Press, 2012); and Bob Becking, *Ezra, Nehemiah and the Construction of Early Jewish Identity* (FAT, 80; Tübingen: Mohr Siebeck, 2011), pp. 58-73.

41. So e.g. Karla Bohmbach. Bohmbach differentiates between names that express the identity of a person, eponymous names that 'identify a real or created person for whom a place, clan, or tribal group is named', names that function as a symbol for the whole people, e.g. the names of the children of Hosea and Gomer (Hos. 1.4-9) and names that are linked to a certain person and are used in order to activate this link, e.g. the common reuse of Mary in reference to the prophetess Miriam. Karla G. Bohmbach, 'Names and Naming in the Biblical World', in *WiS*, pp. 33-40 (36).

been a somewhat casual, partial and accidental one'.[42] In my view, one must differentiate between the actual naming of newborn children and the naming of a character in a story, which may relate to historical persons but has a focus on the presence of the character in the narrative. In the latter case, names may indeed give additional information about the character; serve as a means of setting the tone of a narrative; and trigger association processes.

The role of names in genealogies is particularly ambiguous since the lists largely lack narrative context in which the meaning of a name could resonate. For example, one of the women in the genealogies of Manasseh bears the name Hammolecheth, which means 'she who reigns' (7.18).[43] On first sight, the name is extremely interesting and may convey that the text includes a woman who indeed reigned. But then, the text in its typical genealogical reticence deprives the reader of this character's story. Still, the text provides clues: Hammolecheth presides over a lineage of descendants. She is introduced as sister rather than as wife, the father of her children not being mentioned. The textual evidence is insufficient to prove that the passage recalls a tradition of a sister of Manasseh who reigned in one way or another. What can be said, though, is that the name Hammolecheth can serve as a starting point for the observation that the text accumulates evidence that could be interpreted in this way; no more, but also not less.

*eponymous
(def.)*   One reaches firmer ground when it comes to the large group of eponymous names, especially in the genealogies of Judah. Eponymous names are names that 'identify a real or created person for whom a place, clan, or tribal group is named'.[44] In general, boundaries between personal names, place names and ethnic names in 1 Chronicles 1–9 are fluid.[45] Hence eponyms, such as Maacah (2.48), Bilhah (7.13), or Sheerah (7.24), affect ethnic and territorial identities and imply geopolitical claims. Wives whose names simultaneously serve as place names or ethnic names have especially important functions in negotiating identity and alterity in segmentation processes. For example, the name of Caleb's secondary wife Maacah probably represents a link between the Calebites and Maacah, the territory and people in the northern Transjordan, which have the same name (2.48).[46]

The function female eponymous names have in negotiating ethnic and territorial identities also applies to wives, who are listed with additional information about their ethnic and/or territorial provenance.[47] For example, the

42. James Barr, 'The Symbolism of Names in the Old Testament', *BJRL* 52 (1969/70), pp. 11-29 (21), emphasis original.

43. Julia Myers O'Brian, 'Hammolecheth', *WiS*, p. 89.

44. Bohmbach, 'Names and Naming', p. 36.

45. Knoppers, *1 Chronicles 1–9*, p. 307.

46. D.G. Schley, 'Maacah (Place)', *ABD* IV, p. 430.

47. For example the Canaanite woman Bath-shua (2.3), Ahinoam the Jezreelite and Abigail the Carmelite (3.1) and the Aramean secondary wife of Manasseh (7.14).

nameless Aramean secondary wife of Manasseh (7.14) links the genealogy of Manasseh to Aram (and attributes to it a secondary importance due to the qualification of the mother as secondary wife).[48] In turn, the Aramean presence in the lineage is continued and supported by additional women of the lineage, who bear Aramean names, for example Maacah.[49]

On a wider scale, wives and secondary wives form the largest group of women in 1 Chronicles 1–9.[50] Most (secondary) wives are mothers of sons (and in few cases also of daughters).[51] Descriptions of women as wives or secondary wives are both relational and functional in character.[52] For example, the description of (secondary) wife is relational inasmuch as it defines a woman in relation to her husband and his lineage, as well as, often, in relation to her descendants. However, the description also indicates functions of the (secondary) wives in the genealogy composition. On the one hand, their function is to procreate. Here, the high number of wives and mothers is in line with the patrilinear reproduction matrix of the genealogies. On the other hand, (secondary) wives have the function to distribute and qualify segments. In this context, mothers play an important role in identifying their descendants.

It is important to note that the explicit listing of wives and mothers, many of them related to ethnic and territorial reference points, is only characteristic of particular parts of 1 Chronicles 1–9, especially the genealogies of Judah (and to a lesser extent Manasseh). Other sections of the genealogies do without reference to wives and mothers, for example the genealogies of Reuben, Gad and Levi. In the genealogies of Judah and the house of David, exogamous marriages with Canaanites, Ishmaelites, Arameans,

---

48. The tradition about Manasseh's Aramean/Syrian secondary wife is also present in Gen. 46.20 LXX but not in Gen. 46.20 MT. See Knoppers, *I Chronicles 1–9*, p. 461.

49. Sara Japhet, 'Conquest and Settlement in Chronicles', *JBL* 98.2 (1979), pp. 205-18 (216).

50. 1 Chronicles 1–9 lists nineteen women and one female group as wives (אשׁה). Four women and one female group are listed as secondary wives (פילגשׁ). Four women are described as being married by means of verb forms of the roots לקח (married, took as wife) or בוא (came to, had intercourse with).

51. Maacah, the wife of Jeiel, the father of Gibeon, is an example of a women who is listed as wife but does not have children (8.29//9.35). Examples of women who have daughters are Matred, mother of Mehetabel (1.50) and Hammolecheth, mother of Mahlah (7.18). In addition to the (secondary) wives who have children, four women who have children are listed as sisters (2.16-17; 4.19; 7.18). In most cases, having children is indicated by verb forms of the root ילד qal (to give birth). In seven cases women are identified as heads of a segment of descendants by means of the opening or closing formulas (2.16-17, 18; 4.5-8, 18 MT, 19). Only two women are directly identified as mothers (אם).

52. See Anna Kiesow, *Löwinnen von Juda: Frauen als Subjekte politischer Macht in der judäischen Königszeit* (Münster: LIT Verlag, 2000), p. 51.

Egyptians, and Moabites, among others, are referred to.[53] This presence of foreign wives (and husbands[54]) is in line with the large number of non-Israelite individuals and groups who are associated with and incorporated into Judah.[55] In conclusion, Chronicles advances a 'multilayered depiction of Judah that underscores its ethnic and social diversity'.[56]

In his discussion of the ethnic and social complexity of Judah, Knoppers brings the discussion back to the issue of mixed marriages. In a final comparison between the genealogies of Judah and Ezra–Nehemiah, he concludes that while 'in Ezra (9.10-15) the people's fragile existence in the lands is threatened by the phenomenon of mixed marriages, in Chronicles the phenomenon of mixed marriages is one means by which Judah expands and develops within the land'.[57] I agree with Knoppers that 1 Chronicles 1–9 conceptualizes Judah as ethnically and socially complex and that women, especially (secondary) wives, play an important part in actualizing this concept. Here, one important function of the gendered references in Judah is evident, namely to identify, distribute, and other segments of the genealogies. In my view, however, inclusiveness and complexity are only one side of the coin. The genealogies of Judah evolve around the lineage of the house of David, which constitutes a strong power center. Distributing lineages always takes place in view of this power center and the concepts of inclusiveness and complexity represent the flipside of powerful hierarchies and othering. Moreover, instances of opening the patrilinear succession to agents who introduce ethnic, social, and gendered complexity, for example the embedded narrative on Sheshan's daughter and the Egyptian slave Jarha (2.34-35), are regularly intertwined with attempts to restrict openness as soon as it is granted, as I show in Chapter 4. In conclusion, inclusiveness and complexity are indeed important aspects of the genealogical self-conception of Judah. However, these aspects need to be interpreted as elements that function in the larger discourse on authoritative definitions of Israel past and present, as I will propose in Chapter 6.

Mixed Marriage in the Context of Female Inheritances. In her analysis of texts from Ezra–Nehemiah and Elephantine examining the life of Jewish women in the postexilic period, Tamara Eskenazi relates the discourse on mixed marriages to the issue of female inheritance.[58] At the center of her

---

53. Gary N. Knoppers, 'Intermarriage, Social Complexity and Ethnic Diversity in the Genealogy of Judah', *JBL* 120.1 (2001), pp. 15-30 (22).

54. 1 Chron. 2.17, 34-35.

55. Knoppers, 'Intermarriage, Social Complexity and Ethnic Diversity', pp. 23-27, 30.

56. Knoppers, 'Intermarriage, Social Complexity and Ethnic Diversity', p. 28.

57. Knoppers, 'Intermarriage, Social Complexity and Ethnic Diversity', p. 30.

58. Tamara C. Eskenazi, 'Out from the Shadows: Biblical Women in the Post-Exilic

analysis are references to women in the books of Ezra–Nehemiah, as well as documents that concern women from archives of the Jewish community in Elephantine.[59]

Eskenazi shows that the documents from Elephantine sketch legal and social roles for women that are not usually ascribed to women in biblical or postexilic communities. Among them are activities such as divorcing husbands, buying and selling and especially important here, the possibility of inheriting as a daughter even if there were sons available.[60] Eskenazi argues for continuity between the situations in Elephantine and the Persian province Yehud, which were both under Mesopotamian influence and Persian rule. She supports this argument with her reading of Ezra–Nehemiah. Here, she suggests understanding Ezra–Nehemiah's position against mixed marriages as concern about the loss of land through inheritance, a concern that makes most sense if women were in fact entitled to inherit as was the case in Elephantine.[61] As backdrop for this claim, Eskenazi parallels the postexilic period with the pre-monarchic one. With reference to Carol Meyers's sociohistorical research on the pre-monarchic period, which equates a strong position of the family with more influential positions for women,[62] Eskenazi argues that the uncharted conditions of the return, as well as the resurgence of the household as the fundamental socioeconomic and political unit in the postexilic era, 'likewise led to a greater power for women than was available during the monarchy'.[63]

In my view, the link between the polemic against mixed marriage and the issue of female inheritance is plausible and suggests looking at the daughters and the issue of female inheritance in 1 Chronicles 1–9. In the genealogies,

---

Era', in *A Feminist Companion to Samuel and Kings* (ed. Athalya Brenner; Sheffield: Sheffield Academic Press, 1994), pp. 252-71).

59. Bob Becking has challenged the characterization of the community at Elephantine as Jewish and suggested the alternative term Yehudi. His argument is that the materials under consideration stem from the fifth century BCE, thus from a period that is characterized by a transition from Yahwism to Judaism and antedates the existence of Jewish communities, which he would only term as such from the Hellenistic period onwards. Hence, he argues that labeling the Elephantine community as Jewish would be an anachronism. Becking, *Ezra, Nehemiah and the Construction of Early Jewish Identity*, pp. 123, 129. In contrast to Becking, Eskenazi describes the fifth and fourth century BCE communities in both Elephantine and Yehud as Jewish communities. As this is consistent and in line with her emphasis on the continuity between the two contexts, while presenting her argument, I stick to her vocabulary and use the term Jewish community.

60. Eskenazi, 'Out from the Shadows', p. 259.

61. Eskenazi, 'Out from the Shadows', p. 263.

62. Carol Meyers, *Discovering Eve: Ancient Israelite Women in Context* (Oxford: Oxford University Press, 1988), pp. 173-81, especially p. 174.

63. Eskenazi, 'Out from the Shadows', pp. 260-61.

the second most frequent characterization of women is the characterization as daughter (בת).[64]

In many cases, daughters are introduced in relation to their fathers as well as the place and ethnicity he is linked to; for example, 2.21 lists the nameless daughter of Machir, father of Gilead. In her research on Jewish names in the Second Temple period, Rachel Hachlili shows that the full name of a person, male or female, was composed of a personal name (such as Mariame or Shlamzion) and a patronymic one, that is, the indication of the father for men and the indication of the father, husband, or son for women.[65] Hachlili emphasizes that the full name was the official and formal name of a person that was commonly used in burial inscriptions as well as on legal documents, specifically on storage jars.[66] Against this background, the use of the patronymic for the daughters under consideration exposes a patriarchal structure in which women are defined through a male relative, but likewise attests to the formal status of the women thusly introduced. The assumption of a formal status of these daughters makes sense especially concerning a diplomatic marriage between David and Maacah, the daughter of King Talmai of Geshur (3.2), as well as for a reference to Bithiah, the daughter of Pharaoh (4.18 MT), women who had high social positions and likely had goods at their disposal. Whether this included inheritance or not is not an issue the text addresses.

The issue of inheritance is more clearly addressed in a short reference to the daughters of Zelophehad (7.15), as well as in the reference to Caleb's daughter Achsah (2.49). The respective intertexts recount that Zelophehad's daughters successfully claim a share of their father's inheritance (Num. 27.1-11; 36.1-12). Achsah does not explicitly inherit land, but claims arable land to live on from her father (Judg. 1.11-15; Josh. 15.15-19). The references clearly link daughters to the issues of female land claims and inheritances. However, the fragmentary character of these references seems to repress the issue more than highlight it. In my view, 1 Chronicles 1–9 is not

---

64. Women who are listed as daughters are Mehetabel (1.50); Matred (1.50); the nameless daughter of Machir, father of Gilead (2.21); the nameless daughters of Sheshan (2.34); the nameless daughter of Sheshan (2.35); Achsah (2.49); Maacah, daughter of King Talmai of Geshur (3.2); Bithiah, daughter of Pharaoh (4.18 MT); six daughters of Simeon (4.27); Zelophehad's daughters (7.15); and Sheerah (7.24).

65. Rachel Hachlili, 'Hebrew Names, Personal Names, Family Names and Nicknames of Jews in the Second Temple Period', in *Families and Family Relations as Represented in Early Judaism and Early Christianities: Texts and Fictions* (ed. Jan Willem van Henten and Athalya Brenner; Leiden: Deo Publishing, 2000), pp. 83-115 (84-85).

66. Hachlili, 'Hebrew Names', pp. 84, 86. For Jewish names in the Second Temple period, see also Tal Ilan, *Lexicon of Jewish Names in Late Antiquity Part I: Palestine 330 BCE–200 CE* (Texte und Studien zum Antiken Judentum, 91; Tübingen: J.C.B. Mohr, 2002).

interested in giving voice to the issue of female inheritance, whether linked to the issue of mixed marriage or not.[67]

Even though Eskenazi's argument on female inheritance practices as sociohistorical backdrop to the polemic against mixed marriages does not especially resonate with 1 Chronicles 1–9, her sociohistorical reconstruction of women's lives in the postexilic period is highly relevant for the genealogies. Eskenazi shows that patriarchal societies at the time were quite complex, and that 'patriarchal' is not to be equated with the absence of complex sociopolitical realities of women's lives. By doing so, she provides an important counterpoint to approaches that postulate that, from a sociohistorical viewpoint, women did not play a role in the context of 1 Chronicles 1–9.[68]

3. Reading 1 Chronicles 1–9 as an Archive

Heterogeneity versus Conceptual Coherence

As a last introductory issue I will address the heterogeneous character of 1 Chronicles 1–9. Heterogeneity is a basic characteristic of this genealogy composition. Heterogeneity relates to its type and origin of materials. For example, the genealogies include linear and segmented lineages, town lists and short narratives. Materials stem from biblical literature, extra-biblical sources, and the text's literary engagement.[69] The length and character of the genealogies of the individual tribes is heterogeneous. For example, Judah covers one third of the text while Dan's lineage can only be reconstructed from a fragment in 7.12,[70] and Levi features primarily linear lineages and includes numerous town lists, while Issachar and Asher feature military census lists.[71] In sum, the heterogeneous character of 1 Chronicles 1–9 comes to the fore in what appears on first sight to be an extremely inconsistent and random entanglement of its lineages and other components. Accordingly, the composition has often been characterized as 'garbled, disorderly, corrupt and incoherent'.[72] On the level of methodologies,

---

67. So also Wacker, who rightly emphasizes that the text is more interested in the issue of a possible continuation of the lineage through females, especially daughters, for example in the case of Sheshan's daughter (2.34-35). Wacker, 'Die Bücher der Chronik: Im Vorhof der Frauen', p. 149.

68. So e.g. Oeming, *Das wahre Israel*, p. 209.

69. Japhet, *I&II Chronicles*, pp. 14-26.

70. Knoppers, *I Chronicles 1–9*, pp. 453-54.

71. Marshall D. Johnson, *The Purpose of the Biblical Genealogies with Special Reference to the Setting of the Genealogies of Jesus* (SNTSMS, 8; Cambridge: Cambridge University Press, 1969), p. 65.

72. Gary N. Knoppers, '"Great among His Brothers", But Who Is He?: Heterogeneity in the Composition of Judah', *JHS* 3 (2001), article 4 no pages (section 1.3). A classic

the composition's heterogeneity has led to a focus on source and redaction criticism, and with that, on diachronic readings.[73]

Against this focus, Knoppers has objected that it may expose the heterogeneity of 1 Chronicles 1–9 as such, but it cannot explain why supposed composers and redactors did not work toward a greater consistency of the text.[74] As a consequence, he advocates a reading of 1 Chronicles 1–9 that understands the text as a deliberate composition and recognizes heterogeneity as a central characteristic that has to be made sense of.[75]

Knoppers's plea for research into the conceptual coherence of the composition has hit a nerve: more recent research on 1 Chronicles 1–9 has indeed focused on tracing a deliberate structure of the composition, which confirms that (genealogical) materials have been assessed, reworked, structured and supplemented within a complex composition.[76]

In general, 1 Chronicles 1–9 is divided into three parts: the genealogies from Adam to the sons of Israel (1.1–2.2); the genealogies of the tribes of Israel (2.3–9.2); and the account of the return and the list of inhabitants of Jerusalem with an appendix of the genealogy of Saul (9.3-44).[77] In the second part, the genealogies of the tribes, the tribes are listed in a geographical order that takes a circular shape and brings Jerusalem as a center into focus (2.3–9.2).[78] As a rule, lineages of the tribes are traced back to the

example in this respect is Martin Noth who describes 1 Chron. 1–9 as being in great untidiness and confusion: '[Ein Text,] der sich in seiner überlieferten Form im Zustand einer ungewöhnliche großen Unordnung und Verworrenheit befindet'. Noth, *Überlieferungsgeschichtliche Studien*, p. 117.

73. Knoppers, '"Great among His Brothers"', sections 2-5.

74. Knoppers, '"Great among His Brothers"', section 6.8.

75. Knoppers, '"Great among His Brothers"', section 7.1.

76. So e.g. Beentjes, *1 Kronieken*, pp. 23-24; Knoppers, '"Great among His Brothers"', section 6; Willi, *1 Chr 1–10*, p. 72; Oeming, *Das wahre Israel*, pp. 112-16.

77. Structuring 1 Chronicles 1–9 entails two problematic points. First, v. 9.2 might be allocated either to the second or to the third part of the composition. Second, the last part of chapter 9 (9.35-44) might be considered as part of the genealogy composition or as part of the subsequent story of Saul (10.1-14). In line with Japhet, I allocate 9.2 to the second part of the genealogy composition and consider 9.1-2 as conclusion of the genealogies of the tribes. Likewise in line with Japhet, I consider 9.35-44 as an appendix to the genealogy composition in 1 Chronicles 1–9, which makes it part of the larger composition. Japhet, *I & II Chronicles*, pp. 8-10. This is against Knoppers, who allocates 9.1 to the second part and 9.2, the account of the return, to the third part of the composition (Knoppers, *I Chronicles 1–9*, pp. 487-88). Moreover, Knoppers allocates 9.35-44 to the subsequent story of Saul (10.1-14). Knoppers, *I Chronicles 1–9*, pp. 509-11.

78. Tribes are listed in the following order: Judah opens the list (2.3–4.23), followed by Simeon to the south (4.24-43) and by the Transjordanian tribes Reuben (5.1–10), Gad (5.11-22) and Half-Manasseh (5.23) to the east. This is followed by Levi in the center of the composition (5.27–6.66 MT), as well as by the northern tribes Issachar (7.1-5), Benjamin (7.6-11), [Dan (7.12)], Naphtali (7.13), Manasseh (7.14-19), Ephraim (7.20-29),

ancestral period, thereby emphasizing on the authority of this period, as well as the continuity between the ancestral period and postexilic Israel.[79] Concerning the tribes, the composition puts emphasis on Judah (2.3–4.23), Levi (5.27–6.66 MT) and Benjamin (7.6-11; 8.1-40; 9.35-44), at the beginning, center, and end.[80]

With reference to the gendered fragments in 1 Chronicles 1–9, the degree to which the references are unevenly distributed is striking, even though particular patterns are traceable. The leading genealogies of Judah and the house of David (2.3–4.23) contain references to thirty four individual women and two female groups. This represents more than half of the references to women in the entire composition. Hence, the prominent position of Judah and the house of David at the beginning of the genealogies of Israel overlaps with mention of a noticeable high number of women. This is in stark contrast to the second main tribe, Levi. The genealogies of Levi are emphasized due to their length and their position at the center of the composition. Still, they include only one woman, Miriam, who is listed among the *banîm*, 'sons' (בנים), of Amram (5.29). In contrast to Judah, Levi's prominent position at the center of the genealogy composition comes together with the absence rather than the presence of references to women.

The genealogies of Levi are framed by two groups of tribes that likewise stand out through absence rather than presence of women: the descendants of Simeon (4.24-43) and the Transjordanian tribes (5.1-26) on the one hand, and the genealogies of Issachar, Benjamin, Dan and Naphtali (7.1-13) on the other, list only three women and two female groups (1 Chron. 4.27; 5.29 MT; 7.4; 7.8; 7.13).

This again has a counterpart in a group of small tribes at the end of the inner composition that provide a strikingly dense occurrence of gendered fragments: the genealogy of Manasseh lists seven women and hints at Zelophehad's daughters in no more than five verses (7.14-19). The following genealogy of Ephraim with a summary of the dwellings of Manasseh and

---

Asher (7.30-40) and again Benjamin (8.1-40). Japhet, *I&II Chronicles*, pp. 9-10. A lineage of Dan is not explicitly mentioned but is often reconstructed. See Knoppers, 'Intermarriage, Social Complexity and Ethnic Diversity', p. 16.

79. Knoppers, *I Chronicles 1–9*, p. 261.

80. 1 Chronicles 1–9 operates with different concepts and numbers of tribes. For example, 2.1-2 orders the tribes according to their mothers, a structure that runs alongside the geographical order. Different numbers of tribes in 2.3–9.2 occur because the text replaces Joseph through Ephraim and Manasseh, counts Manasseh twice (plus Half-Manasseh) and skips Dan and Zebulon. In addition, Levi is counted twice (Levites and priests). Magnar Kartveit, *Motive und Schichten der Landtheologie in 1 Chronik 1–9* (CBOTS, 28; Stockholm: Almqvist & Wiksell, 1989), pp. 117-18. I agree with Japhet that the composition thereby synthesizes different views of the identity of the twelve tribes. Japhet, *The Ideology of the Book of Chronicles*, p. 281.

Ephraim (7.20-29); the genealogy of Asher (7.30-40); and the genealogy of Benjamin (8.1-40) include eight women. Many of them hold noteworthy positions and names, for example Sheerah the builder (7.24) and Hammolecheth, the one who reigns (7.18).[81]

While broad consensus confirms the idea of the conceptual coherence of 1 Chronicles 1–9 (even though detailed structures have been identified differently), the challenge to explain why a coherent composition features such significant heterogeneity on the level of form, genre, and semantics has not yet been met. Central questions in this respect are how one may analyze the unity of a text that encompasses significant inconsistency; which linking elements put the text's disparate elements together in a composition; and, in view of my particular research question, what role the female-gendered passages play in this process. In view of these questions, I propose a twofold strategy. First, I suggest a synchronic reception-oriented close reading of the gendered fragments. However, the synchronic reception-oriented approach alone does not make sense of the heterogeneity of the composition. Therefore, as a second aspect of my reading strategy, I suggest conceptualizing 1 Chronicles 1–9 as an archive.

1 Chronicles 1–9 as Archive of Genealogies

A productive impetus for dealing with the composition's heterogeneity results from the process of socializing: the film *My Life Part 2* takes the form of an archive. The form of an archive allows the filmmaker to present disparate contents in a meaningful way and to engage heterogeneity as a form of storytelling, especially in a post-traumatic context. Transferred to 1 Chronicles 1–9, I claim that the challenge to account for both conceptual coherence and factual heterogeneity of the genealogy composition can be met by reading 1 Chronicles 1–9 as an archival text.

Archives are by definition collections of potentially heterogeneous materials that are structured according to a specific taxonomy on the basis of particular interests and ideologies. Archives collect, store, and make knowledge available, but by doing so concurrently produce, contest, and negotiate it.[82] Reading 1 Chronicles 1–9 as an archive allows reading the text as an integral composition without neglecting its disparate constituents. In addition, understanding the genealogy composition as a site of knowledge production and a cross section of contested power rather than a mere storage

---

81. The last part of 1 Chronicles 1–9 lists the first inhabitants of Jerusalem (9.3–34) and provides an appendix of the genealogy of Saul (9.35-44). The list of inhabitants of Jerusalem does not list women at all. The genealogy of Saul mentions a single woman who already occurred earlier (8.29 // 9.35).

82. Ann L. Stoler, 'Colonial Archives and the Arts of Governance', *Archival Science* 2 (2002), pp. 87-109 (87).

of more or less poorly assembled genealogies brings the text's subject character to the fore. It acknowledges that 1 Chronicles 1–9 may have functioned as an initial statement on Israel's origins and identities, which begins Chronicles' account of the history of Israel's monarchy. Finally, conceptualizing 1 Chronicles 1–9 as an archive, places emphasis on engaging knowledge that is repressed or only implicitly present, a focus that may provide a key for analyzing gendered absence in the text. Archive theory may thus be expected to provide important avenues for analyzing how 1 Chronicles 1–9 responds to its traumatic past and what role the gendered fragments play in this response, a thesis that I pursue in Chapter 6.[83]

Conceptualizing 1 Chronicles 1–9 as an archive asks the question, in what respect can the composition be understood as an archive? In Chapter 1, I discussed the different dimensions of the archive notion, first, as a collection of documents, often in the context of an institution and second, as a human and cultural impulse. 1 Chronicles 1–9 is indeed based on a collection of records that are assembled according to a specific system of appraisal and classification. For example, earlier genealogies, town lists, census lists, inner-biblical intertexts and oral traditions on particular tribes are arranged according to a hierarchical classification of tribes, which privileges Judah and Levi. However, this collection is presented in the form of a literary text. This literary text is conditioned by the collection—or archive—but also exceeds it: it is a memory act that presents or performs the underlying archive in the form of a literary text. As such, 1 Chronicles 1–9 demonstrates the fundamental degree to which the archival impulse is at work in society in general and in the production of cultural and religious utterances in particular. Moreover, it shows the diverse forms that the exterior place of an archive can take beyond institutionalized archives.[84] Art works such as the documentary *My Life Part 2* express the cultural impulse toward archiving in a similar way.

In conclusion, I understand 1 Chronicles 1–9 as an expression of a fundamental archival impulse. Moreover, because 1 Chronicles 1–9 is also a manifestation of this impulse at an exterior place, where it collects, appraises, labels, highlights and represses contested knowledge of Israel's past and

---

83. Independently from my research, Kathleen O'Connor pursues a comparable approach with regard to analyzing the 'literary disorder' of the book of Jeremiah. Reading Jeremiah as a response to the trauma of siege warfare, destruction of state and temple and deportations, O'Connor argues that the book's literary disorder aims at supporting the reader's coming to terms with the traumatic past. For example, the confused structure would assign the task of meaning-making to the readers. Kathleen M. O'Connor, *Jeremiah: Pain and Promise* (Minneapolis, MN: Fortress Press, 2012), pp. 128-34.

84. For the priority of the consignation of an archive in an exterior place, see Jacques Derrida, *Archive Fever: A Freudian Impression* (trans. E. Prenowitz; Chicago, IL: University of Chicago Press, 1996), p. 11; and Chapter 1, above.

formulas

Trauma Begets Genealogy

present, I think it is indeed adequate to speak of 1 Chronicles 1–9 in terms of a genealogical archive.[85]

Formulas as a Means to Structure Archival Content. A critical device for labeling and structuring the contents of 1 Chronicles 1–9 is the strongly formalized language of the genealogies. Particular verbal forms and phrases reoccur over and over again and establish characteristic repetitive language patterns and formulas. Patterns and formulas pertain to particular genealogical forms, for example to segmented or linear forms, as well as to particular groups, for example to fathers or sisters. In line with Thomas Willi, I understand the formulaic character of the genealogies as a major device in the purposeful design of 1 Chronicles 1–9.[86] Reoccurring phrases and formulas provide structure and establish hierarchies. They frame the disparate contents of the composition and make it accessible.

variations   Formulas in 1 Chronicles 1–9 come with variations. These variations do not diminish the force of the formulaic language in structuring the composition. On the contrary, variations are an important means of playing out a given formal repertoire and allow the text to emphasize, minimize, or subvert its principles of recall.

Two basic formulas in 1 Chronicles 1–9 are the opening and closing formulas, for example the closing formula in 7.8b: כל־אלה בני־בכר, 'All these were the sons of Becher'.[87] The opening and closing formulas convey that a lineage pertains to a name/person. By doing so, these formulas induce what Julie Kelso calls 'genealogical ownership', the attribution of a segment of a genealogy to a particular name, who functions as owner of that segment of the lineage.[88] As a rule, opening and closing formulas attribute lineages to males. However, in some cases, women are the subjects of the formulas. For example, 1.33b concludes the list of the sons of Keturah with the closing

---

85. With regard to text collections of the ancient Near East, the distinction is often made between archives and libraries. As a rule, archives would include most diverse types of documents that were used to record day-to-day activities of the time. In contrast, libraries would include mostly literary texts and were linked to the existence of a scribal class that maintained, controlled and preserved the literary texts. Against this distinction, Jaqueline du Toit argues for a continuum between the different types of text collections of the time (archives, libraries, genizas, foundation deposits, etc.) and suggests referring to them by the umbrella term 'textual deposit'. Jaqueline S. du Toit, *Textual Memory: Ancient Archives, Libraries and the Hebrew Bible* (The Social World of Biblical Antiquity, Second Series, 6; Sheffield: Sheffield Phoenix Press, 2011), pp. 79-81, 153.

86. Willi, *1 Chr 1–10*, pp. 72, 99.

87. Other instances of the closing formula are 1.23, 33; 2.23; 4.4, 6; 5.14; 7.8, 11, 17, 33, 40; 8.38//9.44.

88. Julie Kelso, *Oh Mother, Where Art Thou?: An Irigarayan Reading of the Book of Chronicles* (London: Equinox, 2007), pp. 112-13.

formula: כָּל־אֵלֶּה בְּנֵי קְטוּרָה, 'All these were the sons of Keturah'.[89] In these instances segments pertain to women who function as genealogical owners of the lists of descendants.

The occurrence of women in the opening and closing formulas undergoes a striking marginalization in the exegetical discussion. For example, the references to the co-wives Helah and Naarah, who are both listed in opening and concluding formulas which attribute lists of descendants to them (4.5-8), are regularly passed over without any comment.[90] If the passage is discussed, scholars seem to apply double standards in their assessment of linguistic patterns and formulas: both Japhet and Knoppers argue that the passage provides no formulas at all, an assessment that falls short of their otherwise detailed and thorough commentaries.[91]

Next to formulas which usually pertain to men, the genealogies provide typically female formulas, for example the sister formula in 3.19b: וּבֶן־זְרֻבָּבֶל מְשֻׁלָּם וַחֲנַנְיָה וּשְׁלֹמִית אֲחוֹתָם, 'The son(s) of Zerubbabel: Meshullam and Hananiah; and Shelomith: their sister'.[92] Listing sisters in a reoccurring formalized pattern draws attention to them and suggests relating the individual fragments to each other, all the more so as the formula determines their being sisters in a somewhat laborious way.[93] Instead of directly listing them as daughters of PN1 (first listed personal name), the formula identifies them as sisters of the sons of PN1.[94]

One reason for the identification of women as sisters is the relation of the sister role to the linear structures of the genealogies. Sisters belong to the lineages of their fathers and brothers and potentially relate their descendants to these lineages. For example, Zeruiah is introduced as a sister of David, who presides over a segment of descendants which are attributed to her by means of the opening formula (2.16-17). In this case, the combination of the

---

89. See also 4.6b (Naarah) and 7.13 (Bilhah).

90. For example Oeming, *Das wahre Israel*, p. 105.

91. Japhet, *I&II Chronicles*, p. 105; Knoppers, *I Chronicles 1–9*, p. 345.

92. See 1.39 (Timna); 2.16 (Zeruiah and Abigail); 2.49 (Achsah/daughter); 3.9 (Tamar); 3.19 (Shelomith); 4.3 (Hazzelelponi); 7.18 (Hammolecheth); 7.30 (Serah); and 7.32 (Shua). See also 1.19 for the use of the same phrase to list a male as a brother; Japhet, *I&II Chronicles*, p. 107.

93. The group of sisters (אֲחָיוֹת) forms the third largest group of women after the groups of (secondary) wives and daughters. It comprises ten named women and one nameless woman, four of which have sons and daughters. Six out of the sisters only occur in 1 Chronicles 1–9.

94. Wacker devotes a section of her discussion of women in 1 Chronicles 1–9 to the sisters of brothers. She likewise points to the long-winded form in which the sisters are introduced and concludes that research on the functions of these sisters is still required. Wacker, 'Die Bücher der Chronik: Im Vorhof der Frauen', p. 150.

sister formula and the opening formula attribute the descendants of Zeruiah to the Davidic lineage, as I will argue in Chapter 4.

The function of attributing descendants to the lineage of the sisters is only relevant in the case of sisters who indeed have children (four out of eleven). It is difficult to account for the function of the remaining larger part of the sister group. In the subsequent close readings, I will approach them by means of exploring the function of gaps in the composition.

Another element of the formulaic language of the genealogies is the identification of men—and sometimes women—as sons of PN1. In the text, seven women are listed as בן / *ben* ('son'), or appear in lists of non-gender-specific descendants, which mostly include sons. Most prominent among them is Miriam, the sister of Aaron and Moses (5.29). Miriam is neither listed as sister, nor as daughter, even though numerous biblical references make clear that she is a female figure. Instead, the text lists Miriam among the *sons* of her father Amram. In my view, it is appropriate to translate בן consistently as 'son' rather than with a gender neutral term such as 'descendant' or 'child'.[95] The gender-neutral translation would be imprecise—the text does use the terms 'sister' and 'daughter' in other instances. Moreover, a gender-neutral term would obscure a power structure inherent in the genealogical language that tends to privilege males and to make females invisible.[96] In addition, some interesting details might get lost. For example, female *banîm* ('sons') are the only category of women in 1 Chronicles 1–9 that does not include women who are married or have children. Finally, thinking about female 'sons' emphasizes the functional character of the term and foregrounds the question of whether under particular circumstances, a daughter may have been formally considered a 'son'.

The Verb ילד */ yld as Central Framing Device.* As an alternative to my focus on formulas, Julie Kelso has suggested that the occurrence and use of the verb ילד / *yld* ('to bear, beget') is a central element in framing the contents of 1 Chronicles 1–9.[97] Kelso argues that the occurrence of both the verb *yld* and of women induces a discourse—or fantasy—of a solely male genealogical (re)production and transmission, which goes hand in hand with a repression of the maternal body.[98]

95. So also Wacker, 'Die Bücher der Chronik: Im Vorhof der Frauen', p. 147.
96. Against Van Wieringen who argues that an inclusive rendering ('children' or 'descendants') is appropriate in many cases. Van Wieringen, 'Why Some Women Were Included', pp. 293-94.
97. Kelso, *Oh Mother, Where Art Thou?*, pp. 115-66.
98. Kelso, *Oh Mother, Where Art Thou?*, p. 162. See also Anne-Mareike Wetter, who compares the use of the root *yld* in Chronicles and Samuel–Kings. Wetter observes that while Samuel–Kings uses the verb exclusively with a female subject, Chronicles has an overwhelming number of male subjects. Anne-Mareike Wetter, 'Verschuivende Visies:

Kelso reads the book of Chronicles against the background of the feminist philosophers Luce Irigaray and Michelle Boulous Walker. Kelso's central argument is that, in Chronicles, women are silenced by their association with maternity and the concurrent repression and disavowal of the maternal body. The latter aims at allowing the male subject to imagine himself as a sole producer of his world.[99]

In her analysis of 1 Chronicles 1–9, Kelso focuses on what happens to language and its production when women appear; specifically, what effect the occurrence of the verb *yld*, which she understands to mean 'to bear' in all of its modifications, has on the genealogical form and its contents.[100] Kelso concludes that the sense of continuity of meaning, according to her a central concern of the genealogies, breaks down around both the appearance of women and the verb *yld*. The breakdown includes grammatical and/ or syntactical breakdowns, contradictions and a breakdown of reality.[101] The breakdowns occur in the context of constructing women as mothers of sons and the concurrent dominant discourse of masculine (re)production. The discourse of masculine (re)production is based on the overwhelming dominance of masculine subjects of the verb *yld*. Moreover, it is supported by the discourse of a generative succession of male names that represses any recognition of corporeal maternal origins.[102] Masculine (re)production is thus presented as the standard procedure. At the same time, text-inherent breakdowns expose the repression and disavowal of the maternal body. This comes along with '*the phantasy of mono-sexual, masculine (re)production*' and the conception of male-only reproduction and transmission.[103]

Kelso's most important contribution to understanding 1 Chronicles 1–9 is her observation that women often appear in passages that are text-critically unclear and difficult to make sense of. She shows in a convincing way that something happens with respect to the text structure when women and the verb *yld* appear. However, her interpretation of the phenomenon is

---

De Kronist over de rol van de vrouw', in *Nederlands theologisch tijdschrift* 65.3 (2011), pp. 227-41 (229-30).

99. Kelso, *Oh Mother, Where Art Thou?*, p. 161. To date Kelso provides the only monograph on Chronicles from an explicit feminist perspective. In her reading, Kelso applies the approach of Irigaray by using a specific mode of analysis in which she addresses the text in direct speech. This psychoanalytic 'You–I' discourse aims at enabling the silences of the masculine discourse to be heard. It alternates with a chorus-like poem that aims to generate 'a sense of the [missing] mother–daughter relationship' in the text (p. 113). Her study thus presents an intriguing interplay between highly theoretical philosophical reflection and an experimental close reading of the Hebrew text.

100. Kelso, *Oh Mother, Where Art Thou?*, p. 112.

101. Kelso, *Oh Mother, Where Art Thou?*, p. 113.

102. Kelso, *Oh Mother, Where Art Thou?*, p. 162.

103. Kelso, *Oh Mother, Where Art Thou?*, p. 162, emphasis original.

less convincing to me. Kelso's strong focus on maternity and the maternal body draws attention away from the more complex description of women in 1 Chronicles 1–9. It thereby fails to account for the ambiguity of their appearance. In this context, her methodological frame is a two-sided coin. On the one hand, the engagement of Irigaray and Boulous Walker is extremely productive. It allows her to contextualize the few passages that include women in the overall genealogy composition and to expose its androcentric agenda. In addition, it allows her to reveal the performative character of the genealogies and to analyze the text as a site of production of knowledge, memory, and subjectivity—in this respect, her suggestion to use the verb *yld* as a framing device for the genealogical contents makes sense. On the other hand, her theoretical frame seems to narrow her analysis. The text seems to fit in too easily with the theoretical philosophical discourse she unfolds. Kelso matches text and theory so closely that the multidimensionality of the text tends to fall out of sight. It seems that she does away too easily with contradictions, ambiguities and nuances within the corpus of gendered fragments, rather than working out a way of understanding them.

4. *Assessment with Regard to the Close Reading*

Ambiguity as Guiding Notion
The survey of gendered fragments in 1 Chronicles 1–9 brings into focus an abundance of interesting materials, as well as the complexity of the references to women. Reasons why the women are included are revealed as diverse. Some roles are easier to understand than others. But in any case, the large number of women suggests understanding the functions these references fulfill as an integral part of the composition's memory and identity performance.

Looking at the two elaborate studies that approach 1 Chronicles 1–9 from an explicit gender perspective, Labahn and Ben Zvi and Kelso, it becomes clear that they share a discussion of ideological claims made through the female-gendered references. However, the studies show striking dissent in their evaluation of implied ideologies. Labahn and Ben Zvi hold that references to women contest one-dimensional gender constructions in favour of successful individual transgressions within a patriarchal frame. In contrast, Kelso claims that the references to women constitute a misogynic discourse of monosexual, masculine (re)production. The dissent in evaluation alerts us to a possible two-sidedness of the references. References to women may be analyzed for both their potential to support and re-inscribe ideological aims of the text and their potential to interfere with these very aims. In conclusion, contextualizing the gendered fragments within the exegetical gender-related debate calls attention to the notion of ambiguity. Inherent ambiguities and contradictions may thus be considered an important heuristic tool.[104]

Judah as Main Text for the Close Reading
An excellent set of texts for pursuing my initial interest in fractures and discontinuity as well as the issue of ambiguity are the genealogies of Judah. The genealogies of Judah contain the majority of gendered references, but they are also important in terms of quality: they comprise important references, such as the main gendered embedded narratives, many of the intertextual references to biblical women, and ample gendered formulaic language. Most importantly, however, the genealogies of Judah contain both gendered fragments that are in line with the patrilinear setup of the texts, for example its many wives and mothers, and gendered fragments that disturb and potentially subvert the patrilinear flow, for example the women who own lineages, and the protagonists of the narratives on the patrilinear succession at risk. In other words, the genealogies of Judah will allow for exploring the ambiguity of the gendered fragments. Moreover, their complex character will enable a deeper understanding of how the genealogies of Judah, but also the larger composition of 1 Chronicles 1–9, performs gendered genealogies in view of responding to a fractured past.

There is another reason for focusing the close reading on the genealogies of Judah. Judah is not only a central part of 1 Chronicles 1–9, but also central with respect to the sociohistorical context of the composition in late Persian Yehud. This context makes the interplay between memory performance and self-conception in the present especially important for this section of the genealogies.[105]

The focus on exploring the ambiguity of the gendered passages brings the presence of women into focus. And Judah is indeed about the presence of women. This focus implies that in the following close readings, the issues of the absence, forgetting and repression of women, as for example

104. Labahn and Ben Zvi argue in the same direction with their claim that it is a typical feature of Chronicles that 'theological or ideological claims advanced in some, or even many accounts are informed and balanced by contrasting claims advanced elsewhere in the book'. Labahn and Ben Zvi, 'Observations on Women', p. 473. See also Ehud Ben Zvi, 'A Sense of Proportion: An Aspect of the Theology of the Chronicler', in *History, Literature and Theology in the Book of Chronicles* (ed. Ehud Ben Zvi; London: Equinox, 2006), pp. 160-73.

105. For the exposed position and the representative role of the genealogies of Judah in the larger composition of 1 Chronicles 1–9, see Thomas Willi, 'Late Persian Judaism and its Conception of an Integral Israel according to Chronicles: Some Observations on Form and Function of the Genealogy of Judah in 1 Chronicles 2.3–4.23', in *Second Temple Studies. II. Temple Community in the Persian Period* (ed. Tamara C. Eskenazi and Kent H. Richards; Sheffield: Sheffield Academic Press, 1994), pp. 146-62 (160-62).

represented by the genealogies of Levi, take a back seat. Rather than focusing on the presence and absence of women as central antagonists for understanding the role of gender in the composition, I focus on the ambiguity of the gendered passages, and thus on different, potentially contradictory forms taken by women. In view of the broader frame of socializing, the focus on the ambiguous presence of women in the genealogies ties in with *My Life Part 2*. The film works toward unearthing the past and likewise centers on gender.

In conclusion, I will provide two chapters of close readings of passages of 1 Chronicles 1–9, which will frame the intermediate chapter on the film analysis. In Chapter 4, I will investigate a sample of passages that allow me to address the issue of gendered fragments linked to fractures and discontinuity in the patrilinear organization of the memory performance. This first round of close reading focuses on cracks in the smoothly functioning patriarchal succession. It investigates indications of social, ethnic, and gendered complexity within the continuation of the line and reflects on how the texts deal with this complexity. By doing so, it focuses on the subversive potential of the gendered fragments, specifically in interrelation with notions of ethnicity and of social/legal status (e.g. widows, slaves). The texts for this first round of close readings are the genealogies of Judah, specifically two narratives that address a threat to the continuation of the line of Judah (2.3-4 and 2.34-35); two sets of passages that introduce Ephrathah and Zeruiah in genealogical key roles and by means of genealogical formulas (2.19, 50; 4.4 and 2.16-17); and two passages that feature breakdowns of syntactical coherence and meaning around a cluster of references to women (2.18-19 and 4.17-18).

After these first close readings, I will turn to the film and provide an analysis of *My Life Part 2*, with a focus on how the film deals with gender as well as with fractures and discontinuity in the genealogy performance.

I will then turn back to the Bible text and investigate gendered fragments in Judah on a more structural level and with the additional perspectives gained from the film, as well as concepts from anthropology and sociology (e.g. concerning identity and alterity). In this part, the genealogies of Judah are again the primary reference frame for the close reading, especially for the investigation of structures in this central part of 1 Chronicles 1–9. In the synthetic interpretations of the materials, however, I will broaden my perspective and draw lines into the larger web of gendered fragments in 1 Chronicles 1–9. In this section, wives and mothers on the one hand and sisters on the other will take center stage. Moreover, I will take up the concept of archive and show how it advances my specific research question.

Chapter 4

CRACKS IN THE MALE MIRROR: GENDERED FRAGMENTS
AS CHALLENGE TO THE PATRIARCHAL SUCCESSION

Contextualizing the gendered fragments of 1 Chronicles 1–9 in their literary and sociohistorical context, as well as assessing the gender-related exegetical debate about them, has revealed the ambiguity of the passages. The
female-gendered references seem to be in line with the patrilinear flow of
the genealogies in some cases and interfere with this very flow in others.
Starting with this observation, I begin the close reading with three sets of
texts that indicate fissures in the patriarchal succession. These texts consist
of two embedded narratives on the jeopardized lineage (2.3-4 and 2.34-35);
a set of passages that refer to Ephrathah and Zeruiah as eponymous ancestor
(2.19, 50-51; 4.4) and head of lineage (2.16-17) respectively; as well as passages in which difficult text-critical situations obscure the agency of women
(2.18-19 and 4.17-18).
   The notion of patrilinear succession is a key notion of transfer in the
genealogical memory performance of 1 Chronicles 1–9: names and affil-
iations, continuity and identity, offices and inheritance rights—in short,
the *line*—is passed down from father to son and from male group to male
group. As a consequence, patrilinearity designates males as central agents
for the continuation of the line. It communicates the idea of a patriarchal
society that reserves central sociopolitical and economic positions for male
adult Israelites and sustains the power of its beneficiaries. Hence, the patrilinear succession is likewise a patriarchal one.[1] As the patrilinear/patriar-
chal succession is a central notion for the transfer of memory as performed
in the genealogies, fissures in this succession are situated at the core of the
transfer. They are central in view of how the text performs Judah's memory
and identity.
   Given the centrality of the notion, this chapter investigates the character of fissures in the patrilinear succession and analyzes how the text deals

   1. Kelso goes even further and argues that the genealogical discourse in Chronicles
would not only present patrilineage as the standard but would 'present masculine reproduction as the standard through the overwhelming dominance of masculine subjects of
the verb "to bear"'. Kelso, *Oh Mother, Where Art Thou?*, p. 162.

with these fissures. It explores the interplay of fissures and form, embedded narratives on the one hand, and genealogical formulas on the other. And it discusses the impact of the fissures on the character and status of the patrilinear succession as a key notion of transfer in the Judah genealogies and beyond, specifically in view of their ability to contest and break open the priority of patrilinear succession on the one hand, and their supporting and confirming it on the other.

1. *Narratives on the Jeopardized Lineage*

The genealogies of Judah contain two short embedded narratives that address a threat to the continuation of the patrilinear line.[2] The first narrative tells a short version of the story of Tamar and Judah in Genesis 38. The second is distinct to Chronicles and addresses the endangered continuation of the lineage of sonless Sheshan.[3]

Tamar
Before the first lineage of Judah is properly spelled out, the text immediately recounts a small embedded narrative (2.3-4). It reads as follows:

> The sons of Judah: Er, Onan and Shelah; these three were born to him by Bath-shua the Canaanite. And Er, the firstborn of Judah, was displeasing to YHWH, and he put him to death. And Tamar his daughter-in-law bore to him Perez and Zerah. All sons of Judah: five.

The narrative closely refers to two Genesis passages: the genealogy in Gen. 46.12, and the narrative in Genesis 38. Even though Gen. 46.12 has been emphasized as a *Vorlage* for 2.3-4,[4] I would like to stress the importance of Genesis 38 for the analysis of the passage under consideration.[5] In contrast to Gen. 46.12, 1 Chron. 2.3-4 refers to names and characteristics of

---

2.   Short embedded narratives are a genuine part of genealogies. As original elements of larger genealogy compositions, they are to be found in Mesopotamian, Israelite and Greek genealogies. These traditions likewise feature a 'basic pattern of interlacing lineages with stories and explanatory comments'. Knoppers, *I Chronicles 1–9*, p. 256.

3.   The genealogy of Levi in 1 Chron. 23 provides a third embedded narrative on the jeopardized lineage. 1 Chron. 23.22 recounts that Eleazar died without having sons, only daughters and that the daughters married their cousins. Wacker argues that the marriages of Eleazar's daughters to their cousins implied that they remained in the extended family and contributed to its continuance. Marie-Theres Wacker, 'Die Bücher der Chronik: Im Vorhof der Frauen', in *Kompendium Feministische Bibelauslegung* (ed. Marie-Theres Wacker and Luise Schottroff; Gütersloher Verlagshaus: Gütersloh, 3rd edn, 2007), pp. 146-55 (149).

4.   E.g. Sarah Japhet, *I&II Chronicles: A Commentary* (London: SCM Press, 1993), p. 69.

5.   So also Willi, *1 Chr 1–10*, p. 84.

Bath-shua the Canaanite and Tamar the daughter-in-law of Judah.[6] By doing so, the text directly refers to Genesis 38. Moreover, 2.3b quotes Gen. 38.7. The quote explains why Judah's firstborn Er is not able to continue the line. It also emphasizes YHWH's agency in this critical situation for the succession.[7] 1 Chron. 2.3 provides the first reference to YHWH in the book of Chronicles. This sheds additional light on the narrative and may connote the underlying concern of whether Judah, as sociohistorical and political entity, will remain.

Let me briefly recall Genesis 38 from a viewpoint that is primarily interested in the genealogical aspect of the story. Judah and his wife, the Canaanite daughter of Shua, have three sons. Firstborn Er is married to Tamar (38.1-6). However, the lineage that might be expected to spring from this marriage is threatened. The threat unfolds in three steps. In the first step, Er, being 'displeasing to YHWH' (רע בעיני יהוה), is put to death and Tamar becomes a sonless widow (38.7). In the second step, Tamar is given to her brother-in-law Onan, so that he may fulfill the duty of levirate and beget a son for Er.[8] The aim is the continuation of the lineage of Er. Onan is told, 'bring about offspring for your brother' (והקם זרע לאחיך, 38.8). Onan refuses to properly act out his levirate duty and YHWH likewise puts him to death. Tamar remains a sonless widow once again (38.8-10). In the last step, Judah keeps his third son from fulfilling the levirate duty with Tamar and thus puts the continuation of the lineage further off (38.11). Now, the focus of the narrative shifts from Judah to Tamar.[9] Tamar brings about an unexpected move in the narrative: she does not submit herself to the fact that she has been deprived of the right of the levirate. Instead, the marginalized widow engages her resources —her wit and cunning, her social and argumentation skills, her body and sexuality—and takes the action into her own hands. Tamar dresses up as a prostitute. She has sex with Judah who does not recognize her, but leaves an unmistakable pledge with her. Tamar becomes pregnant. When Judah demands her death for adultery, she reveals to him his identity as father of the expected child. Judah recognizes Tamar's point: 'she is more righteous than I am / she is righteous in relation to

---

6.   Strikingly, Oeming in his standard monograph on 1 Chronicles 1–9 entirely passes over the mentioning of Bath-shua and Tamar. Oeming, *Das wahre Israel*, p. 211.

7.   Verse 3b quotes Gen. 38.7 word for word with the only difference that it leaves out the second occurrence of the Tetragrammaton ('*he* put him to death' instead of '*YHWH* put him to death'). Compare 5.1-2 which explains how Ruben dismissed the status of firstborn. Knoppers, *I Chronicles 1–9*, p. 303.

8.   The text assumes the institution of a levirate duty which aims to secure a son for the deceased husband, but does not necessarily imply a levirate marriage. Claus Westermann, *Genesis 37–50* (BKAT, I/3; Neukirchen–Vluyn: Neukirchener Verlag, 1982), p. 46.

9.   Jürgen Ebach, *Genesis 37–50* (HThKAT; Freiburg: Herder, 2007), pp. 134-35.

me' (צדקה ממני, 38.26).[10] The narrative ends with the birth of Tamar's twins Perez and Zerah and their naming through a 'he' (Judah) or a 'she' (Tamar or the midwife).[11]

The text-critical decision between a male or a female subject of the naming is important from a genealogical viewpoint. If Judah is understood as the one who names the twins, this naming may imply legally recognizing them as his sons. So Jürgen Ebach, who consequently understands 'the genealogical-legal incorporation of the sons of Tamar as sons of Judah' as a basic theme of Gen. 38.27-30, which is then taken up in later texts such as 1 Chron. 2.3-4.[12] In my view, Ebach is right in pointing out the genealogical dimension of the narrative. However, his claim of a genealogical climax of the narrative overstates the text-critically debated naming of the boys by Judah. Moreover, this claim loses sight of the fact that the plot centers on doing justice to Tamar and the name of her deceased husband Er.

In conclusion, Genesis 38 is a complex narrative that, along with the theme of the genealogical succession, addresses issues of outsiders and social justice, ethnic difference, sexuality, female agency and female trickery. The short version in 1 Chron. 2.3-4 brings the genealogical aspect of the story into focus, without losing sight of the other issues addressed in Genesis 38.

Comparing the original narrative in Genesis 38 and its short version in 1 Chron. 2.3-4, three important shifts stand out. First, the intention underlying the efforts to produce a son by Tamar changes. While Genesis 38 primarily aims at producing offspring for Er in the context of the levirate institution, the Chronicles' account suggests that the sons of Tamar are sons for Judah ('All sons of Judah: five'). In the context of setting out the lineage of Judah, the receiver of offspring through Tamar thus shifts from Er to Judah.[13] This shift was already prepared for in Genesis 38; however, it is only completed in the Chronicles' account.[14]

The shift regarding the receiver of offspring through Tamar implies a second one. Not the firstborn but the fourth-born of Judah is the one to

10. ממני may be translated with a focus on the comparative aspect or with a focus on the relational/connective aspect of the utterance. Ebach, *Genesis 37–50*, p. 150.

11. Different text witnesses and editions have the root קרא as qal perfect singular masculine (*BHS*) or qal perfect singular feminine (e.g. a few Hebrew manuscripts, Samaritan Pentateuch, Peshitta and Targum Pseudo-Jonathan).

12. Ebach, *Genesis 37–50*, pp. 152-53, my translation.

13. The same shift is made in Gen. 46.12: 'Judah's sons: Er, Onan, Shelah, Perez and Zerah—but Er and Onan had died in the land of Canaan; and Perez's sons were Hezron and Hamul' (JPS).

14. Against Ebach, who claims that the end of the Genesis narrative (Gen. 38.27-30) is genealogically motivated and is as such the actual climax of the narrative. Ebach, *Genesis 37–50*, p. 150.

continue the line. The primacy of the firstborn is thus suspended, as in Genesis 5.[15]

The third shift concerns the agency of the protagonists of the narrative. Genesis 38 foregrounds the agency of Tamar and introduces numerous additional agents, for example Judah's friend Hirah and the midwife. In contrast, 1 Chron. 2.3-4 emphasizes the agency of YHWH and Judah's owning of sons.

Beyond these shifts, 1 Chron. 2.3-4 shares the central themes of Genesis 38, namely ethnic difference, social justice and female trickery. These themes are mainly communicated through the references to Bath-shua and Tamar. This is noteworthy, especially since the genealogical notice in Gen. 46.10 leaves out the women altogether.

The issue of ethnic difference is introduced through Bath-shua, who is introduced as 'the Canaanite' (2.3). Bath-shua the Canaanite stands at the beginning of the genealogies of Judah (and thereby the genealogies of the tribes), immediately after the genealogies of the nations (1 Chron. 1.1–2.2). In the genealogies of the nations, ethnic groups provide the context in which the central lineage emerges and eventually leads to Israel.[16] The reference to the Canaanite Bath-shua at the beginning of the Judah genealogies introduces another focus. It establishes the fact that ethnic differences play a role within, rather than before or alongside, Judah/Israel.[17]

The reference to Tamar, possibly also a Canaanite, adds to the same issue, but reaches further.[18] Tamar is characterized as daughter-in-law of Judah. Identifying her as the daughter-in-law of the father of her sons recalls the unusual circumstances of her pregnancy and broaches the issues of social justice, legislation for widows and the levirate. Moreover, it engages the theme of trickery as related to female sexuality and agency.

The notion of trickery in biblical literature refers to 'characters of low social status who improve their situation through use of their wit and

15. For the motive of suspending the primacy of the firstborn in the Hebrew Bible, see Frederick E. Greenspahn, *When Brothers Dwell Together: The Preeminence of Younger Siblings in the Hebrew Bible* (Oxford: Oxford University Press, 1994).

16. For a discussion of the genealogy of the nations see Gary N. Knoppers, 'Shem, Ham and Japheth: The Universal and the Particular in the Genealogy of Nations', in *The Chronicler as Theologian: Essays in Honour of Ralph W. Klein* (ed. M. Patrick Graham, Steven L. McKenzie and Garry N. Knoppers; London: T. & T. Clark, 2003), pp. 13-31.

17. Knoppers emphasizes that the text does not moralize against the important role that non-Israelites played in the memory of Israel but calls attention to it. Knoppers, *I Chronicles 1–9*, p. 302.

18. For the identification of Tamar as a Canaanite see Knoppers, *I Chronicles 1–9*, p. 303; and Athalya Brenner, *I Am…Biblical Women Tell Their Own Stories* (Minneapolis, MN: Fortress Press, 2005), p. 134. Against Ebach, *Genesis 37–50*, pp. 125-26.

cunning'.[19] Tamar may be read as a trickster inasmuch as she achieves off-spring and thus a living for herself through her wit and readiness to take unconventional action. As Melissa Jackson puts it, '[a]s with Lot's daughters, Tamar's character has the traits of a trickster. She has little status, and so uses the means she has—her cleverness and her sexuality—to secure her future'.[20]

Reading Tamar as a trickster reflects the exceptional way in which Genesis 38 contextualizes female sexuality with female originality and agency. Rather than displaying Tamar as an immoral harlot or a helpless victim, she is sketched as a resourceful agent who counters her marginalization for her own benefit, the benefit of her deceased husband Er, and that of the Judah line.

Reading Tamar as a trickster is but one possibility that is offered by the text. However, the impact of the presence of Tamar and her story in 1 Chronicles 1–9 with all its overtones should not be underestimated. Tamar is not written out of the text, as for example in Gen. 46.12. Instead, her name and her identity as daughter-in-law of the father of her children recall female subjectivity in the ancestral age. Apart from Keturah (1.32-33) and Bilhah (7.13), Bath-shua and Tamar are the only women of the ancestral period to be listed in the entire genealogy composition in 1 Chronicles 1–9. Tamar is thus *the* matriarch in the composition. The text, which broaches the themes of female resistance to disenfranchisement, female sexuality and trickery, among others, thus provides a critical key to the memory of the matriarchs. Trickery is not restricted to Tamar, but is characteristic of several biblical figures, among them Abraham, Jacob, Rachel and Ruth.[21] The embedded narrative on the jeopardized lineage engages the themes of resistance, trickery and humor as vital elements of the memory and hence identity of Judah.[22]

---

19. Melissa Jackson, 'Lot's Daughters and Tamar as Tricksters and the Patriarchal Narratives as Feminist Theology', in *JSOT* 98 (2002), pp. 29-46 (29). See also Susan Niditch, *A Prelude to Biblical Folklore: Underdogs and Tricksters* (Urbana, IL: University of Illinois Press, 2000); and Ann W. Engar, 'Old Testament Women as Tricksters', in *Mappings of the Biblical Terrain: The Bible as Text* (ed. Vincent T. Tollers and John Maier; Lewisburg, PA: Bucknell University Press, 1990), pp. 143-57.

20. Jackson, 'Lot's Daughters and Tamar as Tricksters', p. 34. For the typical link between female biblical tricksters and the issues of sexuality and female agency, see Jackson, 'Lot's Daughters and Tamar as Tricksters', p. 32. See also Susan Niditch, 'Genesis', in *The Women's Bible Commentary* (ed. Carol Ann Newsom and Sharon H. Ringe; Louisville, KY: Westminster/John Knox Press, 1998), pp. 13-29 (24-26).

21. Typical trickster narratives are the three 'Wife-Sister Tales' (Gen. 12.10-20; 20.1-18; 26.1-11) and many of the stories about Jacob, e.g. Gen. 27 (Niditch, *A Prelude to Biblical Folklore*, pp. 23-69, 93-125). See also Rachel (Gen. 31.19-35) and Ruth (Ruth 3) (Engar, 'Old Testament Women as Tricksters', pp. 147, 159-60).

22. Jackson shows convincingly that the trickster story of Tamar (and of Lot's

What does 1 Chron. 2.3-4 imply for the patriarchal succession as a key notion of the memory transfer in 1 Chronicles 1–9? Genesis 38 and its reflection in 1 Chron. 2.3-4 provide ample indications of cracks in the patriarchal succession. The primacy of the firstborn is renounced. The levirate law malfunctions; instead, a widow achieves offspring through her father-in-law. A central lineage is blocked and only restored through female agency and trickery. Finally, Judah is fundamentally linked to the Canaanites.

How are these fissures dealt with in the text? On the one hand, 1 Chron. 2.3-4 overtly exposes them. Listing Bath-shua as a Canaanite and Tamar as the daughter-in-law of Judah keeps open fissures that already appeared in Genesis 38 and sharpens them in view of the genealogical succession. Here, 1 Chron. 2.3-4 appears as an exponent of ethnic, social and gendered complexity. On the other hand, 1 Chron. 2.3-4 closes with a statement that sharply counters such an assessment. The closing formula states, 'All sons of Judah: five' (2.4b). It thereby unambiguously attributes to Judah all five sons, who are then not distinguished from each other anymore.[23] By doing so, the closing brings an end to all irregularities that became apparent in the embedded narrative. The offspring of a complex and ambiguous situation is clearly attributed to the paterfamilias. The text thus provides a dynamic to channel complexity and ambiguity in a way that seems to include its devitalization. Fissures are exposed but at the same time put into perspective or even closed down again.[24]

The Nameless Daughter of Sheshan
The second story that addresses the patriarchal succession at risk is distinct to Chronicles. It takes its starting point from the absence of sons who might continue the lineage.

> Sheshan had no sons, but daughters. And Sheshan had an Egyptian slave and his name was Jarha. And Sheshan gave his daughter as wife to his slave Jarha. And she bore him Attai (1 Chron. 2.34-35).

The narrative on sonless Sheshan takes up a motif that has already been introduced in the preceding verses. Twice, a lineage ends with sonless

daughters) may be read as comic. Jackson, 'Lot's Daughters and Tamar as Tricksters', pp. 44-46.

23. 1 Chron. 2.4b is the only part of 2.3-4 that is not worked out in closely relation to Gen. 46.12 or Gen. 38 (Japhet, *I & II Chronicles*, p. 70). The verse thus sets an original accent and ending to the story.

24. In accordance with my assessment, Labahn and Ben Zvi call attention to the tendency to 'tame' the character of Tamar in later literature, for example in Pseudo-Philo (D.C. Polanski, 'On Taming Tamar: Amram's Rhetoric and Women's Roles in Pseudo-Philo's Liber Antiquitatum Biblicarum 9', *JSP* 13 [1995], pp. 79-99). Labahn and Ben Zvi, 'Observations on Women', p. 470.

males, a circumstance that is laconically expressed by a final 'no sons' (2.30, 32). The theme comes to a climax in the narrative under consideration. In contrast to the preceding instances of sonlessness, where lineages stop, the sonlessness of Sheshan occasions a small narrative.[25] Sheshan has no sons but daughters. Moreover, his household includes the Egyptian slave (עבד) Jarha. Sheshan draws on the persons at his disposal in order to solve his problem. He marries one of his nameless daughters to his slave Jarha. She bears Attai 'to him'. Attai will be the first link in the subsequent, notably long linear genealogy (2.36-41).

The text recalls Genesis narratives in which slave women (אמה/שפחה) are given to the husbands of their mistresses in order to procreate, for example Genesis 16. Genesis 16 recounts that Sarah gives her Egyptian slave Hagar to Abraham, so that she could achieve offspring through her.[26]

The passage closely parallels Genesis 16, but features a reverse gender configuration. An Egyptian male slave is given to a woman of the Judahite lineage. The Israelite insider is thus female, the Egyptian outsider male. While the son of Hagar clearly belongs to Sarah and Abraham, the claim upon Attai is less clear. 1 Chron. 2.35a does not clearly specify whether Sheshan's daughter bears Attai to her husband Jarha or to her father Sheshan. 2.35 reads:

ויתן ששן את־בתו לירחע עבדו לאשה ותלד לו את־עתי

And Sheshan gave his daughter as wife to his slave Jarha. And she bore *him* Attai.

The verse leaves open to whom Attai belongs in terms of genealogical ownership. The ambiguity has inspired different interpretations of the identity of the genealogical owner of Attai. For example, Antje Labahn and Ehud Ben Zvi argue that, 'structurally speaking', the narrative casts Sheshan's daughter in the role of the son who passes on the line.[27] This argument seems to suggest that she bears Attai to her own generation and thus to Jarha. In contrast, Sara Japhet argues that Sheshan's daughter bears Attai to her father. He remains the owner of the son of his slave Jarha.[28] In this read-

---

25. The preceding list mentions a certain Sheshan and his son Ahlai (2.31). This reference has given rise to various theories about the relation between the two Sheshans and the provenance of the passages. I follow Knoppers who argues that it may be most useful to accept that we indeed have a contradiction, which, however, does not have to be resolved. Knoppers, *1 Chronicles 1–9*, p. 310.

26. See also Bilhah and Zilpah, who are given to Jacob by their mistresses Rachel and Leah (Gen. 30). The status of Hagar, Bilhah and Zilpah is described with the terms שפחה and אמה (slave-woman/maidservant). For Jarha, the term slave/man-servant (עבד) is used.

27. Labahn and Ben Zvi, 'Observations on Women', p. 465.

28. Japhet, *I&II Chronicles*, p. 84.

ing, Sheshan's daughter gives birth to the generation of her father; her own generation is skipped.

Japhet's argument seems to be more convincing. First, identifying Attai as the son of Sheshan has a strong basis in the syntax of the passage. Throughout the passage, Sheshan is kept in the position of the subject of action. He is the dominant *major participant* in the narrative.[29] As major participant, Sheshan can be referred to by means of a pronoun or inflectional affix, even if local instances of other potential referents stand closer to the pronoun under consideration.[30] Even though the minor participant Jarha stands closest to the suffix pronoun *him* (לו), the pronoun is most likely assigned to Sheshan, who has been established as major participant in the preceding sentences.[31]

Identifying Attai as the son of Sheshan also ties in with the parallels in Genesis. Here, the son of Hagar remains the son of her masters.[32] Finally, it ties in with the namelessness of Sheshan's daughter. The namelessness reduces the subjectivity of the daughter throughout the narrative, especially since all other protagonists bear personal names. The reduction of subjectivity easily ties in with the role of carrier of her father's son. It is less fitting to interpret her as the one to continue the lineage.

The genealogical ownership of Attai by his grandfather Sheshan constitutes a parallel to the narrative of Tamar, whose sons are also assigned to their grandfather-father Judah. Both stories seem to suggest a similar way of dealing with fissures in the patriarchal succession. Twice, narratives address

29. For the concept of major and minor participants in Hebrew Bible texts see L.J. De Regt, *Participants in Old Testament Texts and the Translator: Reference Devices and their Rhetorical Impact* (Assen: Van Gorcum, 1999). Thank you to Arian Verheij for introducing me to De Regt's approach.

30. De Regt, *Participants in Old Testament Texts*, p. 24. Minor participants would more likely be referred to by proper names that would then 'be reserved for re-establishing antecedents into a central role' (De Regt, *Participants in Old Testament Texts*, pp. 23-24).

31. For a parallel case, see Judg. 15.19. The word וישת 'and he drank' refers back to Samson even though other potential referents are in closer proximity. As De Regt puts it: 'In such a global strategy, the pronoun or affix is assigned to one of the major participants early in the story and is retained throughout the discourse as referring to this entity, even if there are intervening local instances of other potential referents'. De Regt, *Participants in Old Testament Texts*, p. 44.

32. Japhet and Willi analyze the passage against the backdrop of Israelite slave legislation. Japhet refers to Exod. 21.4, which states that the children of a Hebrew slave belong to his master, as the legal basis for attributing Hagar's son Ishmael to her mistress Sarah, as well as for attributing Attai to Sheshan. (Japhet, *I & II Chronicles*, p. 84). Willi argues that the text more likely refers to Lev. 25.39-54, which distinguishes between Israelite and non-Israelite slaves, because it makes explicit the Egyptian identity of Jarha (Willi, *1 Chr 1–10*, pp. 98-99).

obstacles in the ongoing genealogical stream. Twice, they suggest solutions that involve unusual agents (women, foreigners, slaves) and unconventional actions (marriage between a woman from Judah and an Egyptian slave; female agency and trickery). Twice, proposed solutions bring about sons who continue the line. And twice, sons are eventually attributed to their grandfather-generation while the parent-generation is skipped.

Giving Birth for the Father Generation: Establishing and Curtailing Complex Genealogical Agents

Reading the two narratives together reveals a twofold dynamic in dealing with fissures. On the one hand, the narratives openly admit that the patriarchal succession might be endangered through inadequate male behavior and cases of sonlessness. As a solution, they suggest opening up the patriarchal succession and engaging additional members of the sociopolitical life of Israel who may contribute to overcoming deadlock and break-up. In this respect, the texts perform the identity of Judah as complex and inclusive. On the other hand, sons that spring from this opening are eventually attributed to the Israelite male patriarch of their grandfather's generation. The generation that represents a multifaceted identity performance is dispossessed of offspring and collapses. As a consequence, new genealogical agents are deprived of the possibility of forging their own generation; their potency to effect ongoing change is substantially weakened. Instead, admitting fissures, proposing unconventional solutions, and drawing on complex agents eventually leads to a growth of potency on the part of the paterfamilias. The texts thus display ambiguity toward their own proposed solution; developments are, to an extent, withdrawn.[33]

The scenario just described concerns gender positions but also involves ethnic and social difference. The genealogical agency of an Egyptian and possibly a Canaanite, as well as a slave and a widow, is recognized, but its potential is mitigated. In the narratives on the jeopardized lineage, ethnic and social difference becomes manifest through individual figures. Beyond these individual agents, the text addresses ethnic difference and social stratification of larger groups that make up part of Judah. Groups that are depicted as independent from Judah in other places are listed as fully integrated with Judah (e.g. the Jerahmeelites in 2.25-33) or loosely affiliated to it (e.g. the Qenizzites in 4.13-14).[34] The integration of these

---

33. A third passage that shows a similar dynamic is 1 Chron. 2.21-23, the lineage of Caleb and the daughter of Machir. The latter belongs to a different tribe and territory and is thus illustrative of the complex identity of Judah. Her descendants, however, are eventually attributed to the generation of her father: 'All these were the sons of Machir' (2.23).

34. Knoppers, 'Intermarriage, Social Complexity and Ethnic Diversity', pp. 26-27.

groups seems likewise to challenge an exclusive patriarchal succession from Israelite male to Israelite male in favor of a broader picture of subjectivities constitutive for the memory and identity of Judah. Accordingly, Knoppers claims a concept of 'ethnic diversity and social complexity' in the genealogies of Judah.[35] But what type of genealogical participation does this broader picture involve and how do the interests and agencies of groups at the periphery become apparent? Beyond the picture of social and ethnic stratification, genealogical segmentation and ramification bring about a hierarchical relationship between periphery and center. This includes othering groups by means of detaching them from the main lineage as I will show in Chapter 6. The double movement of granting complexity and concurrently devitalizing its impact on the level of individual agents thus seems to have a parallel on the level of larger groups.

The text's inherently ambiguous pattern of dealing with fissures through female-gendered references impacts the character and authority of the constructed notion of patrilinear succession. On the one hand, patrilinear succession appears as a concept that is secure enough to deal with shortcomings self-critically and effectively. This includes the involvement of social and ethnic 'outsiders' as solutions to problems in the sucession. Moreover, it contains the ability to refer to the memory of the group and to activate it in view of actual memory performances. Patrilinear succession thus appears as a potent and authoritative notion which is able to acknowledge and respond flexibly to crises. In the passages under consideration, this potential becomes especially apparent in the form of embedded narratives and intertextual references. These genealogical forms are employed to stimulate discussion, to trigger themes present in the narrative intertexts and to forward possible solutions.

On the other hand, the ambiguous pattern of dealing with fissures has a flipside, which highlights another aspect of the potency of the patrilinear succession concept. It is constructed as able to withdraw power from new genealogical agents in favor of the paterfamilias. Here, genealogical formulas in particular are used to restrict complexity and to overtly reinstitute the patriarchal order. In dealing with fissures, the texts can deactivate and repress potential for sociopolitical change, which may evolve from the solutions the texts themselves suggest. In other words, the notion of the patrilinear succession serves as a basis to regulate the impact and potency of admittedly complex genealogical agents that are brought into the textual action.

In conclusion, the ambiguous take on fissures in the patrilinear succession exposes a balancing act between its different qualities. Positively speaking, patrilinear succession appears as a notion of transfer that secures a given structure and order, which enables mapping the roots and relationships of

---

35. Knoppers, 'Intermarriage, Social Complexity and Ethnic Diversity', pp. 29-30.

the community over a long time span. Part of this order is to involve different group members in times of crisis and change. Negatively speaking, patrilinear succession appears as an authoritarian concept. It reduces the richness of transfer by repeatedly depriving involved agents of their genealogical agency, participation and power, as soon as their contribution has been adduced. From the latter perspective, the concept only pretends to be flexible and innovative. But in practice, it brings the transfer to the limits of being relevant beyond a certain group whose privileges it secures.

2. *Women as Eponymous Ancestors and Heads of Lineages*

The narratives just discussed are embedded in formalized genealogical language, but, as embedded narratives, they also transcend it. Moreover, they feature protagonists who constitute part of Judah/Israel, but who are also outsiders due to gendered, ethnic and social difference. Other passages refer to women in regular genealogical formulas and provide them with positions at the core of the lineage. In the next step, I will complement the previous analysis with such examples and discuss the passages on Ephrathah, eponymous ancestor of a major Davidic clan (2.19, 50; 4.4), and Zeruiah, sister of David and head of a segment of the Davidic genealogy (2.16-17). Both characters hold key genealogical positions. Moreover, they are referred to in clear genealogical formulas. By doing so, female characters seem to fill classical genealogical positions and forms usually reserved for men.[36]

Ephrathah
Ephrathah stands out as eponymous ancestress of the clan of the same name. The clan settled in and around Bethlehem and brought forth the Davidic dynasty.[37] As an eponymous ancestor, Ephrathah may be identified as a 'real or created person for whom a place, clan, or tribal group is named'.[38] In the genealogical context, eponymous ancestors function specifically as founding ancestors of lineages. The occurrence of Ephrathah in the genealogies of Judah merges with traditions, narratives and places that are linked to her

36. Labahn and Ben Zvi, argue that '1 Chronicles 1–9 presents some women in roles that were commonly assigned to mature males in the society', primarily the roles of head of the family and builder of cities. Labahn and Ben Zvi, 'Observations on Women', pp. 473-75.

37. For an introduction to the traditions related to Ephrathah as a person and as a place, see Lamonette M. Luker, 'Ephrathah (Person)', *ABD* II, p. 557; Lamonette M. Luker, 'Ephrathah (Place)', *ABD* II, pp. 557-58; and Aaron Demsky, 'The Clans of Ephrath: Their Territory and History', *Journal of the Institute of Archaeology of Tel Aviv University* 1 (1986), pp. 46-59.

38. Karla G. Bohmbach, 'Names and Naming in the Biblical World', *WiS*, pp. 33-40 (36).

name. Among them are the location-bound origins of the Davidic dynasty and one of various traditions on Rachel's tomb.[39] In addition, other biblical texts place Ephrathah so close to Bethlehem that Ephrathah appears as an alternative name for Bethlehem (e.g. Gen. 35.16-20).[40]

The genealogies of Judah refer to Ephrathah three times.[41] The first reference to Ephrath(ah) introduces her as wife of Caleb and mother of Hur (2.19b):

> And Caleb took for himself Ephrath. And she bore him Hur.

The second reference to Ephrathah lists her in connection with Caleb and Hur again (2.50-51):

> These were the sons of Caleb. The sons of Hur, the firstborn of Ephrathah: Shobal, the father of Kiriath-jearim, Salma, the father of Bethlehem, Hareph, the father of Beth-gader.

In this second reference, the relations between the protagonists change slightly. Ephrathah and Caleb are linked through Hur; their identification as husband and wife is implicit. Hur is listed after Caleb and thus possibly as his son. However, there is no logical transition from v. 50a to v. 50b. Instead, the passage makes sense when v. 50a is read as a concluding summary of the previous section, the lineage of Caleb (2.42-49). Hence, in accordance with Knoppers and the JPS, I take v. 50b as an opening formula that marks a beginning.[42] If v. 50a is attributed to the previous section, the connection between Caleb and Hur and thus between Caleb and Ephrathah takes a back seat. In contrast, the passage closely relates Ephrathah and Hur. While Hur is listed as the son that Ephrathah bore to Caleb in 2.19b, the actual passage introduces him as the firstborn of Ephrathah. This identification is repeated in the third reference to Ephrathah (4.4):

> And Penuel, the father of Gedor, and Ezer, the father of Hushah. These were the sons of Hur, the firstborn of Ephrathah, the father of Bethlehem.

The passage confirms the status of Hur as the firstborn of Ephrathah as a critical feature of his identity. This is supported by the reference to Bethlehem.

---

39. Luker, 'Ephratha (Place)', pp. 557-58.

40. See also Judg. 19 for the strong connection between Ephrathah and Bethlehem; Japhet, *I & II Chronicles*, p. 82.

41. See also the occurrence of the place Caleb-Ephrathah in 2.24. It states that Caleb's father Hezron died in Caleb-Ephrathah. An alternative text-critical interpretation suggests that Caleb went into Ephrathah after the death of Hezron, see e.g. Knoppers, *I Chronicles 1–9*, p. 299.

42. So Knoppers, *I Chronicles 1–9*, pp. 310-11 and the JPS. Against the Masoretic text demarcation, which, by means of a setuma, suggests reading 2.50a as a—rather clumsy—opening phrase to the subsequent lineage of Hur.

Verse 4b identifies either Ephrathah or her firstborn Hur as 'father' of Beth-lehem.[43] In both cases the tradition to link or identify Ephrathah and Beth-lehem is activated in determining Hur's identity.

The shifting connections between Ephrathah, Hur and Caleb shed light on the different ways the text deals with Ephrathah's position as eponymous ancestor. Where emphasis is on the relation between Ephrathah and Hur, the text recognizes Ephrathah as mother of Hur, with far-reaching implications. Ephrathah is identified as the one who provides Hur with the status of first-born and links his identity to Bethlehem. Hur is primarily qualified as the son of his mother and only secondarily as the son of his father. Ephrathah appears as a mother with the potency to qualify her son as a/her firstborn and to link him to a central place.

Where emphasis is on the relation between Ephrathah and Caleb the text seems to pursue another picture of Ephrathah. She is then introduced as the wife of Caleb and Hur appears primarily linked to Caleb: Caleb takes Ephrath(ah) for himself and she bears him Hur (2.19b).[44] However, the arrangement appears clumsy in 2.50-51 and disappears altogether in 4.4. The assertion that Ephrathah bore Hur to Caleb (2.19b) is countered by the double formula in 2.50 and 4.4 ('Hur firstborn of Ephrathah'). The image of Ephrathah as (dependent) wife of Caleb again takes a back seat in favor of her characterization as a potent founding mother.

Shifting connections may be read as an attempt to channel and limit Ephrathah's authority by way of depicting her as relational to her husband Caleb and attributing her firstborn to him (2.19b). However, this attempt is not successful. Instead, in their entirety, the references bring into focus the fact that Ephrathah occupies a central position in the genealogies of Judah. The patriarchal clan was remembered as emerging from a female charac-ter. Moreover, her repeated occurrence in the genealogies activates the pool of traditions, narratives and places evolving around her. It makes this pool available as a resource for the formation and expression of memory and identity. Ephrathah is a female figure who is placed in the critical genea-logical position of eponymous ancestor, equipped with formalized gene-alogical language ('Hur firstborn of Ephrathah'), and bound to central traditions of Judah. The references to her bring into focus a challenge to the

---

43. Strictly speaking, 4.4b lists Ephrathah as the father of Bethlehem (בני־חור בכור אפרתה אבי בית לחם). Considering Hur as the one who is meant to be the father of Beth-lehem would be possible by interpreting 'the firstborn of Ephrathah' and 'the father of Bethlehem' as two appositions to Hur. The *BHS* apparatus deals with the problem by introducing היא and deleting בי (בי would then be read as a dittography). This would result in the reading 'that is Bethlehem'.

44. Willi understands the marriage between Ephrathah and Caleb as an expression of the fact, that Caleb gains influence in Northern Judah. Willi, *1 Chr 1–10*, p. 95.

exclusiveness of patrilinear succession that is at the center of the Judah traditions and narratives.

Zeruiah

The second example of a female-gendered passage that centers on a woman in a key genealogical position and employs formalized genealogical language is a passage on Zeruiah. Zeruiah appears with her sister Abigail at the end of a lineage that reaches from Hezron to the generation of David (2.9-16a). The lineage terminates with a list of David and his brothers. At its end is a reference to their sisters Zeruiah and Abigail (2.16a).[45]

> The sons of Hezron who were born to him: Jerahmeel, Ram and Chelubai. Ram begot Amminadab; Amminadab begot Nahshon, prince of the sons of Judah. Nahshon begot Salmon; Salmon begot Boaz; Boaz begot Obed; Obed begot Jesse; Jesse begot Eliab his firstborn. And Abinadab the second; Shimea the third; Nethanel the fourth; Raddai the fifth; Ozem the sixth; David the seventh. Their sisters: Zeruiah and Abigail (1 Chron. 2.9-16a).

The reference to Zeruiah and Abigail is set in a standard formula that recurs throughout 1 Chronicles 1–9.[46] Zeruiah pertains to the five out of eleven sisters, who are known from inner-biblical intertexts. In addition, the genealogies themselves elaborate on her position in the lineage. The text continues as follows:

> The sons of Zeruiah: Abishai, Joab and Asahel, three. 17 Abigail bore Amasa. And the father of Amasa was Jether the Ishmaelite (1 Chron. 2.16b-17).

2.16b marks a new beginning with the opening formula and lists the sons of Zeruiah: 'The sons of PN1: PN2, PN3, PN4, three'. This is followed by a note on the son of Abigail and his Ishmaelite father (2.17). At this point in the text, the sons of Zeruiah and Abigail are the only ones to carry the lineage from Hezron to David into the next generation.

The list of the sons of Zeruiah is noteworthy. It employs the opening formula that is regularly used for listing male heads of lineages and their sons (see e.g. 2.6; 3.23; 4.1). In 2.16b Zeruiah occupies the formal slot of father and head of linage. In addition, the father of the sons of Zeruiah, in other words the one who might be expected to be listed as head of the lineage, is not referred to.[47]

---

45. The view that Zeruiah and Abigail were Jesse's daughters contradicts 2 Sam. 17.25, which recounts that Abigail was the daughter of Nahash. The same passage also mentions a different father of Abigail's son Amasa. Japhet, *I& II Chronicles*, p. 77.

46. See Chapter 3 below, for the details of the formula and the sisters occurring in this formula.

47. Wacker emphasizes that the sons of Zeruiah regularly occur as 'sons of Zeruiah' (e.g. 2 Sam. 18). For example, Joab, commander of David, is always referred to as 'son of Zeruiah' (e.g. 1 Chron. 11.6, 39; 18.15; 26.28; 27.24). Wacker, 'Die Bücher

Parallel cases are passages that list mothers in comparable formulas, for example Helah the mother of Zereth, Izhar and Ethnan (4.7), and Naarah the mother of Ahuzzam, Hepher, Temeni and Haahashtari (4.6).[48] However, in these instances, the father (and husband) is listed as well. The only other sister and mother listed without any reference to the father of her children is Hammolecheth, the sister of Machir (7.18).

It is difficult to assess the implications of the occurrence of Zeruiah (and other women) in the formal position of head of a lineage. Labahn and Ben Zvi summarize the duties attributed to the head of the family as including the duties 'to lead the family, represent it in public, manage its properties and the goods it produces, participate in trades as required and the like' and to participate in the 'local, "political" life of their community'.[49] Among these tasks, they consider it probable that women were in exceptional cases responsible for the 'economic life of the household' and held 'decisive authority within the household on internal matters'. In contrast, they consider it less likely that women could represent the family in the public sphere and in political positions.[50] In conclusion, the passage may hint at a possible powerful position of sisters (of the king) in terms of political, administrative, economic and/or territorial autonomy, action and possessions. However, this must be discussed in a broader textual framework as well as in light of extra-biblical sources.[51] On the level of the genealogy composition, however, the text is quite clear. Zeruiah fills the key genealogical position of head of lineage. This implies genealogical ownership of her sons—they are attributed to her name. Moreover, her name and position as sister of David serve as central reference points for the identity of her sons, comparable to the position of Ephrathah as reference point for the identity of her firstborn son Hur.

Exceptions that Prove the Rule versus Exceptions that Set New Rules
Zeruiah and Ephrathah are intriguing figures who indicate fissures at the center of Judah's patrilinear succession. They make sure that key genealogical and power positions that are usually attributed to men are not exclusively

der Chronik: Im Vorhof der Frauen', p. 150. For Zeruiah and her sons see also Athalya Brenner, 'My Sons, the Generals; I Am Zeruiah Sister of David', in *Biblical Women Tell Their Stories*, pp. 147-54.

48. Helah is likewise listed in the opening formula. In the case of Naarah, the concluding formula summarizes the list of her sons: 'All these were the sons of Naarah'. See also 1 Chron. 1.33.

49. Labahn and Ben Zvi, 'Observations on Women', pp. 473-74.

50. Labahn and Ben Zvi, 'Observations on Women', pp. 473-74.

51. For a careful assessment of the status of women at the Jerusalem court, especially female kin and spouses of the king and female administrative personnel, see Anna Kiesow, *Löwinnen von Juda: Frauen als Subjekte politischer Macht in der judäischen Königszeit* (Münster: LIT Verlag, 2000), pp. 80-95.

reserved for them. The positions of eponymous ancestor
are 'male mostly' rather than 'male only' positions. M;
quality that is regularly but not necessarily required tc
positions.

The explosive potential of the references to Ephrathah and Zeɪ ʋ.
sharp contrast to the manner in which they are presented in the text. The
text seems to handle their presence in the genealogies as a matter of course.
They are listed without further characterization or comment. Instead, the
text uses available formulas in order to position them in the lineages. The
matter-of-fact integration of Zeruiah and Ephrathah may easily result in
understanding the passages as exceptions that prove the rule. And indeed,
secondary literature often qualifies the passages under consideration as
exceptions or selective transgressions.[52] Against this assessment, I claim
that the text actively works toward presenting the women figures as exceptions that prove the rule, thereby downplaying their impact. This claim was
as its starting point the significant differences between the passages on Ephrathah and Zeruiah and the embedded narratives on Tamar and the nameless
daughter of Sheshan.

In a comparison between the two sets of passages, several aspects stand
out. First, Ephrathah and Zeruiah are referred to in formalized genealogical language rather than in embedded narratives. Next, Ephrathah and Zeruiah occur in instances of functioning patrilinear successions rather than in
instances of blocked or jeopardized lineages. In this context, Ephrathah and
Zeruiah occupy respectable patriarchal positions (eponymous ancestor and
head of lineage). They are insiders and located at the center of the self-conceptions and power of Judah and the house of David. In contrast, Bath-shua,
Tamar and the nameless daughter of Sheshan occupy genuine female roles
(mother, wife and daughter). Moreover, the women as well as the Egyptian slave Jarha hold insecure social positions (foreigner, widow, nameless
daughter and slave). They are outsiders in terms of gendered, ethnic, and
social difference.

Finally, Ephrathah and Zeruiah do not represent their generation (this is
done by Caleb and by David) but insitute the next generation: their sons are
identified as 'firstborn' and 'sons of Ephrathah' and Zeruiah respectively. In
contrast, Tamar, the daughter of Sheshan and Jarha temporarily represent
their generation but are prevented from establishing the next one.

The comparison highlights features in the passages that allow for the
smooth integration of Ephrathah and Zeruiah into the text. The use of formalized genealogical language in the context of functioning patrilinear
succession provides an excellent setting for slipping in women such as

52. See e.g. Knoppers, *I Chronicles 1–9*, p. 358; and Labahn and Ben Zvi, 'Observations on Women', pp. 458, 473.

ₑphrathah and Zeruiah in an inconspicuous way. Moreover, situating them at the center of self-definitions of Judah, providing them with respectable patriarchal positions, and pairing them with male protagonists who unambiguously represent their generation decreases the provocative potential inherent in the narratives. All these features work toward introducing Ephrathah and Zeruiah in a way that makes it easy to read them as exceptions and by doing so, to downplay their impact.

The References to Ephrathah and Zeruiah Provoke Echoes that Tend to Permeate the Authority of the Patriarchal Succession. The mechanism of downplaying the explosive potential of female figures such as Ephrathah or Zeruiah initiates yet another dynamic. The integration of women in central positions as a matter of course recurs throughout the genealogies of Judah and beyond. The references to Ephrathah and Zeruiah are thus part of a wider web of passages in which the fissures they indicate provoke echoes.

The fissures echo in two directions. First, the passages link up with female figures who likewise occupy the syntactical position of head of lineage.[53] Second, the passages connect Zeruiah with a structure of sisters throughout the genealogies of Judah and beyond. The references to Zeruiah and Ephrathah gain significant power through these echoes in the wider context of 1 Chronicles 1–9. Echoes are sustained by the use of the same genealogical formulas that confirm and strengthen fissures evolving around the female figures under consideration. They indicate scope for female agency and instances of powerful women that were seen as exceptional begin to look like permanent fissures in the patriarchal succession.

The mechanism of dealing with outstanding female figures by means of integrating them as exceptions that prove the rule invokes a delicate balance in the texts. On the one hand, the concept of patrilinear succession appears as a prevailing concept that is inherently linked to central constituents of the genealogies in order to remain predominant. Most important in this respect is the use of formalized genealogical language. On the other hand, the notion of patrilinear succession is permeated by 'exceptions' that institute a dynamic that magnifies their impact by means of echoing throughout the genealogy composition. Again, formalized language is crucial for this process. Patrilinear succession thus remains a leading concept of genealogical memory transfer. However, its authority is fragile. Echoes of the references to Ephrathah and Zeruiah bring numerous comparable passages to the fore. Brought into focus, they may permeate patriarchal succession to a point that its authority is significantly diminished.

53. E.g., 1.32 (Keturah); 4.6 (Naarah); 4.7 (Helah); 4.18 ᴍᴛ (Bithiah).

3. *Obscured Female Agency in Text-Critically Difficult Passages*

The last set of female-gendered passages that indicate fissures in the patrilinear succession stand out because of the collapse of syntactical coherence and meaning around a cluster of references to women (2.18-19 and
4.17-18). The examples thus reinforce the centrality of form and formalized language; they deconstruct the formalized language in the text. At the
same time, the theme of a potential loss of control is pursued on the level
of language.

My analysis of 2.18-19 and 4.17-18 builds on Julie Kelso's observation
that women often appear in passages that are text-critically unclear and difficult to make sense of. In this context, Kelso likewise elaborates on 2.18-19,[54]
which serves as an important basis for her argument that in 1 Chronicles
1–9, the occurrence of women, as well as the verb *yld*, induce 'grammatical and/or syntactical breakdowns', 'contradictions' and 'a breakdown of
realism'.[55] For Kelso, observations on breakdowns of grammar, coherence
and realism are part of her larger conclusion that the text advances a fantasy of male mono-sexual (re)production; my interest, however, is in how
these passages address female agency and the matter of fissures in the patriarchal succession.[56] My argument will be that these passages aim to actively
obscure negotiations at the basis of the texts and prevent the texts being
contested, now or in the future.

Women in 1 Chronicles 2.18-19
Let me begin with 1 Chron. 2.18-19:

וכלב בן־חצרון הוליד את־עזובה אשה ואת־יריעות ואלה בניה ישר ושובב וארדון
ותמת עזובה ויקח־לו כלב את־אפרת ותלד לו את־חור

> And Caleb son of Hezron begot (with) Azubah, a woman, and (with) Jerioth.
> These were her sons: Jesher and Shobab and Ardon. And Azubah died; and
> Caleb took for him Ephrath; and she bore him Hur.

Verse 18a starts out with the recurring phrase 'PN1 begot PN3'. The phrase
is frequent in 1 Chronicles 1–9 (e.g. 2.10-13, 36-41). As a rule, it begins
with a masculine subject followed by the verb ילד hiphil (to beget).[57] This
is followed by one or several masculine direct objects, often marked by the
object-marker את. In the passage under consideration, the phrase is modified inasmuch as the object marker את is followed by two feminine objects,
Azubah and Jerioth. One of them, Azubah, is explicitly identified as אשה

---

54. Kelso, *Oh Mother, Where Art Thou?*, pp. 129-39.
55. Kelso, *Oh Mother, Where Art Thou?*, p. 156.
56. Kelso, *Oh Mother, Where Art Thou?*, p. 162.
57. Kelso translates the hiphil form of *yld* causatively as 'caused to bear', Kelso, *Oh
Mother, Where Art Thou?*, pp. 130-31, 160.

(woman/wife). Verse 18b continues with the opening phrase 'these were her sons' followed by a list of sons. The subject of the opening phrase is indicated by means of a suffix pronoun in the first person feminine singular (בניה). The pronoun may refer to Azubah or to Jerioth. Verse 19a records Azubah's death. It is the only instance in 1 Chronicles 1–9 that records the death of a listed woman. After the death of Azubah, Caleb marries Ephrathah, who bears Hur to him (2.19b).

The passage raises plenty of questions. Does the text indeed record that Caleb begot Azubah, a woman, and Jerioth, and recall that sons were attributed to one of them? If so, what is the status of Azubah, a character that the text makes sure to state is female, whose death is recorded, and who is succeeded as wife of Caleb by Ephrathah, mother of Hur? As an alternative reading, the object marker את may be regarded as a preposition (with).[58] This may be combined with the text-critical reconstruction of the apposition 'a woman' as 'his woman/wife'.[59] In this alternative reading, either Caleb would beget with Azubah and with Jerioth, or Caleb would beget Jerioth with Azubah. The modification raises additional questions. If Azubah and Jerioth are indeed listed as wives of Caleb with whom he fathered sons, what is the impact of the fact that this information is given in a phrase that is usually reserved for fathers who beget sons? How is the agency of reproduction divided between Caleb, Azubah, and Jerioth in this form of collaboratively begetting sons? The same questions have to be raised if one assumes that Caleb and Azubah begot Jerioth, who would then appear as a daughter who continues the line and owns the subsequent list of sons.

The benefits of modifying and text-critically reconstructing the passage seem to be limited. Alternative readings are not entirely able to sort out the relationships between Caleb, Azubah, Jerioth and Ephrathah. Nor do they succeed in entirely clarifying role and agency for the women involved. Instead, the syntax of the passage remains odd. The genealogical associations of its protagonists remain ambiguous. The problems of interpretation are displaced. The ambiguity of the passage makes it difficult to analyze the position of the women it refers to. One may advance assumptions about their position and reputation. However, the complicated condition of the passage keeps them hypothetical. Azubah may have been an important ancestress in the Calebite lineage—or just a wife of Caleb. Jerioth may

58. E.g. Jacob M. Myers, *I Chronicles* (AB, 12; New York: Doubleday, 1965), p. 10; and Japhet, *I&II Chronicles*, p. 72. Against this reading, Kelso argues that in all other cases in which the hiphil of *yld* is used, the direct object of the verb is marked with an את. As a consequence, she reads the passage as 'a slip pointing to the fantasy of male birth; in this case, a man bears those who 'in reality' are the only ones who can bear'. Kelso, *Oh Mother, Where Art Thou?*, p. 160.

59. *BHS* apparatus suggests reading את אשתו instead of אשה ואת with reference to the Peshitta, Targum and Arabic translations.

have been a daughter who passed on the line—or just a secondary wife of Caleb. Ephrathah may have been Azubah's successor in a highlighted position—or just another wife of Caleb. The difficult condition of the text primarily communicates ambiguity toward the gendered position and agency of the protagonists in question.

The Women in 1 Chronicles 4.17-18

The unclear state of 2.18-19, and the consequent ambiguous presentation of its female agents, seems to be mirrored in a passage in the second part of the genealogies of Judah. 1 Chron. 4.17-18 is even more difficult to understand and has a similarly elaborate history of text-critical reconstruction. The text reads as follows:

ובן־עזרה יתר ומרד ועפר וילון ותהר את־מרים ואת־שמי ואת־ישבח אבי אשתמע
ואשתו היהדיה ילדה את־ירד אבי גדור ואת־חבר אבי שוכו ואת־יקותיאל אבי זנוח
ואלה בני בתיה בת־פרעה אשר לקח מרד

The son of Ezrah: Jether, Mered, Epher and Jalon. She conceived Miriam, Shammai and Ishbah, the father of Eshtemoa.
His wife, the Judahite, bore Jered, the father of Gedor, Heber, the father of Soco, and Jekuthiel, the father of Zanoah.
These are the sons of Bithiah, the daughter of Pharaoh, whom Mered married.

Verse 17 begins with a list of sons, including Mered who reappears at the end of the passage. Verse 17a announces only one son (בן, singular); however, a list of sons follows. Verse 17b states that a certain 'she' conceived (הרה, qal imperfect consecutive third feminine singular), and opens a second list of descendants. Among them are Miriam, probably a daughter, and Ishbah, the 'father' of a place. The verb הרה (to conceive) disturbs the reading process and raises questions. First of all, it is not clear who the female subject of the verb is. Second, הרה qal is a verb that does not require a direct object, as, for example, ילד (to bear) would. It is thus an odd replacement of the verb ילד (to bear), which is dominant in the context. The subsequent verse is even more striking. It begins with a list of sons, all three also being 'fathers' of a place. They are born by 'his' wife, the Judahite, where 'his' identity again remains obscure. Even more striking is the fact that the list of the sons of 'his' wife, the Judahite, is summed up by a formula that attributes these very sons to Bithiah, daughter of Pharaoh and wife of Mered.

I am once again not primarily interested in an attempt to reconstruct a more coherent version of the text.[60] Rather, I am interested in the paral-

---

60. For a common reconstruction see Japhet: 'The generally accepted reconstruction of these lines is that proposed by Curtis... The words "These are the sons of Bithiah, the daughter of Pharaoh, whom Mered married" are transposed from v. 18b to after v. 17a, "son" (17a) becomes "sons" (following some MSS and the Versions) and in v. 17b wattēled ("and she bore") is added, for the reading "and she conceived and bore Miriam,

lels to 2.18-19. As in 2.18-19, difficulties in terms of coherence and meaning appear in a passage that provides a dense web of references to women.
Difficulties concentrate around the gendered references. 4.17-18 additionally involves the issues of ethnicity and place. As in 2.18-19, female agency
in procreation and female genealogical ownership are hinted at. And as in
2.18-19, an assessment of this agency and ownership has to remain provi-
sional and ambiguous.

Collapses of Genealogical Forms and the Patriarchal Succession in Crisis
Both passages hint at fissures in the patriarchal succession inasmuch as
they allow for assumptions about female agency in procreation and for
the attribution of lineages to women. The women under consideration are
recipients of male begetting or themselves involved in begetting a daughter (Azubah); they identify segments of a lineage (Jerioth; Bithiah); they
conceive sons and daughters ('she'); they represent ethnic and territorial
interests in the Judahite lineage (the Egyptian Bithiah);[61] they build up successions between mother and daughter (Azubah–Jerioth, 'she'–Miriam);
they embody links to related tribes (Ephrathah to Benjamin); and as eponymous ancestresses they embody foundational traditions (Ephrathah). By
attesting to all these activities, the passages reveal a dense web of fissures
in the patrilinear succession. However, these fissures remain intangible and
vague due to extremely difficult and incoherent syntax. The occurrence of
what Kelso terms 'grammatical and/or syntactical breakdowns' establishes
ambiguity and a lack of transparency.[62] It counters female genealogical
agency and ownership by means of rendering it fragmentary and invisible.
As a result, gender-related interests and power dynamics are not openly
negotiated. The passages do not make a clear statement concerning the
identities and positions of Azubah, Jerioth, Ephrathah, Miriam, the Jehudite wife, Bithiah daughter of Pharaoh, and several other 'shes'. Instead,
intangibility obscures possible negotiations and contest in the texts. In the
same way, ambiguity represses potential negotiations at the level of textual
reception.[63]

---

etc."' (Japhet, *I&II Chronicles*, p. 114). The NRSV translates accordingly: 'The sons of
Ezrah: Jether, Mered, Epher and Jalon. These are the sons of Bithiah, daughter of Pharaoh, whom Mered married; and she conceived and bore Miriam, Shammai and Ishbah
father of Eshtemoa. And his Judean wife bore Jered father of Gedor, Heber father of
Soco and Jekuthiel father of Zanoah'.
    61. Knoppers, *I Chronicles 1–9*, p. 350.
    62. Kelso, *Oh Mother, Where Art Thou?*, p. 156.
    63. An additional tension in the text emerges from the name 'Bithiah'. Bithiah is
clearly an Israelite name, which means 'daughter of God'/'daughter of YHWH'. The
name in combination with the title 'daughter of Pharaoh' hints at the negotiation and

The passages thus expose a double dynamic and ambiguity in how the text handles fissures in the patrilinear succession through female-gendered references. The passages let the reader gaze at fissures in the patrilinear succession but at the same time employ mechanisms for closing or obscuring these fissures and for devitalizing their impact.

The collapse of syntactical coherence and meaning in the passages prevents the texts from being contested, now or in the future. It may attest to an interest in actively obscuring negotiations that undergird the texts. Such interest would testify to an authoritarian dimension in the patrilinear succession.

However, the double dynamic of the passages also points in another direction. In the passages, formalized language is in crisis. Established phrases and formulas are not adequately filled and appear emptied of meaning. At the same time, the coherence of the passages' content (names, genealogical attributions, places) falls apart. Logic and coherence of the patrilinear succession are in crisis as well. The moment patrilinear succession and formalized language fall apart, in other words, the moment in which patrilinear succession loses formalized language as a partner in the memory transfer, seems to mark a crisis of its authority and meaning. This crisis is characterized by uncertainty in judgment and weakness in taking a stance. Not taking a stance in interplay with the crisis of form and logic hints at a crisis of authority of patriarchal succession as a key notion of transfer.

4. Conclusion

The Pattern of Exposing Fissures and Restricting their Implications

The analysis of three illustrative sets of female-gendered passages in the genealogies of Judah has exposed fissures in the patrilinear succession. Even though the passages address dysfunctions and limits of the patrilinear succession in distinct ways, a general pattern may be traced. The passages admit to fissures in surprisingly explicit ways. At the same time, they feature movements to limit, downplay, or obscure them—more or less successfully.

In the first sample of passages, the narratives on the jeopardized lineage, the text deals with the threat of a dead end in the patriarchal succession by means of integrating genealogical agents that introduce gendered, ethnic and social complexity. However, this is countered by depriving these agents of the descendants they bring forth, thereby curtailing the impact of their integration.

In the second sample of passages, the text admits to the presence of women in central genealogical roles that are usually reserved for men,

maybe integration of Judean and Egyptian traditions in this female figure and her exog-amous marriage (see Susan Tower Hollis, *WiS*, p. 62).

namely the roles of eponymous ancestor, head of house, and owner of lineages. However, the text presents the women as exceptions that prove the rule, thereby downplaying their impact.

In the third sample of passages, the text may allow a glimpse of negotiations concerning the presence of women as important genealogical agents. However, these negotiations are obscured by the unclear syntax and difficult text-critical situation of the passages.

The attempt to restrict the impact of fissures in the patriarchal succession is not always successful. For example, in the passage on Zeruiah, both her presentation as sister and her presentation as owner of a segment of the Davidic lineage create echoes in the larger composition of 1 Chronicles 1–9. These echoes undermine the tendency to limit the impact of fissures and work toward the subversion of the notion of patrilinear succession.

The characteristic back and forth between admitting to fissures and countering their implications confirms my hypothesis that ambiguity is a leading aspect of the memory performance in 1 Chronicles 1–9. The use of form and formalized language, as well as the institution of a gendered subtext, are central in playing out this ambiguity.

The Primacy of Form

Skilful use of genealogical forms frames the contents of the passages under consideration. This use of form is a significant factor in establishing the interplay between admitting to fissures and acknowledging the contribution of complex agents on the one hand and limiting their impact on the other.

In the passages on Tamar and the daughter of Sheshan, the form of embedded narrative is used to stimulate discussion and suggest solutions. In this context, a narrative intertext is employed to communicate viewpoints and connotations beyond the possibilities of a genealogical structure. On the other hand, genealogical formulas are used to restrict complexity and to overtly reinstitute the patriarchal order.

In the passages on Ephrathah and Zeruiah, standardized formulaic language is used to inconspicuously integrate outstanding women into the genealogical structure. Genealogical form is used to restrict the impact of these women by labeling them as exceptions. At the same time, the use of formulaic language creates echoes, which may bring the phenomenon of exceptions to a point where they may develop a life of their own.

In the passages that attest to a breakdown of coherent form around the mention of Azubah, Jerioth, Bithiah, and others, formalized language is used as a basis to vary and even shatter form. By doing so, formal breakdowns obscure possible negotiations about the position of women in the genealogical memory performance. At the same time, the shattering of form occurs at the expense of taking clear stances and weakens the authority of patrilinear succession.

The text uses different formal tools of the genre of genealogy. None of the forms work fully and successfully against or in favor of exposing fissures in the patrilinear succession. Strict formal patterns seem to work against women in sets 1 and 2, but also institute powerful echoes within the genealogical structure and prompt potent memories such as the female trickery of the matriarchs. In turn, embedded narratives and 'syntactical chaos' work to concede complexity but are also open to counter-movements in the shape of clear-cut formulas. In conclusion, the use of genealogical forms in order to handle fissures and complexity is done in a multilayered and powerful manner. Still, it results in a tightrope-walk between remaining in charge and risking a loss of control through echoes that, as part of a gendered subtext, develop a life of their own.

Ambiguity and the Female-gendered Subtext
Fissures in the patriarchal succession establish a gendered subtext that adds complexity to the memory performance and challenges the primacy of patrilinearity. The subtext changes the genealogy composition. It makes clear that women participated in the continuation of the lineage within and beyond their reproductive capacities, both at the center and at the margins of the genealogy composition. It adds a multilayered dimension to the genealogical memory act and makes it more rich and interesting. In this respect, different groups must have been able to identify with the genealogical memory performance. In fact, the genealogies of Judah may be read as an invitation to various groups to integrate.

But the subtext is also problematic. The text seems to work toward an opening of the patriarchal succession and toward granting complexity only as long as this serves the purposes of the main text and its leading ideologies. As the close readings have demonstrated, admitting to fissures and granting complexity triggers counter-dynamics that restrict them as soon as the patriarchal agenda is fulfilled. This leads to the problematic dynamic of inviting complex agents and then silencing them.[64] In other words, the subtext has a function for the main text and is in danger of being exploited by it.

Even though the subtext has a somewhat ambivalent status in the text, I hold that it creates a dynamic in the genealogies that cannot be entirely monopolized. Countering and trying to exploit the subtext does not undo it. In this context, the third dynamic that evolves in the process of a back and forth between admitting to complexity and denying its impact is critical. Gendered fragments that are rendered as exceptions but echo throughout the genealogical composition deconstruct the authority of the patriarchal succession from within, as do gendered fragments whose meaning is obscured

---

64. A similar dynamic occurs in the genealogies of Ruth 4: after Ruth's marriage and the birth of her son, Ruth and Naomi disappear from the genealogy.

at the cost of taking clear stances. This third dynamic bears an important and stable potential for subversion.

Authority and Ambiguity of the Patrilinear Succession

In conclusion, focusing on fissures in the patrilinear succession through references to women reveals the character and functions of the concept of patriarchal succession as constructed in the texts. On the one hand, the patriarchal succession as a key aspect of the memory transfer allows for a relatively complex memory act. The enacting of the patriarchal succession seems to involve the ability to actively address crises in the ongoing lineage and to employ different members of the community to develop solutions. This goes hand in hand with an ability to recognize the diversity of the community and to integrate its diverse participants. Next, the patrilinear succession seems to be able to establish and maintain a certain symbolic order. This order seems to coherently correlate Israel's past to its present in a way that is relevant for different groups and interests within the community. Analyzing fissures in the patrilinear succession thus reveals how much patriarchal succession benefits from the gendered fragments and the complexity they contribute to the memory act.

On the other hand, patriarchal succession comes into focus as a notion that tends to tilt toward the authoritarian and diminishes the relevance of the genealogical act of memory. This backlash, as it becomes apparent in the various counter-movements of the relevant texts, undermines the authority of the patrilinear succession and diminishes its relevance as the key notion of transfer. It tends to reduce genealogical transfer to an act of memory that is only relevant to those who are privileged by the patriarchal structure.

Finally, patriarchal succession appears as a notion that struggles to balance its impulses to open and to restrict. This struggle is enacted by means of the text's skilful handling of genealogical forms. It is successful inasmuch as the main text retains control over the subtext. However, there is also a tendency to lose control in what I have described as a third dynamic, evolving from the ambiguity of back and forth between opening and restriction. Reading the genealogies of Judah from the perspective of its female-gendered references highlights fissures in the male mirror. At the same time, it points to the fragility of the material of the mirror itself.

While the genealogy composition in 1 Chronicles 1–9 features gendered fragments that are embedded in a male memory act and a male self-conception in the present, the film *My Life Part 2* performs its genealogical memory act by means of establishing a female lineage. How does this female mirror function? What are its key notions of transfer, and how are its contents structured and framed? What do the fissures in the female mirror reveal and how does it respond to a traumatic past?

Chapter 5

GYNEALOGY PERFORMANCE IN *MY LIFE PART 2*

This film analysis focuses on the memory performance in the documentary film *My Life Part 2*, specifically on how the film conceptualizes and uses gendered genealogies.[1] By doing so and in accordance with the film's intent to unearth the past, I focus on genealogical memory production rather than on forgetting, repression, and displacement of memories. Moreover, in line with the context of socializing *My Life Part 2* and 1 Chronicles 1–9, I draw special attention to the role of fissures and fractions in the genealogy performance, as well as to the issue of ambiguity, both themes that came to the fore in the previous text analysis.

The chapter develops five themes. Section 1 surveys the contents and formal elements of the film and provides information about the filmmaker. By discussing the film's use of time and space, it introduces the intersection of personal and public memory performances and the concept of the paradox as key coordinates for the film's gendered genealogies. Section 2 addresses the quality of gendered genealogy performance in *My Life Part 2*. It delineates the main lineage of the film, namely the lineage of Levi women, and explains why it can be appropriately identified as a *gynealogy*. Section 3 highlights fractions and discontinuities at the center of the lineage, as they complicate the film's gynealogy performance. In the film, discontinuity mainly relates to the challenge of dealing with the Shoah. Hence, I will suggest understanding the film as a gynealogical memory project that aims to come to terms with the legacy of the Shoah. I will argue that the film brings discontinuity to the fore without abandoning the genealogy project, thereby locating discontinuity within rather than outside the

1. Original title: *Mein Leben Teil 2*, DE 2003; original version: German; subtitled version: English. Screenplay, director and editor: Angelika Levi; production: Angelika Levi/ *celestefilm* in cooperation with ZDF (*Das Kleine Fernsehspiel*); distribution by ZDF and *celestefilm* (Metzer Sraße 20, 10405 Berlin, Germany). Additional information about the film at http://www.berlinale.de/external/de/filmarchiv/doku_pdf/20031008.pdf and http://www.arsenal-berlin.de/forumarchiv/forum2003/katalog/mein_leben_teil_2.pdf (accessed June 8, 2013). Trailer and an interview with the filmmaker on YouTube at http://www.youtube.com/watch?v=IMarqtWIowY and http://www.youtube.com/watch?v=0neLtUTdJ3o (accessed June 8, 2013).

genealogy form. Section 4 emphasizes the moment of mediation of the cultural memory and focuses on the film's reception and the role of the viewer. It discusses the film's ability to open up spaces of otherness and to convey affects of concern. An emphasis on the role of film as a medium will lead me to suggest political agency and shared identities as a second setting for gendered genealogies in response to trauma, along with the motivation of identity formation and utterance. Section 5 assesses the film's contribution to the understanding of gendered genealogies in response to trauma and identifies the central themes explored in both *My Life Part 2* and 1 Chronicles 1–9 that will form the basis of my intertextual analysis.

1. *'My Life Part 2' and Its Location in Time and Space*

Contents of 'My Life Part 2'
My Life Part 2 covers the filmmaker's family history as well as political history from the beginning of the twentieth century to the mid-1990s. Its central locations are Germany and Chile. The story is told chronologically, but events are illuminated by home movies, audio records and interviews from different time periods. Ursula Levi, mother of the filmmaker and main protagonist, is born in Hamburg in 1926 to Karla Levi Heins, who was raised without denomination, and Robert Levi, the son of a wealthy Jewish merchant's family. For Ursula, the family name Levi constitutes a link to the biblical Levi and is a powerful element of her self-conception. Ursula's father emigrates to Chile in 1938. Rather than placing his emigration into a political context, the film explains that he had to leave Germany because of a non-Jewish lover, an incoherence that is never resolved. Threatened with deportation, Ursula's grandmother commits suicide. The other paternal family members are murdered by the Nazis. A virtual memorial album commemorates the dead with photographs and voice-over testimonies. Ursula, her mother Karla and her brother Jürgen (born in 1924) survive the Nazis in Germany. Photographs from the beach at the Baltic resort of Boltenhagen and an audio record of Karla from the 1980s only hint at this period. The film repeatedly emphasizes that neither Ursula's daughter Angelika, the filmmaker, nor Ursula's husband Johannes, know exactly how Ursula, Karla, and Jürgen survived. As an adult, Angelika encounters the time of persecution in distorted ways. For example, she finds a yellow sifter in a Hamburg office building, where an uncle of hers worked until the 1930s. Angelika recognizes the mesh as a Star of David pattern. She cleans it and takes a photograph.

In 1947, Ursula and Karla join Ursula's father in Chile. After ten years of separation and vastly different experiences, their reunion proves difficult. Moreover, Ursula struggles with her identity as being at the same time Jewish and non-Jewish. In Chile, she studies biology and becomes the country's first female ecologist. She researches plants that survive in extreme conditions by adapting to their environment. In 1956, Ursula's brother Jürgen dies in a car accident in the United States. The time period is represented by a series of photographs that Ursula and Karla took of each other at the same location and in the same postures. Two years later, Ursula and Karla return to Germany on a research grant from the Alexander von Humboldt Foundation. The return is marked by a photograph of the Polylepis tree Ursula does research on. The photograph shows a pile of gnarled tree trunks beside a barrack. It strongly resembles the photographs of piles of corpses taken at the Nazi concentration camp Bergen-Belsen after the liberation in April 1945. In a voice-over, Angelika identifies the photo as a turning point, causing Ursula's return to Germany, 'back to the site of her trauma'.

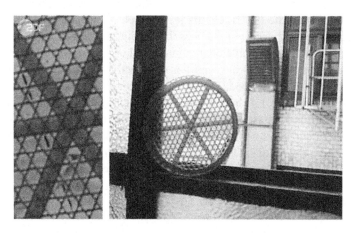

Fig. 1. *The yellow sifter ('My Life Part 2', 00:07:45)*

Fig. 2. *Cut Polylepis trees ('My Life Part 2', 00:37:45)*

In Bonn, Ursula meets her future husband, a Protestant minister. His name, Johannes Becker, does not appear in the film, but is given in the credits. The church approves of their marriage as an act of reconciliation. They have two children, Angelika (born in 1961) and her younger brother Thomas (date of birth not given; name given in the credits only). Ursula turns from Jewish émigré and scientist to a minister's wife.

Shortly after the wedding, Ursula falls ill. For several years, her complaints are dismissed as hysterical. Finally, however, she is diagnosed with Hodgkin lymphoma. Throughout long hospital stays, chemotherapy and the diagnosis that she will shortly die, Ursula meticulously documents her physical and emotional condition. She falls into a severe depression and is pushed to spend time in a psychiatric institution before eventually coming home. Back with the family, Ursula feels extremely isolated. The traumatic past resurfaces and deeply influences the family situation. Ursula perceives housework as an unbearable charge put onto her as a means of tormenting her. She cries while cooking, and her daughter Angelika, fearing that the tears might poison the food, cannot eat anymore. Ursula accuses her husband of planning to kill her by psychological torture. She insults herself with Nazi terms such as 'Jewish pig'. The account of these years is complemented by interviews with Angelika's father and Ursula herself, providing retrospective reflections. Ursula links her situation to the years of persecution by the Nazis. The subjective similarity of excessive distress and pain causes her to associate the situations and re-enact the trauma.

At this point Ursula's story disappears from view. There is a gap in her story in the 1980s and early 1990s. Instead, a metadiscourse is inserted. Television footage of the German discourse about the Nazi past is juxtaposed with further domestic scenes from the 1970s. Television footage includes Margarete Mitscherlich's plea to work through the past after the screening of the *Holocaust* series in 1979; Martin Walser's justification of a culture of looking away in 1998; and Guido Knopp's public opinion poll on whether Germans should put away the past (50% positive, 44% negative). The footage is contrasted with a Christmas feast where Ursula gives her children the necessary documents and money for a flight to Chile that might become necessary because of new anti-Semitic persecution. The metadiscourse continues with an interview with Berlin Rabbi Rothschild, who reflects on ways to cope with the Shoah and on being Jewish. He suggests having children and going on with life as one possible answer to the Shoah; life/*Chaim* as another. Angelika reflects on these suggestions in a voice-over. She wonders whether she is the answer of her mother and also of her father to the Shoah. Her own answer will not be a biological one. She and her brother are lesbian and gay, without a wish for children.

The plotline continues with Angelika's journey to Chile in the 1990s. The journey deeply challenges her views of her mother and her own political agenda. Visiting old family friends, who are Jewish emigrants like her grandfather, Angelika discovers that many of them sympathized with Chilean dictator Augusto Pinochet. Angelika recounts that the clash between anticipation and reality broke open her fixed perpetrator-victim scheme and allowed her a fresh perspective on her mother's story. After this turning point, the film carefully takes up earlier themes, slightly alters them and brings them to a close. The yellow sifter with the Star of David pattern reappears as a bread basket in a café in Santiago de Chile. The beach of early family photographs at Boltenhagen transforms to shots of Angelika among women friends at the Chilean beach. Interview sequences with Ursula readdress themes such as the impact of the name Levi. Whenever themes are taken up, a change in atmosphere occurs.

The film ends with Ursula's résumé of her life: it was her life and it was okay. Ursula died in 1996 at the beginning of Angelika's work on the film.

Formal Elements of the Film. My Life Part 2 uses specific formal elements; it presents its story as a montage of archival materials. Materials include photographs, home movies and television footage, objects and documents, interview sequences, and audio records. Among the archival material, family photographs, home movies, and objects are most characteristic. The silent home movies of the 1960s and 1970s represent the domestic sphere as a place of traumatic recall and the struggle to come to terms with loss, grief and isolation. Domestic scenes are juxtaposed with public footage, for example the television footage on the contemporary German debate on National Socialism. The juxtaposition embeds the family story in its cultural-political context. Domestic realities are contrasted with public debates, and the interplay of private and public processes in the formation of cultural memory is emphasized.

Objects play an important part, for example the yellow sifter, laundry with name boards, pages of Ursula's herbarium, official documents, letters, notebooks and a silver goblet. These objects serve as prisms for points the filmmaker wants to make. For example, the silver goblet is a family heirloom that ancestor Leon Levi received as a gift of honor from the city of Neustadt in 1871. In the 1930s, Ursula's grandmother asks the girl Ursula to bring her the goblet so she can use it to commit suicide. In the 1990s, Angelika travels to Neustadt, where she finds a continuity of anti-Semitism and racism, which she identifies as typical for West Germany before and after reunification. The goblet serves as a symbol for the widespread ignorance of the past in contemporary West Germany.

The use of archival material is combined with a second critical element of the film, the voice-over. The personal voice-over explains the archival material and serves as the main narrative device of the film. Most characteristically, *My Life Part 2* is an extremely personal film, in which the personal is accompanied by a meta-level history it both recounts and produces.

Additional narrative devices of the film are audio records and interview sequences, notably an interview with Ursula from the early 1990s. The interview introduces and reflects key themes of the film before bringing them to a close. It also serves to both indicate and bridge a gap in the film. The development of the mother in the 1980s is not directly addressed. But the interview shows Ursula narrating and reflecting on the past, thereby indicating that she went through a process of overcoming traumatic reenactment and depression. The viewer learns about the outcome of a process that has not been directly addressed or explained.

A last critical element of the film is its soundtrack, which mainly consists of spoken language and voice-over and sparingly used guitar music. The guitar music includes a characteristic theme that reoccurs throughout the film: a poetic melody, picked on a classical guitar. It occurs four times at central moments of the film. For example, during the opening scene, Angelika Levi recounts how she and her brother used to look at the memory objects of her mother and the photographs of relatives murdered by the Nazis. The first reference to the traumatic experiences of the mother is concluded by the guitar theme. The film then uses additional guitar music, for example a single stroke, to indicate the turn from a seemingly happy family to the cancer diagnosis and the resurfacing of the trauma. Along with voices and guitar music, the film includes many sequences with either barely audible sound (e.g. wind or clapping beach chairs) or silence.

The Filmmaker. The filmmaker Angelika Levi was born in Bonn in 1961. She studied film at the German Film and Television Academy Berlin (1986–1992). Levi lives in Berlin where she works as a filmmaker and film editor. Her films include six short films and two documentary features.[2] Levi's documentary features start out from personal relationships, which are then located in the context of political and cultural discourses. This is true of her most recent film *Absent Present* (2010). The film traces the journey of a friend from Namibia, who was deported from Germany after reunification. Starting out from the story of a friendship, the film addresses migration, denationalizing people and globalization in Germany and beyond. In

2. *Ariel* (short, 1984); *S.A.R.K. or Traversing the Block as Stations on the Cross of the Footpath* (*S.A.R.K. oder die blockdurchquerende Fusswegachse als Stationenweg*, short, 1987); *Fist in Your Eye* (*Faust aufs Auge*, short, 1988); *Off We Go. But Where?* (*Auf geht's. Aber wohin?*, short, 1989); *The Little Object a* (*Das kleine Objekt a*, short, 1992); *Desireé & Polylepis* (short, 1994); *My Life Part 2* (*Mein Leben Teil 2*, documentary feature, 2003); and *Absent Present* (documentary feature, 2010). Source http://www.german-films.de/app/filmarchive/film_view.php?film_id=975 (accessed June 8, 2013).

a similar way, *My Life Part 2* addresses the legacy of the experience of the Shoah in the second and third generation against the foil of her own family story.

Time in 'My Life Part 2': Cultural Memory Performance at the Intersection of Private and Public Time

The female-gendered genealogy of *My Life Part 2* is intimately interwoven with the film's uses of time and space. Analyzing how they are used is imperative to identify central coordinates of the genealogy and to understand its function and meaning.

The most specific aspects of time in *My Life Part 2* are established using archival footage, especially home movies. The use of archival footage in documentaries engages the date of the archival record, the period of compilation during filmmaking and the time of viewing. Intervals between the time layers need to be bridged in the attempt to correlate past and present. The use of home movies increases the significance of the interval between the date of the recording and the moments of compilation and viewing, because of the difference between the home movie's orientation to the personal and private and the filmmaker and viewer's interest to contextualize it in light of historical developments and public discourses.[3] The ignorance of the future of those posing in holiday shots or in home movies stands in particularly strong contrast to the historical knowledge of both filmmaker and viewer.[4] One possible way of dealing with the contrast is to expose it. For example, 'The Maelstrom' by Péter Forgács (1997) repeatedly superimposes the historical time of the compilation onto the personal time of the home movie, working toward a 'staged clash' between personal and historical time.[5]

My Life Part 2 likewise uses this strategy to contrast personal and historical time. However, its main focus is on interrelating different time layers. This is initiated by involving additional time layers. First, the film adds a period of trauma reenactment in the 1960s and 1970s. During this intermediate time layer, Ursula's trauma resurfaces and unleashes its power a second time, as manifested in home movies from this period. The same home movies show the childhood of the next generation, thus not only pertaining to Ursula's trauma, but also to the next generation's present. The displacement of the trauma from the past to the present of the next generation creates a situation in which the trauma is passed on from parent to child.

---

3. Malin Wahlberg, *Documentary Time: Film and Phenomenology* (Minneapolis, MN: University of Minnesota Press, 2008), pp. 112-13.

4. Wahlberg, *Documentary Time*, p. 113.

5. Ernst J. van Alphen, 'Toward a New Historiography: Péter Forgács and the Aesthetics of Temporality', in *Resonant Bodies, Voices, Memories* (ed. Anke Bangma *et al.*; Rotterdam: Piet Zwart Institute, 2008), pp. 90-113 (103).

The second additional time layer is the layer of recollected time. It encompasses the personal family story as well as its historical context; it suggests perspectives from which to look at the personal and the historical time periods. Those additional time layers work toward intermeshing past and present, personal and historical, linear and distorted time. In conclusion, the use of time in *My Life Part 2* highlights the continuity and interconnectedness of all time layers involved.

Working with home movies and other private materials, such as photographs or personal objects, brings with it the potential to use 'alternative archives of amateur film'.[6] These archives can provide accounts that serve as an alternative to dominant history and memory established by official representations of political events.[7] In *My Life Part 2*, alternative archives pertain to the filmmaker's own family. The film's most characteristic way of editing the material is Levi's autobiographical voice-over. The voice-over relates the family story and historical elements from a personal and engaged insider perspective. This insider perspective chronicles the family story, while reflecting on political history and juxtaposing it with public footage and discourses. The result is a film that is extremely personal but likewise 'fully entangled with public discourses'.[8] In this characteristic aspect of the film, the use of amateur film archives works toward emphasizing the productivity of crossing private and public perspectives of history, memory and politics. Not the contrasts between personal time and historical time, but the crossing points between the personal time of the private home movies and the historical time of the retrospective perspective of the filmmaker, are brought into focus. The film's specific uses of time suggest that intersections between personal and historical time, and between private and public discourses, are productive locations of cultural memory production.

Space in 'My Life Part 2': Slipping In and Out of Homeland and Exile
The story of *My Life Part 2* unfolds between two critical places, Germany and Chile. Germany is the native country but also the site of the trauma. It's the place where Ursula and Angelika are at home but also alienated—insiders and outsiders at the same time. Ursula expresses this paradox through her choice of nationality. Even while living in Germany,

---

6. Wahlberg, *Documentary Time*, p. 109.

7. Wahlberg, *Documentary Time*, p. 102. See also *Mining the Home Movie: Excavations in Histories and Memories* (ed. Karen L. Ishizuka and Patricia R. Zimmermann; London: University of California Press, 2008).

8. Hilde Hoffmann, '*Mein Leben Teil 2—My Life Part 2* (2003): Reflections about Recent Autobiographical Documentaries', in *Gendered Memories: Transgressions in German and Israeli Film and Theatre* (ed. Vera Apfelthaler and Julia B. Köhne; Vienna: Turia & Kant, 2007), pp. 128-43 (132).

she keeps her Chilean passport under the name of Ursula Levi Heins de Becker (00:26:33[9]):

> I have no interest in becoming a German citizen again. No, I feel different, even now. Yes, I was born here and I speak the language. And yes, I'm at home here. Germany is my home, of course. But still... I just couldn't.[10]

Germany is the place of the traumatic past and the place haunted by displaced trauma. It is also the place where the fear of a recurrence of the terror dwells: when Ursula provides her children with the necessary money and documents for a possible flight to Chile, her gesture expresses her fear. At the same time, it constructs Chile as a safe place.

In contrast to Germany, Chile appears as the place of exile and the reunion of the family in 1947. It is the place of Ursula's studies and pride; the place Angelika returns to in the 1990s. But just like Germany, Chile is the site of a paradox. Home to a large number of the Jewish diaspora, it is also the place of the Pinochet dictatorship. During her first journey to Chile in the 1990s, Angelika painfully encounters this paradox. She realizes that many old friends of her family sympathized with the Pinochet regime (01:13:50).

Chile and Germany are constructed as antagonists. Throughout the film, the transition between the two places is marked as a dramatic and radical experience. It indicates central moments for the development of relationships, stories and memory. When Ursula and Karla emigrate from Germany to Chile in 1947, Ursula's father resents the close bond between mother and daughter, which makes the reunion of the family extremely problematic. Ursula experiences the rejection as a major shock, 'a bigger shock even than the Nazis. I don't know, I'd almost say it made me into a different person' (00:28:14). When the women return to Germany ten years later, footage of transatlantic ships and the voice-over on the journey back is suddenly replaced by a black-and-white photograph of piles of gnarled corpse-like shapes beside a barrack. Only after a few painful seconds does the voice-over explain that the photograph shows piles of cut Polylepis trees (see Fig. 2). The voice-over explains that, for Angelika, this is the photograph that brought her mother back to Germany, back to the site of her trauma. And indeed, Ursula's marriage and life in Germany will become the site of her illness and depression, of the re-enactment of her trauma and her recurring fears.

Ursula and Karla do not go back to Chile, but Angelika travels there in the 1990s, a journey that deeply affects her perception of her mother as well

9. Time indications mark the beginning of the sequence in question. The sequences are to be found in the scene protocol (Appendix 2).

10. All English quotes are according to the English subtitles of the subtitled version of *My Life Part 2*.

as her political stance. Finding that many German exiles had sympathized with Pinochet disrupts her black-and-white understanding of past and present. Angelika always thought of her mother as wanting to go back to Chile. For her, her mother was not German but Jewish and a survivor. There was no way to explain her return to Germany except as a victim (01:13:15). Angelika's journey to Chile unsettles this perception: 'This contradiction changed my view, my black-and-white notions of victims and perpetrator' (01:13:50). The change in perspective indicates the second critical turning point in the film.

Germany and Chile accommodate Ursula's and Angelika's experience and self-conception of being alienated at home, of concurrently belonging and being apart. Both places exemplify the paradox of a homeland that is likewise a kind of exile. Moving between the two places facilitates the expression of this paradox and informs the identity of the women and their lineage, beyond a diffuse feeling of being different. In addition, slipping in and out of Germany and Chile is a central engine for exploiting the paradox for processes of identity performance and emotional and political developments. In this way, the paradox serves as an impulse for development and change.

Slipping in and out of homeland and exile provides an important link to the genealogies in 1 Chronicles 1–9 and beyond. Being at home but still a returnee, a returnee but still an alien, is a motif both film and text share. However, the motif is not entirely in parallel. The biblical returnees from Babylonian exile eventually take a central role in the memory and the present life of the biblical community,[11] while the Levi family remains at the fringe of both the post-Shoah and the German memory discourse. Still, the parallel highlights the paradoxical challenge of belonging to a home community in which one is alien as a possible driver for gendered genealogy performance in response to trauma.[12]

2. *Gynealogy Composition: The Lineage of Levi Women Unfolds*

Gynealogy Performance versus Gendered Fragments
First, genealogy composition in *My Life Part 2* pertains to the family lineages of the filmmaker. These lineages encompass the filmmaker's maternal lines, namely the Heins and Levi lineages and her paternal line, namely the Becker lineage. The genealogy is established through narratives on and by

11. See Bob Becking, 'Exilische identiteit als post-exilische ideologie: Psalm 137 opnieuw gelezen', *Nederlands theologisch tijdschrift* 64.4 (2010), pp. 269-83.

12. The book of Ruth is another example of a biblical text that combines the motif of slipping in and out of the homeland and gendered genealogy composition. Here, Naomi is the returnee, who belongs to her home community at Bethlehem but is also alien to it.

family members of different generations and through audio-visual family trees. The audio-visual family trees assume the simple and skeleton-like form of the genealogies in 1 Chronicles 1–9: photographs are switched one for the other, while the voice-over provides names and dates. Photographs and extremely limited information condense the narratives. The resulting audio-visual ancestor trees reach beyond the form of family saga.

In addition to the family lineages, the film revolves around a central symbolic lineage, the lineage of Levi women. The central lineage integrates the stories of the main female characters into a thread that runs throughout the film. It is based on kinship but goes beyond it, as it is likewise constituted by shared identities, political commitments and the dedication to recall and to construct a past. Being a critical element of the film, the lineage of Levi women is a central structuring device that serves as a prism for the film's most vital themes. Its protagonists are Angelika Levi's great-grandmothers Sophie Cecilia Heins and Recha Levi, her grandmother Karla Levi Heins, her mother Ursula Levi Heins de Becker and Angelika Levi herself. Even though the women come from the Heins, the Levi, and the Becker families, the central lineage is constructed as a Levi lineage. The name Levi stresses that belonging to a Jewish German family has an ongoing impact on the women's lives, memories, and self-conceptions. Speaking of a lineage of Levi women, then, accounts for its being constituted as a female-gendered and as a Jewish lineage.

Fig. 3. *Family photographs at Boltenhagen beach from the 1940s to the 1990s ('My Life Part 2', 00:20:28 and 00:23:16)*

While the female-gendered genealogies in 1 Chronicles 1–9 appear as female-gendered fragments within a predominately male-gendered genealogy, the female-gendered genealogy in *My Life Part 2* has women at its very center. Here, gendered genealogies appear as groups of women standing in a biological, symbolic, and ideological succession. The succession is characterized by the subjectivity and agency of its female protagonists. What is foremost a male and androcentric project in 1 Chronicles 1–9 is here reconceptualized as a female endeavor.

To highlight the fundamental difference between the female-gendered genealogies in 1 Chronicles 1–9 and those in *My Life Part 2*, I suggest the term *gynealogy* for the women-centered female-gendered genealogy of the film. The notion of gynealogy stands in opposition to the female-gendered fragments of 1 Chronicles 1–9: while the female lineage is a visible and central aspect of the film's genealogy project, the gendered fragments of 1 Chronicles 1–9 are hidden in the overwhelmingly male-oriented text. Beyond the two cases, the notion of gynealogy indicates the performance of a genealogy that has female subjectivity and agency at the center of succession. In this respect, the notion is also opposed to the concept of genealogy performance, which I understand as inherently male-gendered. Just as male-gendered genealogies are not exclusively male, the gynealogy of *My Life Part 2* is not exclusively female. On the contrary, the murdered members of the family, male and female, and the biblical figure Levi play central roles. Moreover, gender is intimately interwoven with additional subject positions such as Jewish identities. Still, at its core, the film's gynealogy establishes a space in which the often complicated memory, subjectivity and agency of the participating women can take centre stage.

Grandmother–Granddaughter Relationships: Unearthing the Trauma

The central lineage of Levi women is handed down in the relationships between the women of the family. The grandmother–granddaughter and the mother–daughter relationships involve political empathy and bodily practices that I will discuss in the next sections. They are decisive building blocks of the film's gynealogy performance.

My Life Part 2 puts special emphasis on the grandmother–granddaughter relationships between Ursula and her grandmother Recha, and between Angelika and her grandmother Karla. Both relationships are imprinted with the experience of the Nazi terror and develop between silence and solidarity.

The relationship between Ursula and her grandmother Recha is addressed in the first minutes of the film. Ursula documents the events around the suicide of her grandmother Recha on audio tape (00:07:50). When Recha receives the call for deportation to Theresienstadt, she addresses Ursula, as Ursula recounts it:

> Ursula, in the cupboard at home, there's a lovely wine goblet, that used to belong to grandfather, a large one. Could you bring that along tomorrow? I want to put the pills in there and drink from that lovely old goblet when I die.

Ursula does not dare to tell anyone but decides not to take the goblet to her grandmother.

> I just looked at the goblet and thought, 'If you take it, she'll kill herself. If you don't, maybe she'll think about it and go to Theresienstadt after all'.

But Recha, seeing that her granddaughter comes back without the goblet, looks at her sadly and says, 'Oh, child, now I have to drink it out of a toothbrush glass'. The following day, the family learns that Recha has indeed died of an overdose. Ursula's story underlines her speechlessness and helplessness in the face of the threat of Nazi terror. At the same time, it testifies to the attempt to recall and overcome the silence.[13]

Later, in the voice-over to the footage of an early amateur film of hers, Angelika describes how the traumatic incident disseminates through the lineage (00:56:52).

> This footage of the stairwell dates from much later. I wanted to evoke how I had slid down the red banister as a little kid. But the mood expressed is another. My mother tried to commit several times suicide with pills, like her grandmother in 1942.

When Angelika embarks on a journey to Neustadt, planning to donate the family goblet to the local museum, she finds that the museum is located in the former Nazi district office. From there, Joseph Bürkel organized the deportation of the Jews of the region (00:10:44). At the fun fair of the traditional Neustadt wine festival, she bumps into a booth with a tin can alley. Balls are thrown at cylinders of stereotyped Black, Jewish and Roma figures. The employee advertises it as a game from their grandparents' time (00:11:57).

> Try your luck at winning prizes! Play along and win! A game for the whole family, for young and old! Who wants to play with me? Stay for a minute and check it out! A game our grandparents played. Just hit three hats with four balls. Play along, join in the fun! Don't get left out!

Not only the trauma of the Nazi terror, but also everyday German anti-Semitism is transmitted down the lines. The film links the silver goblet to two very different moments in German history. It is central to the relationship between a Jewish girl and her grandmother threatened by the Nazis. At the same time, it points to widespread ignorance of the past in contemporary West Germany. Juxtaposing the situations counters silence and repression. But this time, Angelika's political analysis provides a strong incentive for unearthing the past.

---

13. The wish of Ursula's grandmother to drink from the special goblet when she dies may evoke the death of Socrates as recounted in Plato's 'Phaedo', as well as the prayer of Jesus on the eve of his death: 'Let this cup pass from me' (Mk 14.36). However, the reference is not made explicit in the film.

Fig. 4. *Tin can alley booth at the Neustadt fun fair ('My Life Part 2', 00:11:57)*

Political analysis and solidarity play an even more explicit role in the grandmother–granddaughter relationship between Angelika and her grandmother Karla. Again, the relationship is dominated by anti-Semitism, past and present. The key scene deals with the voices Karla started to hear in her old age (00:24:06).

> In 1991, my grandmother began hearing voices. They threatened her, talking and singing their way into her thoughts. She called the voices 'Telekom'. She called me often, believing that, as long as we were on the phone, the voices couldn't come through the line. But they were also in the wall by her bed, taunting her. They were Nazis, insulting her and saying things like, 'Off with her arms and her legs! Off into the pond!'… In 1994, she dropped the name, Levi, in favor of her maiden name, Heins. That subdued the voices somewhat.

The voice-over is accompanied by sequences that show Angelika on the telephone, talking to her grandmother, and an elderly Karla in a wheelchair, with Angelika caressing her forehead. The voice-over contextualizes the voices with the political situation in Germany after reunification, where a resurgence of nationalism occured in tandem with anti-Israel sentiments during the Gulf War and the first reports of neo-fascist violence. The resurfacing trauma is again related to a continuity of anti-Semitism in post-war Germany. While Ursula tries to reenact the suicide of her grandmother and later starts to break the silence, Angelika tries to express solidarity and to actually support her grandmother. For this strategy, her political analysis and her second-generation position are critical. They allow her to contextualize the resurfacing trauma and assume a more distant position.

The Daughter–Mother Mirrors

The relationships between mother and daughter are likewise affected by the traumatic experience of the Nazi terror and by the tension between silence and recall. Additionally, mothers and daughters initiate the gynealogy in a concrete bodily form with the practice of mirroring. *My Life Part 2* provides two parallel scenes in which mother and daughter assume similar poses, gestures and facial expressions. The first pertains to Karla and Ursula. The scene takes place in Chile, just before their joint return to Germany (00:36:17). The mirror consists of a series of photographs, in which Ursula and Karla assume the same positions, standing at a window sill, beside a tree, on a bridge and in a square, feeding doves. The order of photographs changes: twice, the photograph of the mother is shown first, and twice, the one of the daughter is shown first. The mirror is followed by shots of the first pages of Ursula's scientific work, all dedicated to her mother, and by an account of their return to Germany. The characteristic poetic guitar theme, which reoccurs throughout the film, is added to the sequence. Photographs, dedications and the joint return convey an extremely close relationship between mother and daughter. As Ursula puts it in an interview sequence: 'We had almost become one person' (00:28:14). Yet, the bodily practice of the mirror also facilitates distance. The closeness of the duo is not represented in biological terms but in the form of staging intimacy. The staging has an artificial component, which implies distance. The mother–daughter mirror indicates the moment at which mother and daughter risk becoming one. At the same moment it facilitates distance and keeps generations apart.

Fig. 5. *The first mirror: Ursula and Karla standing at the window sill ('My Life Part 2', 00:36:17)*

In the second mother–daughter mirror the focus shifts from play to entanglement. It pertains to footage from a Dutch summer cottage in 1993. In the kitchen, Ursula and Angelika filmed each other with a Bolex (00:02:58). The duo again assumes similar poses. Both women are bent over. Both sport a dark, curly and somehow wild haircut. Both women's hands are busy, one cutting bread, the other switching on the cooker. While the first mirror plays with the question of who takes the posture of whom, the second mirror has a more determined hierarchy. Ursula sets the posture and haircut: she is bent over the cooker in the fashion of an elderly lady, a posture that exposes her wild hair. Angelika is bent over in a similar way. She has her hands in her hair and tousles it in what may be an attempt to bring it into a shape that resembles her mother's. The second mirror seems to quote the first one. However, while the first mirror expresses a relationship that conveys closeness on equal terms, the second mirror expresses Angelika's desperate attempt to belong to her mother and communicates enmeshment or even compulsion in the process of mirroring.

Angelika's attempt to resemble her mother resumes in a subsequent home movie from the 1970s. The footage shows her as a girl, sitting at a table and drawing black curls onto a photograph that shows her with straight brown hair. The voice-over explains that she always wanted to resemble her mother and to share attributes that were Jewish in her mother's eyes, 'hair, names, noses, words, humor, facial expressions and gestures' (00:06:41).

The mirror as a bodily practice between mother and daughter is ambivalent. On the one hand, it matches extreme closeness with a sense of play and initiates gynealogy in a way that accommodates intimacy but also facilitates distance between the generations. On the other hand, it conveys entanglement and compulsion in a relationship in which trauma is transferred from mother to daughter. In the first case, the duo went through the trauma together. In the second case, the duo must deal with the crossover from experience to legacy.

Compared to the grandmother–granddaughter relationships, the mirrors convey the presence of trauma in a less outspoken and more bodily way. Only the two-generation distance of the grandmother–granddaughter relationship seems to provide the necessary space for unearthing trauma and confronting it with political analysis.[14] Yet, the film deals with unearthing the past in the context of a relationship between mother and daughter. Here, the gynealogical structure of the film supports opening the mirrors toward recall and reflection.

The different relationships between the female protagonists of the lineage of Levi women form the context within which processes of unearthing

---

14. This ties in with the work of Paul Connerton, who identifies the relationship between grandparents and grandchildren as the central location for the transmission of memory. Paul Connerton, *How Societies Remember* (Cambridge: Cambridge University Press, 1989), p. 38.

the past emerge. Important stimuli for these processes are provided by polit-ical perspectives, love, and affection. Moreover, adding relationships that extend over more than one generation to the central mother–daughter rela-tionship between Ursula and Angelika provides an important inducement toward taking distance, telling stories, and forging cultural memory.

My Life Part 2 provides a third mirror scene, in which Angelika and her father walk on the beach (00:42:26). Father and daughter sport simi-lar outfits and walk in synchrony. However, the voice-over does not frame the sequence in a way that would pair it with the other two mirrors. On the level of gestures, Angelika seems to seek distance. While her father closes his hands behind his back, she has her hands in the pockets of her trousers. Still, in its ambiguous way, the footage is a trace of a subtext to the domi-nant mother–daughter narrative.

The Jewish Identity of the Lineage of Levi Women

The lineage of Levi women becomes manifest in the relationships between its members. The contents of transmission are strongly linked to the trauma of the Nazi terror, to the political perspective on it and to ways of respond-ing to it. All these aspects are related to the Jewish identities of the women. These are not easy to define. The women belong to a Jewish family. At the same time, they also have non-confessional and Protestant lines of descent. These lines are responsible for Karla and Ursula surviving the Nazis; they forge experiences that differ from those of the Jewish part of the family. The film addresses the complicated Jewish identity of the women by interplay-ing their given and their imagined ancestors, namely the murdered relatives and the biblical figure Levi.

Commemorating the Murdered Relatives. The dead of the family are present in photographs and narratives. A central sequence in this respect is the *vir-tual memorial album* that commemorates the murdered relatives of the Levi family (00:18:40). The virtual memorial album consists of photographs, portraits and snapshots, which are explained by the voice-over. The series starts with a portrait of Angelika's great-grandmother Recha:

> Recha Levi, née Bodenheimer. Committed suicide.

The following portrait shows Angelika's great-grandfather Eugen:

> Her husband Eugen Levi. Thrown down a flight of stairs by the Nazis.

At the center of the virtual memorial album is a postcard sent to Franz Levi. It shows the *Reichstag* with the caption 'Deutschland, Deutschland über alles!' The voice-over comments:

> I often wonder what happened to the anger, the fear, the despair of those who were murdered?

The next photograph shows Angelika's uncle Franz in a rowing boat.

> Their sons… Franz Levi, murdered in Dachau.

The following snapshot shows her uncle Rudolf, standing on a beach promenade, smiling at the woman beside him.

> Rudolf Levi, deported to Lodz. May 10, 1942, deported to Chelmno.

The virtual memorial album makes a political statement by listing the names together with the circumstances of violent death and murder. Not the dead per se, but the murder victims are commemorated. The memorial album, a small genealogy on its own, makes the murder victims visible and honors them. It reinstalls their place in the lineage and bestows upon them the role of ancestors.[15]

The virtual memorial album is framed by two sequences about the sons of the family, Robert Levi and Rudolf Levi. The preceding sequence recounts the journey of Ursula's father Robert to Chile in 1938. The subsequent sequence recounts the deportation of her uncle Rudi (00:19:29). In an audio record from the 1970s, Ursula recalls a scene at Hamburg Central Station, the assembly point for deportation: a girl of her age clung to her and repeatedly asked why she, as the daughter of a non-Jewish mother, did not have to go. The focus of the account is entirely on Ursula herself. Rudolf's situation and emotions remain out of perspective. The dead of the family are recalled in view of the survivors and inheritors of the traumatic past, who are coming to terms with past and present.

The Imagined Lineage from Biblical Levi to Ursula Levi. For the women of the Levi lineage, coming to terms with past and present is connected with coming to terms with both a Jewish and a non-Jewish past in Nazi Germany and post-war Germany. The difficult situation between the lineages forms the backdrop for taking biblical Levi into the gynealogy. On the basis of the name Levi, Ursula draws a lineage from the biblical figure to herself and establishes Levi as her ancestor. The opening of the film introduces the link by reading from a paper with ten principles Ursula passed on to her daughter (00:00:00).

---

15. From the perspective of the Chronicles genealogies, the last photograph in the memorial album stands out. Uncle Rudolf and an unidentified woman look at each other smiling. They may be friends, kin, or even husband and wife. The woman remains without name and story, as many of her biblical counterparts are in 1 Chronicles 1–9. But whereas the latter are introduced as sisters, wives, or daughters, thus in relation to someone, the film as a visual medium allows for presenting the woman without indicating her relational status.

Item one reads: 'The meaning of life lies in evolving toward perfection. Nothing that is created and is good should be discarded. Build on what's already been achieved. You are descended from Joseph's brother Levi, who lived 3000 years ago'.

The following interview sequence takes up the issue (00:00:56).

> Ursula: 'The two of one, Ruben and Levi, twins; sons of Jacob; there the story begins'.
> Interviewer: 'So the Name has a power for you?'
> Ursula: 'Yes, a real power. I feel it in my genes'.
> The interviewer continues to talk but Angelika and Ursula start to laugh.
> Ursula: 'Yes it is in my genes. It is there'.
> Angelika: 'I thought you feel it in your jeans'.
> Ursula: 'In my genes—how do you say that?'
> Interviewer: 'Yes it is genes'.
> Ursula laughs again: 'This is too funny I don't even own any jeans'.
> Interviewer: 'That's correct English'.

Ursula addresses the descent from biblical Levi again at the end of the film (01:21:27).

> The Levis weren't a tribe you know. The other brothers all got their own tribe. Each brother founded a tribe, most of which were later lost. Levi is the only one without a tribe. He became a priest.

In the scenes, Ursula describes Levi in close relation to his brothers and father. Their family cohesion marks the beginning of 'the story'. On the other hand, Ursula identifies Levi as being clearly set apart from his brothers. They founded tribes, but Levi did not. Most of the tribes got lost in time, but Levi became a priest and this tradition lives on until today.

The biblical account confirms Ursula's sense of Levi's belonging to the house of Israel while at the same time being set apart. Levi is one of the twelve sons of Jacob and eponymous ancestor of a substantial part of Israel. In opposition to Ursula's account, however, the Levites did form a tribe. Yet, they did enjoy special status. They did not receive their own territories but inhabited cities in the territories of the other tribes. Moreover, they were appointed for service at the sanctuary and as priests. Their demarcation from the other tribes was substantially based on their privileges and duties as Levites.[16]

---

16. John R. Spencer, 'Levitical Cities', *ABD* IV, pp. 310-11 (310); and Merlin D. Rehm, 'Levites and Priests', *ABD* IV, pp. 297-310 (300-305). For the distinction between the Levites and the other tribes, see also Claudia V. Camp, 'The Problem with Sisters: Anthropological Perspectives on Priestly Kinship Ideology in Numbers', in *Embroidered Garments: Priests and Gender in Biblical Israel* (ed. Deborah W. Rooke; Sheffield: Sheffield Phoenix Press, 2009), pp. 119-30 (121).

Establishing a lineage begining with the biblical Levi on the basis of her last name allows Ursula to link herself to the heart of the Hebrew Bible and Jewish tradition. The lineage confirms Ursula's Jewish identity. However, things are more complex. The imagined lineage links Ursula to a very particular element in the Jewish tradition. In the Hebrew Bible, priests and Levites belong to Israel, but likewise hold a special status that sets them apart. Linking herself to the bearers of this tension allows Ursula to confirm her Jewish identity while leaving space for the experience of difference and separation. Constructing the lineage on the basis of the name Levi serves an additional function. It supersedes the traditional affiliation criterion in Judaism (a Jewish person is the child of a Jewish mother) and therefore provides an alternative mode of affiliation. Being Jewish per orthodox rule is replaced by being Jewish per imagined lineage on the basis of a name. Still, both modes of affiliation remain abstractions. In concrete terms, Ursula's Jewish identity has mostly to do with actual family bonds, shared histories and the experience of persecution—a situation that was true for the majority of Jews at the time.

Angelika confirms the importance of the link to the biblical Levi in a sequence on the name change of various family members. After German reunification, she assumed the maiden name of her mother, Levi, as an artist name (*Künstler- und Ordensname*) in order to express a difference. She adds, 'Somehow this was also in accord with the tribal ideology of my mother, the descent of the tribe of Levi' (00:26:13). The scene confirms the importance of the Jewish name, Levi, for Angelika. It demonstrates her Jewish heritage and allows her to articulate the complexity of her identity. In a twisted way, this again includes the situation of belonging (to German society), while at the same time being set apart (as a member of a partly Jewish family). Last but not least, including the tribe of Levi in the lineage of Levi women introduces a paradox. It incorporates the extremely male-gendered priestly Levite tradition into the ancestry of a gynealogy performance.

Given and imagined ancestors are both important in the gynealogy composition of *My Life Part 2*. They intersect in the struggle of the main protagonists to develop Jewish German identities that can accomodate their multilayered subject positions and the complexity of the family story. The interplay between given and imagined ancestry also highlights that gynealogy composition in *My Life Part 2* does not merely follow traditional lines of kinship. Instead, political commitment, imagination and ideology play major roles.

Standpoint-Based Gynealogy Composition
Along with the specific relationships and references to the ancestors, the lineage of Levi women is decisively shaped by the subjectivity and agency

of its female protagonists. The different protagonists of the lineage confront their past and present lives in particular ways. Features such as political sensibility and humor are characteristic of all women of the Levi lineage, even though these characteristics are realized in individual ways. In order to understand the character of the gynealogy and its function in the film, it is important to fully acknowledge its ideological foundation. The women are related through kinship ties. However, shared subjectivities are critical to establish, confirm and engage the succession in view of identity and memory formation.

The women's characteristic take on past and present first of all concerns what Madeleine Bernstorff calls their 'political sensibilities'.[17] The term 'sensibilities' is appropriate, since it points less to direct political engagement than it does to refusing to allow a certain normality to take over. This becomes explicit in Karla's refusal to divorce her Jewish husband during Nazism, as well as in the many instances in which Ursula and Angelika expose continuities between Nazism and post-war Germany. A case in point is Ursula's reflection on two colleagues from the local paper's senior citizens page, where she publishes her stories (01:20:33).

> Among those who write for the paper, there are two Nazi women. I wanted to quit at first. There are two who keep saying, 'Things used to be much better'. 'There was no crime'. Right, there was no crime—[Pauses, then laughs]—Ha, that's a laugh!

Rejecting a normality that tolerates latent anti-Semitism and downplays continuities between German fascism and post-war Germany goes hand in hand with the commitment to recall. At the basis of the film is a family story that contradicts the basically non-Jewish story constructed as the norm in post-war Germany. Recalling this family story is an act of counter-present memory and a political statement. Working against neglecting and silencing the past is not self-evident, not even within the Levi–Becker family. The film repeatedly emphasizes that Angelika and her father do not have intimate knowledge of the past. For example, Angelika does not know if the family of her grandfather tried to emigrate and did not manage to do so in time (00:17:19). Recalling is also a struggle against a dynamic of silence, pain and maybe shame.

Shared subjectivity and agency are closely linked to the women's sense of humor. Ursula and Karla, the two Levi women who survived the Nazi terror, meet the challenge to recall and recount with their characteristic humor. Ursula's humor and infectious laughter are introduced in the opening interview. Ursula explains that she feels the power of the name Levi in her genes—misunderstood by Angelika as 'in her jeans'. Ursula turns

---

17. Madeleine Bernstorff, 'MEIN LEBEN TEIL 2 von Angelika Levi, D 2003', http://www.madeleinebernstorff.de/seiten/leben_tx.html (accessed June 8, 2013).

the confusion into a joke, 'that's too funny, I don't even own any jeans' and bursts into laughter (00:00:56). The same humor is evident in Ursula's account of her colleagues at the newspaper. In both cases, Ursula's laughter pertains to existential issues. The power of the name Levi is bound to Ursula's struggle for her Jewish identity. The incident at the local newspaper concerns the fragile visibility of her subjectivity within West German society. Humor and laughter are coping strategies and tools for the balancing act required by recounting and reflection. Part of this is a moment of self-irony, which becomes especially visible in the genes/jeans scene.

Fig. 6. *Ursula laughs about the jeans/genes joke ('My Life Part 2', 00:00:39)*

Karla's humor comes through in her account of a flight to Austria in an audio recording from the 1980s. Karla recounts how she and her children had to flee after a confrontation with an SS officer. Finding her destination crowded with Nazis, she takes her children to the best hotel on site and claims a room. The receptionist refuses because of her name, but when she explains that Levis with an 'i' are all 'Aryan', they indeed get a room (00:20:28). The story is a typical trickster story in which she faces a life-threatening situation with all her wit and cunning. Karla plays on the absurdity of racial politics and acquires a place, as safe as possible, right in the lion's den. Karla's ironic account ridicules the Nazis and highlights her own agency. Her humor is crucial in the actual situation, as well as with regard to the difficult task of recall. This becomes evident in Karla's late name change from Levi back to Heins. She was able to establish an ironic distance from the haunting memories in the 1980s. But in her old age, and under the pressure of the political developments in the 1990s, the spell of her courageous joke delivered on the hotel staff in Austria breaks and she has to look for other ways of dealing with the past.

For Angelika, humor takes a slightly different shape. It comes in home movies of the girl/teenager Angelika, who plays the guitar, dances and fools around and plays the clown together with her brother. Adding this footage to the film testifies to a self-deprecating humour that resembles the self-irony with which Ursula comments on her missing jeans. Still, her clownish ways are quite different from the humor of her mother and grandmother. For them, humor seems to facilitate recall. For second-generation Angelika, humor seems to be a means of dispelling the haunting specter of the traumatic past. In one home movie, Angelika's father joins in the clownish dance. He, too, has a sense of humor. Without explicitly commenting upon it, the visual footage aligns him with the Levi women and sets another note in the male-gendered subtext underlying Angelika Levi's gynealogy.

The women of the lineage actively deal with trauma. At the same time, they are deeply affected by what they experienced or inherited. The film presents its protagonists as complex personalities: humorous and headstrong on the one hand, injured and uncompromising on the other. *My Life Part 2* exposes the multilayered and sometimes complicated personalities of its female protagonists. It does not ignore the fact that trauma may turn a person into someone who is everything but nice and easy to get along with. The women are the heroines of the film. At the same time, they are anti-heroines, making it difficult for the audience to extend immediate empathy and solidarity. But it is exactly this aspect—revealing both sides of the women—that works toward taking them seriously and guaranteeing their integrity.

Complex Layers of Reality beyond a Strict Reality-Representation Divide. Classical documentary filmmaking and theory clearly distinguishes between reality and representation. Reality is expressed by a record that touches on the recorded events as closely and factually as possible. In contrast, representation is expressed by the narrative and is a place for interpretation, subjectivity and invention.[18] However, this strict distinction has increasingly been questioned. Film theorist Bill Nichols has argued that performative documentaries, such as *My Life Part 2*, give up the reality/representation divide in favor of communicating a sense of the complexity of the world. This is linked to combining the actual with the imagined, highlighting 'the subjective qualities of experience and memory that depart from factual recounting'.[19] Film theorist Stella Bruzzi goes a step further by questioning

18. Stella Bruzzi, *New Documentary: A Critical Introduction* (London: Routledge, 2000), p. 13.
19. Bill Nichols, *Introduction to Documentary* (Bloomington, IN: Indiana University Press, 2001), p. 131.

the differentiation between reality and representation. Bruzzi critiques the hierarchy inherent in such differentiation and claims that the document at the heart of the documentary film is always open to 'reassessment, re-appropriation and even manipulation without these processes necessarily obscuring or rendering irretrievable the document's original meaning or content'.[20]

My Life Part 2 likewise rejects a strict boundary between reality and representation. It is less interested in facts than in subjective realities and memory production. This stance in the discourse on reality and representation is a major strategy in securing the integrity of the anti-heroines of Angelika Levi's gynealogy. The film carefully establishes space for different layers of reality within the family, especially as perceived by the mother and grandmother. An example is how the film addresses the hostility of the family, as perceived by Ursula during her time of illness and depression. The voice-over reads aloud from Ursula's diary, in which she accuses her family of making her do endless housework because they are too cowardly to 'immediately kill the Jewish pig'. Angelika Levi's lending her voice protects Ursula in this difficult statement and works against exposing her perception as fictitious. In addition, the scene is followed by a retrospective interview, in which Ursula describes her attitude then as one of psychological 'association'. The diary notes are placed in the context of traumatic reenactment. It is made clear that they are not about 'objective' facts. However, by letting Ursula reflect on the events, her personhood and truth is taken seriously. The film never denounces the subjective reality of Ursula as wrong or unreal. Instead, it highlights the powerful impact of experiences. Traumatic experiences are particularly suited to creating realities whose vitality depends on factors other than their factuality.

The Male Protestant Becker Line

The lineage of Levi women is strongly female-gendered. It is carried by the stories and struggles of the women of the family; female relationships and female succession are central to the lineage. Men do play vital roles when it comes to determining the Jewish identity of the lineage. Both the murdered male family members and the biblical Levi are installed as important ancestors. Other males, especially Angelika's father and brother, have quite a different status. Both remain without name—their names are given in the credits only—and the family of the father is never mentioned. Instead of his own lineage, the father brings the Protestant tradition into the family.

20. Bruzzi, *New Documentary*, p. 16. For the negotiation of reality and representation in the depiction and interpretation of biblical figures such as the figure of King David, see Bob Becking, 'David between Evidence and Ideology', in *History of Israel between Evidence and Ideology* (ed. Bob Becking and Lester L. Grabbe; *OTS*, 59; Leiden: Brill, 2011), pp. 1-30.

Footage shows him as a minister during a church service, and interview sequences sketch him as rooted in Protestant tradition. In addition, the church seems to supplement his family and lineage. At the wedding at the Protestant seminary at Bad Kreuznach, his male colleagues seem to function as his family (00:41:15). The sense of family also emerges in his critical reflection on the minister who baptized Ursula in 1940 (00:39:19). Here, he conducts a dispute typical of the Christian German post-war generation and its parents.

The lack of name and proper lineage together with his identification with the Protestant church *others* Angelika's father and his tradition. The process of othering has a strong gendered aspect: the central lineage is female-gendered, while the Protestant context of the father is exclusively male. In addition, the process of othering involves the contrast between the Jewish and the Protestant side of the family. Protestant tradition, as embodied by the father, is not restricted to the family, but it is linked to the dominant West German culture. In an interview, the father articulates the wish to let a 'healing thing' grow over the past: 'Why should we bring up things that are so deeply disturbing? It's better to let bygones be bygones so that healing can take place' (00:59:03). In a voice-over, Angelika assesses this position as a 'sentimental desire for reconciliation, but blindness toward the actual effects of divergent histories' (01:08:07). The position of the father is aligned with the German mainstream interest in repressing the past. Othering the father and the Protestant line keeps this position outside the dominant storyline of the family.

Along with processes of othering, other traces point to a subtext that interferes with the division between the dominant lineage of Levi women and the male Protestant line of the other. The subtext becomes visible through the visual materials. Many photographs and home movies are far more gender-inclusive than the voice-over narrative would have it. In addition, the subtext appears in allusions to relationships that cross the male/female and the Jewish/Protestant divide, for example in the third mirror between Angelika and her father. Finally, it surfaces between the lines of the narrative. One example is a short sequence about Angelika's grandfather. The voice-over narration relates that he visited his family in Germany every other year. In his view, it was anything but surprising that Ursula became ill in Germany. Why would she go back? Later in the film, Angelika herself asks the same question in an elaborate reflection on her attitude toward her mother. A perspective unfolds that illustrates a trace of an affinity between Angelika and her grandfather, which exists alongside the much foregrounded succession of headstrong, humorous and original women. The trace testifies to the complexity of the genealogy established by Levi and hints at its possible subversive layers.

Malin Wahlberg defines the trace as the 'presence of absence and as an incentive for both imagination and historical representation'.[21] The trace is part of the poetic enactment of a documentary film, but also part of its selection of source material, and of the narrative strategies of representing and invoking the past. As a historian, the filmmaker uses material vestiges of the past to recreate and narrate the historical event. Recorded images and sounds are framed as mnemonic signs.[22] As part of the creative work of the documentary filmmaker, the trace is less an imprint of what happened in the past than 'a constituting sign in the narrative reinvention of history'.[23] Understood as such, the traces of the male-gendered subtext are signs in the narrative—and gynealogical—reinvention of the family story. They enforce the process of othering but at the same time hint at a subversive subtext in the gynealogy performance. The trace of a subtext suggests understanding othering and subversion as two sides of the same coin. The male-gendered subtext in *My Life Part 2* mirrors the female-gendered subtext in the Chronicles' genealogies. In both cases, gender is significantly involved in processes of othering and hence in establishing the 'us'. In addition, in both gendered genealogies, further categories are linked to the gender category. They are concerned with ethnicity, religion, culture and/or social position. Gender seems to function as a category that takes the lead in differentiating, othering and subverting more complex circumstances.

3. Discontinuity with and Inscription to the Lineage of Levi Women

Discontinuity with the Mother Role

The lineage of Levi women conveys a strong sense of continuity: continuity between biblical traditions and present conceptions of being Jewish; continuity between the murdered and those who live in their memory; continuity between the years of persecution and the time of the trauma coming back to haunt; continuity between the women's struggle to survive and their struggle to recall. Yet *My Life Part 2* also contains moments of discontinuity. On a most practical level, the Levi and Heins lineages are about to come to an end. Ursula is the last member of her generation. Her children, Angelika and Thomas, chose not to have children of their own. The actual situation of the Levi lineage seems to be an expression of a more profound sense of discontinuity that gleams through the prevailing sense of continuity.

The impulse toward or even desire for discontinuity is articulated by both Ursula and Angelika. Ursula articulates her longing to let the line go in an interview (01:08:46):

21. Wahlberg, *Documentary Time*, p. 103.
22. Wahlberg, *Documentary Time*, p. 101.
23. Wahlberg, *Documentary Time*, p. 103.

Ursula: 'I am the last, the last from the family'. [Laughs] 'Except for them'.
[Pauses] 'The last of the family who went through all that'.

In her statement, Ursula refers to the shift from first to second generation. Her children, she hopes, will not go through the same traumata. On
a second level, the sequence communicates an end that widens the gap
between the generations. The difference in experience is perceived as a
divide between her and 'them'. It leads to a moment in which the sense of
belonging together as a family is secondary. It is replaced by an impulse not
to trace the family line further, but rather to let go of the line, bringing the
attempt to forge a family to an end. Ursula does not give up family and lineage, but for a moment articulates the desire to let it go.

Angelika takes up the sequence in a statement about the film. She quotes
her mother, but not fully: '"I'm the last member of my family", my mother
said. "And now they come along". She was referring to my brother and I.'[24]
Skipping her mother's explanation adds a moment of distance and exclusion to the scene. It confirms the impulse to let go of the line, along with a
sense of discontinuity. The film combines the interview with home movie
footage of Angelika and her brother, which slowly fades into close-up views
of trees and sky. 'They' are shortly touched upon but then die away. The
characteristic reoccurring guitar theme is added to the footage. The theme
indicates central moments of the film: Angelika's confrontation with the
traumatic family story in the opening scene (00:01:42); the performance of
gynealogy in the first mirror between Ursula and Karla and the subsequent
return to Germany as the site of trauma (00:36:17); Ursula's impulse to let
go of the line in the sequence under discussion (01:08:46); and the eventual
blurring of images and memories on a video screen in a hotel room in Santiago in the closing scene (01:27:28). Combining the guitar theme and the
impulse to let go of the line highlights the latter and integrates it into the key
thematic triangle of trauma, gynealogy performance and memory.

Ursula's statement on being the last one of the family is part of a larger
sequence about the challenge of coming to terms with the Shoah and Jewish
identities (Sequence Eight). It comprises the interview with Berlin Rabbi
Rothschild and further reflections by Ursula and Angelika. The sequence
begins with the Rothschild interview (01:07:25):

> The answer of many survivors was to marry and have children. I am the
> answer of my parents to the Shoah. I was born in 1954 and carry the name
> of my grandfather who was in Dachau. It is possible to mourn and com-
> plain the whole life long, have problems and struggle for one's identity. Or
> I can say, it was really shit what happened but I will build something new
> for the future. Founding a family, having children—not everybody wants
> it, not everybody can do it, but it is a matter of a positive view.

24. For this statement as well as a longer interview with the filmmaker see http://home.
snafu.de/fsk-kino/archiv/Mein%20Leben%20Teil%202.htm (accessed June 8, 2013).

The scene shifts to a home movie of the Levi–Becker family. Angelika, aged thirteen or fourteen, is playing the guitar with a fast and rhythmic beat. Her brother and father dance around wildly, playing clowns. The voice-over responds to Rothschild (01:08:07):

> Am I my mother's answer to the Shoah? Was voluntary adaptation, starting a family with my father, her answer? Am I also my father's answer? With his sentimental desire for reconciliation, but blindness toward the actual effects of divergent histories? I decided my answer would not be biological. My brother's wasn't either. We were girl and boy, according to plan, and today we're both gay and don't want any children.

The next sequence is the one in which Ursula states that she is the last of the family. The scene then shifts to a discussion of the meaning of being Jewish.

Horizontal Memory Production versus Vertical Genealogical Reproduction
In the voice-over quoted above, the filmmaker states that she and her brother are both gay and do not want any children. Her answer to the Shoah will not be a biological one (01:08:07). This rejection of the biological reproductive continuation of the lineage of Levi women marks a moment in which the film's gynealogy opens into a horizontal same-generation dimension. The horizontal dimension results from a movement away from a 'biological answer'; it foregrounds the relationship between Angelika Levi and her brother; and it is conceptualized as a homoerotic context. The latter is spelled out in subsequent scenes that take up key motifs from the family lineage and contextualize them in female relationships. For example, the yellow sifter with the Star of David pattern returns as a bread basket at a table of women friends on one of Angelika's Chilean journeys.

Fig. 7. *The yellow sifter reappears as a bread basket ('My Life Part 2', 01:19:09)*

The horizontal dimension accompanies or even replaces the vertical linear dimension of the gynealogy that prevailed so far. The rejection of a reproductive kinship-based continuation of the lineage is presented as a second generation decision. Ursula states that, with her, the line of those who experienced Nazi persecution ends. Angelika takes the point further and marks the shift from first to second generation with the decision to work out a different non-biological answer to what is not her experience but her legacy.

The horizontal dimension allows a distancing from the vertical succession as embodied in the intergenerational relationships between grandmother and granddaughter and between mother and daughter. It involves a chosen rather than received community. The horizontal dimension focuses less on what is handed down by whom and in what way, or on how the past puts a stamp on the present. Instead, it explores the present in view of discovering which communities, social frames and discourses are helpful in creating a present that can accomodate past traditions and traumata, but goes beyond them. In other words, passing on what one receives is subordinated in favor of interpreting, interfering and bringing about change. This is conceived as an intra-generational dynamic. It takes place in one generation, which is in communication with previous and later generations. In *My Life Part 2*, the horizontal dimension is also conceptualized as a homoerotic, particularly a lesbian context. In my view, the lesbian context here stands for the production of relationships, culture and memory beyond reproduction. Alison Landsberg has suggested analyzing homoerotic intergenerational relationships as a productive context for memory performances. In situations in which memories would be too painful and too shameful to pass on between parents and children, homoerotic intergenerational relationships may occur as productive sites for recall, narrative and memory acts.[25] Landsberg emphasizes that the homoerotic dimension of such a context is critical inasmuch as it releases the generation of memory from the 'heterosexual matrix'. The generation of memory is then located in the logic of production and not in the heterosexual logic of reproduction.[26]

In *My Life Part 2*, the horizontal homoerotic dimension does not become manifest in a single relationship. Instead, footage of the moving hands or the streaming hair of women friends and/or lovers hint at its presence and mark the inner development of Angelika while pursuing her gynealogy. The footage pertains to the second part of the film, after Angelika's first journey to Chile initiates a process that challenges and eventually breaks down the fixed victim-perpetrator scheme that had prevailed in the perception of

25. Alison Landsberg, *Prosthetic Memory: The Transformation of American Remembrance in the Age of Mass Culture* (New York: Columbia University Press, 2004), p. 85.
26. Landsberg, *Prosthetic Memory*, p. 85.

Angelika's mother so far. After this turning point, the film takes up themes introduced at the beginning of the film. For example, the yellow sifter with the Star of David pattern reappears as a bread basket in a café in Santiago de Chile. The yellow sifter, shot as a static object on a window sill in the first minutes of the film, initially symbolized Angelika Levi's strong bond to the family story and the pressing experience of disenfranchisement and murder. Now, the yellow sifter reoccurs as a basket filled with bread, touched and explored by the moving hands of women friends. Here the horizontal lesbian dimension of the gynealogy composition comes in as a force to transform and animate the symbols of the past.

In a similar way, the motif of the beach is taken up. In the first part of the film, the Boltenhagen beach family photographs convey the pain of absence and stand for the attempt to establish continuity between the generations. Among the Chile footage is a sequence at the beach with women friends that is all wind, water, streaming hair, movement and light. The footage recalls the static Boltenhagen materials, but adds a dimension of swiftness, flexibility and movement. Both the footage of the moving hands and the footage of the streaming hair do not afford clear views of their owners. The lesbian horizontal dimension of the gynealogy is spelled out as a location inhabited by potential and plural relationships rather than a site of clear-cut bonds and family. It serves above all as a hint at a site of memory that interrupts the established gynealogy and at the same time enables the gynealogy to be productive in the face of its traumatic contents.

The lesbian context allows for the conceptualization of relations between women in the genealogical context beyond the mother-daughter or grandmother-granddaughter pattern and beyond relations that depend on the heterosexual matrix, for example sisters or sisters-in-law. In this respect, the lesbian context is consequently a follow-up to the gynealogy project, which constitutes a lineage of women. Still, *My Life Part 2* does not suggest that the horizontal dimension of gendered genealogies necessarily has to be a lesbian one. What the film does is challenge the viewer to imagine and create the present in a way that allows for formulating, engaging and passing on the legacy and the character of a lineage in a more comprehensive way than a merely kinship-based genealogy can.

The Answer of Chaim (Life)

The discussion between Rothschild and Angelika brings up an additional possibility for confronting the Shoah and life beyond it, namely life or *Chaim*. Rothschild addresses Angelika and suggests (01:11:36):

> A 'dose' of Jewishness might be good for you if it helps you to solve your problem. Otherwise, you might seek for other answers. One traditional Jewish answer has been *Chaim*: Life.

The statement is followed by sequences of a live recording of the lesbian rock band Subsonic in Berlin (Blockschock, live, 1984), which alternates with another live recording of a lesbian performance (maybe another performance of Subsonic). The next sequence shows Angelika in a winter cloak at the beach, arms stretched out and slowly spinning round. A wind turbine casts the shadow of its rotating blades on the spot where Angelika spins round. The shadow and Angelika rotate in opposite directions, so that blades and stretched arms form a dance pattern. Both sequences remain uncommented—a rarity in the film. They seem to illustrate what *Chaim* might mean for Angelika. However, in their uncommented way, they test possibilities rather than seizing them. Both facets of life are familiar to Angelika—diving into the urban lesbian subculture as well as the intense expression of individuality that becomes visible in the shadow dance. Still, *Chaim* is beyond what Angelika Levi is aiming at in her film. *My Life Part 2* is about building a lineage and responding to the legacy of her mother's traumatic memories. Angelika Levi seeks to understand the past of her family and how it affects her life and perception. She seeks to find an answer to her legacy, which makes sense at the intersection of family story and political history, and which allows her to draw her gynealogy into her own generation.

The Answer of Levi's Gynealogy Project
One way in which filmmaker Angelika Levi confronts her legacy is the film *My Life Part 2*. In the following, I propose to analyze Angelika Levi's decision to engage her position as artist and filmmaker in order to address her family story and mediate it to the public cultural discourse as a response to her legacy and as a continuation of the gynealogy she establishes. This gynealogical memory project encompasses the aspects of recalling, appropriating the past and projecting the appropriated past into the future in a mediated memory act. All three aspects are intimately interwoven through the making of the film. They are especially linked to its personal female voice-over, to its archive performance and to its location at the intersection of family story and public discourse.

Recall as Facilitated by the Personal Female Voice-Over
Recall, the first aspect of Angelika Levi's genealogical memory project, takes place on different levels. For example, interviews and audio recordings include direct accounts and testimonies, and archival records tell stories and facilitate memory. However, the main narrative device of the film is the personal voice-over of the filmmaker.

The voice-over in *My Life Part 2* is personal, subjective, reflexive and female. It is in overt contrast to the 'voice-of-God commentary' of classical documentary film.[27] The personal voice-over marks *My Life Part 2* as a performative documentary. Nichols highlights that performative documentaries use the personal voice-over to support their emphasis on the intersection between private and public processes as the location where knowledge is produced and negotiated.[28] Knowledge and memory are presented as subjective, embodied, and gendered. In turn, their contingence is identified as a critical starting point for further political analyses.[29] The category of performative documentary helps to understand the concept of recall in *My Life Part 2*. In the film, knowledge largely refers to knowledge of the past. The personal voice-over is a critical means of stressing the contingent character of this knowledge of the past and hence cultural memory. In *My Life Part 2*, the contingent and subjective character of cultural recall involves the filmmaker's viewpoints. However, it is likewise related to her mother and additional protagonists of the film. Successfully engaging their perspectives is made possible due to the multilayered character of the voice-over. First of all, the voice-over chronicles the family story and relates it to political history. It provides the context for all other versions. In addition, the voice-over presents the mother's materials by means of carefully placed explanations and lends her its voice. Presenting her materials accommodates Ursula's characteristic way of recollecting and presenting her story in the form of an archive. It lets the materials speak and acknowledges the mother's ways of recall beyond direct testimonies. One way of presenting her mother's materials consists of the filmmaker lending her voice to Ursula by reading aloud from journals and letters. This technique is used especially in sensitive cases. For example, the voice-over reads from the diary entries in which Ursula links the attitude of her family to how the Nazis treated her many years ago. Lending her voice lends the authority of the filmmaker to the statement. Later on in the film, Ursula herself will reflect on the statement, but for the time being it is under the authoritative guard of the voice-over.

The voice-over communicates how her mother recalls, but also conveys the viewpoint of the filmmaker herself. It integrates the perspective of the daughter Angelika into the film and provides space for the philosophical and political reflections of the filmmaker. The analytical character of these reflections makes sense in the context of categorizing *My Life Part 2* as an 'informal film essay'.[30] Erik Barnouw describes the informal film essay as a form of compilation documentary that combines historical footage with

---

27. Nichols, *Introduction to Documentary*, p. 101.
28. Nichols, *Introduction to Documentary*, p. 101.
29. Nichols, *Introduction to Documentary*, p. 133.
30. Erik Barnouw, *Documentary: A History of the Non-Fiction Film* (Oxford: Oxford University Press, 2nd edn, 1993), p. 336.

testimonies of the surviving participants of the documented events.[31] This is achieved by combining the use of historical footage and testimonies with first-person narrative and observations.[32] Understanding *My Life Part 2* as a film essay defines the film's strategy of recall as a strategy that advances a contingent take on memory performance while insisting on an understanding of personal recall in the context of political history and public discourses on memory. Hence, recall as the first aspect of Angelika Levi's gynealogical memory project encompasses the subjective contingency and the structural political dimensions of knowledge and memory production. The personal, subjective, reflexive and gendered voice-over serves to open these different dimensions of recall.

Archive Performance as Appropriation of a Traumatic Legacy
Next to the female personal voice-over, the second aspect of Angelika Levi's gynealogical memory act is her appropriation of the family story.[33] Appropriation is fundamentally linked to the film's use of archival footage. The use of archival material in documentary is usually analyzed along two lines, either illustratively or critically. Used illustratively, archival material completes the narrative of the voice-over or interview. The viewer absorbs the material while following the narrative. Used critically, archival material is a distinct part of the argument. Extracts of reality are recontextualized and juxtaposed to effects of polemics, irony, absurdity, or confrontation.[34] Angelika Levi uses archival materials to both ends. For example, Angelika Levi juxtaposes German television footage of Martin Walser justifying a culture of looking away with home movies of the Levi–Becker family dominated by the oppressive presence of the traumatic family past. Contrasting such materials exposes a public discourse dominated by the legacy of perpetrators and bystanders and points to the marginalization of the memory of the victims.[35] The confrontation makes a strong point on its own, which also confirms the voice-over narrative.

31. Barnouw, *Documentary*, p. 319.

32. Barnouw, *Documentary*, p. 336.

33. By appropriation, I refer to a process of bestowing meaning to something and adopting it for one's own purpose. For example, appropriating information means to adapt and integrate information in a way that makes it meaningful for oneself and enables using the achieved knowledge as one's own.

34. Bruzzi, *New Documentary*, pp. 26-27.

35. For a critical reflection on the German post-war discourse about National Socialism and the Shoah with a focus on the notions of continuity, genealogy and generation, see Sigrid Weigel, '"Generation" as a Symbolic Form: On the Genealogical Discourse of Memory since 1945', in *The Germanic Review* 77 (2002), pp. 264-77 (on Walser specifically, see p. 273).

new archive

Angelika Levi uses archival materials in a third most characteristic way. She combines existing archival footage and original footage toward establishing a new archive, the documentary *My Life Part 2* itself. In the new archive, archival materials serve particular functions. For example, the film includes photographs and home movies of the family at Boltenhagen beach from the 1940s until the 1990s. Over the course of the film, they come to symbolize the lineage of Levi women from its roots in the 1940s to its performance in the 1990s. In the process of archiving, the materials acquire this specific meaning through repetition, variation and juxtaposition. The visual motif of the family at Boltenhagen beach also prepares for a later contrast with the Chile beach footage, which indicates the shift from the vertical to the horizontal dimension of gynealogy performance.

The notion of archive in relation to *My Life Part 2* was first introduced by Madeleine Bernstorff.[36] However, Bernstorff stresses the archive Angelika inherits from her mother. She suggests understanding *My Life Part 2* as a process in which Angelika Levi leads the viewer through the archive of her mother.

> She inherited a huge archive from her mother and now guides us through this archive with her film. The vehicles of memory are BASF C60 audiotapes from the seventies, 16 mm film, super8 film, digital video, S-VHS video, photographs, written documents, a cup, a sieve, diaries, pieces of laundry, pressed and dried plants: tokens that point into history at the transition between the material and the immaterial. She comments on this in her conversations with the collected, selected and precisely organized material, keeping the suspense between the unspoken and that which can be said.[37]

In contrast to Bernstorff, I find it crucial to emphasize that *My Life Part 2* does not primarily represent the moment in which Angelika Levi leads the viewer through the archive of her mother. Instead, the film is about setting up her own archive. This new archive contains materials apart from the archive inherited from her mother. It also draws on public archives, for example television footage, as well as on the family archive in a broader sense, for example the home movies shot by Angelika's father and on Angelika's own archive. The new archive also includes footage pertaining to the production of the film itself. This footage is often not entirely in focus, filmed on 8 mm film. It is rendered as archival material and supports the understanding of the film as an archive.

In her new archive, Angelika Levi appropriates the family past in an effort to give her own account of it. The process of appropriating the family story and presenting it anew can best be described as a performance of the

---

36. Bernstorff, 'MEIN LEBEN TEIL 2 von Angelika Levi, D 2003'.

37. Bernstorff, 'MEIN LEBEN TEIL 2 von Angelika Levi, D 2003', translation Marianne Löwisch, Jutta Brettschneider and Barbara Becker.

archive. With this identification, I align with a broader tendency in Archive and Memory Studies to use notions of performance and performativity in order to conceptualize archives.[38] Claire Waterton has highlighted that engaging notions of performance and performativity in archival theory can be seen as a move toward focusing on contingencies and politics prominent in the archive, and as an expression of taking the 'guts of our archives' into the center of analysis.[39] This refers both to what archives reveal and what they hide.[40] The notion of performativity especially communicates ideas of process, activity, open-endedness, and change. It conveys that archiving is about producing rather than merely describing reality.[41] As Waterton emphasizes in reference to Gilles Deleuze and Félix Guattari, understanding archives as performances conveys that archives are not only about describing the world but also about creating the conditions under which new things come into existence.[42] As Ann Laura Stoler puts it, archives are not storerooms of knowledge, but sites of contested knowledge production.[43]

Conceptualizing *My Life Part 2* as an archive performance highlights the fact that Angelika Levi, while collecting, recontextualizing, and arranging her materials, sets up something genuine and new. *My Life Part 2* goes beyond presenting the story of the filmmaker's mother and family. The moment of performance implies a process of appropriating and digesting family narratives and memory objects in order to perform a memory act that responds to the past to which they bear witness. Performing her archive takes her from narrating the traumatic story of her mother to claiming it as her own legacy; to appropriating it; and to linking it to her own story, ideas and political position. In other words, performing her archive presents a powerful memory act that opens up the private family story to the public discourse on the memory of the Shoah.

Mediating Cultural Memory at the Intersection of Family Story and Public Discourse

The third aspect of Angelika Levi's gynealogical memory act, after personal voice-over and appropriation, pertains to the film's function as mediator of cultural memory. Angelika Levi performs her memory act as an artist and filmmaker. This position allows her to bring the appropriated past into dialogue with public cultural discourse. As a publicly screened film, *My*

38. Claire Waterton, 'Experimenting with the Archive: STS-ers As Analysts and Co-Constructors of Databases and Other Archival Forms', in *STHV* 35.5 (2010), pp. 645-76.

39. Waterton, 'Experimenting with the Archive', p. 647.

40. Waterton, 'Experimenting with the Archive', p. 648.

41. Waterton, 'Experimenting with the Archive', p. 650.

42. Waterton, 'Experimenting with the Archive', p. 653.

43. Ann L. Stoler, 'Colonial Archives and the Arts of Governance', *Archival Science* 2 (2002), pp. 87-109 (87).

Life Part 2 mediates the family past with public discourse and discloses Angelika Levi's answer to her legacy to the next generations. Angelika Levi mediates the past of her family and beyond to the present and the future. Mieke Bal has convincingly emphasized the importance of the mediation of cultural memory in literature, media and artworks for the recall of traumatic histories.[44] Mediation implies an active choice for the second personhood in the memory act. Artists or critical readers who bear witness and facilitate memory as second persons create artworks, photographs, or published texts that function as mediators between 'the parties to the traumatizing scene and between these and the reader or viewer'.[45] Such mediation takes place in sociocultural reference frames and may constitute an 'act of memory that is potentially healing, as it calls for political and cultural solidarity in recognizing the traumatized party's predicament'.[46]

Bal's notion of mediation works with a clear distinction between the first and the second personhood involved in the memory act. The second personhood of those who mediate cultural memory is characterized by witnessing and confirming the testimony of those who experienced directly the events remembered and hold the first personhood of cultural memory. In *My Life Part 2*, the distinction between first and second personhood in the memory act is not clear cut. Angelika Levi takes on a double role. As filmmaker, she takes the position of second personhood. As daughter, she is affected by the impact of the trauma on her mother's life. In an indirect way, she participates in the traumatizing scene and occupies a first person position. The voice-over explains the motivation for the film accordingly: 'I wanted to understand how a trauma I hadn't experienced myself was passed on to me and colored my perception' (00:03:24). Angelika Levi shares her position between first and second personhood of the memory act with a number of mostly female filmmakers of the second generation, who likewise address their complex family stories in 'autobiographical documentaries' that combine family story and public history.[47] Hilde Hoffmann's comparative analysis suggests an understanding of the legacy of a family story that interferes with dominant narratives of the past as an important impetus for working through the personal family story in communication with public discourses. In this context, the position between first and second personhood is made productive in order to

44. Mieke Bal, 'Introduction', pp. vii-xvii.

45. Bal, 'Introduction', p. x.

46. Bal, 'Introduction', p. x.

47. Hoffmann, '*Mein Leben Teil 2*', p. 128. Hoffmann also analyses *Familien Geheimnis: Geschichte einer gefährlichen Liebe* (Anja Krug-Metzinger, DE 2002), *IMA* (Caterina Klusemann, DE 2001), *Meine 'Zigeuner' Mutter* (Therese L. Ràni and Egon Humer, AT 1998) and *Unterwegs als sicherer Ort* (Dietrich Schubert and Peter Finkelgrün, DE 1997).

'enact identities—fluid, multiple, even contradictory—while remaining fully entangled with public discourses'.[48]

By way of telling the story of her mother, Angelika Levi also relates a facet of her own story. *My Life Part 2* serves as a mediator between the experiences and stories of the women of the family lineage and the audience. Angelika belongs to this lineage, but as the one who performs it, she has an intermediate position. This particular permutation of taking the role of mediator of the filmmaker's own family story operates at the intersection of private and public memory. This intersection has been established as a productive location of cultural recall throughout the film. Here, it acquires an additional critical meaning. Due to the double position as daughter and filmmaker, the mediation of the family story and the public discourse affects Angelika Levi's position within the family story and family lineage. In my view, the moment in which Angelika Levi performs her memory act marks the moment in which she herself steps into the lineage of Levi women. She decides not to enter the Levi lineage as a mother, but does so as an artist and mediator of cultural memory. While a frequent answer of the first generation to the experience of the Shoah was to have children and build a new life, Angelika's second generation answer to the legacy of the Shoah is an act of memory, in which she mediates the traumatizing past of her mother and family to audiences involved in recent public discourse on cultural recall. In *My Life Part 2*, Angelika Levi places the essence of the female lineage at the center of the family story and projects it toward a future existence beyond her control in the public discourse. By doing so, the decision against having children and the concomitant break in the lineage is accompanied by another form of continuing the lineage and passing on her legacy to future generations. As a memory act, the film articulates a break and discontinuity. At the same time, it performs an act of enfolding the gynealogy's very constituents, it commemorates the murdered; it intertwines factual and imagined ancestry; it consitutes an act of political resistance and it passses down the line to future generations. The memory act is an answer that addresses ruptures and discontinuity as crucial elements in the continuation of the gynealogical transmission.

Angelika Levi's way of inscribing herself into the lineage of Levi women implies a double paradox. First, she establishes the lineage of Levi women but then decides not to enter the lineage as a mother. Instead, she lets the lineage end and does something new. Second, the moment of breaking the lineage is exactly the moment in which she steps back into the lineage as an artist and mediator of the family story. Strikingly, Angelika Levi's names seem to represent the double paradox. The filmmaker's first name, Angelika, means 'the female messenger' and seems to have anticipated the

48. Hoffmann, '*Mein Leben Teil 2*', p. 132.

Wow!

role of mediator. A Christian name, it may also connote and symbolize the dynamic of the Protestant Becker lineage and context as it is involved in the paradox of establishing a Jewish female lineage that then opens into something quite different. The second twist is connoted by the name Levi, which the filmmaker assumes as an adult as her artist name. Angelika Levi fills the meaning of her first name Angelika by inscribing herself into the lineage of Levi women as an artist and filmmaker.

4. *The Political Impact of Mediating Cultural Memory*

Conveying the Space of Otherness

Highlighting Angelika Levi's act of mediation in confronting her legacy of the Shoah emphasizes the film's reception along with its production. The focus on the viewer and on reception broadens the perspective on the functions of gendered genealogy performances in response to trauma, toward political agency and shared identities beyond the female Levi lineage.

In order to conceptualize the position of the viewer in the film, I am working with Thomas Elsaesser's concept of subject positions and speaking positions in post-Shoah films.[49] Elsaesser aims at exploring the possibilities of the cinema for contributing to the process of transforming historical periods and events from arid data into elements of history, memory and culture. Crucial in this undertaking are strategies of representation that encourage forms of empathy which reject indifference and self-centeredness and work toward the ability to 'reconcile memory and hope, commemoration and forgetting, or mediate between pity, sentiment and shame'—in other words, strategies of representation able to open up the 'space of otherness'.[50] Elsaesser argues that one effective cinematic strategy of doing so is to create subject positions for the viewers that disturb and challenge their well-established and coherent identities through 'affects of concern' (*Betroffenheit*). Affects of concern are meant to be affects of identification and empathy that involve contact with the space of otherness and result in empowerment and activity.

> This concept…tries to convey subject positions that lie beyond sentimentality and yet touch a point where the self itself knows and can experience otherness. In the face of narcissistic forms of identification in conventional narrative and fictional dramatization, such an 'affect of concern' is meant to

49. Thomas Elsaesser, 'Subject Positions, Speaking Positions: From *Holocaust*, *Our Hitler* and *Heimat* to *Shoah* and *Schindler's List*', in *The Persistence of History: Cinema, Television and the Modern Event* (ed. Vivian Sobchack; New York: Routledge, 1996), pp. 145-81.

50. Elsaesser, 'Subject Positions, Speaking Positions', p. 172.

break through any coherent and thus comforting subject position and shock the spectator into recognition.[51]

Elsaesser argues that fiction film and documentary film have different means of sustaining ambiguous and disturbing subject positions. Of the two, fiction film is especially able to 'shatter' subject positions by means of using its typical tools such as 'aesthetic strategies, resources of narration and identification, strategies of contrast, excess, violence'.[52]

As for documentaries, Elsaesser discusses works by Marcel Ophüls and Claude Lanzmann.[53] Both filmmakers create nuanced speaking positions for their protagonists by means of holding back their own emotions and convictions in favor of restricting their role to a 'quasi fictional character' (Ophüls) or to 'something like his subjects' super-ego, at once insistent and firm' (Lanzmann).[54] As a consequence, these documentaries account for the need to create complex subject positions for the viewer and indeed provoke affects of concern because they fill the mind with voices that 'will forever speak of a history for which there is neither redemption nor exorcism'.[55] Still, the documentaries' speaking positions keep the subject position of the viewer intact and do not threaten the coherence of the viewer's identity. Comparing the two genres, Elsaesser concludes that 'if fracturing the viewers' identity is the very condition that makes the radical otherness of an extreme historical experience representable, then there may be a limit to the documentary methods employed by Lanzmann and Ophuls.'[56]

Subject and Speaking Positions in 'My Life Part 2'
The documentary *My Life Part 2* works quite differently from the documentaries discussed by Elsaesser. Filmmaker Angelika Levi does not hold back her convictions. On the contrary, she provides the film with a radical personal perspective. This personal perspective is established through the

51. Elsaesser, 'Subject Positions, Speaking Positions', p. 173.

52. Elsaesser, 'Subject Positions, Speaking Positions', p. 175. For example, Joseph Losey's 'M. Klein' (FR 1976) is built around establishing and then shattering a particular subject position: 'Identification, historical foreknowledge and the logic of classical narrative have here conspired to lull the senses into 'accepting' the transported Jews as normal, until the moment we want to rescue our hero and realizing that we need to rescue them all, we are shattered by the knowledge of our total impotence; but which is also the knowledge of our own collusion and complicity'. Elsaesser, 'Subject Positions, Speaking Positions', p. 175.

53. Elsaesser discusses 'The Sorrow and the Pity' by Marcel Ophüls (FR 1969) and 'Shoah' by Claude Lanzmann (FR 1985). Elsaesser, 'Subject Positions, Speaking Positions', pp. 173-74.

54. Elsaesser, 'Subject Positions, Speaking Positions', p. 173.

55. Elsaesser, 'Subject Positions, Speaking Positions', p. 174.

56. Elsaesser, 'Subject Positions, Speaking Positions', p. 174.

autobiographical character of the film and is enforced especially by the personal female voice-over. In this personal perspective, the filmmaker creates a fundamentally hybrid speaking position that is located in a sociocultural interim space, characterized by difference. At the same time, by means of providing ample space for the female protagonists to speak in audio records, home movies and in interview sequences, the film creates speaking positions for the women of the Levi lineage, particularly for Ursula Levi and Karla Levi. These speaking positions are established with a clear attitude of sympathy on the part of the filmmaker. On this basis, they can be drawn out as complex and ambiguous, as well as located in a sociocultural interim space.

In my view, by doing so, the filmmaker creates a complex subject position for the viewer. This position is not shattered, as Elsaesser describes it in fiction film. But neither does it remain untouched. Instead, this complex subject position is challenged by means of constantly confronting the viewer with the narrowness of their position. The film provokes affects of identification and empathy, but likewise conveys the limitation of these affects and thereby implies a contact with the space of otherness, which may indeed result in empowerment and agency.

The confrontation with the narrowness of the (complex) subject position created by the film evolves from the speaking position of the female protagonists. They are portrayed as humorous headstrong survivors on the one hand, but as injured, difficult and sometimes unfair anti-heroines on the other, an ambiguity that challenges continuous affects of empathy.

Moreover, the viewer is confronted with the narrowness of their complex subject position through the film's engagement of the filmmaker's hybrid speaking position. This dynamic becomes visible in the screening and reception of the film, which is not a mainstream cinema film, but a film that has been mostly screened at festivals and in film-series.[57] The reception of *My Life Part 2* mirrors the subject positions created in the film. Locations of screening, announcements, reviews and awards document how these positions are assumed, rejected and transformed by the viewers.

My Life Part 2 has been screened at festivals that tie in with particular aspects of the hybrid speaking positions of the filmmaker, namely Jewish

---

57. *My Life Part 2* had its premiere at the *International Forum of New Cinema* of the *Berlinale* on February 11, 2003. It was screened by German public broadcaster *ZDF* and at numerous national and international film festivals. Film festivals between 2003 and 2005 include *San Francisco Jewish Film Festival 2003*; *27. Duisburger Filmwoche 2003* (awarded with the *Preis der Stadt Duisburg*); *5th Jewish Film Festival Jerusalem 2003*; *14. lesbisch schwule filmtage hamburg* 2003; *The 6th Annual Barcelona Jewish Film Festival 2004*; *2nd Jewish Film Festival Warsaw* (awarded with the second price for documentary feature, member of the festival jury in 2005); *8th Women's Film Festival Seoul 2004*; *Queer Film Festival Vienna 2005*.

film festivals, queer film festivals and women's film festivals. In this context the complex identities of filmmaker and protagonists come to the fore.
For example, the sixth Annual Barcelona Jewish Film Festival in 2004
screened Levi's film under the headline of Complex Jewish Identities. The
festival advertisement read as follows:

> Under the title 'Identity, Diversity', the Sixth Annual Barcelona Jewish
> Film Festival investigates the deeper meanings of Jewish identity and, par-
> adoxically, the enormous cultural, national and intellectual diversity that
> exists in its midst. At the same time, the Festival will cover some of the
> topics that worry, concern and confront Jews whatever their nationality or
> sociocultural situation.[58]

Including *My Life Part 2* in the program testified to the anticipation that the
film would contribute to exploring the complexity of Jewish identities. The
film was assessed as being able to convey the recognition of otherness from
an inside perspective. For example, Rabbi Rothschild's suggestion that he
is the response of his parents to the Shoah is a statement with which many
Jewish viewers will identify. However, the voice-over then reframes the
issue by answering in a very different way, creating a moment in which the
viewer can touch the space of otherness.

In a similar way, screening *My Life Part 2* at queer film festivals invites
the viewer to identify with the lesbian and gay speaking positions of the
filmmaker and her brother. However, viewers who align themselves with
the subject position of the cosmopolitan and politically engaged lesbian
Angelika are quickly confronted with the complexity of Angelika Levi's
speaking position (both as protagonist of the film and as filmmaker). The
confrontation challenges viewers to recognize a space of otherness within
lesbian and gay culture and politics. In both cases, the complexity of the film
conveys subject positions where the viewer is confronted with otherness.

Subject positions as conveyed by *My Life Part 2* are also related to the
film's inhabiting of the intersection between personal story and public discourse. As the program of the San Francisco Jewish Film Festival puts it,
the film provides the 'portrait of a family whose story is both its own universe and a microcosm of European history'.[59] The intersection of family
story and broader cultural and political discourses makes the family story
relevant. For the jury of the Duisburg Documentary Film Festival in 2003,
which awarded Angelika Levi with *The Award of the City of Duisburg*, the
location at this intersection was the major reason for its positive assessment

---

58. Festival advertisement, http://www.accesomedia.com/display_release.html?id=
16885 (accessed November 17, 2010). Unfortunately the text is no longer available
online.

59. http://www.sfjff.org/film/detail?id=2074 (accessed June 8, 2013).

of the film.[60] At the same time, it provides access to the personal story and enables the viewer to touch upon its otherness. This works in two ways. Looking at the microcosm from a macroscopic perspective facilitates a more comprehensive understanding of its complexity. Going back from the microcosm to the macrocosm sharpens the view of its structure and dominant discourses. Both movements add to subject positions that evoke the recognition of otherness and might provoke affects of concern.

Looking at the reception of *My Life Part 2* reveals how the complex speaking positions of the film's protagonists convey subject positions that facilitate recognition of otherness and affects of concern. Getting intellectually and emotionally involved in the film through a specific angle of identification inevitably results in a confrontation with the space of otherness established by the complexity of Angelika Levi's speaking position. Engaging the dynamics between the microcosm of the family story and the macrocosm of political history constitutes affects of concern that challenge one's worldview and political analysis and raises questions about strategies of political solidarity.

Stimulating Political Alliances and Shared Identities
Angelika Levi performs her gynealogy in communication with cultural memory performances and audiences. This broadens the scope of her gynealogy performances in response to trauma toward political agency and shared identities. In its communication with its audiences, *My Life Part 2* opens up spaces of otherness, evokes affects of concerns and shatters comforting subject positions. Following Elsaesser, I understand these qualities as a foundation for political activity and coalition building. An example of this dynamic is the role of the film in the political discourse on the memory of the Shoah and beyond. *My Life Part 2* has been repeatedly screened in film-series that aim toward a nuanced form of counter-present memory, either by bringing marginalized positions to the center and/or by bringing together positions that are usually strictly divided. For example, the film-series *Divided History: The Meaning of the Shoah in the Life of the Descendents of Persecutors and Survivors* (Vienna 2004) reflects on the impact of the National Socialist past on second and third generation descendants of survivors, perpetrators, and bystanders and on lineages that are situated between the lines.[61] The series addresses the powerful impact of the past shared by the different groups while at the same time carefully keeping divisions and differences in focus. It expresses a political interest shared by the second and third generation to perform a transformed and nuanced form of counter-present cultural memory. Such a performance is a highly political

60. http://www.duisburger-filmwoche.de/festival03/ (accessed June 8, 2013).
61. See http://www.kinoki.at/mikrokino/pro/p112.htm (accessed June 8, 2013).

act and may feed into shared identities between formerly divided groups and individuals. *My Life Part 2* is an important film in this context because it is able to convey subject positions that touch upon the space of otherness. Moreover, it is relevant in this context because it does not present a completed story, but comprises traces, paradoxes and open ends that invite discussion, debate, engagement and conflict.

The analysis of 1 Chronicles 1–9 has suggested identity formation and expression as central motivation for gendered genealogies in response to trauma in *My Life Part 2* and beyond.[62] The focus on the context of communication with audiences and a shared desire for counter-present acts of cultural memory brings a second critical motivation for gendered genealogy composition in response to trauma into focus. Mediating the lineage of Levi women with the public discourse on memory introduces the context of political agency and shared identities as a crucial context for the performance of gendered genealogies in response to trauma.

5. *Conclusion and Crossover with 1 Chronicles 1–9*

Alternative Female Succession
My Life Part 2 presents a gynealogical memory project in which gendered genealogies are conceptualized as a female succession, which is established by the subjectivity and agency of its female protagonists. By doing so, the film proposes a concept of memory transfer that is alternative to the concept of patriarchal succession as employed in 1 Chronicles 1–9. The alternative gynealogical succession is established through a consistent focus on a lineage of protagonists who do not stand at the structural junctions of transmission, like the women in a patrilinear genealogy. The succession is characterized by an amalgamation of kinship and ideology based succession and an interplay of received and imagined ancestry from the viewpoints and based on the needs of the female protagonists.

The film's alternative form of succession complicates both lineage and memory performance and works toward recognizing complexity. Starting from the subjectivity of the female protagonists allows for an emphasis on the continuity of all time and reality layers involved, and involves complex subject positions. Thus the alternative succession provides an entry to the complexity of the traumatic past.

Recognizing the complexity of the traumatic past and the challenge of responding to it is also supported by the film's readiness to retain paradoxes and unresolved ends. Paradoxes and open ends convey the character of the gynealogy as multilayered and open. Unresolved issues include open ends

---

62. See also Hoffmann who likewise takes a strong identity based approach to Angelika Levi's film (Hoffmann, '*Mein Leben Teil 2*').

in the family story; the male-gendered subtext; the tension between wanting to know and not wanting to know; the paradox of establishing a female Jewish lineage of mothers and then doing something new; and the paradox of being alienated returnees at home.

In *My Life Part 2* the complexity of the gynealogy performance is not achieved through fissures in the dominant principals of recall, as in 1 Chronicles 1–9. Instead, complexity is a basic feature of the alternative female succession and an important aspect of the agenda of the filmmaker.

Next to complexity, alternative succession facilitates counter-present memory. Gynealogical succession re-evaluates the story and memory of the female protagonists. Persons, stories and archives that are at the margins of hegemonic memory discourses come to the fore. The re-evaluation of center and fringe is intimately interwoven with the female-gendered quality of the alternative gynealogical succession. It expresses a clear position concerning negotiations of power relations, gender hierarchies, and hegemonic memory discourses.

The counter-present character of the gynealogy performance is supported by the form of the film as an alternative archive. The form of an alternative archive draws on materials outside the main sources of historiography and takes account of marginal perspectives. Moreover, it allows the juxtaposition of perspectives and involves layers of meaning beyond the dominant narrative. Here, the presentation of narrative and gynealogy in the form of an archive reflects the interest in paradoxes and open ends.

The form of the archive has yet another implication. It shows that the gynealogy of the film is fragmentary in character even though it is a female lineage and it is in this respect analogous to the gendered fragments of 1 Chronicles 1–9. This link suggests understanding female genealogies in the patriarchal context of male lineages of power, authority and inheritance as fragmentary by definition—yet not necessarily fragmented. For example, the gynealogy of *My Life Part 2* resists being fragmented in the way the female lineages of 1 Chronicles 1–9 are. Still, it is based on fragments that are put together in Angelika Levi's archive performance.

The counter-present character of the memory performance in *My Life Part 2* is in contrast to the ambiguity that became visible in the close reading of 1 Chronicles 1–9 in the previous chapter. Still, a sense of ambiguity may be perceived in the film's employment of paradox. But where ambiguity in the biblical text pertains to a back and forth between granting openness and curtailing it, and to denying clear stances, the use of paradox in the film means that two opposing elements are spelled out and simultaneously adhered to. In other words, where the ambiguity of 1 Chronicles 1–9 works toward supporting the patriarchal succession and contesting a multilayered memory act, the paradox in *My Life Part 2* works toward acknowledging the multilayered and contradictory character of the gynealogy performance, favoring complexity.

Appropriating the Traumatic Past

The film's alternative female succession is characterized by yet another feature of the film: the filmmaker does not only establish the lineage of Levi women in the course of the film, but also inscribes herself into it. The process of inscribing herself into the lineage comes into being the moment the filmmaker establishes discontinuity with this lineage. Angelika Levi refuses to enter the line by means of becoming a mother herself. But then, paradoxically, this moment of discontinuity does not break the female lineage, but allows the filmmaker to inscribe herself into it and to appropriate the traumatic past as her own legacy.

The centrality of discontinuity in the female succession constitutes a parallel to 1 Chronicles 1–9. Admitting to discontinuity as a central element in the gendered genealogy performance in response to trauma is an element that both genealogies share. Moreover, in both cases, breaks, either in the form of discontinuity with the central lineage or in the form of fissures in the patriarchal succession, convey an opening that implies an invitation to protagonists who transgress the norms of the lineages they occupy. In the case of *My Life Part 2*, breaking the lineage of mothers inheres an invitation to the daughter Angelika Levi to inscribe herself into the lineage of Levi women, an invitation she accepts.

In the film, discontinuity as an engine for appropriating the past comes with a focus on horizontal memory production as a counterpart to vertical genealogical reproduction. *My Life Part 2* conceptualizes the horizontal intergenerational context of memory performance as a homoerotic one. However, instead of making this homoerotic component imperative, the film issues a challenge to imagine relationships that are able to accommodate and facilitate the production of cultural memory in response to trauma, for example friendships, partnerships, colleagueships, or political alliances. In 1 Chronicles 1–9, the characteristic occurrence of sisters hints at such a position beyond the genealogical reproduction matrix and includes traces of the horizontal dimension of genealogy production, as I will argue in Chapter 6.

In *My Life Part 2*, appropriating the past is enacted through archive performance and through mediating the past and the public discourse on post-Shoah memory. In the film, the archive performance is a means for the filmmaker to appropriate her traumatic legacy rather than to merely present it. Hence, the archive performance implies a shift from recounting the past to claiming it as her own and, by doing so, to linking it to her own story, ideas and political positions.

? appropriate traumatic legacy

The filmmaker performs her archive in the context of mediating the past and the public discourse in the form of a documentary film. The context of mediating memory renders her archive performance into a powerful memory act in which she introduces the family story as her own legacy to the public discourse on the memory of the Shoah. The mediation of memory at the intersection of personal and public memory points to a specific setting of gendered genealogy performance, beyond the setting of self-conception and identity performance, namely the context of political agency and shared identities.[63]

The location of gendered genealogy performance at the intersection of personal story and public discourse cannot be transferred to 1 Chronicles 1–9, because differentiating between personal and public domains is a modern concept. Still, the shift from identity to agency is important for understanding the Chronicles genealogies. The shift highlights the fact that genealogy performance does not end with proposing identity conceptions, but also has a clear political scope. By doing so, it emphasizes the importance of 1 Chronicles 1–9 in the discourses on exile and return and on mixed marriages at the time. It confirms my understanding of genealogy performance as a potent tool in the debate about who owns tradition and past, who is able to appropriate it for her/his needs and who has the power to (normatively) define identities of Israel at the time of the creation of the Chronicles genealogies.

63. The shift from identity to agency is important to note, because it highlights the uses of genealogies, especially in response to fractured pasts, in hegemonic or fascists contexts, for example in the fascist ideology of the Nazis. See Chapter 1.

Chapter 6

STRUCTURAL FUNCTIONS OF WOMEN IN THE GENEALOGIES OF JUDAH

This chapter aims to understand the structural functions fulfilled by references to women in the genealogies of Judah. It stems from the first round
of close reading of the Judah genealogies in Chapter 4, which had two main
results. First, it demonstrated that gendered fragments in the genealogies
of Judah interrupt and challenge patrilinear succession on a regular basis.
By doing so, the fragments establish a subtext to the dominant patrilinear
succession, adding complexity to the lineages. However, the analysis also
established that complexity is regularly restricted; that outstanding women
are presented as exceptions that prove the rule; and that the agency of
women is obscured. Hence the analysis showed that the memory act is fundamentally ambivalent. Second, the sample analysis in Chapter 4 showed
that some references to women occur in standardized formulas. For example, identification of Zeruiah as a sister, as well as formal attribution of a
lineage to her name, both take the form of a reoccurring formula (1 Chron.
2.16). Selected passages—on Zeruiah and others—revealed a larger web of
occurrences of the same formula, echoing the single occurrence of the formula and reinforcing its impact.

  Both results hint at broader patterns and structures formed by the gendered fragments. My primary interest in this chapter is to describe these
structures and to analyze their role in the overall genealogy composition.
Working on structures aims to complement the close reading of individual
passages to create a comprehensive and nuanced picture of the functions
of female-gendered references in the memory performance of the genealogies of Judah. It will include relevant approaches from Cultural Studies,
for example anthropological concepts of exogamous marriage, as well as
additional perspectives derived from film analysis, for example the notion
of paradox, and the focus on the political character of gendered genealogy
performance.

  The task of investigating fragments with regard to their structural functions involves some challenges. First of all, it requires a basis for the interpretation of a handful of fragments as structures pertaining to the core
message of the larger composition, whether they are induced by formulas or
not. Next, in order to more fully understand the dynamic of interrupting the

patriarchal succession and setting up a subtext, the analysis needs a strategy to investigate in what respect gendered references coincide *with* the patriarchal flow and which functions they fulfill in relation to the dominant drive of the text. Finally, it requires an approach that is able to interpret the dynamic force of the composition that became apparent in Chapter 4, and which enables engagement of the results with the issue of memory acts in response to trauma.

While the close reading of a sample of female-gendered references in the genealogies of Judah in Chapter 4 left me with an interest in structural functions, the context of socializing 1 Chronicles 1–9 with *My Life Part 2* gave rise to ideas on how to address the challenges involved, namely on how to employ the notion of the archive. I have suggested transferring the archive concept from *My Life Part 2* to 1 Chronicles 1–9 in Chapter 3. There, I analyzed formulas and patterns in the Chronicles genealogies as framing devices within the genealogical archive. Building on this argument, I now use the archive as a model of interpretation for analyzing the genealogies of Judah (and the broader composition of 1 Chronicles 1–9) with reference to the structural functions of the gendered fragments it contains.

Employing the archive concept will enable integrating the corpus of female-gendered fragments into the wider composition by means of understanding patterns of the female-gendered references as instances of the taxonomy of the archive. The taxonomy of an archive is the sum of its structures, labels, organizing principles and hierarchies.[1] It describes the way in which an archive produces knowledge and advances its interest. The close reading in Chapter 4 brought to the fore that female-gendered references form patterns and building blocks of structures. The concept of the archive suggests reading these patterns as instances of the taxonomy of the archive of genealogies—specifically of the genealogies of Judah, which constitute a critical part of the larger composition. Doing so integrates them with the overall genealogy composition and is an excellent means of assessing both their implications for the presentation of female figures in the text and their impact on the composition as a whole.

In order to keep track of the composition's ambivalence, as well as the involvement of the gendered fragments in both generating the subtext and the dominant layer of the text, I follow Ann Stoler, who insists on the need to read archives *along the grain*.[2] Stoler argues that any attempt to read an archive *against* the grain should be based on a reading *along* the grain. This means to read an archive 'for its regularities, for its logic of recall, for its densities and distributions, for its consistencies of misinformation,

---

1.   Ann L. Stoler, 'Colonial Archives and the Arts of Governance', *Archival Science* 2 (2002), pp. 87-109 (98-103).
2.   Stoler, 'Colonial Archives', p. 100.

omission and mistake' and in view of these principles' specific production of knowledge.[3] Stoler insists that such an analysis reflects a critical reading practice that likewise aims at disclosing power dynamics in the text. It acknowledges 'that archival production is itself both a process and a powerful technology of rule'.[4] The approach of reading *along the grain* will allow me to pursue ways in which female-gendered references help to form the dominant dynamic of the text. At the same time, keeping an eye on implicit structures and dynamics, as well as on regular omissions and gaps, will help to simultaneously keep track of the reference's involvement in the subtext.

The decision to employ the concept of the archive draws not only on the general principles of the archive concept. It is also linked to the specific way in which *My Life Part 2* functions as an archive. In the film analysis, I have argued that Angelika Levi not only leads the viewer through the archive of her mother, but that she performs her own archive and, by doing so, generates something genuine and new. This act is critical for appropriating the family story, claiming it as her own legacy, and presenting it anew with reference to her own convictions and political positions. The film analysis thus suggests exploring the potential of the archive in the context of memory performance in response to trauma. Hence, using the archive concept for the analysis of female-gendered references in the genealogies of Judah is done on the basis of the following hypothesis: the archival character of the genealogies of Judah (its organized heterogeneity) lets the text go beyond merely recalling and ordering the tribes and their lineages. Rather, establishing this archive of genealogies is a genuine response to a traumatic past, which makes a strong statement in the discourses on memory, identity, and power dynamics at the time of composition.

For the actual text analysis I will use two starting points. First, I will look at the occurrence and frequency of formal/relational terms that define women, for example as wives and as sisters. Here especially, the many wives and co-wives who occur in the genealogies of Judah, as well as their involvement in processes of segmentation, are brought into focus.

The second starting point will be marked by formulas and the structures they induce. Formulas primarily concern the formal affiliation of segments to women, as wives or/and sisters. This involves the affiliation of segments of the genealogies to the house of David, and with that to the power center of the genealogies of Judah and of 1 Chronicles 1–9. In this context, special attention will be paid to the wives and sisters included in this power center. The second important formula that induces structures is the formula that introduces sisters. Here, my focus will be on gaps and gap filling.

---

3.   Stoler, 'Colonial Archives', p. 100.
4.   Stoler, 'Colonial Archives', p. 100.

In light of the previous chapter's film analysis, the focus on wives and sisters might be striking. In *My Life Part 2*, mothers and daughters are central. Even though most mothers are married, they are identified mainly as mothers and grandmothers. In the genealogies of Judah, the opposite is the case. Most women figures are listed as wives and sisters. The majority of them also have children. Still, they are introduced as wives and sisters rather than as mothers. The difference in focus, here the focus on sisters and wives, there the focus on daughters and mothers, reflects the different setups of the genealogies. Still, it is important to bear in mind that, in each case, the (repressed) roles are implicitly present.[5]

The chapter is divided into four main sections. Section 1 addresses segmentation through wives. I give an overview of the scholarly debate on segmentation through wives and respond to it in the subsequent close readings. The text analysis is divided into passages that address segmentation through wives and others that address segmentation through secondary wives. Section 2 addresses the formal attribution of lineages to women on the basis of formulas. I discuss the function of the opening and closing formulas to induce genealogical ownership and demonstrate how this function is brought into play with regard to the female-gendered references. The subsequent close readings are divided into passages that attribute lineage segments to wives; passages that attribute lineage segments to sisters; and passages whose text-critically uncertain condition obscures possible attributions of lineages to women. Section 3 addresses the role of sisters. I start with a general discussion of sisters (and wives) in the genealogies of David. I then focus on Shelomith, listed in the succession of kings, and suggest understanding her as the center of a larger structure of sisters in the genealogies of Judah. I then interpret the character of this structure of sisters as a structure of shaped gaps. In a next step, I discuss the issue of gap filling

---

5.   In her Irigarayan reading of the book of Chronicles, Julie Kelso deals with the absence of the mother–daughter relationship by means of adding to the analysis a chorus-like poem in order to generate 'a sense of the mother–daughter relationship' in the text. Julie Kelso, *Oh Mother, Where Art Thou?*, p. 113. For a general reflection on the depiction of the relationship between mothers and daughters in biblical literature, including a discussion of the terms 'mother' and 'daughter' as metaphors for describing the relationship between God and Israel, as well as a discussion of the term 'mother's house', see Leila Lea Bronner, 'The Invisible Relationship Made Visible: Biblical Mothers and Daughters', in *Ruth and Esther: A Feminist Companion to the Bible (Second Series)* (ed. Athalya Brenner; Sheffield: Sheffield Academic Press, 1999), pp. 172-91. See also Cheryl Kirk-Duggan for a reading of the stories of Esther and Ruth through the lens of mother–daughter poems and stories by African American writers; Cheryl A. Kirk-Duggan, 'Black Mother Women and Daughters: Signifying Female-Divine Relationships in the Hebrew Bible and African American Mother–Daughter Short Stories', in *Ruth and Esther: A Feminist Companion*, pp. 192-210.

with an analysis of the references to Tamar and Bathsheba/Bath-shua serving as a model. Finally, I relate the structure of shaped gaps to the horizontal dynamic of memory production that became evident in *My Life Part 2*. Section 4 provides a concluding discussion of the gendered fragments in 1 Chronicles 1–9. I identify two groups of ideas in the text and discuss them one after another. The first group advances the goal of achieving a monopoly in defining Judah and Israel. The second group conveys the readiness to establish a gendered subtext that introduces complexity, discontinuity and the paradox of the memory act. I then discuss for a final time the ambiguity of the memory act and end drawing conclusions concerning 1 Chronicles 1–9 and the process of socializing 1 Chronicles 1–9 with *My Life Part 2*.

1. *Segmentation through Wives*

Segmentation through Wives in Chronicles Scholarship
Most women listed in the genealogies of Judah are introduced as wives (אשה) and secondary wives (פילגש). Most often these wives induce segmentation, which means the horizontal, ostensibly contemporaneous branching out of lineages. Segmentation indicates interrelations within a community as well as between neighboring communities.[6] It expresses relatedness and affiliation on the one hand, demarcation and difference on the other. It works toward performing identity with a focus on conceptualizing the self and the other and establishing complex 'us'–'them' relations.

Segmentation processes in the genealogies of Judah stand out for two reasons. First, they are strongly linked to territorial references and ethnic differentiation.[7] Second, and central for the investigation of the gendered fragments, they are in many instances facilitated by women, especially wives. The strong presence of women involved in the segmentation process is by no means self-evident. As a rule, segmentation in genealogies is realized through males, especially through sons and brothers. Many biblical genealogies realize segmentation in exclusively male terms. For example, the Table of Nations in Genesis 10 and the genealogies of Levi in 1 Chron. 5.27–6.66 MT bring about segmentation without the help of females, whether they are wives, daughters, or sisters.

In recent Chronicles scholarship, the strong involvement of women in the segmentation processes of the genealogies of Judah has been discussed from the perspectives of integration, mapping complexity, and othering. Sara Japhet has proposed analyzing segmentation through wives in terms of

---

6. Robert R. Wilson, *Genealogies and History in the Biblical World* (New Haven, CT: Yale University Press, 1977), pp. 18-21.

7. Knoppers, 'Intermarriage, Social Complexity and Ethnic Diversity', pp. 15-30.

integration. She argues that the status of wife and secondary wife allows the text to present 'non-Israelite elements' as organic parts of Israel:

> Indeed, one of the goals of these genealogies is the inclusion, rather than exclusion, of the non-Israelite elements in the people of Israel, by presenting them as an organic part of the tribes, mainly in the status of 'wives' or 'concubines'. [8]

Segmentation through wives and secondary wives would then not only facilitate integration but also function as a means of absorbing more independent groups into mainstream Judah.

In addition to the focus on integration, Gary Knoppers has interpreted segmentation through women, especially through secondary wives, in terms of mapping complexity.[9] This places emphasis on explaining ethnic and social stratification in Judah as depicted in Chronicles.[10] For example, concerning the genealogy of Caleb (1 Chron. 2.42-50), Knoppers argues that 'by organizing portions of the Calebite lineages by secondary wives (vv. 46, 48-49) and presumably spouse (vv. 42-45), the writer explains social differentiation within the larger group'.[11]

Antje Labahn and Ehud Ben Zvi likewise emphasize differentiation between wives and secondary wives, but do so with an additional focus on othering groups within Judah.[12] They argue that the text uses the differentiation between wife and secondary wife to create an 'ideological hierarchy'.[13] Listing a wife as a 'concubine' (2.46, 48) or 'other wife' (2.25) would then function to other the genealogical segment pertaining to her.[14]

My analysis builds on these approaches. However, I think it is necessary to adapt these explanatory models in two ways. First, any analysis needs to explain when and why the text achieves integration as well as stratification by means of segmentation through wives rather than by means of other features at its disposal. For example, the genealogies also integrate groups into Judah by listing them as sons. The Kenites are a case in point. They are recalled as ethnically distinct from Israel in the Hebrew Bible (Gen. 15.19; Judg. 4.17-21; 5.24-27; 1 Sam. 15.6), but are in the book of Chronicles integrated into Judah by means of listing them among the sons of Salma (1 Chron. 2.55).[15] This move represents an instance of genealogical

---

8. Japhet, *I&II Chronicles*, p. 74.

9. Knoppers, *I Chronicles 1–9*.

10. Knoppers, 'Intermarriage, Social Complexity and Ethnic Diversity', pp. 19-23.

11. Knoppers, *I Chronicles 1–9*, p. 312.

12. Labahn and Ben Zvi, 'Observations on Women', *Biblica* 84 (2003), p. 464.

13. Labahn and Ben Zvi, 'Observations on Women', p. 460.

14. Labahn and Ben Zvi, 'Observations on Women', p. 460.

15. See Japhet, *I&II Chronicles*, p. 90; and Knoppers, 'Intermarriage, Social Complexity and Ethnic Diversity', p. 26.

fluidity: fluidity occurs in cases in which genealogies change according to the needs of the situation in which they are performed. It implies that different genealogies that process the same data can exist side by side, both being equally true but responding to different contexts and settings.[16] In the case of the Kenites, genealogical fluidity plays a major role in integrating and absorbing this group into Judah. Again, the situation in the Judah genealogies is specific rather than general. It is necessary to ask about the specific impact of segmentation through women, an impact that may not have been achieved simply by segmentation through males and other forms of genealogical affiliation and distribution, for example through fluidity.

Second, I think it is necessary to adapt the analytical approaches described above with respect to the identity of the addressees of integration, diversification and othering. In the postexilic period, demarcations between 'us' and 'them' were complex. They involved demarcations for foreigners, but likewise concerned the relationship with Samaria, as well as conflicts between the former land-owning aristocracy that returned from exile and the peasants who had remained in the land.[17] In other words, demarcations that ostensibly took place between 'us' and 'them' most often concerned demarcation that in fact took place *within* the 'us' group. For a nuanced interpretation of segmentation in this context, I follow Gerd Baumann and Andre Gingrich's approach to identity.[18] Baumann and Gingrich conceptualize identity as something that necessarily includes alterity.[19] Difference is not to be located outside, but inside of identity. As a consequence, 'othering and belonging are mutually constitutive components of identity'.[20] Collective identities are 'multidimensional', 'contradictory' and fluid,[21] rather than 'stable', 'coherent' and 'almost homogeneous'.[22] For the genealogies of Judah, this means that integration, ethnic and/or social stratification and othering by means of segmentation through wives will in most cases not pertain to 'non-Israelite elements', as Japhet claims,[23] but concern processes

---

16. Wilson, *Genealogies and History*, pp. 27-36.

17. Claudia V. Camp, *Wise, Strange and Holy: The Strange Woman and the Making of the Bible* (JSOTSup, 320; Sheffield: Sheffield Academic Press, 2000), p. 31.

18. Gerd Baumann and Andre Gingrich, 'Foreword', in *Grammars of Identity/Alterity: A Structural Approach* (ed. Gerd Baumann and Andre Gingrich; New York/Oxford: Berghan Books, 2004), pp. ix-xiv.

19. Baumann and Gingrich, 'Foreword', p. x.

20. Andre Gingrich, 'Conceptualising Identities: Anthropological Alternatives to Essentialising Difference and Moralizing about Othering', in *Grammars of Identity/Alterity*, pp. 3-17 (4).

21. Gingrich, 'Conceptualising Identities', p. 6.

22. Gingrich, 'Conceptualising Identities', p. 14.

23. Japhet, *I&II Chronicles*, p. 74.

that take place within the multidimensional, fluid and dialogical identities of emerging Judaism.[24]

Having explained the state of affairs in the exegetical literature, I proceed to the text analysis and discuss passages that realize segmentation through wives. I start out with discussing segmentation through Atarah in the genealogy of Jerahmeel (2.25-33) and then discuss the parallel case of segmentation through Abijah and the nameless daughter of Machir in the genealogy of Hezron (2.9-55).

2. *Segmentation through Wives in the Text Itself*

Segmentation through Atarah: Visible Othering in the Genealogy of Jerahmeel (2.25-33)

One of the central passages in the genealogies of Judah that realizes segmentation through women is the genealogy of Jerahmeel (2.25-33):

> And Jerahmeel, the firstborn of Hezron, had sons: Ram the firstborn, and Bunah and Oren, and Ozem, Ahijah. And Jerahmeel also had another wife. And her name was Atarah; she was the mother of Onam. And the sons of Ram, the firstborn of Jerahmeel, were Maaz, and Jamin, and Eker. And the sons of Onam were Shammai and Jada. And the sons of Shammai were Nadab and Abishur. And the name of Abishur's wife was Abihail. And she bore him Ahban and Molid. And the sons of Nadab: Seled and Appaim. And Seled died without sons. And the sons of Appaim: Ishi. The sons of Ishi: Sheshan. The sons of Sheshan: Ahlai. And the sons of Jada, the brother of Shammai: Jether and Jonathan. And Jether died without sons. And the sons of Jonathan: Peleth and Zaza. These were the descendants of Jerahmeel.

The passage begins with the opening formula ‏ויהיו בני־ירחמאל בכור חצרון‎, 'And Jerahmeel, the firstborn of Hezron, had sons': The formula is followed by a list of five sons, among them Jerahmeel's firstborn, Ram (2.25). The text then introduces Atarah, ‏אשה אחרת‎, 'another wife' of Jerahmeel (2.26). The focus of the list that follows is on the descendants of Atarah's son Onam. His descendants reach into the eighth generation, even though some of them remain sonless. The genealogy concludes with the closing formula ‏אלה היו בני ירחמאל‎, 'These were the descendants of Jerahmeel', which attributes all listed sons to Jerahmeel (2.33).

---

24. Katherine Southwood makes a comparable argument concerning the mixed marriage crisis in Ezra 9–10, which she locates inside emerging Judaism rather than between Jewish and foreign groups. Katherine Southwood, 'Die ‚heilige Nachkommenschaft' und die ‚fremden Frauen': ‚Mischehen' als inner-jüdische Angelegenheit', in *Zwischen Integration und Ausgrenzung: Migration, religiöse Identität(en) und Bildung—theologisch reflektiert* (ed. Johanna Rahner and Miriam Schambeck; Bamberger Theologisches Forum, 13; Münster: LIT Verlag, 2011), pp. 61-82 (75-76).

Of the wives of Jerahmeel, Atarah is the first to be mentioned. While the mother of Jerahmeel's firstborn is passed over, Atarah and her descendants stand out. First, Atarah's name is emphasized with a reoccurring phrase. The text reads ושמה עטרה, 'And her name was Atarah'.[25] Next, she is one of only two women in 1 Chronicles 1–9 who are explicitly listed as mother (אם).[26] Finally, she is introduced with the phrase אשה אחרת, 'another wife' of Jerahmeel.

The phrase is noteworthy because it describes Atarah as beyond the distinction between wife (אשה) and secondary wife (פילגש).[27] The *Dictionary of Classical Hebrew* suggests translating אשה אחרת as another/other/additional wife of Jerahmeel, whereas אחר would indicate a relation of similarity (rather than of contrast).[28] In contrast, Japhet reads אשה אחרת, 'another wife', as a title, which would point to the foreign origin of Atarah.[29] Ethnic expansion in the genealogy of Jerahmeel would then be expressed through 'the assimilation of outside elements, designated "wives"'.[30] Japhet supports her argument with a reference to the parallel phrase in Judg. 11.2 and 1 Kgs 3.22. In these passages the phrase 'another wife' has a negative connotation linked to ethnic difference.[31] I agree that the phrase 'another wife' has a negative connotation in Judg. 11.2 and 1 Kgs 3.22. However, this does not necessarily involve ethnic difference. On the contrary, ethnic otherness for women in biblical literature is usually indicated with the adjective נכרי, 'foreign, alien, strange',[32] or with a form of זר, 'foreign, forbidden'.[33] Neither of these terms is employed to describe Atarah. Moreover, the context

25. The phrase that draws attention to the name of a woman likewise occurs in 1.50; 2.29; 4.3; 7.15; 8.29//9.35.

26. Only two women are listed as mothers: Atarah in 2.26 and the nameless mother of Jabez in 4.9.

27. The *Dictionary of Classical Hebrew* translates אשה as 'wife' and adds that the term refers to the 'legitimate sexual partner of a man and mother of his children'. 'אשה', *DCH*, I, pp. 404-11 (404). It translates פילגש as 'secondary wife' with the addition '(rather than concubine)'; 'פילגש', *DCH*, VI, pp. 681-82 (681).

28. See 'אחר', *DCH*, I, pp. 192-93 (193).

29. Japhet, *I&II Chronicles*, p. 74. See also Willi, who qualifies Atarah as 'fremde[s] Element' (alien element), Willi, *1 Chr 1–10*, p. 97. Labahn and Ben Zvi interpret the status of 'other wife' in terms of a 'lower status'. Labahn and Ben Zvi, 'Observations on Women', p. 461.

30. Japhet, *I&II Chronicles*, p. 83.

31. Japhet, *I&II Chronicles*, p. 82. *DCH* translates Judg. 11.2 as 'another, other, different', where another refers to a contrast (rather than similarity). 'אחר', p. 192.

32. *DCH* translates the adjective נכריה (feminine singular) as 'foreign, alien, strange', specifically as 'attributively of women' in 1 Kgs 11.1, 8; Ezra 10.2; and Neh. 13.27. It translates the corresponding noun as 'foreigner, alien, stranger' and refers to Ruth 2.10 as an example of a female foreigner. 'נכרי', *DCH*, V, p. 695.

33. *DCH* translates the 'participle (זר) as adjective' as 'foreign (and hence, sometimes,

of genealogies suggests reading the phrase in parallel to phrases such as זרע אחר, 'another seed', in Gen. 4.25 and בן אחר, 'another son', in Gen. 30.24, where the connotations are positive.[34] Contextualized as such, the phrase indicates the status of a second—albeit not necessarily secondary—wife without indicating ethnic difference or providing a negative connotation. The emphasis on Atarah's name, her listing as mother, and the depth of the lineage stemming from her (eight compared to three generations of the main segment of the genealogy of Jerahmeel), as well as her identification as 'another wife', highlight Atarah. In my view, at this stage of the text it is not clear to what end she is thusly exposed; it is a question that needs to be pursued further by looking at the lineage deriving from her.

The most striking feature of the lineage deriving from Jerahmeel and Atarah is its link to Edom. The list provides a set of names with striking similarities to names from the Edomite and Seirite genealogies in 1 Chron. 1.35-54, lending to the lineage Edomite and Seirite connotations.[35] Moreover, the names correspond with extra-biblical evidence of the mutual presence of Edomite and Judean groups in Southern Judah and Edom/Idoumea.[36] Knoppers convincingly concludes that the 'author's genealogies and lists may function as a tacit acknowledgement and affirmation of numerous ties between Judean and Edomite (Idoumean) circles'.[37] The lineage springing from Atarah acknowledges these ties. At the same time, the Edomite groups still belong to genealogies of Esau in 1 Chron. 1.35-54. They remain part of the other, which here, and only at this point of the lineage, is an ethnic other as well.

The link to the Edomite genealogy in 1 Chron. 1.35-54 also evokes the story of the eponymous ancestors Jacob and Esau in the book of Genesis. Hence, the link to Edom not only involves actual sociocultural circumstances but also the mythic/literary memory of Israel. In the memory of Israel, the Edomites are seen as patriarchal brothers through Esau. Esau is the brother who held primogeniture but lost it to Israel—thus to the 'us'—by

---

forbidden)' with an explicit reference to women in Prov. 2.16 and 7.5 where it is combined with נכריה; 'זור', *DCH*, III, pp. 98-100 (98).

34. *DCH* translates זרע אחר, 'another seed' (Gen. 4.25), as 'another, other, different' seed in terms of contrast and בן אחר, 'another son' (Gen. 30.24), as 'another, other, additional' son in terms of similarity, as in the case of 'another wife' Atarah. 'אחר', *DCH*, I, pp. 192-93.

35. For example Onam (Onam in 1.40) and Shammai (Shammah in 1.37). See Knoppers, *I Chronicles 1–9*, pp. 309-10 and Willi, *1 Chr 1–10*, p. 96.

36. Knoppers, *I Chronicles 1–9*, pp. 309-10. On the archaeological evidence of Edomite inscriptions in the South of Judah see John R. Bartlett, *Edom and the Edomites* (JSOTSup, 77; Sheffield: Sheffield Academic Press, 1989), pp. 209-11.

37. Knoppers, *I Chronicles 1–9*, p. 310. Knoppers locates these ties in the Persian period while Willi opts for either earlier or later relations. Willi, *1 Chr 1–10*, p. 96.

fraud but according to God's will (Gen. 25.29-34; 27.1-45). The reoccurrence of Esau/Edom in the genealogy of Jerahmeel is a means of expressing the paradoxical relatedness as well as the necessary differentiation between Judah and Edom/Idoumea: Esau/Edom is the 'us' inasmuch as it represents the brother with original primogeniture. But it is also 'them', because the primogeniture shifts to the younger brother, who is now the 'us'.[38]

The names in the lineage deriving from Jerahmeel and Atarah do not include place names. Names refer to families or clans, rather than to locations or territories.[39] The lack of place names has often been interpreted in terms of the semi-nomadic tradition of this branch of Judah.[40] However, given the complex conceptions of identity and alterity involved, the lack of specific locations might also aim to ensure that the affiliation with Edomite groups has nothing to do with any geopolitical and territorial claims.

The context of paradoxical relatedness and necessary differentiation, based on Israel's narrative memory, implies a certain ambiguity concerning the ethnic difference depicted in the segment under discussion. There is no clear ethnic othering through Atarah (her name or affiliation to a place) or through territorial references. However, similarities to the Edomite and Seirite names in the genealogies of Esau imply ethnic othering, albeit with a reference to the complex relatedness to this group.

In my assessment of the passage, I agree with Japhet, Knoppers and others, who suggest that, in the case of Atarah, segmentation through wives assimilates an (ethnic) other. However, I disagree with the qualification of this process as an organic one, as Japhet assumes for segmentation through women in general,[41] or as a tacit acknowledgement of ties, as Knoppers argues for this particular case.[42] Both Atarah and the segment deriving from her are exposed by means of a formulaic emphasis on her name; by means of listing her as mother; and by the exceedingly long lineage stemming from her son Onam. Segmentation through Atarah indeed facilitates the integration of Edomite groups into the self-conception of Judah. However, this integration is not complete. The identification of Atarah as 'another wife' highlights the lineage as a second or secondary segment of the lineage of

---

38. See also Bartlett who emphasizes the 'peculiar relationship' between Edom and Judah. Bartlett argues that Edom is regularly depicted as 'a fierce' as well as 'particularly treacherous enemy' of Judah and that the relationship between Judah and Edom seems to have been worse than those with the other Transjordanian states. Still, Edom is called in several places 'brother' to Israel and Judah, a position not granted to Moab or Ammon. Bartlett, *Edom and the Edomites*, pp. 175-86, especially p. 175.

39. Willi, *1 Chr 1–10*, p. 96; and Japhet, *I&II Chronicles*, p. 83.

40. Willi, *1 Chr 1–10*, p. 96. See also 1 Sam. 27.8-10 and 30.26-30; Knoppers, 'Intermarriage, Social Complexity and Ethnic Diversity', p. 25.

41. Japhet, *I&II Chronicles*, p. 74.

42. Knoppers, *1 Chronicles 1–9*, p. 310.

Jerahmeel. It requires the specification of a mother, which is not necessary in the primary segment of the lineage of Jerahmeel, which is listed without an indication of the mother it springs from.[43] The status of affiliation is not on par with the status of affiliation in a first segment. Hence, segmentation through Atarah facilitates integration into Judah, but the segment remains visible as 'other'.

My claim that segmentation through Atarah aims at explicitly and visibly defining the place of the segment springing from her is supported by the tacit and organic integration taking place concurrently: Jerahmeel himself is recalled as a non-Israelite in other biblical books (e.g. 1 Sam. 30.29) but is entirely incorporated into Judah in Chronicles.[44] His integration is achieved by means of listing him as a son of Hezron and by means of fluidity. Fluidity allows integrating Jerahmeel into Judah while concurrently communicating a subtext of ethnic difference. It is here that ethnic affiliation and demarcation are negotiated through implicit and tacit means.

In conclusion, my close reading of the lineage of Jerahmeel *along the grain* results in the following claim about the structural function of segmentation through wives in the Judah genealogies: Lineages springing from segmentation through wives are integrated into Judah by means of an explicit (rather than tacit or organic) discussion of both their ambiguous and paradoxical relatedness to Judah. The explicit character and paradoxical dimension of this integration negotiates identity and alterity in a specific way. Groups are integrated into the matrix of the genealogies of Judah, but are concurrently identified as others. This mechanism is reinforced by the parallel integration of males through listing them as sons and through fluidity, which takes place implicitly and tacitly.

Parallels in the Genealogy of Hezron (2.9-55). In order to further substantiate my conclusion concerning the function of segmentation through wives, I will briefly discuss a second case of segmentation through wives as it occurs in the genealogy of Hezron (2.9-55). The genealogy of Hezron structures the first part of the genealogies of Judah and presents its central families (one of them is the genealogy of Jerahmeel, which I have just discussed). The genealogy of Hezron features segmentation through wives in a way that displays noticeable parallels to the segmentation through the wife Atarah in the genealogy of Jerahmeel.

Hezron has five sons in total. Initially, the text lists his sons Jerahmeel, Ram (the forefather of David) and Chelubai/Caleb (2.9).

> And the sons of Hezron, who were born to him: Jerahmeel, and Ram, and Chelubai.

43. Labahn and Ben Zvi, 'Observations on Women', p. 461.
44. Willi, *1 Chr 1–10*, p. 82.

The existence of their mother(s) is only hinted at by means of the phrase אֲשֶׁר נוּלַּד־לוֹ, 'who were born to him'. As sons and brothers, they themselves bring the segmentation of the lineage into effect. The text proceeds with the genealogy of Ram (2.10-17) and the first part of the genealogy of Caleb (2.18-20). The text then returns to Hezron and lists further sons: Segub and Ashhur (2.21-24). These additional sons are both introduced with a reference to their mother. Segub springs from the nameless daughter of Machir (2.21), and Ashhur, father of Tekoa, springs from Abijah (2.24). In both cases, the text realizes segmentation through wives.

> And afterward Hezron went in to the daughter of Machir, father of Gilead. And he married her when he was sixty years old. And she bore him Segub. And Segub begot Jair, who had twenty-three towns in the land of Gilead. But Geshur and Aram took from them the towns of Jair, with Kenath and its daughter villages, sixty towns. All these were descendants of Machir, father of Gilead. And after the death of Hezron in Caleb-ephrathah, Abijah wife of Hezron bore him Ashhur, father of Tekoa.

Segmentation through wives in the genealogy of Hezron provides some important parallels to segmentation through Atarah in the genealogy of Jerahmeel. First of all, the genealogy of Hezron likewise provides main and secondary lineages. The primary lineage is listed without a clear reference to its mother(s), while the secondary lineages are listed with explicit references to the wives who give rise to them. Next, as in the genealogy of Jerahmeel, the secondary character of the additional lineages is indicated by describing them as segments that are later/following/other (אחר) segments: Hezron marries the daughter of Machir after the previously listed events (וְאַחַר בָּא חֶצְרוֹן אֶל־בַּת־מָכִיר אֲבִי גִלְעָד), 'And afterward Hezron went in to the daughter of Machir, father of Gilead'), and Abijah gives birth to Ashhur after the death of Hezron (וְאַחַר מוֹת־חֶצְרוֹן, 'And after the death of Hezron').[45]

In the case of the daughter of Machir, the segment that springs from her likewise involves groups that are related to Judah both in terms of sociopolitical circumstances and in terms of literary/mythological memory. Given that the daughter of Machir is the granddaughter of Manasseh, the lineage stemming from her marriage with Hezron represents ties between the Hezronites and Manasseh in the northern Transjordan.[46] Moreover, it claims a Judahite connection to large parts of Gilead, one of the core territories of Manasseh and Machir.[47] At the same time, the (implicit) reference to Manasseh alludes to both the relation of and the difference between Judah

---

45. In contrast to the passage on Atarah, the characterisation of the events as events after/following a primary event has here a temporal meaning. 'אחר', *DCH*, I, pp. 193-95 (193-94).

46. Japhet, *I&II Chronicles*, p. 80.

47. Japhet, *I&II Chronicles*, p. 80.

and Manasseh as eponymous sons/grandsons of Israel.[48] The lineage spring-ing from the daughter of Machir belongs to Judah, but is also distinct from it—a fact underlined by the eventual attribution of all the descendants to Machir, father of Gilead. The segment is integrated into Judah, not in terms of full integration but in terms of secondary affiliation.

Differences between the genealogy of Jerahmeel and the genealogy of Hezron relate to the description of the respective wives. While Atarah is listed with a reoccurring phrase that puts emphasis on her name, the name-less daughter of Machir and Abijah are not. In addition, the daughter of Machir remains nameless, but is identified via her father and the place to which he pertains. Differences also relate to the involvement or lack of places. In contrast to the genealogy of Jerahmeel, the lineages deriving from the daughter of Machir and from Abijah provide ample references to places. The segment deriving from the daughter of Machir addresses ter-ritorial conflicts and has a prominent geopolitical scope.[49] In the segment deriving from Abijah, her son Ashhur, father of Tekoa, represents ties with northern Judah.[50]

In conclusion, the genealogy of Hezron confirms the analysis of segmen-tation through wives in the genealogy of Jerahmeel, in spite of the differ-ences. Most important in this respect is the observation that, in both cases, segmentation through wives qualifies a lineage in complex ways. Again, belonging and alterity are negotiated in an overt process of integrating a segment into Judah, yet keeping it visible as other.

Analyzing key passages that feature segmentation through wives leads me to a first preliminary conclusion about the structural function of the female-gendered references in the genealogies of Judah. Segmentation through wives provides a means of visibly affiliating groups to Judah, in contrast to implicitly integrating groups by means of granting them the status of sons and by means of fluidity. This visible affiliation allows for integrating seg-ments in an explicit process of othering, which involves negotiating their ambiguous relatedness and difference to the central parts of Judah. Pro-cesses of othering are concerned with ethnic difference, geopolitical claims and determining relationships according to the ancestral narratives. Same-ness and otherness are presented as complex, ambiguous and sometimes paradoxical. Being located in both cultural memory and contemporaneous sociocultural relations, they are ambivalent rather than clear-cut. This par-ticular form of affiliation enables the acknowledgement and facilitation of

48. See the narrative on Joseph and his brothers in Gen. 37, the birth of Joseph's son Manasseh in Gen. 41.50-52 and the blessing of the sons and grandsons by Jacob in Gen. 48–49.

49. Japhet, *I&II Chronicles*, p. 80.

50. Knoppers, *1 Chronicles 1–9*, p. 308.

different shades in determining sameness and otherness. By doing so, it contributes a central feature to the genealogical identity performance. The function of segmentation through wives, facilitating shades of sameness and otherness, is in line with the broader interest of the text to define the position and status of its constituents. It runs along the grain of the overall genealogy composition.

Segmentation through Secondary Wives

So far, I have addressed segmentation through wives that negotiates ambiguous and paradoxical forms of identity and alterity. In a second step, I now focus on cases of segmentation through wives, and especially through secondary wives, that negotiate identity and alterity of groups more overtly distant from Judah, both in terms of ethnic and territorial difference. An example of such a form of segmentation is the segmentation through Bithiah, who is introduced as the (Egyptian) daughter of Pharaoh and who probably represented traditional Egyptian interests in Southern Judah.[51]

Segmentation through wives that focuses on ethnic and territorial difference occurs against the backdrop of a fundamental interest in 1 Chronicles 1–9 in space and territories.[52] In the genealogies of Judah, numerous references to places and territories, as well as plenty of toponyms in which personal names, male and female and names of places and/or communities overlap, expose the intimate link between places and identity conceptions in genealogical memory performance. One central concern of these genealogies is to set up a geopolitical identity map.[53]

In the genealogies of Judah, the most prominent gender position in the context of spatial references is the male-gendered position of the father of a place. Fathers of places are referred to in the formula 'PN1 father of PN2', for example, מְכִיר אֲבִי־גִלְעָד, 'Machir father of Gilead' (2.23). In 1 Chronicles 1–9, the formula is most frequently used in the genealogies of Judah.[54]

---

51. Knoppers, *I Chronicles 1–9*, p. 350.

52. For the interrelation of notions of space, territories and identities, see Magnar Kartveit, *Motive und Schichten der Landtheologie in I Chronik 1–9* (CBOTS, 28; Stockholm: Almqvist & Wiksell, 1989); and *Constructions of Space I: Theory, Geography, Narrative* (ed. Jon L. Berquist and Claudia V. Camp; LHBOTS, 481; New York: T. & T. Clark, 2007). For an archaeological study of the places mentioned in 1 Chronicles 1–9 see Israel Finkelstein, 'The Historical Reality behind the Genealogical Lists in 1 Chronicles', *JBL* 131.1 (2012), pp. 65-83.

53. For the interaction of genealogy, geography and history as constitutive for the description of the tribes see Manfred Oeming, *Das wahre Israel*, p. 130. For a general discussion of Chronicle's attitude to the 'Land of Israel', see Sara Japhet, *The Ideology of the Book of Chronicles and its Place in Biblical Thought* (BEATAJ, 9; Frankfurt: Peter Lang, 1997), pp. 275-307 275-77).

54. Of 33 instances of the father formula in 1 Chron. 1–9, 29 instances occur in the

Against the background of the formula's wide use in other biblical books (Genesis, Joshua, Judges), the formula is used here to express relationships between lineages and places, genealogy and geography.[55] In her nuanced analysis of the formal character of references in the text, Japhet argues that the formula maps processes of 'expansion, absorption and dispersal, all expressed in the code of genealogical structures'.[56] She convincingly analyzes the references to (the descendants of) fathers of places as a particular means of negotiating processes of affiliation and demarcation in view of the text's geopolitical identity map.

As a rule, fathers of places are listed in the vicinity of women, mainly wives and secondary wives.[57] The wives are the (grand)mothers of the fathers of places and the places/communities are listed as their sons. Many of the 'grandmothers' have toponyms or come with attributes that contain spatial and/or ethnic information. For example, Ephah bears the Midianite name of an Arabian tribe (2.46), Naarah carries the name of a town at the border between Benjamin and Manasseh–Ephraim (4.5), and Bithiah is listed as the (Egyptian) daughter of Pharaoh (4.18 MT). Moreover, some of the women are listed as secondary wives and introduce the dimension of social hierarchies and stratification.[58] In many cases, wives and secondary wives thus indicate and specify the context in which founding fathers and

genealogies of Judah. Here, fathers of places appear in 12 genealogical segments: 1 Chron. 2.21-23, 24, 42-50a, 50b-55; 4.3-4, 5-7, 11-12, 14, 17-18, 19, 21-23. The father formula frequently occurs together with a significant number of toponyms, for example in 1 Chron. 2.42-50a and 2.50b-55. The second name of the formula (PN2) regularly indicates localities, 16 of which appear as towns also elsewhere in biblical literature. See James T. Sparks, *The Chronicler's Genealogies: Toward an Understanding of 1 Chronicles 1–9* (Academia Biblica, 28; Atlanta, GA: Society of Biblical Literature, 2008), p. 220.

55. Willi, *1 Chr 1–19*, p. 100. Against Martin Noth, who suggested that the 'father formula' (*Patroniziumsformel*) points to an originally integral source (*Grundschrift*). This source would have been structured by the 'father formula' but was later lost and integrated into the Chronicles' genealogies. Martin Noth, 'Eine siedlungsgeographische Liste in 1. Chr 2 und 4', *ZDPV* 55 (1932), pp. 97-124 (100).

56. Japhet, *I&II Chronicles*, p. 85. Against Oeming, who understands the function of the formula as outlining the settlements of the early monarchy and as a means to link them to particular tribes. Oeming, *Das wahre Israel*, p. 129.

57. From the passages mentioned above, nine of twelve are linked to women: 2.21-23 is linked to the daughter of Machir, 2.24 to Abijah, 2.46-49 to Ephah and Maacah, 2.50-55 to Ephrathah, 4.3 to the brothers of Hazzelelponi, 4.4 to Ephrathah, 4.5-7 to Naarah and Helah, 4.17-18 to the nameless wife the Judahite and to Bithiah, the daughter of Pharaoh and 4.19 to the wife of Hodiah sister of Naham. Passages that mention founding fathers without a link to women are 4.11-12, 14, 21-23.

58. Knoppers, *I Chronicles 1–9*, p. 312. 1 Chron. 1–9 lists four women and one anonymous group as secondary wives: Keturah (1.32-33), Ephah and Maacah (2.46, 48), the secondary wives of David (3.9) and the Aramean secondary wife of Manasseh (7.14).

places/communities are listed. As 'grandmothers' they open up a wider geo-political scope.

Having introduced the priority of geopolitical references and the gen-dered position of founding fathers as a context for segmentation through secondary wives, I now proceed to the text analysis.

Negotiating Ethnic and Territorial Difference: Segmentation through Sec-ondary Wives in the Genealogy of Caleb (2.42-50a). The most prominent passage that addresses segmentation in the context of providing a wider geopolitical scope is in the second part of the genealogy of Caleb. The gene-alogy of Caleb is divided into two parts. The first part (2.18-24) has its place among the three main segments of the genealogy of Hezron (2.9-41). The second part occurs as a sort of addendum after these three main segments of the genealogy of Hezron (2.42-50a).

> And the sons of Caleb brother of Jerahmeel: Mesha, his firstborn, who was father of Ziph. And the sons of Mareshah father of Hebron. And the sons of Hebron: Korah, and Tappuah, and Rekem and Shema. Shema begot Raham, father of Jorkeam. And Rekem begot Shammai. The son of Shammai: Maon. And Maon was the father of Beth-zur. And Ephah, Caleb's secondary wife, bore Haran, and Moza, and Gazez. And Haran begot Gazez. And the sons of Jahdai: Regem, and Jotham, and Geshan, and Pelet, and Ephah, and Shaaph. The secondary wife of Caleb, Maacah, bore Sheber and Tirhanah. And she bore Shaaph, father of Madmannah, and Sheva, father of Machbenah, and the father of Gibea. And the daugh-ter of Caleb: Achsah. These were the sons of Caleb.

The passage starts out with a list of the sons of Caleb and a woman who is not mentioned (2.42-45). It then segments through Caleb's secondary wives Ephah and Maacah (2.46-49a). As in the case of Jerahmeel and Hezron, the genealogy begins with the descendants of a woman who remains anon-ymous. Only the secondary lineages feature references to the wives they spring from. However, in this case, the 'main' segment already constitutes an addendum. On this basis, the additional segments undergo a second form of othering through the qualification of their mothers as secondary wives (פילגש).[59]

The passage contains ample geopolitical references (toponyms, ethnic names, fathers of places). This includes the two secondary wives, whose names are clear territorial and/or ethnic references. The Midianite name Ephah serves as the name of an Arabian tribe, one of the offspring of Mid-ian.[60] The name Ephah thus suggests connections with a related ethnic or

---

59. In fact, Ephah and Maacah are the only secondary wives in the genealogies of Judah who are listed by name.

60. Knoppers, *1 Chronicles 1–9*, p. 312.

political population group in the Southern Transjordan.[61] Maacah is the name of a Syrian kingdom and connotes relations in the Northern Trans-jordan.[62] Hence, the references to Ephah and Maacah open up a space in which a particular sector of geopolitical interests and relationships—further elaborated by fathers of places and other geopolitical references—can be negotiated.

In conclusion, the comparison with the aforementioned segmentation through wives (Atarah, Abijah and the daughter of Machir) highlights that segmentation through secondary wives as well as the context of opening wider geopolitical spaces works toward establishing more independent ter-ritories and related groups. This argument is supported by the parallel case of segmentation through the secondary wife Keturah (1 Chron. 1.32-33). In this passage, Keturah functions as a genealogical reference point for descendants of Abraham, who are associated with 'areas to the south and southeast of Israel', on the basis of their toponymous names.[63] Interestingly, Keturah is introduced as a later wife of Abraham in Gen. 25.1 (ויסף אברהם ויקח אשה ושמה קטורה, 'And Abraham went on. And he took a wife. And her name was Keturah'), but is listed as a secondary wife (פילגש) of Abraham in Chronicles.[64] The shift from wife to secondary wife seems to foreground the distance to Arabia. Hence, again, segmentation through a secondary wife facilitates more overly articulated and less ambiguous othering in terms of territorial, ethnic and mythic relations.[65]

Hints to Female Inheritance and Land Claims in the Genealogy of Caleb and Beyond (2.49; 7.15; 7.24). Segmentation through the secondary wives Ephah and Maacah relates to the aim of the text to establish a geopolitical identity map. The second genealogy of Caleb provides yet another passage

---

61. Knoppers, 'Intermarriage, Social Complexity and Ethnic Diversity', p. 24. Knop-pers specifies that 'Midian' is associated with people to the southeast of Israel, e.g. the Ishmaelites (Judg. 8.24), the Medanites (Gen. 37.28, 36), the Moabites (Num. 22–25) and the Edomites. Sources testify to important links as well as continuous animosities. Knoppers, 'Intermarriage, Social Complexity and Ethnic Diversity', p. 24 n. 43.

62. D.G. Schley, 'Maacah (Place)', *ABD*, IV, p. 430.

63. Knoppers, *I Chronicles 1–9*, p. 280.

64. The shift from wife to secondary wife has been also discussed by Willien van Wieringen, 'Why Some Women Were Included in the Genealogies of 1 Chronicles 1–9', in *Rewriting Biblical History: Essays on Chronicles and Ben Sira in Honour of Pancra-tius C. Beentjes* (ed. Jeremy Corley and Harm van Grol; DCLSt, 7; Berlin: De Gruyter, 2011), pp. 291-300 (295).

65. The fourth reference to a secondary wife in 1 Chronicles 1–9 is the reference to the nameless Aramean secondary wife of Manasseh (7.14). This nameless Aramean sec-ondary wife opens the genealogies of Manasseh (7.14-19). Here, the status of secondary wife, together with the identification as an Aramean wife, functions to marginalize the tribe of Manasseh.

that likewise links the gendered fragments to the theme of geopolitical identities and claims, namely the reference to Caleb's daughter Achsah (2.49). At the very end of the genealogy, the text states that the daughter of Caleb was Achsah.[66] The reference to the daughter Achsah alludes to the narratives connected to her. Judges 1.11-15 and Josh. 15.15-19 recount that Achsah claimed arable land from her father after he had married her into the desert.[67]

This narrative background broaches the issue of female claims to land. Moreover, it is related to a second reference to daughters outside the genealogies of Judah. 1 Chron. 7.15 lists Zelophehad as one of the descendants of Manasseh and, as a sort of afterthought, adds that Zelophehad had daughters (ותהיינה לצלפחד בנות). Without explicitly referring to the story in which the daughters of Zelophehad claim a share of their father's inheritance (Num. 27.1-11; 36.1-12), the issue of female inheritance is broached.[68] In 1 Chronicles 1–9, the term 'daughter' most often occurs as a substitute for a name (the nameless daughter of Machir) or as a means of qualifying a woman (Bithiah, daughter of Pharaoh). The explicit listing of women in their role as daughters is rare. It seems to echo issues of female inheritance and land claims.

This possibility is further supported by yet another reference to a daughter: 7.24 lists Sheerah, the daughter of Ephraim (or daughter of his son Beriah) as a builder of the cities Upper Beth-horon, Lower Beth-horon and Uzzen-Sheerah.[69] Sheerah's building of cities might have involved actual,

---

66. In the case of Achsah, genealogical fluidity is at stake. While the Achsah of Judg. 1.11-15 and Josh. 15.15-19 is identified as the daughter of Caleb, son of Jepunneh, Chronicles lists her as daughter of Caleb, son of Hezron. The inclusion of Achsah conveys that the Caleb of the conquest is (also) meant. Hence, Achsah, as daughter, identifies and integrates her father into the lineage.

67. For a discussion of the narratives in Judges and Joshua see Danna Nolan Fewell, 'Deconstructive Criticism: Achsah and the (E)razed City of Writing', in *Judges & Method: New Approaches in Biblical Studies* (ed. Gale A. Yee, Minneapolis, MN: Augsburg–Fortress, 2nd edn, 2007), pp. 115-37; Lillian R. Klein, 'Achsah: What Price this Prize?', in *Judges: A Feminist Companion to the Bible (Second Series)* (ed. Athalya Brenner, Sheffield: Sheffield Press, 1999), pp. 18-26; and Judith McKinlay, 'Meeting Achsah on Achsah's Land', in *The Bible and Critical Theory* 5.3 (2009), pp. 39.1-39.11.

68. For a discussion of the narratives of the sisters in Numbers see Ankie Sterring, 'The Will of the Daughters', in *A Feminist Companion to Exodus and Deuteronomy* (ed. Athalya Brenner; Sheffield: Sheffield Academic Press, 1994), pp. 88-99.

69. Lower and Upper Beth-Horon are among the best known Ephraimite cities (Sara Japhet, 'Conquest and Settlement in Chronicles', *JBL* 98.2 [1979], pp. 205-18 [213]; Uzzen-sheerah is not attested elsewhere (M. Stephen Davis, 'Sheerah [Person]', *ABD*, V, pp. 1190-91).

manual labor, or the activity of founding or bestowing cities.[70] Either way, she is referred to as a female who extends her specific legacy to the cities.[71]

In conclusion, the second genealogy of Caleb highlights the interrelation between gendered fragments and the text's interest in spatial references and related geopolitical claims. This is accomplished in different ways, on the one hand along and on the other hand against the grain of the text. Segmentation through secondary wives determines relationships with groups that are ethnically and territorially distant to Judah, thereby negotiating identity and alterity in the context of broader geopolitical scopes than segmentation through wives does. Like segmentation through wives, segmentation through secondary wives operates along the grain of the text. In contrast, the reference to Caleb's daughter Achsah works against the grain of the text by providing a glance at the negotiation of female land and inheritance claims. The issue echoes in additional references to daughters in the genealogies of Manasseh and Ephraim, but is not elaborated on in the text.

Concluding Discussion

Based on my analysis of the key passages on segmentation through wives and secondary wives in the genealogies of Judah I come to the following conclusions. The close reading has demonstrated that segmentation through wives and secondary wives allows for addressing identities of and alterity within Judah in a nuanced manner. Nuanced and multilayered positions are enabled by the visible and explicit character of segmentation through wives and secondary wives. They include negotiating paradoxical and ambiguous relations in the case of segmentation through wives, as well as correlating and othering more overtly articulated ethnic and territorial differences in the case of secondary wives.

Interpreting segmentation through wives as an overt negotiation of integration and othering gains additional plausibility against the backdrop of Israelite marriage practice. Marriage arrangements then involved 'female

---

70. For women who engaged in manual building activities see Neh. 3.12, which states that the daughters of Shallum worked on the city wall next to their father. In spite of this evidence, Kiesow argues that the reference probably refers to the founding or funding of the cities. Anna Kiesow, *Löwinnen von Juda: Frauen als Subjekte politischer Macht in der judäischen Königszeit* (Münster: LIT Verlag, 2000), p. 50.

71. The passage is assessed differently by Labahn and Ben Zvi and Wacker. While Labahn and Ben Zvi interpret the building of cities by Sheerah as a divine blessing, Wacker argues that it could also be negatively connoted in line with negative connotations of building cities in Gen. 4 (the genealogy of Cain) and in Gen. 11 (Babel). Labahn and Ben Zvi, 'Observations on Women', p. 475; and Marie-Theres Wacker, 'Die Bücher der Chronik: Im Vorhof der Frauen', in *Kompendium Feministische Bibelauslegung* (ed. Marie-Theres Wacker and Luise Schottroff; Gütersloher Verlagshaus: Gütersloh, 3rd edn, 2007), pp. 146-55 (149).

mobility and male stability'.[72] Gender-related determination of mobility and stability pertains to both exogamous marriages between ethnic groups and endogamous marriages between tribes and paternal houses. In both cases, wives are objects of exchange, but subject to crossing community boundaries and negotiated sociocultural values.[73] Therefore, they mediate, integrate and channel the other.[74] Attributing to a particular ancestress a segment of genealogy that involves negotiating ethnic, geographical and/ or cultural boundaries makes sense against this background. The genealogy composition then builds upon a social practice with the aim of forming a genealogical tool that acknowledges and negotiates difference through segmentation. By doing so, the genealogies point to the sociopolitical and cultural-religious impact of women on communities when they cross community boundaries through exogamous and endogamous marriages.[75] Thus, in the postexilic period and beyond, wives emerge as critical agents in negotiating and integrating complex identity processes.[76]

Negotiating sameness and otherness through wives exposes female agency in processes of identity formation. However, there are two sides to this coin. Whereas references to wives mediate and channel the other, women are simultaneously othered by being attributed to secondary segments. Wives have an important function in the text, but fulfilling this function links them to marginalized parts of the Judah genealogies. This problematic side of the coin becomes even more apparent in the case of segmentation through secondary wives, where the secondary status of the wife adds a second level of othering

72. Carol Meyers, *Discovering Eve: Ancient Israelite Women in Context* (Oxford: Oxford University Press, 1988), p. 133.

73. Meyers, *Discovering Eve*, pp. 184-88. The understanding of marriage as a mode of exchange was first proposed by Claude Lévi-Strauss. He argued that in small-scale societies, marriage does not only affect the spouses, but constitutes a system of exchange, which involves 'material goods, social values such as privileges, rights and obligations and women'. Marriage as exchange system produces and shapes relations between groups. Claude Lévi-Strauss, *The Elementary Structures of Kinship* (ed. Rodney Needham; trans. J.H. Bell, J.R. von Sturmer and Rodney Needham; Boston, MA: Beacon Press, 1969), p. 115.

74. Camp, *Wise, Strange and Holy*, pp. 24-25.

75. For the sociopolitical and cultural-religious impact of women's informal groups or networks, see Carol Meyers, '"Women of the Neighborhood" (Ruth 4.17): Informal Female Networks in Ancient Israel', in *Ruth and Esther: A Feminist Companion*, pp. 110-27 (116-19).

76. The notion of wives as critical agents in negotiating complex processes of identity formation is also relevant to the gynealogy composition of *My Life Part 2*. However, discussing the issue would have to be done in a clear historical framework which would allow contextualizing the film with the history of Jewish assimilation in Germany, as well as with National Socialist race politics and the history of 'mixed marriages' in Nazi Germany. Such a strong historical focus goes beyond the scope of this project.

to the process of othering already underway through the female-gendered segmentation. In conclusion, the structural functions of segmentation through wives add important patterns of both explicit and nuanced othering to the genealogical fabric. However, these functions do not change the patterns, but belong to the dominant agenda of the text.

Overt othering through the wives and secondary wives in Judah stands in contrast to the concurrent implicit integration of segments through the status of sons and fluidity. The genealogies use both forms of integration side by side. This double strategy especially makes sense for the genealogies of Judah, an entity whose territorial, ethnic, sociopolitical and religious constitution was critical for the self-conception of Jewish identities at the time. In this context, segmentation through wives and secondary wives provides a tool to define identity/alterity in a much more nuanced way than a genealogy without gendered passages may have done. This might explain why so many wives are listed in this particular part of 1 Chronicles 1–9.

The passages discussed under the heading of segmentation through wives concern structural and functional matters. Such structural and functional matters are to be achieved most effectively through women figures without preceding stories in the cultural memory reflected in biblical literature. Here, women figures function as road signs for developing a larger genealogical map, rather than as individual female ancestors who consolidate traditions and can serve as identification figures, as for example Ephrathah. This function may be one clue as to why 1 Chronicles 1–9 lists so many unknown women that are distinct to the genealogy composition.[77]

3. Women as Subjects of Opening and Closing Formulas

Formulas that Induce 'Genealogical Ownership'
While the previous analysis was focussed on the functional/relational terms of wives and secondary wives, close readings in this section explore structural functions of female-gendered passages that are induced by formulas. The focus of analysis is on the opening and the closing formula, thus on formulas that attribute descendants to a name. As I have explained in Chapter 3, I understand the formulaic character of the genealogies as a significant feature of the genealogy genre in general, as well as a major device in the purposeful design of 1 Chronicles 1–9.[78] In the

---

77. Against Oeming, who argues that the lack of names of prominent women reflects the unimportance of women in the postexilic period, especially concerning the cult. Oeming, *Das wahre Israel*, p. 208.

78. My emphasis on the genre builds on the work of John Barton, who argues that the meaning of a biblical text depends on its genre and suggests 'genre-recognition' as a key aspect of critical Bible scholarship. John Barton, *Reading the Old Testament: Method in*

context of understanding 1 Chronicles 1–9 as an archive, I understand the use of formulas as a critical device in structuring, labeling and framing the contents of the composition, thereby setting up the taxonomy of the genealogical archive. For example, the opening and closing formulas attribute lineages to names, places and traditions. Moreover, they distribute segments in view of power centers such as the lineage of the house of David. By doing so, the formulas give shape to organization principles, establish regularities and enact hierarchies. They are an important tool in determining the archive's 'logics of recall'[79] and are critically involved in the genealogical process of memory performance. Analyzing the genealogy composition with reference to its formulas follows these logics of recall and is a form of reading the genealogy composition along the grain—even though the results of the analysis might seem to contradict the predominant aim of the text.

The opening and closing formulas attribute lineages to a name, and thereby establish 'genealogical ownership'.[80] The term *genealogical ownership* has been coined by Julie Kelso and refers to the attribution of a lineage to a name.[81] The name defines and identifies the lineage. In turn, the lineage belongs to the name. Genealogical ownership first of all concerns the distribution of names (rather than historical persons) and establishes a certain order on the level of (literary) genealogy performance. Sociopolitical circumstances are connoted, but the concept does not aim to describe legal or social relations in the first place.

As a rule, genealogical ownership is induced by opening and closing formulas. The opening formula attributes a list of descendants to the subject of the formula. For example, the opening formula בני יהודה, 'The sons of Judah', in 1 Chron. 2.3 opens a list of descendants who are attributed to Judah. In a similar way, the closing formula concludes a list by means of attributing the previously listed descendants to the subject of the formula. For example, אלה היו בני כלב, 'These were the descendants of Caleb', in 1 Chron. 2.50a.

In the patrilinear genealogies of Judah, female names are usually attributed to male names. Likewise, genealogical ownership is usually awarded to males. However, the genealogies of Judah feature instances in which males are attributed to female names and females occur as owners of lineages. This applies to wives, but also sisters, for example Zeruiah, one of the sisters of David (2.16). In the following close readings, I will analyze

Biblical Study (Louisville, KY: Westminster/John Knox Press, 2nd edn, 1996), pp. 16-19 (19).

79. Stoler, 'Colonial Archives', p. 100.
80. Kelso, *Oh Mother, Where Art Thou?*, pp. 112-13.
81. Kelso, *Oh Mother, Where Art Thou?*, p. 135.

passages that feature female subjects of opening and closing formulas. The close readings are structured according to passages that depict wives as genealogical owners; passages that depict sisters as genealogical owners; and passages in which women as genealogical owners appear in text-critically uncertain passages.

Wives as Genealogical Owners

The most important passage that features wives as owners of lineages is the passage on the co-wives Helah and Naarah (4.5-7). This passage lies at the center of this section. Next to Helah and Naarah, wives that own genealogies appear in passages that are text-critically uncertain. I will discuss the latter in the section on female ownership of genealogies in text-critically uncertain passages.

1 Chron. 4.5-7 introduces Helah and Naarah as co-wives of Ashhur and genealogical owners of lineages.

> And Ashhur father of Tekoa had two wives, Helah and Naarah; And Naarah bore him Ahuzzam, and Hepher, and Temeni, and Haahashtari. These were the sons of Naarah. And the sons of Helah: Zereth, Zohar, and Ethnan.

The text states outright that Ashhur, father of Tekoa, had *two* wives (4.5). By doing so, it introduces the co-wives Helah and Naarah without indication of a social, legal or relational hierarchy.[82] Naarah gives birth to four sons for Ashhur. All four sons are attributed to her name by means of the closing formula (4.6):

ותלד לו נערה את־אחזם ואת־חפר ואת־תימני ואת־האחשתרי אלה בני נערה

> And Naarah bore him Ahuzzam, and Hepher, and Temeni, and Haahashtari. These were the sons of Naarah.

The next verse begins with the standard opening formula. The formula gives the name of the mother Helah and the list of three sons attributed to her name (4.7):

ובני חלאה צרת יצחר ואתנן

> And the sons of Helah: Zereth, Izhar and Ethnan.

---

82. A parallel case occurs in the genealogy of Cain, which lists the co-wives Adah and Zillah (Gen. 4.17-24). Phyllis Silverman Kraemer provides an analysis of biblical women that come in pairs, which unfortunately does not include the genealogical references to co-wives and co-secondary wives, but nevertheless provides an interesting backdrop to the passages. Phyllis Silverman Kraemer, 'Biblical Women that Come in Pairs: The Use of Female Pairs as Literary Device in the Hebrew Bible', in *Genesis: A Feminist Companion to the Bible (Second Series)* (ed. Athalya Brenner; Sheffield: Sheffield Academic Press, 1998), pp. 218-32.

The text attributes the descendants of Ashhur, father of Tekoa, to his co-wives Helah and Naarah by means of the opening and closing formulas. While these formulas are usually used in the context of males and their sons (for instance in 4.1, 4b, 13, 15, 16), they are here used for females and their descendants. This striking feature of the text has lead to different interpretations. Willi acknowledges the significance of the use of these formulas in reference to Helah and Naarah and argues that the co-wives represent two main segments of the genealogy of Ashhur. Moreover, he explains this configuration with a reference to Tekoa as a town that maintained a reputation as a home of intellectually superior men and women throughout the monarchy.[83] Other scholars deny the impact of the formulas. For example, Knoppers states that the passage provides no opening or closing formulas at all.[84] This surprising statement seems to presuppose that otherwise unambiguous formulas only fulfill their function in the text if they describe the attribution of sons to a male name. In my view, this presupposition is based on extra-textual biases and is not convincingly supported by the Judah genealogies themselves. The text has sufficient linguistic tools at its disposal to indicate segmentation through wives and to attribute sons of several wives to the same father (see above). Still, the genealogy of Ashhur goes beyond this repertoire and unambiguously attributes Ashhur's sons to either Naarah or Helah by means of the relevant formulas. Therefore, in line with Willi, I understand the passage as an outstanding example of attributing descendants to wives by means of an opening and closing formula.

Using an opening and/or closing formula for females rather than males adds a new dimension to the issue of segmentation through wives. Even though Naarah and Helah are mothers of sons whose names have strong geopolitical implications,[85] the genealogy lacks a movement toward integrating and at the same time othering segments, which prevailed in the previous cases. Instead, the sons of Ashhur are directly attributed to his two wives, who are introduced without hierarchy, and who preside over two parallel main branches of the genealogy of Ashhur.[86] In contrast to the strong aspect of othering in the previous cases, here segmentation through co-wives works to express an equal status.

The expression of an equal status has sociocultural implications with respect to the paternal household (בית־אב / *bēt 'āb*). The text conveys a

---

83. For example, the prophet Amos (Amos 1.1) and the wise woman of Tekoa (2 Sam. 14.2). Willi, *1 Chr 1–10*, p. 124.

84. Knoppers, *I Chronicles 1–9*, p. 345.

85. See the names of their sons, which indicate the geopolitical impact of the segments: Temeni and Haahashtari are gentilic names (Japhet, *I&II Chronicles*, p. 108) and Ethnan might refer to Ithnan (Josh. 15.23) in the Negev (Japhet, *I&II Chronicles*, p. 108).

86. So also Willi, *1 Chr 1–10*, p. 124.

coequal dimension of the *bēt 'āb* in which two wives and their descendants have equal status. By doing so, it questions the conceptualization of the *bēt 'āb* in strictly hierarchical terms.[87] This is supported by the parallel mention of the co-wives Adah and Zillah in Gen. 4.17-24 and perhaps also by the mention of the co-secondary wives Ephah and Maacah (2.46, 48), as well as by the references to the co-divorcees Hushim and Baarah (8.8-11).

In conclusion, the passage under consideration unambiguously attributes lineages to the wives Helah and Naarah, who consequently own these lineages. As Helah and Naarah are listed as wives, the passage likewise addresses the issue of segmentation through wives. In this context, the passage stands out for introducing Helah and Naarah as co-wives without indicating a hierarchy between the two. Therefore, the co-wives and owners of lineages initiate a segmentation that conveys difference that is not hierarchically arranged. This function significantly differs from the previously discussed cases of segmentation through wives and secondary wives. In this case, the combination of segmentation through wives and formula-induced genealogical ownership adds a dimension to the discussion of segmentation through wives that was not previously addressed.

Sisters as Genealogical Owners

So far, I have addressed occurrences of wives owning genealogies. In a second step, I shall address occurrences of sisters owning genealogies. The genealogies of Judah attribute lineages to Zeruiah, listed, together with Abigail, as a sister of David (2.16-17), and to the nameless wife of Hodiah, sister of Naham (4.19). I begin with Zeruiah and then proceed to the sister of Naham.

Zeruiah. 1 Chron. 2.16-17 introduces Zeruiah and Abigail in the following way:

> Their sisters: Zeruiah and Abigail. The sons of Zeruiah: Abishai, Joab and Asahel, three. Abigail bore Amasa. And the father of Amasa was Jether the Ishmaelite.

---

87. For the constitution and importance of the *bēt 'āb* see C.J.H. Wright, 'Family', *ABD*, II, p. 762; and *Families in Ancient Israel* (ed. Leo G. Perdue, Joseph Blenkinsopp, John J. Collins and Carol Meyers; The Family, Religion and Culture Series, 7; Louisville, KY: Westminster/John Knox Press, 1997). For the term 'house of the mother' (*bēt 'ēm*) see Bronner, 'Biblical Mothers and Daughters', pp. 187-89; and Athalya Brenner, 'Alternative Families: From the Hebrew Bible to Early Judaisms', unpublished essay based on the paper of the same name delivered at the ISBL in Tartu, Estonia, in July 2010, http://www.uva.nl/over-de-uva/organisatie/medewerkers/content/b/r/a.brenner/a. brenner.html (accessed June 8, 2013).

Zeruiah is listed in the opening formula and assumes the position of head of family, as I have shown in Chapter 4. A most prominent feature in the reference to Zeruiah is that she is listed as a sister and mother of sons without revealing the identity of the father of her sons.[88] Zeruiah's sons are attributed to her name, whereas she is not attributed to a male husband. Instead, the identification as sister attributes Zeruiah to her original family lineage as represented through her brothers (and sister).[89] Zeruiah is introduced side by side with her sister Abigail (2.16-17). Abigail is not listed with an opening or concluding formula. Still, the text makes sure that her son belongs to her lineage by indicating that she gave birth to her son Amasa. This statement integrates Amasa into the Davidic birth line of Abigail. Only then does the text add that Amasa's father was Jether the Ishmaelite. Here, the text does not use a concluding formula, which would eventually attribute Abigail's son to his father. Instead, Jether is mentioned in a gloss, which explains the circumstances but leaves attribution of Amasa with his mother.

In the cases of the sisters Zeruiah and Abigail, female genealogical ownership fulfills the function of linking sons to the lineage of their mothers. This does not concern just any given lineage, but the royal lineage of the house of David. Here, female ownership of the genealogy as realized through sisters achieves situating their descendants in greater proximity to the power center of the genealogies of Judah. The sisters are thus located at a nerve center of the genealogical distribution of power in terms of both domination and participation.

Linking sons to the royal lineage throws a spotlight on the court as a context for possible female agency. The listing of Zeruiah in particular points to a possible presence of women in the political, cultural, religious and administrative life of the court and beyond it. Even though the genealogies of 1 Chronicles 1–9 do not aim to account for particular sociohistorical circumstances, these passages contribute to a discussion of the sociohistorical situation of women at the court and in the upper-class in exilic and postexilic times.[90]

In conclusion, the passage on Zeruiah and Abigail presents the sisters as owners of lineages in order to affiliate these lineages with the power center of the house of David. It brings segmentation through females into effect, even though in this case, they are not listed as wives but as sisters. Again, the combination of segmentation through females and female genealogical ownership adds a genuinely new aspect to the discussion on genealogical ownership.

---

88. A parallel instance of a sister who has sons but is listed without reference to a husband is Hammolecheth, who pertains to the genealogies of Manasseh (7.18).

89. Camp, *Wise, Strange and Holy*, p. 191.

90. For a detailed and nuanced study on the situation of women at the court see Kiesow, *Löwinnen von Juda*, pp. 64-95.

The Nameless Wife of Hodiah, Sister of Naham. The second case of a sister as genealogical owner occurs in the last part of the genealogies of Judah (4.1-23), which includes branches less firmly integrated into Judah than those listed in the first part of its genealogies.[91] In 4.19, the nameless wife of Hodiah, sister of Naham, is the subject of the opening formula.

> The sons of the wife of Hodiah, sister of Naham: the fathers of Keilah the Garmite and Eshtemoa the Maacathite.

The phrase 'wife of Hodiah, sister of Naham' replaces an actual name in the opening formula.[92] The formula attributes to the nameless woman a list of sons, namely the (also nameless) father of Keilah the Garmite and Eshtemoa the Maacathite.[93] The short lineage belongs to a series of short sequences that are only loosely linked together. The strong geopolitical references reinforce the character of loosely arranged sequences by suggesting a certain independence from the main lineages of Judah. Attributing the lineage to the wife of Hodiah, sister of Naham and thus to the birthline of the nameless sister, might be connected to the tendency to indicate independence from the main Judahite lineages.

Female Ownership of Genealogies in Text-Critically Uncertain Passages
Having discussed genealogical ownership of wives and sisters in passages that unambiguously attribute lineages to these women, I next turn to passages that feature female genealogical ownership in text-critically uncertain passages. Next to the passage on the nameless wife of Hodiah, sister of Naham (4.19) discussed above, this concerns the passage on Azubah and Jerioth (2.18-19) and the passage on Bithiah, daughter of Pharaoh (4.17-18). In Chapter 4, I have already discussed the latter passages with regard to fissures in the patriarchal succession and specifically in view of obscured female agency in text-critically difficult passages. The discussion made clear that these passages are extremely difficult to analyze and that, to a certain extent, their meaning remains hidden.

2.18-19. The first case concerns the unclear attribution of sons to either Azubah or Jerioth. In 2.18-19, the opening formula attributes a list of descendants to an ambiguous 'she'.

91. Knoppers, *1 Chronicles 1–9*, pp. 352-56.

92. The Masoretic Text reads אשת הודיה, 'the wife of Hodiah', but the *BHS* suggests reading אשתו היהדיה, 'his wife the Judahite', with reference to the Greek translation and the mentioning of a Jehudite wife in v. 18. See Leslie C. Allen, *The Greek Chronicles: The Relation of the Septuagint of I and II Chronicles to the Masoretic Text, Part 2: Textual Criticism* (VTSup, 25.2; Leiden: E.J. Brill, 1974), p. 137. In line with Japhet, I follow the MT (Japhet, *I&II Chronicles*, p. 103).

93. The number and names of the descendants of the sister of Naham differ in the different textual witnesses. For an overview, see Knoppers, *1 Chronicles 1–9*, p. 342.

וכלב בן־חצרון הוליד את־עזובה אשה ואת־יריעות ואלה בניה ישר ושובב וארדון
ותמת עזובה ויקח־לו כלב את־אפרת ותלד לו את־חור

And Caleb son of Hezron begot (with) Azubah, a woman, and (with) Jerioth.
These were her sons: Jesher and Shobab and Ardon. And Azubah died; and
Caleb took for him Ephrath; and she bore him Hur.

The subject of the formula is indicated by a suffix pronoun in the first person
feminine singular (בניה). As the previous sentence is syntactically unclear,[94]
who owns the lineage, Azubah or Jerioth, must remain open.

4.17-18. The second case concerns the unclear identity of the descendants
of Bithiah, daughter of Pharaoh. In 4.18 MT, the closing formula attributes
descendants to Bithiah, daughter of Pharaoh.

ובן־עזרה יתר ומרד ועפר וילון ותהר את־מרים ואת־שמי ואת־ישבח אבי אשתמע
ואשתו היהדיה ילדה את־ירד אבי גדור ואת־חבר אבי שוכו ואת־יקותיאל אבי זנוח
ואלה בני בתיה בת־פרעה אשר לקח מרד

The son of Ezrah: Jether, Mered, Epher, and Jalon. She conceived Miriam,
Shammai, and Ishbah, the father of Eshtemoa. His wife, the Judahite, bore
Jered, the father of Gedor, Heber, the father of Soco and Jekuthiel, the
father of Zanoah. These are the sons of Bithiah, the daughter of Pharaoh,
whom Mered married.

The passage clearly presents Bithiah as genealogical owner of a family of
sons. However, the difficult state of the text makes it impossible to identify
who the sons of Bithiah in fact are.[95] As in the passage on Azubah and Jerioth, the potential impact of the fact that women own lineages is defused by
the uncertainty of the passages.

Hints of Female Lineages. The uncertain status of the passages has yet
another impact. Both passages may contain hints of a female line from
mother to daughter. In 2.18-19, Jerioth may be listed as the daughter of
Azubah (2.18). In 4.17-18 MT, a certain Miriam may be listed as the daughter of an unidentified 'she' (4.17).

The identification of women as mothers of their daughters and vice
versa indeed occurs in 1 Chronicles 1–9, yet outside of the genealogies
of Judah. The most explicit examples are the genealogies of Esau, which
list the female succession of Mehetabel, daughter of Matred, daughter of
Me-zahab (1 Chron. 1.50).[96] Furthermore, the genealogies of Manasseh
feature a mother–daughter relationship when recounting that Hammolecheth bore Mahlah (1 Chron. 7.18). This passage also stands out because

94. See Chapter 4, pp. 109-11.
95. See Chapter 4, pp. 111-12.
96. Labahn and Ben Zvi, 'Observations on Women', p. 463.

Hammolecheth's daughter Mahlah bears the name of one of the daughters of Zelophehad, who are briefly referred to in 7.15.

In contrast to these examples, the passages on Azubah and Jerioth, as well as on Miriam and a certain 'she', provide only traces of mother–daughter relationships. The uncertain status of the passages prevents this argument from taking shape. This is especially noteworthy as the daughters in the genealogies of Judah and beyond are related to the issue of the continuation of the succession (Sheshan's daughter), as well as to the issue of inheritance (Achsah and the daughters of Zelophehad). Repressing the occurrences of daughters also makes remote the possibilities of female succession and female inheritance, especially in the genealogies of Judah.

Concluding Discussion

The close reading of passages that attribute lineages to women on the basis of opening and closing formulas has shown that female genealogical ownership works in two directions, depending on whether its protagonists are introduced as wives or as sisters. In the case of wives, specifically the co-wives Helah and Naarah, genealogical ownership facilitates distribution of lineage segments on equal terms. In the case of sisters, specifically the sisters Zeruiah and Abigail, genealogical ownership affiliates lineage segments to the power center of the house of David.[97]

Next to the actual functions fulfilled by the attribution of lineages to women in the text, the occurrence of genealogical ownership has a socio-cultural impact. The passages show that the genealogies use references to women to particular ends, and, in the course of doing so, do not shy away from listing them as genealogical owners. Listing women in the position of owners of lineages does not make the text illogical or absurd. It seems that the idea of women who were critically important to the status and identity of their descendants made perfect sense within the horizon of contemporaneous authors and readers.

Attributing segments of a lineage to a name denotes a specific instance of segmentation through women. However, segmentation through wives and sisters who own lineages is less about visibly negotiating identity and alterity, or explicitly othering groups, than is the case in the examples of segmentation through wives and secondary wives I discussed earlier. Instead, the combination of segmentation through women and female genealogical ownership aims to convey equal status and to express unambiguous affiliation with central lineages. Given the usual discourse on female

---

97. A third way of linking the identity of a descendant to a female is his/her naming through his mother. The genealogies of Judah feature one instance of naming through the mother in 4.9-10. Here, the nameless mother of Jabez names her son in a speech act (4.9).

segmentation in Judah, these latter functions come as a surprise and are not usually remarked upon. Both the functions to convey parity and to affiliate segments with central lineages exceed the classical descriptions of segmentation through women and draw a nuanced picture of female involvement in segmentation processes.

4. *Sisters and Shaped Gaps*

The discussion of formal genealogical ownership has shifted attention from wives to sisters. This shift implies a shift in attention from segmentation and horizontal genealogical structures to depth and vertical linear genealogical structures. Linear structures allow a genealogy to stretch back in time and to potentially expand into the future.[98] They are formally described as the depth of a genealogy. In the genealogies of Judah and beyond, the depth of a lineage serves to legitimize power claims on the basis of continuity, (male) succession and reference to ancestral traditions. Such claims might concern public offices and cultic authority and also normative memory. Especially in ancient Near Eastern cultures, the identities of individuals and groups were intimately linked to their roots and social context. As a consequence, '[c]urrent social relationships or political hierarchies may be claimed, explained, or ratified by recourse to genealogy'.[99]

The gendered fragments of the genealogies of Judah involve linear structures and the depth of a lineage in relation to the relational/functional role of sisters. Sisters are related to a given linear segment by birth.[100] They belong to the father/son cohesion until they relocate themselves to a new cohesion through marriage. In the previously analyzed passage on Zeruiah and Abigail (2.16-17), their participation in linear structures by birth has enabled their attributing of descendants to the Davidic lineage.

The shift from wives to sisters also implies a focus on the royal lineage, as demonstrated by the fact that the functions fulfilled by the sisters Zeruiah and Abigail are closely linked to their being members of the Davidic family. Before I turn my full attention to the role of sisters in the genealogies of Judah, I will therefore discuss more generally the references to females, both wives and sisters, in the Davidic power center.

The Wives and Sisters of the House of David
The genealogy of the house of David is divided into two parts. The first part (3.1-9) lists wives and sons of David according to their place of birth—Hebron or Jerusalem. While the six wives who gave birth to David's sons

---

98. Wilson, *Genealogies and History*, p. 21.

99. Knoppers, *I Chronicles 1–9*, p. 251.

100. Camp, *Wise, Strange and Holy*, p. 191.

at Hebron are listed one by one (3.1-4a), the mother of Solomon is the only
wife listed by name for Jerusalem (3.4b-9). 1 Chron. 3.5 lists the mother
of Solomon as 'Bath-shua daughter of Ammiel' rather than as 'Bathsheba
daughter of Eliam' as she is called in Samuel–Kings (e.g. 2 Sam. 11.3). Both
pairs of names, Bath-shua/Bath-sheba and Ammiel/Eliam, may be read as
variations on the same names.[101] However, rendering Bathsheba as Bath-
shua also introduces a subtext, which links the Bathsheba of 2 Samuel 11 to
the Bath-shua of Genesis 38 already referred to in 1 Chron. 2.3.[102]

The first part of the genealogy of the house of David concludes with
the statement that all these were the sons of David, except for the sons of
his secondary wives (3.1-9a). It then adds ותמר אחותם, 'and their sister:
Tamar' (3.9b). Like Bath-shua/Bathsheba, Tamar is one of the few women
in 1 Chronicles 1–9 who has a pre-existence in biblical literature. Listing her at this point adds the narrative of the rape of Tamar by her brother
Amnon as recounted in 2 Samuel 13 to the female-gendered backdrop,
which has already been introduced by the reference to Bath-Shua/Bath-
sheba. Moreover, it reinforces the reference to 2.3-4, since the genealogies
of Judah refer to the pair Bath-shua and Tamar twice.

The second part of the genealogy of the house of David provides a
mainly linear genealogy (3.10-24). It includes the list of kings from Solomon to Josiah (3.10–14) and the lineage from Josiah to the sons of Elioenai
(3.15-24). The latter includes several sons—and one sister—for each generation. The lineage brings to the fore the vital and unbroken succession of
the Davidic lineage.[103] As the 'centerpiece' of the genealogies of Judah,[104] the
succession of Davidic kings and heirs establishes a power center. The sole
woman who is listed in this inner power center is Shelomith (3.19). The
text introduces Shelomith as the sister of three of the sons of Zerubbabel by
means of using the sister formula.

> And the sons of Pedaiah: Zerubbabel and Shimei. And the sons of Zerub-
> babel: Meshullam and Hananiah. And Shelomith: their sister. And Hashu-
> bah, and Ohel, and Berechiah, and Hasadiah, and Jushab-hesed, five (1
> Chron. 3.19-20).

The question of why Shelomith is listed in the succession of Davidic heirs
can be approached from different angles. A first approach would identify
her as a historical person of some importance.[105] This assumption may be

---

101. Japhet, *I&II Chronicles*, p. 96.
102. The link has already been highlighted by Japhet (Japhet, *I&II Chronicles*, p. 96).
103. Knoppers, *I Chronicles 1–9*, p. 334.
104. Knoppers, *I Chronicles 1–9*, p. 336.
105. So Japhet, who argues that the listed daughters and sisters are, in general, important figures (but see Hazzelelponi in 4.3 or the sister of Naham in 4.19). Japhet, *I&II
Chronicles*, p. 100.

backed up by the Shelomith seal, which dates from the late sixth century and says 'Belonging to Shelomith handmaid of Elnathan the governor'.[106] The term אמה, 'handmaid/maidservant', has been interpreted as indicating the status of a high-standing functionary, parallel to the term עבד, 'manservant'.[107] This is especially plausible given its location, an official archive, where it was found together with the seal of the province Yehud and those of other male dignitaries.[108] If the owner of the seal were identified with the Shelomith of 3.19 as suggested by Eric Meyers, the genealogical reference would indeed point to a high-ranking female functionary of Davidic descent.[109] In my view, based on available evidence, it is not possible to clearly identify the owner of the seal as the Shelomith of 3.19.[110] Still, it is important to bear in mind that individual female figures may have been so important in the memory of emerging Judaism that it was not possible to leave them out of the genealogical identity performance.

Willi provides an alternative approach, arguing on a text-immanent level. He explains the listing of Shelomith as a means of explicitly closing the first group of sons of Zerubbabel. The reference would then divide the sons of Zerubbabel into two groups, one born in captivity, one born back in Jerusalem, a division that would establish a parallel with the two groups of sons of David, one born in Hebron, one in Jerusalem.[111] Willi's argument is interesting, especially because it draws on the formulaic character of the reference to Shelomith, even if not explicitly so. Still, the argument does not explain why the division is not realized by means of a different mother or a direct geographical note. Moreover, it does not contextualize the reference to Shelomith with parallel references to sisters in the genealogies of Judah and beyond, for example with the reference to Tamar, who is listed with the same formula in 3.9.

In my view, none of the suggested explanations provide a satisfactory explanation as to why Shelomith is included on the list. Still, two important preliminary observations are worth noting. First, Shelomith is listed in formulaic language. Second, because of its openness, the phrase provokes speculation about the meaning and story behind the reference. In my view, the openness of the passage holds a certain potential, especially in view of

---

106. Kiesow, *Löwinnen von Juda*, p. 95.

107. Eric M. Meyers, 'The Shelomith Seal and the Judean Restoration: Some Additional Considerations', *Eretz Israel* 18 (1985), pp. 33-38 (35).

108. See Kiesow, *Löwinnen von Juda*, p. 186; and Hennie M. Marsman, *Women in Ugarit and Israel: Their Social and Religious Position in the Context of the Ancient Near East* (Leiden: E.J. Brill, 2003), pp. 653-54.

109. Meyers, 'The Shelomith Seal', p. 34.

110. So also Japhet, who notes that Avigad would make the identification, but does not reveal her own position (Japhet, *I&II Chronicles*, p. 100).

111. Willi, *1 Chr 1–10*, p. 117.

its combination with formulaic language. It serves as a springboard for further investigation into the inclusion of seemingly dysfunctional sisters and will eventually lead to my proposition of a structure of shaped gaps.

Sisters in the Genealogies of Judah

Tamar and Shelomith are but two of six sisters in the genealogies of Judah. After the Davidic succession, the text turns back to Judah (4.1a). It first provides a linear lineage from Judah to Ahumai and Lahad with a depth of eight generations (4.1-2). The text then changes style and provides a series of loosely connected segmented genealogies. The first of these segmented genealogies lists the descendants of the father of Etam, as well as their sister Hazzelelponi (4.3b).[112]

> And these were the sons of Etam: Jezreel, Ishma and Idbash. And the name
> of their sister: Hazzelelponi.

Hazzelelponi is introduced in formulaic language and with special emphasis on her name.[113] She is not otherwise known in biblical literature.[114] Again, it remains an open question why she is included in the genealogy.

The three remaining sisters in the genealogies of Judah are Zeruiah and Abigail, sisters of David and mothers of sons, and the nameless sister of Naham, wife of Hodiah and likewise mother of sons (4.19). Zeruiah, Abigail and the nameless sister of Naham were discussed earlier under the theme of segmentation and genealogical ownership. In contrast to Tamar, Shelomith and Hazzelelponi, who primarily pertain to linear structures, these mother-sisters engage both linear and segmented structures. As mothers, they enable and determine lineage segments. As sisters, they link these segments to their own birth line. The potential of this double position is acknowledged in the formal genealogical ownership awarded to Zeruiah (and Abigail) and the sister of Naham. Zeruiah and Abigail and the nameless sister of Naham are figures who marry the potential of linear and segmented structures. In this

---

112. I read 4.3a as 'And these (are the ones of) the father of Etam...' (MT: ואלה אבי עיטם יזרעאל וישמא וידבש) without adopting the change of אבי to υἱοί in LXX*. See Willi, *1 Chr 1–10*, pp. 70, 111.

113. 4.3b reads ושם אחותם הצללפוני, 'And the name of their sister: Hazzelelponi'. The last element of her name may be a dittography of the following name 'Penuel' (4.4). See Japhet, *I&II Chronicles*, p. 107.

114. Cheryl Exum borrows the name Hazzelelponi for the nameless mother of Samson (Judges 13) in line with Midrash Rabbah on Num. 10.5. Exum gives names to the nameless women in Judges in order to 'restore' them to their 'full subject position'. J. Cheryl Exum, 'Judges: Encoded Messages to Women', in *Feminist Biblical Interpretation: A Compendium of Critical Commentary on the Books of the Bible and Related Literature* (ed. Luise Schottroff, Marie-Theres Wacker and Hans Martin Rumscheidt; trans. Lisa E. Dahill; Grand Rapids, MI: Eerdmans, 2012), pp. 112-27 (121).

context, genealogical agency and ownership inherent to the position of sisters is activated through procreation.[115]

In contrast to the sisters who are also listed as mothers, the potential attribution of genealogical agency and ownership to the sisters who do not procreate seems to be trapped in a gap (Shelomith and Hazzelelponi) or in disenfranchisement (Tamar). Tamar and Hazzelelponi are both listed at the formal transition from segmented to linear structures. Tamar is listed at the transition from the rich beginnings of the Davidic reign in 3.1-9 to the linear succession in 3.10-24. Hazzelelponi is listed at the transition between the linear structures of the Davidic succession and the second genealogy of Judah in 3.10-24 and 4.1-2 on the one hand and the segmented, loosely affiliated portions in 4.3-23 on the other. These positions may allude to the potential inherent in the crossroads between linear and segmented structures, which may possibly—and ideally—be filled by sisters who also identify segments of sons. However, the sisters who stand close to the power center of the genealogies of Judah and the house of David do not utilize the potential of genealogical agency and ownership. Instead, the potentially powerful position of sister as related to depth but not segmentation remains void and is indicated by a gap.

The difference between sisters who procreate and own lineages on the one hand, and sisters who are listed as sonless on the other, can also be traced in the remaining references to sisters throughout 1 Chronicles 1–9.[116] The genealogies of Manasseh list Hammolecheth as a sister who has children (7.18) and also holds a prominent position, as I have discussed in Chapter 3. In contrast to Hammolecheth, the remaining sisters are listed without indication of descendants: Timna (1.39, part of Edom), Maacah (7.15, part of Manasseh), as well as Serah and Shua (7.30, 32, both part of Asher). Additional attributions such as the information that daughter Sheerah built three cities (7.24) are likewise absent. The potential of their position as sisters is not realized but remains enclosed in a gap.

The Sister Formula and the Structure of Shaped Gaps
The discussion of the references to sisters in the genealogies of Judah brought into focus the difference between sisters who fulfill functions in relation to their descendants and sisters whose function in the text has so far remained open. In a next step, I shall focus on the latter category of

---

115. The potential of the double position of sister and mother may involve issues of inheritance, for example in the case of Zeruiah and in the case of the daughters of Zelophehad.

116. In addition to the six sisters listed in the genealogies of Judah, 1 Chron. 1–9 lists two sisters in Manasseh (7.15, 18), two sisters in Asher (7.30, 32) and one sister in Edom (1.39).

sisters both within and beyond Judah. 1 Chronicles 1–9 generally includes a significant number of sisters who are listed without further indication of why they are included. Still, they are included and not only by name but in characteristic formalized language. This formalized language constitutes a space in the text, which persists even though it is not filled by further information but remains as a gap.

The *sister formula* in 1 Chronicles 1–9 lists sisters as the last item in a list of sons. The name of the sister is then supplemented by an apposition (the noun אחות with a pronominal suffix third person masculine plural), which identifies her as the sister of the previously listed sons (3.9, 19; 7.30, 32). Syntactically, the sisters are presented as part of the respective group of sons. Only after having been listed as one of the sons does the apposition qualify them as a sister. For example, 7.32 reads וחבר הוליד את־יפלט ואת־שומר ואת־חותם ואת־שועא אחותם, 'Heber begot Japhlet, and Shomer, and Hotham; and Shua: their sister'. In a variation, the sister formula first provides the relational/functional term אחות (again with a pronominal suffix third person masculine singular/plural) and then provides the name of the sister(s) (1.39; 2.16; 4.3; 7.15, 18). In 4.3 and 7.15 ושם is added (and *the name* of their/his sister was PN1).[117]

The concurrence of formalized language and a lack of indication of the function of the sisters institutes a phenomenon that I have called a structure of 'shaped gaps'.[118] The notion of *shaped gaps* does not primarily refer to the often tacit and implicit gaps in the logical progression of the text, as Meir Sternberg has described them.[119] Instead, the notion refers to gaps that are specifically pointed out to bring them into focus. Shaped gaps indicate formal vacancies in the text. They explicitly mark the absence of information pertaining to the figures at their center.

In the genealogical context, the occurrence of shaped gaps has a particular impact. Segmented and linear genealogies convey the idea of a genealogical stream that branches out in a process of continuous movement. In contrast, the notion of shaped gaps represents the idea of still-water areas. These still-water areas do not bring the entire genealogical stream to a halt. Rather, they convey a sense of standstill or downtime as part of the movement, a paradoxical dynamic of stillness within the genealogical stream.

---

117. In the particular case of 1.39, the reference to Timna, the sister of Lotan, concludes the list of Lotan's sons (rather than brothers).

118. Ingeborg Löwisch, 'Genealogies, Gender and the Politics of Memory: 1 Chronicles 1–9 and the Documentary Film "Mein Leben Teil 2"', in *Memory in Biblical Narrative and Beyond* (ed. Athalya Brenner and Frank Polak; Sheffield: Sheffield Phoenix Press, 2009), pp. 228-56 (243-44).

119. Meir Sternberg, *The Poetics of Biblical Narrative: Ideological Literature and the Drama of Reading* (Indiana Studies in Biblical Literature; Bloomington, IN: Indiana University Press, 1987), pp. 186-90, 222-37, 258-63.

Claudia Camp has identified a similar paradox with regard to the sisters of the priestly lineages.[120] Camp describes the sisters of the priestly line as the other within. They are part of the lineage by birth. At the same time, they are distinct from the ideology of male priestly succession by gender. This paradox is unbearable, and as 'strangers-within-the-family' the sisters have to be narratively transformed into outsiders. Miriam, sister of Aaron and Moses, is a case in point.[121] Camp's analysis is most convincing. In terms of Chronicles, it highlights the peculiarity of the structure of shaped gaps in the Chronicles genealogies. Here, the sisters are not (narratively) transformed into outsiders who channel the other. Instead, the structure of shaped gaps opens a space for the paradoxical women who belong to the lineage in terms of birth, while at the same time are other in terms of gender. Shaped gaps embody a static moment in a process that is otherwise presented in terms of movement. The sisters represent something that belongs to the genealogies but is also alien to them.

The example that proves the rule is the reference to Miriam in the genealogies of Levi. Here, Miriam, sister of Moses and Aaron, is listed among the בנם, 'sons', of Amram (5.29 MT). The paradox is not tolerated and Miriam is integrated into the lineage as בן, 'son'.

The structure of shaped gaps encompasses another paradox. Shaped gaps repress information. But they simultaneously mark that moment of repression. Shaped gaps work in two directions. As gaps, they repress knowledge about the functional and maybe also sociohistorical impact of the women figures who are identified as sisters. As explicit formulas, they indicate that there is more to remember than the texts actually disclose. Recurring again and again, they invite projection and gap filling at the level of reading and reception.

In conclusion, reading 1 Chronicles 1–9 for its use of formulaic language, thus along the grain, shows that in the case of the sister formula, the purposeful use of formulaic language results in a structure of visible and persisting gaps. The explicit character of the gaps suggests gap filling, which enables different interpretations, as well as the renegotiating of stories and meanings in the process of gap filling. The openness of the shaped gaps and the invitation to gap filling and projection is important because it is an invitation to make sense of repressed memories in an active way. This is especially important for the memory act in response to trauma because it encourages the active addressing of the past. By doing so it works toward appropriating the past and inscribing oneself into it. In order to demonstrate how this might work, I now focus on one particular shaped gap, the reference to the sister Tamar (3.9) and suggest a way of filling this gap.

120. Camp, *Wise, Strange and Holy*, p. 191.
121. Camp, *Wise, Strange and Holy*, p. 191.

Gap Filling: Tamar and Bathsheba/Bath-shua

Tamar is the sister of the sons of David. She has a pre-life in 2 Samuel 13. Thus, in her case, gap filling has a clear starting point. Even though this is not the case with most shaped gaps, the example of Tamar can serve as an example of the powerful impact of gap filling.

Tamar is listed at the end of the first part of the genealogy of the house of David in close proximity to Bathsheba, here listed as Bath-shua, daughter of Ammiel (3.5, 9). As pointed out earlier, rendering the name Bathsheba as Bath-shua draws a connecting line to the beginning of the Judah genealogies (2.3-4). Both passages now provide the same name pair, Tamar and Bath-shua. The first pair consists of Tamar and Bath-shua, daughter-in-law and wife of Judah (2.3-4). The second pair is Tamar and Bath-shua/Bathsheba, daughter and wife of David (3.4b-9). The two woman figures of the family of Judah come to form an intertextual background for the reading of the two woman figures in the house of David.[122] The related narratives of Genesis 38 (Tamar and Bath-shua), 2 Samuel 11 (Bath-shua/Bathsheba), and 2 Samuel 13 (Tamar) form part of this background. All three narratives have sexuality at their center. Moreover, they all address sexual encounters that go beyond proper normative sexuality.[123] But the narratives differ significantly in their depiction of deviant sexuality. The narratives of Tamar and Bathsheba in 2 Samuel 13 and 11 are narratives of sexual violence and of neglected female sexual agency and decision-making.[124] In contrast, the story of Tamar in Genesis 38 exposes self-determined female sexual agency and trickery.[125] In the former case, the intertexts address sexual violence at the expense of the woman who is made the object of this violence (2 Samuel 11 and 13). In the latter case, the intertext addresses sexual intercourse that is initiated by the woman herself and forms part of her agency and trickery (Genesis 38).

Establishing Genesis 38 as a background for the references to Bath-shua/ Bathsheba and Tamar in the genealogies of the house of David enables

---

122. Japhet explains the occurrence of Bath-shua as the adaptation of the name of Judah's wife 'following a general inclination to parallelism between David's household and that of Judah' without further discussing the implications of the adaptation (Japhet, *I&II Chronicles*, p. 96).

123. Susan Niditch, 'The Wronged Woman Righted: An Analysis of Genesis 38', *HTR* 72 (1979), pp. 143-49 (149).

124. For a thorough analysis of 2 Sam. 11 see J. Cheryl Exum, 'Raped by the Pen', in *Fragmented Women: Feminist (Sub)Versions of Biblical Narratives* (ed. J. Cheryl Exum; JSOTSup, 163; Sheffield: Sheffield Academic Press, 1993), pp. 170-201. For an analysis of 2 Sam. 13 see Mieke Bal, Fokkelien van Dijk-Hemmes and Grietje van Ginneken, *Und Sara lachte: Patriarchat und Widerstand in biblischen Geschichten* (Münster: Morgana-Frauenbuchverlag, 1988), pp. 51-74.

125. See my analysis of Gen. 38 in Chapter 4.

an important shift in understanding the nature of the sexuality involved. 2 Samuel 11 and 13 as primary intertexts for the references to Tamar and Bath-shua/Bathsheba in 1 Chron. 3.5, 9 connote sexual violence and disenfranchisement. Reading Genesis 38 as a further intertext adds connotations of female sexual agency and trickery.

The implications of this shift may be analyzed from opposing perspectives. It may function to imbue the Tamar and Bathsheba of 2 Samuel with sexual agency and imply their trickery. From this perspective, the link between 3.4b-9 and 2.3-4 leads to a reassessment of the sexual violence in the Samuel narratives as seduction and can easily lead to blaming the victims. It likewise unburdens Amnon and David and trivializes their actions. Such a perspective corresponds with Anne-Mareike Wetter's readings of women figures in 1–2 Chronicles.[126] Wetter argues that the books notoriously work in favor of David, thereby diminishing negative aspects of this figure even at the expense of the female figures connected to him.[127]

From a second perspective, the shift in connotation of sexuality may function as a critical comment on the narratives in 2 Samuel 11 and 13 from the perspective of Genesis 38.[128] Such a perspective is adopted by Susan Niditch in her reflections on the relationship between 2 Samuel 11 and 13 and Genesis 38. Niditch addresses the shift in modes of sexuality but then focuses on the crucial differences in terms of social fabric. The sexual incidents in 2 Samuel 11 and 13 result in the murder of Bathsheba's husband, Uriah, and in strife and murder within the royal family. They lead to the destruction of the social fabric. In contrast, the sexual incident as provoked by Tamar in Genesis 38 eventually repairs the social fabric and reconstitutes the line.[129] From this second perspective, establishing Genesis 38 as an intertext for the references to Tamar and Bath-Shua/Bathsheba in the genealogies of the house of David implies the re-empowerment of the women and a critical comment on the house of David.

In conclusion, the dissimilar directions the gap filling may take in the case of Tamar and Bath-shua/Bathsheba illustrates that gaps provide scope for divergent interpretations and may serve as a focal point for renegotiations of power. Dealing with the issue in text-critical terms would present yet another position in the (re)negotiation of power. Even though Niditch's focus on the difference in social fabric speaks more to me than Wetter's

---

126. Anne-Mareike Wetter, 'Verschuivende Visies: De Kronist over de rol van de vrouw', in *Nederlands theologisch tijdschrift* 65.3 (2011), pp. 227-41.

127. Wetter, 'Verschuivende Visies', pp. 240-41.

128. See Fokkelien van Dijk-Hemmes, 'Tamar and the Limits of Patriarchy: Between Rape and Seduction', in *Anti-Covenant: Counter-Reading Women's Lives in the Hebrew Bible* (ed. Mieke Bal; Sheffield: Sheffield Academic Press, 1989), pp. 135-56; and Niditch, 'The Wronged Woman Righted', pp. 143-49.

129. Niditch, 'The Wronged Woman Righted', p. 149.

approach, my interest is not in arguing for one of the different possibilities, or proposing a third analysis. Rather than aiming for a coherent analysis, my position is that the ambiguity and the consequent possibility of adapting various positions is the function of the shaped gap.

The 'not having to decide' is a quality of the genealogies that is different from the ambiguous back and forth between granting complexity and curtailing it that I brought into focus in Chapter 4. This new quality is closer to the notion of the paradox that became apparent in the film analysis than to the ambiguity that regularly prevails in the text. In Chapter 4, I argued that the ambiguous character of the memory act tends to make it relevant only for those privileged by the patriarchal rules of succession. The gaps' openness and the paradoxical character of the structure of shaped gaps are counterpoints to this tendency and provide a starting point for a counter-present memory act.

Concluding Discussion

In conclusion, references to sisters form a web of references throughout the genealogies of Judah and beyond. The web has strong nodes (the sister-mothers), weak nodes (the disenfranchised sister), and nodes with potential (the shaped gaps). Significant differences exist between sisters who procreate and sisters who do not. The former embody cross-points between dynamics of segmentation and depth. They fulfill central genealogical functions. The latter pertain to dynamics of depth, but their position and function is difficult to grasp. However, the use of formulas establishes a structure of shaped gaps, which marks the repression of functions and narratives pertaining to the sisters who do not procreate. The explicit marking of absence consitutes the paradoxical character of the structure of shaped gaps. The paradoxical character of the structure continues in its introduction of static moments as part of the otherwise dynamic genealogy genre. Finally, the structure of shaped gaps invites renegotiation of power by a process of gap filling.

The context of socializing 1 Chronicles 1–9 and *My Life Part 2* provides another perspective for understanding the structure of shaped gaps. The analysis of *My Life Part 2* has highlighted that the filmmaker's gynealogy performance implies a shift from the vertical dimension of genealogical succession and reproduction to a horizontal dimension of memory production. The shift is important because it opens up space for appropriating the traumatic past and eventually for the filmmaker's inscribing of herself into her gynealogy. In the film, the horizontal dimension of memory production is conceptualized as a homoerotic intra-generational context and represents a second-generation site of memory performance.

In the Chronicles genealogies, sisters represent a genealogical position that stands apart from the vertical dimension of genealogical succession.

Being presented as sisters rather than daughters, wives, or mothers (even though they might be married and have children) places them beyond the heterosexual reproduction matrix. The horizontal dimension of gendered genealogy composition, as suggested in *My Life Part 2*, invites reassessment of their meaning in 1 Chronicles 1–9. Standing outside the genealogical stream, the structure of sisters might symbolize a trace of the idea of a location of the production of memory beyond reproduction. Following Malin Wahlberg's definition of the trace as 'a constituting sign in the narrative reinvention of history' rather than an imprint of what happened in the past, this line of thought brings this function of the sisters and the accompanying gaps in the text to the fore without diving into historical speculation.[130] Instead, the notion of the shaped gap that conveys a sense of standstill amid the imagery of a genealogical stream can be reconsidered as a marker of a horizontal dimension of genealogy performance, which can function as a paradoxical counterpart to the vertical focus on the genealogy and historiography of the book.

In conclusion, the reoccurrence of sisters in the genealogies of Judah as well as the structure of shaped gaps throughout 1 Chronicles 1–9 add crucial aspects to the functions of the gendered fragments in the genealogy composition. First, sisters are the women who are most directly related to the linear structures of the genealogy composition. In this position, they attribute descendants to the linear lineages they belong to. Second, sisters feature in the structure of shaped gaps (especially those sisters who do not have children). The structure has a paradoxical character because it represses memories while at the same time highlighting the repression and because it conveys standstill in the genealogical flow. This paradox adds to the ambiguity that prevails in the text, thereby changing the quality of the memory act. In this context, the structure of shaped gaps enables gap filling and the negotiation of interpretations. By doing so, it encourages an active engagement with the past that is especially important for memory acts in response to trauma, as well as for the possibility of appropriating a traumatic past. Finally, the position of the sisters provides a trace of knowledge of the importance of a horizontal location of memory production along with the vertical genealogical succession. The functions of sisters in the text are closely linked to the use of formulas. In the case of the sisters, reading along the formulas, and thus along the grain of the text, has led to understanding a new dimension of the text and a critical taxonomical structure of the archive.

130. Malin Wahlberg, *Documentary Time: Film and Phenomenology* (Minneapolis, MN: University of Minnesota Press, 2008), p. 103.

Archives

5. *Patterns of the Genealogical Memory Act*

Eric Ketelaar has described archives as 'repositories of meaning', which contain obvious as well as manifold hidden meanings. As repositories of meaning, archives can yield new significance over and over, and it is in this openness and potentiality of archives that their power lies.[131] Ketelaar's definition of the archive is an excellent description of the archive of genealogies in 1 Chronicles 1–9, as well as of the process I have initiated by reading the genealogies from the angle of their gendered fragments. Exploring the gendered fragments has indeed revealed hidden meanings in a cluster of passages that are usually passed by. Specifically, analysis of the taxonomy of female-gendered fragments of the genealogies of Judah has revealed two main groups of ideas active in the archive's memory performance. In a first group of ideas, female-gendered passages operate in a system of normatively prescribing relationships. They work in line with the broader attempt of the text to gain dominance in defining Israel. Examples of this dynamic are processes of othering by means of segmentation through wives, as well as the attribution of segments to the Davidic power center by means of formally attributing lineages to sisters in the Davidic family. In a second group of ideas, female-gendered passages initiate a dynamic of disrupting and complicating the continuous genealogical flow by means of adding gaps, fissures and ambiguities. They work toward establishing a subtext that introduces the notions of fraction, complexity and paradox to the genealogical memory act.

These groups of ideas relate to the gendered fragments. At the same time, they are starting points for understanding the ways in which 1 Chronicles 1–9 as a larger unit deals with the literary and sociopolitical inheritance of Israel. They are central for understanding how the archive of genealogies functions in order to make sense of the past in a way that allows advancing proper interests in the present. Therefore, engaging hidden meanings of the gendered fragments in the understanding of 1 Chronicles 1–9 also allows for reassessing the significance of the genealogical archive within the literature of the Second Temple period.

Advancing Predominance in Defining Israel
The close reading has shown that references to women create structures that are involved in establishing a system of highly nuanced relationships. These structures serve to overtly negotiate belonging and difference in the context of ambiguous and paradoxical relations; to include and simultaneously other segments that are more obviously different in terms of ethnic

---

131. Eric Ketelaar, 'Tactic Narratives: The Meanings of Archives', *Archival Science* 1 (2001), pp. 131-41 (139).

and geographical difference; to convey parity between segments of a lineage; and to link lineage segments to the Davidic power center. All these functions participate in identifying, locating and assessing segments of the lineages of Judah and beyond. Hence, the gendered fragments are significantly involved in performing identity and alterity, specifically in establishing hierarchies and determining the position of singular segments in these hierarchies.

Establishing hierarchies and determining positions takes place on the basis of a well-defined distinction between center and periphery. In the genealogies of Judah, the Davidic lineage and Jerusalem have the status of an undisputed center (3.1-24). Additional lineages of Judah are divided into central lineages (2.3-55) and marginal ones (4.1-23).[132] This centrality of David and Jerusalem continues throughout 1 Chronicles 1–9. The concurrence of integrating segments into Judah on the one hand and clearly defining center and periphery on the other, increases the text's normative power of definition. Both the inclusion of groups into Judah and providing them with particular and nuanced positions turns Judah into an ethnically and socially complex entity.[133] However, this process is not innocent. On the contrary, it involves the normative determination of the status of the individual segments of the Judah genealogies in relation to its undisputed center. As Knoppers puts it with regards to the author(s) of 1 Chronicles 1–9: 'Writers are not only shaped by their circumstances, they also seek to shape those circumstances.'[134] As a consequence, genealogical memory production is revealed as intimately linked to the struggle for predominance in defining both Judah and Israel.

That the power of definition is inherent in the genealogies is further supported by the broader layout of 1 Chronicles 1–9. The genealogies stretch back into the narrative past. This provides a potent tool to legitimate any claim the text might make with references to the time of David, the ancestral period, or even the time of creation. The genealogies likewise stretch out horizontally. They map an all-inclusive picture of Israel, constituted by its many tribes as well as numerous additional groups and locations far beyond the actual territories of the Persian province Yehud.[135] Stretching back and branching out, while at the same time focusing on Jerusalem as the center of Davidic and priestly traditions, makes manifest the claim that those who represent the Davidic and priestly traditions in Jerusalem are the legitimate inheritors of the entire tradition and represent Judaism in its entirety. For example, the archive of genealogies makes a strong case for the

---

132. Knoppers, *I Chronicles 1–9*, p. 356.
133. So Knoppers, 'Intermarriage, Social Complexity and Ethnic Diversity'.
134. Knoppers, *I Chronicles 1–9*, p. 105.
135. Japhet, 'Conquest and Settlement', pp. 208-210.

claim that all inhabitants of Samaria and Yehud are part of Israel—as long as they accept that it centers on Jerusalem and stands under the hegemony of circles that can (genealogically) substantiate their claim to the Davidic and/or priestly inheritance.

An identity performance that addresses the 'who-is-who' and 'who-is-where' of Judah for the purpose of defining the position of groups within Judah (and Israel) is extremely relevant to the sociopolitical concerns that form the backdrop of the archive of genealogies.[136] For example, gaining predominance in defining the memory and identity of Judah (and Israel) helped to achieve predominance in negotiations concerning political and religious offices and land claims. Many structural functions of the gendered fragments are at the center of bringing this twofold interest into effect. In other words, the genealogies provide a blueprint for the self-conception of Judah (and Israel) at the time of the manufacture of the text. Significant parts of the gendered fragments are involved in setting up this self-conception. Their structural functions add to advancing the related claim to predominance in defining Judaism when it had just begun to emerge.

The participation of women in continuing the line and developing a nuanced picture of Israel is intimately bound to the need of the texts for a variety of agents in defining Israel. In consequence, I think that the inclusion of women is functional rather than politically motivated. Yet the extensive use of women figures, for segmentation purposes or in cases of endangered lineages, creates a strong presence of women that initiates its own dynamics. This strong presence fuels a dynamic of including women, which, at times, seems to develop a life of its own. Women figures without clear-cut functions slip in, and indications of different realities behind the texts become visible. In fact, the many and different occurrences of women communicate a process of competing for participation on different levels of sociopolitical, economic and religious life.

In conclusion, I see a mainly functional motivation as the basis of the broad involvement of women in the genealogy composition. However, the references to women unfold with a certain independence, which allows a glimpse of a multilayered and contested reality behind the texts. This twist in the texts adds a second facet to the quality of the memory act, which I have described as gendered subtext. Hence, along with the text's primary concern in achieving predominance in defining Israel, the genealogical archive features a second group of ideas that evolve around the text's gendered subtext. This second group of ideas makes the memory act complex and ambiguous, and, by doing so, adds to its meaning in response to the fractured past.

136. See Chapter 3 above.

Establishing a Gendered Subtext

Having discussed the first central group of ideas that are characteristic of the genealogical memory act, I now discuss the second group of ideas that are central to it. The genealogies of Judah describe relationships in meticulous ways. Yet, they also leave things open and contain unresolved aspects. Most important in this respect are patterns of fissures and ambivalences in the patriarchal succession, which I have examined in Chapter 4 and the structure of shaped gaps, which adds connotations of unfilled spaces, stillness, and dysfunction to the archive of genealogies. These notions belong to an aspect of the taxonomy of the archive that exceeds achieving predominance in defining Israel and advancing related power claims.

An example of this aspect of the archive's taxonomy is the genealogy of the house of David in 3.10-24. It conveys a strong sense of continuity and the unbroken vitality of the Davidic lineage.[137] It clearly participates in the textual quest to define and control power relations. Yet continuity and vitality are interrupted by a sense of stillness and dysfunction with the inclusion of the sister Shelomith (3.19), as well as additional sisters in this lineage (3.9 and 2.16-17). The occurrence of Shelomith establishes a counterpoint within the Davidic lineage and necessitates an additional understanding of the aim of the genealogy performance.

Reading the Bible text alongside *My Life Part 2* suggests a particular *Paradox* alternative perspective on the interpretation of seemingly dysfunctional structures, namely the notion of paradox. In *My Life Part 2*, paradox is an important way of dealing with breaks and discontinuity in the family lineage. In terms of socializing the Judah genealogies and *My Life Part 2*, the notion of paradox can be engaged as a productive means for making sense of the second aspect of the gendered fragment's taxonomy. Paradoxes are expressions of contradictions, dysfunctions and gaps, which do not lead to a process of deconstruction, but to a process of externalizing and making these very aspects visible. In this respect, they go beyond a process of deconstruction, which Derrida applies to the inner logic of the archive.[138] Paradoxes do not lead to deconstruction, but remain present in the text. For example, the structure of shaped gaps initiates a paradoxical dynamic of stillness as an integral element of the genealogical stream. As the gaps are externalized by means of a reoccurring formula, they do not deconstruct the sense of an ongoing stream or succession, but remain present in the text.

The paradox is not restricted to the gendered structures, but is apparent throughout the archive of genealogies. For example, the text performs the identity of Israel as intimately linked to Palestine in a situation in which the

---

137. Knoppers, *I Chronicles 1–9*, p. 334.

138. Jacques Derrida, *Archive Fever: A Freudian Impression* (trans. E. Prenowitz; Chicago, IL: University of Chicago Press, 1996), especially p. 19.

Diaspora becomes more and more central. It struggles for predominance in defining past and present by means of advancing an inclusive memory performance. Moreover, the text presents a fundamentally patriarchal succession while simultaneously acknowledging the necessary challenge to this structuring principle. All these features imply a paradoxical moment in the memory act and expose the paradox as a critical aspect of genealogy performance in response to fractured pasts.

The concept of the paradox also allows for a look at the issues of continuity and discontinuity from another angle. At first view, the archive of genealogies is at pains to convey continuity. Lineages stretch back to creation and ancestral time (1.1–2.2); they refer to the leading figures of the Exodus and the time in the wilderness (5.29); they encompass the history of the twelve tribes in the land (2.3–8.40); they reflect on the emergence of monarchy and cult (3.1-24 and 5.27–6.38); and they depict exile and return (9.1-34). In other words, they encompass the entire history of Israel. Including all these aspects seems to aim toward continuity. As Johnson puts it, the genealogies attempt 'to assert the importance of the principle of continuity of the people of God through a period of national disruption'.[139] The genealogies, then, respond to the trauma of the exile by means of creating and expressing continuity. But if continuity alone is the major concern of the composition, it is difficult to explain why the genealogy composition admits to a strong taxonomy of gaps, dysfunctions and ambivalences, which interfere with an exclusive sense of continuity and which I have described from different perspectives. Paradoxically, continuity appears to be sustainable and meaningful only if it includes discontinuity as well. The archive of genealogies does not focus on continuity alone. Instead, it simultaneously addresses the fragility of the continuity it establishes. Keeping up this paradoxical dynamic is a crucial aspect of the way in which 1 Chronicles 1–9 performs its memory act in response to trauma.[140]

In my view, this paradoxical dynamic is a key to the strength of 1 Chronicles 1–9, both in view of its performing a meaningful memory act, and in view of its attempt to gain predominance in defining Israel. In this respect, I see the formulaic reference to the sister Shelomith in the royal lineage of 3.10-24 as a turning point in the entire composition. It is here that the moment of paradox comes to a peak, and it is here that the power of the memory act to make sense in response to the traumatic past gains steam.

139. Marshall D. Johnson, *The Purpose of the Biblical Genealogies with Special Reference to the Setting of the Genealogies of Jesus* (Cambridge: Cambridge University Press, 1969), p. 80.

140. Read from this perspective, it is no coincidence that the central genealogies of Judah start with a small narrative on the jeopardized lineage. The reference to Tamar and Judah foreshadows the jeopardized continuation of the larger story of Israel.

The Ambiguity of the Memory Act

The paradoxical dynamic of the archive of genealogies significantly increases the power and impact of the genealogy performance in contemporaneous discourses on memory, identity/alterity and power. In my view, however, this paradoxical dynamic is developed without ever loosing contact with the aim of exerting normative patriarchal power. As a consequence, the impact of the subtext, which emerges on the basis of the second group of ideas relating to the female-gendered taxonomy, is also ambiguous. The subtext is permitted only to a certain extent and only as long as it does not threaten the main text with its patriarchal agenda and its aim of gaining predominance in defining Israel. The subtext invites alternative perspectives and agents. However, these alternative perspectives and agents are eventually domesticated again. The rules of succession and the attempt to define Israel in patriarchal terms are not fundamentally changed.

For the contemporary reader, the ambiguity of the genealogy performance may be a disappointment. The female-gendered fragments bring energy to the text and make it relevant, but in the end, they support the patriarchal aim of the composition. However, I would not agree with such a conclusion. The gendered fragments, by means of setting up a gendered subtext, change the overall composition, which can never be restored to a purely normative condition. Moreover, they significantly contribute to the meaning of the composition in terms of its capacity to respond to a fractured past. In conclusion, the gendered fragments indeed function as a force that is both critical and subversive for the genealogical memory performance.

Conclusion in View of 1 Chronicles 1–9

The analysis of the corpus of female-gendered fragments in the genealogies of Judah in the context of socializing 1 Chronicles 1–9 and *My Life Part 2* has contributed a nuanced analysis of passages that had not previously been thoroughly analyzed. This is a basic benefit of the close readings in Chapters 4 and 6.

Besides this basic benefit, the close reading has accomplished a new understanding of 1 Chronicles 1–9 that concerns the text's conception of identity as well as its memory performance. It has brought 1 Chronicles 1–9 to the fore as a text that expresses a paradoxical dynamic. On the one hand, it capitalizes on the primacy of patriarchal succession for the constitution of Israel, focuses on continuity and aims at asserting normative power relations. On the other hand, 1 Chronicles 1–9 is a text that expresses a gendered subtext that interrupts and subverts patriarchal succession and brings forth moments of discontinuity. This paradoxical dynamic is at the center of the composition's response to the traumatic past. In my view, this dynamic is likewise at the core of how and why genealogy composition is indeed able to perform a meaningful memory act.

The gendered fragments have a leading role in setting up the subtext in the genealogies of Judah and beyond. They constitute a basic element of the taxonomy of the archive of genealogies. However, reading the archive of genealogies 'along the grain' showed that the gendered fragments are also intimately involved in the first aspect of the paradoxical dynamic, namely in establishing predominance in normatively defining Israel. The method of reading along the grain next to reading against the grain thus resulted in an understanding of the identity and memory performance of the genealogy composition that does not establish a dichotomy between male/patriarchal/hegemonic functions on the one hand and female/subversive functions on the other. Instead, it showed that gendered fragments are involved in both aspects of 1 Chronicles 1–9. By doing so, it contributed to an understanding of paradox as central to the genealogical memory performance.

The analysis of the gendered fragments requires relocating 1 Chronicles 1–9 in the contemporary discourse on memory, identity and power: 1 Chronicles 1–9 must be understood as a most important text in this discourse. It performs a memory act that is extremely well equipped to ensure a leading position in the conceptualization of Judaism when it had just begun to emerge.

This analysis has shown that genealogies are an apt genre for negotiating memory and identities. However, it has also made clear that it is the archival form of genealogies that allows for fully engaging fragments and counter-movements in a memory act that makes sense in response to a traumatic past. As the traumatic past of the exile is most central for the discourses on memory and identity at the time of Chronicles' composition (probably even more central to the discourse than to the historical situation), it is critical that the genealogies are able to deal with it. Hence, the form of the archive is no coincidental result of badly assembled heterogeneous materials, but a critical means of giving weight to the gendered genealogy performance.

To conclude, analyzing 1 Chronicles 1–9 from the perspective of its gendered fragments and against the backdrop of socializing it with *My Life Part 2* confirms many aspects of recent scholarly debate on the text, which usually starts with the male-gendered parts of the text. In addition, however, it has brought the understanding of the text one step further. It shows that the originality of the text lies in its paradoxical character: the archive of genealogies is meaningful as a memory act and identity performance in the sociocultural context of the time, because it engages discontinuity, fissures and gaps along with its focus on continuity and patriarchal claims to defining Israel.

Conclusion in View of the Socializing

Socializing 1 Chronicles 1–9 and *My Life Part 2* has resulted in a multitude of singular insights. For example, it has facilitated an understanding of the structure of shaped gaps as a trace of a horizontal dynamic of memory production in the middle of an overwhelming focus on genealogical reproduction. In a review of the process of socializing, I would like to summarize three lines of thought that have set the project apart.

Socializing Bible text and film text has contributed the focus on the archive form in relation to gendered genealogies in response to trauma. It demonstrates that the archive format allows genealogies to tackle two basic needs of a posttraumatic situation. First, it accomodates the need to establish continuity in the aftermath of fragmentation and breaks in continuity through traumata. Second, it allows for acknowledging discontinuity, and by doing so for taking seriously the traumatic past. The capacity to integrate these two basic needs is key for performing meaningful memory acts in response to trauma. In posttraumatic contexts, the genre of genealogies and the concept of the archive go hand in hand and make sense together.

A specific aspect of this contribution of socializing is the focus on discontinuity and an understanding of its priority in genealogy performances in response to trauma. The first round of close reading of the gendered fragments of the Judah genealogies in Chapter 4 brought fissures in the patriarchal succession into focus. This encouraged me to focus on the moment of discontinuity in *My Life Part 2*, and to interpret this moment as a turning point in the film, in spite of its elaborate documentation of a continuous lineage. Analyzing the film from the perspective of discontinuity (and appropriation of the traumatic legacy connected to it) resulted in understanding the paradox as fundamental for the second round of close reading of the gendered fragments of Judah in this chapter. Here, it facilitates an interpretation of the Bible text's contradictory dynamics.

Finally, socializing shows that gender is a basic tool for shaping a memory act in response to trauma. In my view this has to do with the basically gendered nature of genealogies. As the genre requires a gendered rule of succession (patrilineal or matrilineal), genealogy performances that are complex enough to make sense in the aftermath of traumatic pasts necessarily involve gender to facilitate either subversion and complexity (1 Chronicles 1–9) or alternative memory acts (*My Life Part 2*).

Any trauma?
Only trauma

Chapter 7

FROM ANACHRONISTIC LISTS TO MEANINGFUL MEMORY ACTS:
LOOKING BACK IN ORDER TO LOOK FORWARD

1. *Memory Spaces that Comprise Continuity and Discontinuity*

In this final chapter, I argue that the ability of gendered genealogy performances to respond to fractured pasts depends on their setting up memory
spaces that comprise both continuity and discontinuity. I explain why the
genre of gendered genealogies is qualified to set up such memory spaces and
identify the turning points that enable anachronistic lists to transform into relevant memory performances. By doing so, I assess the notions of genealogy
composition that I have discussed in the book and present my conclusion on
the topic of gendered genealogy performance in response to fractured pasts.

Socializing 1 Chronicles 1–9 and *My Life Part 2* has exposed a twofold
dynamic which is active in these gendered genealogy performances. First,
the bare, bony, and somewhat narrow structure of the genealogy is broken open and the breaking subverts this very structure. Second, the genre
can withstand this dynamic without collapsing. I am interested in the very
moment of subverting the genre without imploding it, because it is here
that a space emerges that is of major relevance to cultural memory acts in
response to trauma. Text and film analysis have shown that this memory
space comprises a sense of continuity as well as discontinuity. On the one
hand, it is structured by rules of succession that reflect a particular view
on how life, culture and identity have been continuously passed on. On the
other hand, it simultaneously acknowledges discontinuity in the form of
fractures, gaps and dead ends in this very succession.

Letting the poles of continuity and discontinuity stand side by side, without one deconstructing the other, works toward appropriating a traumatic
past and towards providing it with a place in the present. By doing so, the
dynamic of subverting the genealogy genre without imploding it enables
making sense of the traumatic past and disclosing its resources. At the same
time, it works toward releasing the present from the past's impact. Paradoxically, recounting and recognizing the past in such a memory act helps to let
it go. It is a first step in forgetting, in moving on and in establishing something new.

The ability to provoke counter-movements while simultaneously putting up with them is an essential feature of *female-gendered* genealogies—not of genealogies per se. The genealogy genre is usually realized in a strongly male-gendered memory performance. In this situation, references to women take a leading role in all structural functions that complicate and subvert the succession. Examples of structural functions that take this leading role are as follows. In 1 Chronicles 1–9, female-gendered references indicate fractures in the patrilinear succession and establish a subtext that relates to gender, ethnicity and class, as I have shown in Chapter 4. Next, female-gendered references function as road signs to organize the sociopolitical fabric of the genealogy, as I have demonstrated in Chapter 6. The many mothers and wives in the Judah genealogies are significantly involved in mapping difference, in realizing and nuancing othering and in communicating parity in the context of segmentation processes. The structural dimension of this function is underlined by the fact that many of these women are otherwise unknown in biblical literature. They are not individual female ancestors who embody literary, geographical and other traditions and serve as identification figures, such as, for example, Ephrathah. Instead, they are place holders—road signs—in a memory act that achieves complexity through their structural function.

In *My Life Part 2*, the women-centeredness of the lineage is central in modifying and subverting rules of succession toward a female line, instituting a political succession beyond kinship and presenting alternative ways of being Jewish. Moreover, the women-centeredness of the lineage is a central aspect of performing an alternative memory act, which uses alternative archives, relies on alternative memories and experiences, and performs a shift in margins, and centers, as I have shown in Chapter 5.

In conclusion, both case studies provide ample references to women that complicate and subvert the patriarchal genealogical succession. However, the memory space, which encompasses both continuity and discontinuity, only emerges at the moment in which subversion does not deconstruct the genealogical structure, but in which genealogy performance is able to bear the subversion and maintain the genealogical structure. In other words, it is not the subversion as such that is critical, but the dynamic it enables and encompasses. This argument has an important hermeneutical implication with respect to the biblical genealogies. I am not aiming to demonstrate how subversive—or how patriarchal—individual biblical genealogies are. Instead, the conclusion that I draw from the process of socializing is that in genealogies subversion is a central engine for achieving a meaningful memory act and that gender is at the basis of this drive. For example, the critical point is not that a passage such as 1 Chron. 7.24 mentions a woman, Sheerah, who built three cities. The point is the dynamic this short reference ignites and supports in the larger genealogy composition.

how respond to trauma?

The occurrence of female-gendered references in moments of complication and differentiation in the genealogical succession has been acknowledged for some time, especially with regard to the Genesis genealogies.[1] However, it is critical to also acknowledge that female-gendered references do not enact differentiation and complication after the main argument of a genealogy has been made. Instead, female-gendered references have functions that operate at the core of a genealogy, as I have shown throughout the close readings. Hence, involving a female-gendered dynamic in a genealogy is a central tool in turning genealogies into a form of memory capable of responding to trauma.

Having explained why the genre of gendered genealogies is qualified to set up memory spaces that comprise continuity and discontinuity, I now proceed to identifying three features of the genre I understand to be turning points for the transformation of genealogies from anachronistic lists into relevant memory performances.

① The first feature is the need for continuous decision-making with regard to the inclusion or exclusion and position of the constituents of a genealogy. Continuous decision-making is prompted by the bony structure and by the idea of succession, which needs a primary lineage and secondary lineages and requires the commitment to particular names and qualities. It accounts for the political dimension of gendered genealogies and enables its subversive and alternative uses.

② *Play*

The second feature is the art of play in genealogy composition. By play, I refer to deliberate and often subtle alterations, variations and irregularities in the genealogy composition, as well as imagined segments of a lineage. Play in gendered genealogies means the art of bringing one's point across while remaining fully entangled in the bony structure of the genre. Play is a feature of genealogies that interacts with the scarce non-narrative structure. It allows a flexible use of the structure, adding connotations and repressing meanings, in short, turning it into a meaningful memory act and identity performance.

③ The third feature is the sense of basic relatedness at the basis of genealogy composition. It is due to linking elements such as 'brother' or 'daughter' as basic building blocks of any genealogy. This feature includes the imagery of kinship and the tree model as primary genealogical metaphors.

---

1. See for example Hieke, who identifies the functions of women in the genealogical system of the book of Genesis as 'differentiating' and 'slowing down' the genealogical flow, as 'taking initiative' in situations of crisis, and as representing the proper, i.e. 'endogamous marriage' that is necessary for the lineage to remain under God's blessing. Thomas Hieke, *Die Genealogien der Genesis* (HBS, 39; Freiburg: Herder, 2003), pp. 278-98, especially p. 285. See also Crüsemann, who points out that the often anonymous women of the Genesis genealogies usually occur in central places. Crüsemann, 'Human Solidarity and Ethnic Identity', p. 58.

Both the imagery of kinship and the tree model are ambivalent when it comes to subverting a genealogy succession. Moreover, they indicate the limits of the genre and suggest models such as the rhizome as possible forms to transgress it.

My starting point for the discussion of all features is the reduced and narrow structure of gendered genealogies in their sparse, skeleton-like shape. This means that I start out from an idea that is more closely realized in the biblical genealogies in 1 Chronicles 1–9 and beyond than in the gynealogy performance of *My Life Part 2*. I start out from the sparse, skeleton-like shape of genealogies, because the genre is so specific that even if dispersed in a more narrative archive, such as in the film, its characteristic features allow those who make use of it to work toward the memory space I am interested in.

2. *The Politics of Decision-Making*

Gendered Genealogies as an Inherently Political Genre

The need for continuous decision-making is the first of three features of the genre that play a central part in turning genealogies into memory acts capable of setting up memory spaces that comprise both continuity and discontinuity and thus enable them to respond to a traumatic past. The structure of genealogies requires continuous decisions concerning the priority of its constituents. Genealogies mainly consist of names and functional as well as relational linking elements. These constituents need to be organized—a process that requires a continuous flow of decisions. Genealogies are not merely about facts, whether they are historical, literary, or imagined. They are always about arranging, repressing or highlighting, about prioritizing these facts. The need for continuous decision-making initiates a process of ordering, which involves identifying the essence of the traditions and identities a group wants to pass on. It assesses what is contributed by whom and determines which coalitions are formed or rejected. In sum, such a process of ordering settles what matters most and what comes second. Hence, the need for decision-making moves toward taking a stance in terms of resources, commitments, pragmatics and utopias.

The need for continuous decisions is not merely a characteristic of the genre, but a matter of competence and political practice. Selecting and prioritizing ancestors and relating them to each other requires competence to discuss, negotiate and assess a situation and the factors that influence it, as well as to identify key moments in political, cultural and economic processes, and to embody them in the figures of ancestors, who can serve as prisms for the forces active in those very processes. In this context, forging and selecting, ordering and prioritizing ancestors is a form of enacting the dialogical relationship between sameness and difference. It involves capacities of assessing, appraisal and rejection. In conclusion, the flow of continuous decision-making is at the basis of a form of memory production that likewise represents a political practice.

The flow of constant decision-making accounts for the political dimension of gendered genealogies. Genealogies, which move toward taking stances and establishing a symbolic order, are inherently political. Genealogies cannot be innocent. Instead, the process of genealogy composition necessarily involves interests, power and taking sides.

Insisting on the political character of genealogy composition is critical for the assessment of genealogies in general and biblical genealogies in particular. As I have discussed in the Introduction, academic discourse often passes over genealogies as dry lists, devoid of political impact. Only the priestly lines, if any, are perceived as ideological texts. Against such readings, I want to emphasize that the genealogies in Chronicles and beyond are excellent tools for advancing ideological positions concerning all central sociopolitical, territorial, economic, and religious issues.

Counter-movements. The need to settle definite priorities institutes an additional dynamic, namely the dynamic of questioning these very priorities and of establishing counter-movements. In other words, the need for decision-making and the resulting political character of the genre enables its use in alternative and subversive ways. Counter-movements can employ different mechanisms. A first mechanism is the establishment of a subtext to the dominant structure. The process of genealogical ordering involves dynamics of exclusion and marginalization. This provides fertile ground for subtexts to emerge that challenge and potentially subvert the dominant text. For example, the genealogies of Judah prioritize the Davidic line at the expense of other segments of the Judah genealogies. This is countered by the gendered subtext, which employs tools such as incomplete segments, paradoxes, variations of formulas and crises of form in order to establish a counter-movement in the overall composition.

A second mechanism is the attempt to reorganize centers and margins. The documentary *My Life Part 2* is an example of such a take on genealogy composition. The film draws on alternative archives, for example home movies and the archive of the filmmaker's mother, and moves alternative ancestors to the center, namely the Levi women who are situated at the margins of society and cultural memory discourse. Moreover, the film tries to propose alternative forms of succession, based on imagined lineages, political commitment and specific ways of facing trauma.

On a more general level, echoes and traces form a third mechanism of counter-present genealogies. The genealogy genre accommodates echoes and traces through incomplete segments, paradoxes, variations of formulas and crises of form, to name only a few tools. Diana Taylor has juxtaposed the archive and the repertoire, the archive being what is written down or connected to language and the repertoire being what is otherwise at our disposal or sociocultural practice.[2] I think that the genealogy genre tends toward the archive in its insisting on decisions and establishing and inscribing a symbolic order. Genealogies may aim to communicate an abundance of tradition and past. Still, they capture this in a somewhat closed entity. As a form of memory, they are like clippings of the repertoire that comprises additional layers of reality. Echoes and traces are moments for the fuller repertoire to reenter the genealogical scene.

The Performative Quality

The political orientation of genealogies accounts for the strong presence of ideologies, interests, and agencies in genealogy composition. Throughout this project, I have conceptualized this dimension of genealogy composition in terms of performance. The performance concept insists on activity inherent to the genre—as much as inherent to cultural memory in general. It means that genealogies do not emerge logically from a particular past in inevitable ways. Instead, they are produced, manufactured, created and imagined, in other words, they are performed. Insisting on the priority of activity also highlights negotiation and contest at the basis of genealogy composition. Genealogy composition does not only support an inner formation of memory and identity. Instead, it also insists upon the presentation and negotiation of memory and identity outside of the genealogy, be it in a public or private context.

Bringing activity into focus requires a nuanced understanding of agency. The performance concept does not only take explicit or intended agency into account. Instead, agency in cultural memory performance likewise includes unconscious or repressed agency as well as traumatic recall.[3] As Mieke Bal puts it, 'cultural recall is not merely something of which you happen to be a bearer but something that you actually *perform*, even if, in many instances, such acts are not consciously and willfully contrived.'[4] While taking the agents of genealogy composition into account, it is critical to keep such a broader concept of agency in mind.

---

2.   Diana Taylor, *The Archive and the Repertoire: Reforming Cultural Memory in the Americas* (Durham, NC: Duke University Press, 2003). Thank you to Melva L. Sampson for pointing me to Taylor's approach in her intriguing paper on 'Raising Womanish Girls!: The Implications of Womanist Posturing and the Performance of Motherhood' at the 2011 SBL Annual Meeting in San Francisco.

3.   Mieke Bal, 'Introduction', pp. vii-xvii.

4.   Bal, 'Introduction', p. vii.

Primary and Secondary Agents in Genealogy Performance. Agency in genealogy performance involves primary and secondary agents. First of all, agency in genealogy performance, whether intended and conscious or repressed, re-enacted, and not willfully contrived, involves the actual composers of a genealogy, which I would describe as primary agents of the performance. In the case studies such primary agents are the scribal circles in Second Temple Jerusalem in the case of 1 Chronicles 1–9,[5] and the filmmaker Angelika Levi in the case of *My Life Part 2*. The primary agents are involved in sociopolitical and cultural discourses that give shape to the genealogy performance, for example, the discourse on exile and return in the case of Chronicles and the discourse on the memory of the Shoah in the case of *My Life Part 2*. Such discourses are often controversial and include different sociopolitical groups, individuals and movements. In *My Life Part 2*, representatives of the German memory discourse appear in television footage and interviews. Different positions in the postexilic identity discourse can be grasped through different contemporaneous biblical books, for example Ezra–Nehemiah or Proverbs. Individuals and groups involved in the discourses at the basis of the genealogy composition function as secondary agents of the performance. Which secondary agents are allowed to contribute to forming, selecting and positioning ancestors is determined by contest, negotiation, participation and othering—all key issues of power dynamics in genealogy performance.

Genealogies in the Public Realm and the Shift from Identity to Memory Performance. Next to the involvement of secondary agents, power dynamics in genealogies depend on whether they are performed in the public realm or not. As a rule, the political impact of a genealogy depends on the stage a given genealogy performance enters, in other words, on its involvement in public, ideological, and other discourses, directly or indirectly. Participation in public realms reinforces the political dimension of genealogy performance. Both case studies participate in public discourses and it is here that their powers to disclose the past as a resource for political practices in the present, their capacities to articulate utopias and adhere to commitments and their abilities to wrestle over shared identities and negotiate coalitions become manifest.

In genealogies that participate in public discourses, identity issues are sidelined in favor of memory performances. The biblical genealogies not only make a statement about the identity of Israel or the Jewish people. They represent a deliberately designed memory act, which functions as an argument in a conflict-ridden discourse on the origin, identity and power-balance of a heterogeneous group. The same goes for *My Life Part 2*. The film is part of a memory discourse and reaches beyond the articulation of

---

5. See Chapter 3, above.

identity. This does not mean that the question of identity is not tackled. But it is secondary in the course of performing the genealogical memory act.[6]

The emphasis on memory over identity also highlights the fact that the memory performance is not a mirror of the present identity situation, but a constructed account of the past. This account of the past is not necessarily identical to the implied program for the present. It is important to reckon with the difference between the agenda of the memory performance and the agenda pursued in the present. For example, concerning politics and power in the genealogies of Judah, this means that the political argument that is made in the genealogies is not necessarily identical to the political interest pursued by its composers with regard to contemporaneous concerns. Acknowledging the past in a certain way does not mean that the present should remain the same. For instance, acknowledging the position of a woman like eponymous ancestress Ephrathah in the history of Judah does not mean that the text advocates such a position for women in Judah's present. The opposite might be the case. Relegating the importance of Ephrathah to the past might indeed be a first step in forgetting it.

In conclusion, it is important to consider the timing of the memory act and to ask when and with what interests a memory act is performed. In other words, when and why does the recalling of memories take place? This means highlighting the moment in which a genealogy actually responds to trauma, which is, at the same time, the moment in which a genealogy actually responds to a present context, interest and maybe challenge. Again, concerning the engagement of a female-gendered dynamic in a genealogy, the recalling of memories can work in different directions. In the genealogies of Judah, involving such a great amount of women of different ethnicities and social statuses may aim to link the presence and agency of such women to the past rather than to the present. This corresponds with the situation described in Ezra–Nehemiah, where (foreign) women are pushed out of the congregation (Ezra 9–10; Nehemiah 13).

Power and Participation

Agency in genealogy composition is closely related to the question of who is allowed to take action and thus to the issues of participation and power in

---

6.   See Angelika Levi's corresponding interview statement: 'I found the aspect of the search for an identity less and less important. After all, it's about living your life with all its contradictions, differences and difficulties—which isn't the same as being ambivalent, as I discovered in Chile, for example, where the Jewish-German identity doesn't have such negative connotations. In Chile I began having a more strongly political stance, an attitude that can easily be overlooked when you're dealing with your own past and which I try to allude to with the scene about the elderly Jewish couple'. Interview by Stefanie Schulte Strathaus, http://www.arsenal-berlin.de/forumarchiv/forum2003/katalog/mein_leben_teil_2.pdf (accessed June 8, 2013).

shaping the memory act. Participation and power concern the question of who is in charge of the continuous flow of decision-making. This raises the question of who has a say in settling on resources, commitments and utopias. And it involves negotiating which viewpoints, which arguments and which experiences a genealogy performance attaches importance to and which viewpoints, arguments, and experiences, are deemed of no consequence.

Power Conflicts between Inclusion and Othering. Power in terms of participation in shaping the memory act is reflected in whom a genealogy includes and excludes, as well as in its processes of othering. For example, in the Chronicles genealogies, othering is realized by means of placing particular groups on the sidelines, describing them as descendants of a secondary wife and/or as ethnic others. In *My Life Part 2*, othering of viewpoints and groups involves identifying them with a Protestant male discourse, which is described as hostile to life and latently anti-Semitic.

In genealogies, othering is the flipside of prioritizing and thus a typical feature of the genre. Genealogies require selection, taking in and pushing out from the start. The harshness and permanence of decision-making required by the genre easily leads to silencing minority viewpoints and to excluding parts of a community and its memory. In turn, inclusion and belonging will easily be overemphasized, a dynamic that risks losing track of the interplay between identity and alterity that is so critical for genealogy composition in response to fractured pasts.

On the one hand, the genealogy genre accommodates ruling out minority viewpoints. On the other hand, it is a genre that invites counter-movements and subtexts, as I have argued earlier. The two contrary movements are a source of conflict between allowing for participation of complex genealogical agents in the shaping of the genealogy performance on the one hand, and repressing their agency through othering and silencing them on the other. The two case studies deal with this power conflict in quite different ways.

1 Chronicles 1–9 allows for counter-movements only to a certain extent. In many cases, counter-movements add to the complexity of the genealogy composition. As I have shown in Chapter 4, in the cases of Tamar and Sheshan's daughter, counter-movements are even employed to establish and strengthen the dominant line. However, the moment they get too powerful, they are not welcome any more. As a consequence, counter-movements can function as a subversive force in the genealogy performance, but are not in a position to overthrow the dominant line.

In contrast, in *My Life Part 2*, the entire lineage of Levi women is set up as a counter-genealogy. However, the dominant gynealogy also provides counter elements, for example, hints at the political affinity between the filmmaker and her grandfather Robert Levi. However, these elements remain in the position of traces that add to the complexity of the project, but are not played out to question the dominant line of the film. In conclusion, both case studies contain counter-movements that fulfill important functions. However, both case studies also restrict the impact of these counter-movements and limit their scopes.

Assessing Power Conflicts in Genealogies Depends on their Position within Respective Sociohistorical Contexts. The case studies parallel each other in restricting the counter-movements they insitute. Yet restricting counter-movements has quite different implications in the two case studies and needs to be assessed differently. The different assessment is based on the different locations of the case studies in their respective sociohistorical contexts. While 1 Chronicles 1–9 presents a genealogy composition that is in line with dominant tradition lines and forms of succession, *My Life Part 2* performs a gynealogy that starts out from a minority viewpoint and relies on alternative agents, narratives and rules of succession.

Speaking of 'dominant lineages' and 'minority viewpoints' implies a certain assessment of the position of a genealogy in its sociohistorical context, for example a dominant or marginal position in particular memory discourses or political situations. In the case of the Chronicles genealogies, this has to be elaborated on, as Chronicles forms part of both a dominant and a marginal discourse. From a global perspective, Chronicles and the Jerusalem scribal elite responsible for it occupy a marginal position with regard to the interests, politics and discourses of the great powers of the time. Observed from an inner-biblical perspective, however, it holds a dominant position in advancing its interests on a literary and probably also sociopolitical level. Throughout this book, I have been mainly interested in the inner-biblical perspective. From this perspective, power in terms of negotiating participation is literally palpable. Take the examples of Tamar and of Sheshan's daughter. They exemplify the struggle between subversion and othering: the counter-movements vitalize the genealogy and make it relevant, but there is a strong and effective drive to restrict them. In the course of the close reading, I have argued that the aim of the Chronicles genealogies is to achieve a monopoly in defining the community and its members. This involves a strong process of including while simultaneously othering groups, experiences and viewpoints that might contest the dominant rules of the genealogical archive.

My Life Part 2 is located in a very different discourse and sociopolitical situation. The film and its story are located in a sociopolitical marginal discourse—whether one looks from an inner-German, an inner-Jewish, or an inner-feminist perspective. In *My Life Part 2*, the counter-movement has come out on top and now is the dominant layer in the gynealogy. In this configuration, the male Protestant side of the lineage, a dominant line in the overall memory discourse and the dominant sociopolitical reality, is othered. This is important to state, especially in order to learn something about the functioning of genealogies, but it does not alter the position of the individual viewpoints, whether they are female Jewish or male Protestant, in the overall public memory discourses the film is embedded in.

Conclusion

In conclusion, the need for decision-making and the resulting politically active character of genealogies works toward opening a space in which the past is designed and manufactured rather than merely described and reflected. Such a space is indispensable for memory acts that productively respond to trauma.

The design of a genealogy performance can formulate or sustain a dominant ideology or it can perform a nuanced or subversive account of the past. I am interested in the latter—and have chosen two case studies that (to a certain extent) follow such an agenda. As a consequence, I pursue the genre as it tends toward this direction. In my view this requires special attention to the functions of paradox and play.

3. *Play as a Means of Responding to the Bony Structure of the Genre*

Play in Performance Theory

After the feature of constant decision-making, the art of play is the second feature in a series of three, which I consider central in subverting the genre of gendered genealogies without imploding it and hence critical for opening a memory space that comprises continuity and discontinuity in the formation of a memory act that is capable of responding to a traumatic past. Play refers to strategies such as purposefully employing variations and irregularities, or to interplaying time and reality layers. In genealogy performance, it is the art of making one's point while remaining fully entangled in the bare and bony structure of the genre.

The notion of play is part of performance theory and it is from here that I borrow the term. In performance theory the notion of play describes the innovative, creative and contingent aspects of a performance, which function in opposition to the notion of ritual, which describes the more formal, structured and determined aspects of performance.

> In performance studies, play is understood as the force of uncertainty which counterbalances the structure provided by ritual. Where ritual depends on repetition, play stresses innovation and creativity. Where ritual is predictable, play is contingent. But all performances, even rituals, contain some element of play, some space for variation. And most forms of play involve pre-established patterns of behaviour.[7]

7. Bial, 'Play', in *The Performance Studies Reader*, pp. 135-36.

malleable genealogy

Applying the related definition of performance as 'ritualized behaviour conditioned/permeated by play'[8] to the case of genealogy performance, I use the term *play* in reference to the art of using the genealogy structure for one's needs by means of slight and subtle alterations, variations and additions. This can take the form of deliberate irregularities in the genealogy composition, such as formal variations or altered names, for example in Chronicles. It can also take the form of imagined segments of a lineage, for example the lineage derived from the biblical Levi in *My Life Part 2*.

Both case studies engage the creative, playful, and performative potential of the genealogy genre, each in its individual way and in accordance with its media. 1 Chronicles 1–9 has at its disposal the possibilities of a text. As a creative literary work, it plays out the creative potential of genealogy composition in its virtuoso dealing with form, from formulas to variations and to the breakdown of form; in bringing fluidity into play; and in the skilful juggling of names.

My Life Part 2 has at its disposal the audiovisual tools of a film. It plays out the creative potential of genealogy composition by means of interplaying different time and reality layers: memory, trauma, traumatic re-enactment, biblical myth, and the present. Moreover, it realizes the performative force of genealogy composition in its unconventional ways of establishing succession and defining belonging, both concerning gender and Jewishness.

The different ways of realizing the potential for play expose the intriguing possibilities inherent to the genre as well as the artful ways in which the case studies play out these possibilities. Irregularities and imagination serve to elucidate a position while remaining fully entangled with the bony structure of the genre. Here dwells my fascination with genealogies: the art of using something as strict as genealogies and then beat it with its own weapons. This is fine artistry. This artistry is strongly involved in the dynamic of breaking open and subverting the genre, while remaining committed to it. It is decisive in making a genealogy meaningful in response to trauma.

Play and Paradox: Accomplices in Exposing—and Integrating—Discontinuity
Play in genealogies is a strategy to counter their either/or logic and to prepare for the presence of the paradox. A genealogy in response to trauma needs to confront fractures in order to make sense—either openly or in subversive ways. Appropriating the past cannot be done by means of completely repressing problematic aspects. Instead, a genealogy needs a strategy to include and locate such aspects. In the case studies, play on formations, gender stereotypes and conventional rules of succession are significantly involved in exposing discontinuity and contradictions in the respective

---

8. Richard Schechner, *Performance Studies: An Introduction* (London: Routledge, 2002), p. 79.

Paradox!

Paradox

genealogies—yet without deconstructing the genealogical form, nor the related sense of continuity. Thus play is an effective strategy to expose fractures, contradictions and hybridity within rather than outside of a coherent picture of the past. <u>Play does not deconstruct the rules of the genre it plays within</u>. Instead, it establishes tensions, such as the tension between continuity and discontinuity, or tensions between conflicting hybrid subject positions.

In Chapter 6, I have described the presence of such tensions which resist deconstruction in terms of the presence of paradox. While the genealogy genre with its continuous flow of decision-making presses for either/or decisions, the paradox emerges as a 'figuration of resistance' against this logic of either/or.[9] Here, the art of play and the notion of the paradox function as accomplices in creating space and tension between poles that seem to exclude each other. Play is a critical tool for tapping into the capacity of genealogies to design a symbolic order that houses the paradox. On the other hand, the paradox is a category that is able to make sense of contradictions and hybridity as part of the symbolic order. The interplay between the notions of play and of the paradox makes use of play as an important strategy for actively addressing the need—or the wish—to perform a memory act that integrates hybrid positions and contradictory needs in the enacting of the performance.

The paradox is a means of integrating fractions and hybridity in the aftermath of trauma: the presence of the paradox as part of the symbolic order as designed by a genealogy, and hence the notion of play, are critical for the formation of identity and the determination of alterity in response to trauma. The paradox supports the ability to perform identity as fractured, contradictory and hybrid, yet still coherent. This is extremely important in the aftermath of trauma. It takes the need for a coherent image of the self and the world serious while at the same time respecting the experience that has destroyed such an image. Moreover, it is a way of expressing solidarity with those who have experienced trauma. Acknowledging hybridity and enacting the paradox are not only part of the postmodern *condition humaine*. Instead, they express a political position.

Performing identity as inclusive of paradoxes and hybridity exposes problematic aspects of past and present rather than denying and repressing them. It is orientated toward disclosing resources. At the same time, explicitly recalling injuries and crises of the past may be a necessary step in forgetting them. As Derrida has stated with regard to the need to archive injuries and injustice in the case of the work of the Truth and Reconciliation

---

9. Paul Geyer, 'Das Paradox: Historisch Systematische Grundlegung', in *Das Paradox: Eine Herausforderung des abendländischen Denkens* (ed. Paul Geyer and Roland Hagenbüchle; Tübingen: Stauffenburg, 1992), pp. 11-24 (12).

Commission in South Africa,[10] recalling and storing memories in a safe place may eventually allow for forgetting them. Problematic aspects of the past are not repressed, but are recalled in order to minimize their impact. By doing so, space for moving on to new agendas is created in the present.

The presence of play and the paradox work toward integrating hybrid positions. However, the genealogy genre does not only allow for mapping hybridity, but also channels and limits it. Stories, places, ancestors, or events can be mapped as different by means of identifying them with different roles in the genealogical universe and through positioning them at different locations. However, genealogical roles as well as locations in the genealogical order are determined and limited. Different stories, places, ancestors, or events are mapped as different, but have to somehow fit into the broader picture of a particular genealogy and into the genealogical structure in general. This offers the opportunity to bring things together, the chance to expose hybridity, but at the same time to imagine coherence and integrate it into one picture. On the other hand, this supports and even requires the tendency to harmonize and normalize inherent to the genre. Disparate subject and inheritance positions are assimilated into one shared picture. They cannot be utterly disconnected. Accordingly, the experience of total disconnection does not fit the genre.

Interplaying Fact and Fiction
Another fundamental aspect of the notion of play in genealogy composition is the genre's potential (and habit) to interplay received and chosen ancestry, to pair inheritance and choice, to interweave legacy and imagination. Imagination includes imagining figures and characters, drawing lines across normative ways of succession and developing alternative forms of succession. This is based on the basic category of fluidity and the mutability of genealogies based on changing needs and circumstances. But imagination exceeds fluidity inasmuch as it not only changes what is there, but imagines what is lacking.

In such a play of fact and fiction, imagined ancestors, places and lines of succession are added to a genealogy in order to transform a traumatic past into something that can be grasped, appropriated and made sense of. Yet, the interaction of fact and fiction can be only meaningful if the actual past and legacy remain involved. If this is done, interplaying legacy and imagination is an important element in a memory performance that is oriented toward disclosing resources.

10. Jacques Derrida, 'Archive Fever (A Seminar by Jacques Derrida, University of Witwatersrand, August 1998, transcribed by Verne Harris)', in *Refiguring the Archive* (ed. Carolyn Hamilton *et al.*; Dordrecht: Kluwer Academic Publishers, 2002), pp. 38-80/ even pages (54).

For example, in *My Life Part 2*, the imagined lineage descending from the biblical Levi to the actual Levi women is fascinating and plausible because the gynealogy so deeply engages with the difficulty of the traumatic inheritance. In a similar way, forging their own rules of succession and thereby confirming the identity of the Levi women as a Jewish identity provides the basis for appropriating the experience of having been the target of anti-Semitic persecution and murder. In the film, the gynealogy is deeply committed to the given inheritance, without being narrowed down to it. Here, the playful aspect of the genre allows sounding the interplay between recieved inheritance and imagined ancestry. Both aspects balance and reinforce each other. In conclusion, the lineage of Levi women established by Angelika Levi employs imagination in order to contour silence and to deal with absence. In this context, interplaying fact and fiction is an especially important feature in performing counter-genealogies and alternative memory acts.

In 1 Chronicles 1–9, a resource-oriented interplay unfolds between the inclusions of constructed and claimed tradition on the one hand, and references to groups, places and names that form part of the sociohistorical context of the time on the other. Examples of how the genealogies weave in literary, mythological, and theological traditions are their starting out from the first human, Adam, or the frequent recurrence of the (eponymous) ancestors of the ancestral period. Including these claimed traditions confirms the self-conception of the authors as heirs of earlier biblical traditions and substantiates claims in the present. But there is another aspect to their involvement: the transition between constructed traditions and parameters of the contemporaneous situation is smooth. For example, Adam is a mythological figure but at the same time a direct ancestor. In a similar way, literary traditions are at the same time family history. Drawing on the continuity with claimed traditions works because they are interplayed with the actual sociohistorical context of the time. This interplay conveys to the tradition the status of a legacy and a resource to engage with in the present. By doing so, the repository of experiences, conventions and solutions to conflict and crisis inherent in the biblical traditions is indeed perceived as a resource and used as such. Again, the interplay between created tradition and sociohistorical parameters works toward a resource-oriented memory act.

4. *Metaphors of Relatedness: Kinship, Tree and Rhizome*

The third feature in a series of three, that I think plays a central part in subverting the genre without imploding it, and that is hence critical for turning a genealogy into a memory act that is capable of responding to a traumatic past, is a sense of basic relatedness as expressed in the genealogical imagery of kinship and the tree metaphor.

Genealogies establish and communicate a basic sense of relatedness. This is part of their innate structure—genealogies differ from a mere list of names by means of indicating relations between listed names.[11] Moreover, a basic sense of relatedness is part of the philosophy of the genre: genealogies 'think' in terms of ancestors and relationships.[12]

The focus on relationships also constitutes part of a resource-oriented understanding of the past. For example, ancestors provide knowledge, experience, and stories, in short a legacy to deal with—and a resource for better or worse.

The focus on relationships in genealogies is usually framed in terms of kinship. As a rule, relationships are presented in family terms such as son, sister, father, or wife. In fact, kinship imagery has nearly absolute priority in genealogy composition—a fact that adds to the potential of the genealogy genre, but likewise indicates its limits.

The Imagery of Kinship

The kinship framework conveys a general sense of relatedness. In my view, the great potential of the kinship framework lies in this very feature. This general sense of relatedness is in contrast to the idea of the individual autonomous subject. It suggests that involvement and integration in communities lies at the heart of human life. Such a perception of human life emphasizes that we rely on emotional, physical and social care and communication. In terms of memory performance, it suggests that humans are affected by discourses, characterized by contexts, stand in successions, are confronted with legacies and need to answer them.

Relatedness as conveyed by the kinship framework is a two-sided coin. On the one hand, it concerns involvement and integration. But it also has a more difficult side. Here, relatedness brings about dependency and restricts agency. It includes being overshadowed by histories and legacies, by involuntary inheritances, by repressed issues that are transmitted down generations, by loss.

Even though this flipside may be burdensome, it is extremely important and often informs the drive to engage in memory performances in the first place. It makes clear how important it is to address roots and inheritance positions, and to work through legacies. It also involves the themes of emancipation and commitment.

---

11. Hieke, *Genealogien der Genesis*, p. 18.

12. Rüdiger Lux describes the experience of 'Sozialität in Zeit und Raum' as the basis for a genealogical perception of the world. Rüdiger Lux, 'Die Genealogie als Strukturprinzip des Pluralismus im Alten Testament', in *Pluralismus und Identität* (ed. J. Mehlhausen; VWGT, 8; Gütersloh: Gütersloher Verlagshaus, 1995), pp. 242-58 (246).

Having knowledge of the priority of relatedness and the condition of being deeply involved may be one reason why artists such as filmmaker Angelika Levi work with the genre of genealogy. A genre that is knowledgeable about relatedness and involvement is likely to also be knowledgeable with respect to entanglement and legacy. Both aspects, involvement and entanglement, are important for memory acts in response to trauma.

Another aspect of the kinship imagery is that it narrows down (intergenerational) relationships and role models to the world of the family. Here lurks a limit of the genre, which is especially problematic for the issue of gender. For example, female authority, mentoring, commitment, support and teaching are shaped in the context of motherhood, grandmotherhood and aunthood only. In turn, learning, receiving support and inheriting is conceptualized in the context of the roles of daughter, granddaughter, or niece. Moreover, the kinship imagery promotes particular values. For example, it sets a strong focus on reproduction.

Ideas about kinship-related values, role models and intergenerational relationships depend on the individual cultural contexts. But somehow or other, genealogies are strongly preconceptualized and bring with them ready-made role models and clear-cut ideas about relationships. This problem seriously impacts gender roles and relations but does not end there.

The limits of the kinship notion become even more apparent when thinking about the lack of alternative models for intergenerational relationships in the context of symbolic, religious, artistic, literary, narrative, ideological and/or political successions. Describing succession in such contexts in preconceptualized patterns of mother–daughter, grandmother–granddaughter, or aunt–niece relationships (or the male equivalents) inevitably distorts and reduces them.

Such reduction presents a possible plurality of identification models in terms of gender, capacities and areas of life. For example, 1 Chronicles 1–9 lacks female prophets, female judges, wise women and other leading figures, which are definitely present in biblical literature. In the genealogy composition, these roles and capacities are not relevant. Instead, the genealogies feature women in the roles of wives and mothers, sisters and daughters and dwell on related competences and social positions.

Yet alternatives are possible. The succession of the line could be bound to age, wisdom, locations, activities, or qualifications, to name only a few possibilities. Here, *My Life Part 2* contributes important examples. The lineage of the film is indeed a line of mothers and daughters. However, shared experiences, attitudes and ideologies turn the line into a succession that is able to generate meaning.

Another alternative might be a concept of relations based on affinity and elected family. Here, new conceptions of kinship in cultural anthropology may be helpful to overcome stereotyped concepts of family relations.[13] Still, preconceptualized kinship patterns such as the mother–daughter relationship will exert a strong pull that is not easy to escape.

In sum, the focus on relations as conveyed in the imagery of kinship is highly ambivalent with respect to subversion. On the one hand, it contributes a concept that helps to shape the correlation between relatedness and dependency. At the same time, it limits life areas and role models that could contribute solutions in dealing with them.

Queering Genealogies: Narrow Scopes for Subverting the Gender Notion
Gender in genealogies is closely bound to the kinship imagery. Scope for subverting the gender notion as expressed in its family-related manifestation is narrow but existent. For example, in 1 Chronicles 1–9, the possibility of subverting the gender notion in its kinship-bound manifestation as well as the gender notion itself may become apparent through women figures in 'breeches parts', for example daughters listed as sons. Pursuing these traces is crucial because the analytical focus on gender, as spelled out throughout my analysis, always emanates from the contingent and artificial character of the gender notion itself.

Breeches parts for women in genealogies occur in cases of genealogical roles that are decisively gendered to the point of requiring whoever takes the role to adopt the related gender. In such cases, the role functions as a gendered container. If the gendered container requires a content that is not available, for example a male, the lack may allow for content that is to some extend gender-variable, for example a female or a female who is not married. A prominent instance of such a gendered container is the role of a son who continues the line—a role that is strongly required and strongly gender-bound by the concept of patrilineage. If no male is available to fulfill the container, a daughter might step in and fulfill the male role of son. Labahn and Ben Zvi argue that women may take functional male roles in the Chronicles genealogies, for example the nameless daughter of Sheshan.[14] I agree that such instances of women taking breeches parts takes place in 1 Chronicles 1–9. However, I doubt that this is often done in genealogies without an awareness of the implications of such a move and related restrictions, as I

13. For alternative kinship conceptions in cultural anthropology see Janet Carsten, *After Kinship* (Cambridge: Cambridge University Press, 2004); and Marilyn Strathern, *After Nature: English Kinship in the Late Twentieth Century* (Cambridge: Cambridge University Press, 1992).

14. Antje Labahn and Ehud Ben Zvi, 'Observations on Women', p. 466. On a more general level, Labahn and Ben Zvi argue that 1 Chronicles 1–9 provides references to 'women in roles commonly assigned to mature males in the society', for example the role of head of the family or of builder of cities. Labahn and Ben Zvi, 'Observations on Women', pp. 474-77.

have shown in the case of Sheshan's daughter. Still, this phenomenon indicates a tendency to queer gendered genealogies.

Another impetus for women in breeches parts is the attempt to deny the disturbing presence of women in key positions in narrative traditions and sociohistorical backdrops. This may result in listing women as males straight away, for example in the case of Miriam, who is identified as one of the *banîm*, sons, of Amram (6.3).

My Life Part 2 touches on subverting the primacy of the gender notion by means of redefining genealogical notions, for example and most importantly regarding the concept of succession. This does not primarily mean inverting the notion of patrilineage to a notion of matrilineage, but rethinking qualifications and contents for passing on the line across or beyond gender terms. The gynealogy of Angelika Levi achieves this when highlighting experiences, attitudes and commitment as qualifying factors for standing in, and passing on, the succession of Levi women. At the same time, however, the focus on a succession of women keeps gender in a prominent place.

Tree versus Rhizome: Alliances in the Present

Next to the imagery of kinship, the image of the ancestor tree is characteristic for mapping relations in genealogies.[15] The tree metaphor is able to accommodate vertical as well as horizontal structures, the former represented by main stem and distant branches, the latter represented in the ramifying crown. The tree is a basically hierarchical metaphor. A tree branches out but still has a clear stem from which ramification emerges. In turn, horizontal segments are always dependent on the stem and can be brought back to it. The strictly hierarchical logic of the tree model provides a significant limit to this imagery.[16]

Another limit is the tree's reduced ability to reflect relations in the present, and especially relationships in the present that reach beyond the relational roles of a family. The classical ancestor tree starts out with a couple in the present, maybe maps their children as well as their siblings, but then, by means of depicting parents, grandparents and so forth, inevitably drifts into the past.

Both case studies transgress the tree model, thereby exposing its limits. I suggest that the awareness of the limits of the vertical hierarchical tree

---

15. For an analysis of the visual dimension of various sorts of European family trees, see Mary Bouquet, 'Family Trees and their Affinities: The Visual Imperative of the Genealogical Diagram', in *The Journal of the Royal Anthropological Institute* 2.1 (1996), pp. 43-66.

16. Gilles Deleuze and Félix Guattari, *A Thousand Plateaus* (trans. Brian Massumi; London: Continuum, 2004), pp. 3-29 (13).

structure is directly related to the interest in grasping and mapping fractured pasts and in accommodating fragmented, possibly hybrid presents.

My Life Part 2 starts with the classical tree model. The filmmaker appropriates her family story in an ancestor tree with a focus on her roots. But then, she forms her alliances in the present beyond her stem, reaching into another form of relations, which may be visualized as a rhizome.

The image of the rhizome has been proposed by Gilles Deleuze and Félix Guattari in opposition to the tree metaphor.[17] The rhizome as a botanical phenomenon has a subterranean horizontal stem with ramified surface extensions, as for example couch grass. It serves here as a model for the production of language, knowledge, and sociopolitical circumstances.[18] While the crown always goes back to the stem, the rhizome features variety as laid out on a 'plane of consistency'.[19] On this plateau, it grows from the middle rather than from a start or end point, and develops without pressing toward culmination points such as ancestors in the genealogical tree image.[20] The tree is based on a logic of tracing and reproduction. It forms lineages and functions in terms of cultural memory. In contrast, the rhizome follows a principle of cartography; it forms an open map that is orientated along flight lines.[21] While the tree model illustrates relations on the basis of filiation, the anti-genealogical and 'anti-memory' rhizome illustrates relations on the basis of alliances driven by desire.[22]

For Angelika Levi, the linear structures of the tree image seem to be important to grasp and appropriate her legacy. This is what she starts with. However, the tree seems to be a less practicable model to face her own life and future. Here the rhizome image with its planar structures and a focus on desire and alliances is needed as a complementary structure.

The Chronicles genealogies have a quite different way of transgressing the classical ancestor tree. These genealogies cling to the moment of order—as well as of hierarchy—inherent in the image of branching out from a stem, but reverse the classical tree model. Turning the tree on its head, 1 Chron. 1.1 starts with the first human, Adam and then opens out into a labyrinth of lineages, segments and names, which are connected in many cases, but are just loosely placed together in others. In fact, the text takes nearly indecent liberties to integrate groups into or to exclude them from this labyrinthine crown. By doing so, it forms an entity which goes beyond the scope of the philosophical distinction between tree and rhizome.

17. Deleuze and Guattari, *A Thousand Plateaus*, pp. 5-29.
18. Deleuze and Guattari, *A Thousand Plateaus*, pp. 7-8.
19. Deleuze and Guattari, *A Thousand Plateaus*, p. 23.
20. Deleuze and Guattari, *A Thousand Plateaus*, pp. 23-24.
21. Deleuze and Guattari, *A Thousand Plateaus*, pp. 13-23.
22. Deleuze and Guattari, *A Thousand Plateaus*, pp. 15-27.

Both the tree model in its biblical reversal and the rhizome image as realized in *My Life Part 2* map and initiate relations in the present, yet with different foci. The reversed tree model of the Chronicles genealogies has a focus on identity which is always thought of in connection with the past. It integrates those with whom one has or wants relations in the present into the crown of the tree, thus into the entity that is defined as one's own identity scope. Each individual element of the crown can be brought back to the stem, in other words, back to the primary identity line, which is closely linked to the particular genealogical performance of roots, traditions and history.

In contrast, the rhizome of *My Life Part 2* has a focus on relations in the present that reach beyond roots, traditions and history, but have been identified as decisive for present identities earlier in the film. The rhizome model has a focus on agency. It foregrounds the act of entering deliberate alliances that are not necessarily grounded in an inherited identity but may transgress common origin and social frames.

In both genealogy compositions, however, the fragmentary female lineages hold the puzzle of the past together, both vertically as tree and horizontally as rhizome.

Moving Away from One's Own Stem: A Step Further than Genealogies
The shift from classical tree to reversed labyrinthine tree and further to the form of the rhizome points beyond the genealogy genre. Dealing with a dense, complicated and dominant past may include a movement away from one's roots toward other forms of relations. Such relations would go beyond 'elective affinities' that tend to remain in the kinship imagery,[23] and would be better described as *alliances*, driven by desire and choice, possibly temporary and project-related, spontaneous or coincidental, crossing conventional social frames. Such alliances represent a moment of (temporary) non-connection with the past. The dissociation from the past may occur as a need or as a desire—not as experience alone. But the genealogy genre is limited in is capability to express non-connection with the origins.

The need for and experience of detachment from the past moves toward transgressing the genealogy genre and needs other images, for example the rhizome or the notion of prosthetic memory. Here, again, genealogies are memory acts. As memory acts, genealogies reach into the present and the future, but they cannot replace them.

23. The term 'elective affinity' or 'Wahlverwandtschaft' has been coined by Johann Wolfgang Goethe in his 1809 novel of the same name. Max Weber took up the term and used it in the context of sociology as a metaphor for describing the affinity between particular societal discourses and phenomena, for example Protestant ethics and capitalism. Max Weber, *Die protestantische Ethik und der Geist des Kapitalismus* (Tübingen: J.C.B. Mohr, 1934).

5. *Afterthought*

This chapter directly concerns the analysis of 1 Chronicles 1–9 but also reaches beyond it. Reflecting on the impact that the meta-discussion has on understanding 1 Chronicles 1–9, what strikes me most is that it changes my perception of the text as a reader. Looking at 1 Chronicles 1–9 from the perspective of the meta-discussion, I realize how much I value the text for its multilayered forms and meanings. While the close reading often repelled me, stepping back and looking beyond it makes the text more favorable in my eyes. For example, during the close reading, I took offence at the text's ambivalence, at its introducing of complex genealogical agents only when serving the text's patriarchal agenda and restricting their impact as soon as this aim is fulfilled, and at the constant definition of women in relation to males. Now, stepping back and looking beyond the close reading in the meta-discussion foregrounds that I value 1 Chronicles 1–9 for its skilful use of the genealogy genre, for its permitting paradoxes and contradictions, and for its balancing continuity and discontinuity toward a multilayered memory performance.

This is not only a personal response to the research process. Instead, I claim that reaching beyond the biblical text and reading it as one element among others that contribute to understanding gendered genealogies, as implied by the process of its socialization with Levi's film, works toward a more flexible position vis-à-vis the text—a flexibility that, in my personal case, leads to a certain generosity toward it. This flexibility is not based on downgrading the biblical text as secondary. Instead, it is based on analyzing 1 Chronicles 1–9 in the broader context of the issues that play a role for gendered genealogies in response to trauma, without requiring from it answers to all the complex questions involved. By 'broader context' I refer, among other things, to questions about the role of gender, more recent traumata, the role of public space in our memory acts and our hybrid identities, but also to answers contributed by academic disciplines that explore the present, as well as the film as a cultural expression of it.

In conclusion, this research project has shown that gendered genealogies are an ambitious and intriguing genre, as a biblical genre and beyond the Bible. Specifically, the attempt at socializing has demonstrated that looking at the biblical text as one element alongside other elements does not make it less significant, but is a means of letting the text shine so as to eventually value it as an important voice regarding the relevance of gendered genealogies for meaningful memory acts in response to fractured pasts.

[handwritten annotation:] • does it make sense for biblical text to encode trauma? Is that what we want to recall for generations? • Space & memory: memory creates space

Appendix 1

THE FEMALE FRAGMENTS OF 1 CHRONICLES 1–9
IN THEIR LITERARY CONTEXT

Key for names (names and translation according to the NRSV):

GEN.-AMBIG.	Gender ambiguous name
TOPON.	Toponym
ARAM. / MIDIAN.	Aramean name / Midianite name
ETHN. / GEO.	Indication of ethnic origin / Indication of geographical origin
N. EMPH.	Name emphasized in the text
NAMELESS / NAMELESS GROUP	Nameless woman / nameless group of women
ONLY 1 CHR 1–9 / INTERTEXT	Occurring only in 1 Chronicles 1–9 / occurring in inner-biblical intertext(s)

Reference	Text	Names
1 Chron. 1.1–2.2	**From Adam to the sons of Israel (genealogy of the nations)**	
1.1-4	The descendants from Adam to Noah; the sons of Noah: Shem, Ham and Japhet	
1.5-27	The descendants of Shem; the descendants of Ham; the descendants of Japhet to Abraham	
1 Chron. 1.5-6	5 *The descendants of Japheth: Gomer, Magog, Madai, Javan, Tubal, Meshech and Tiras. 6 The descendants of Gomer: Ashkenaz, Diphath and Togarmah.*	גֹמֶר Gomer GEN.-AMBIG.; INTERTEXT
1.28	The sons of Abraham: Isaac and Ishmael	
1.29-31	The descendants of Ishmael	
1.32-33	The descendants of Keturah	
1 Chron. 1.32-33	32 *The sons of Keturah, Abraham's concubine: she bore Zimran, Jokshan, Medan, Midian, Ishbak and Shuah. The sons of Jokshan: Sheba and Dedan. 33 The sons of Midian: Ephah, Epher, Hanoch, Abida and Eldaah. All these were the descendants of Keturah.*	קְטוּרָה Keturah INTERTEXT עֵיפָה Ephah I GEN.-AMBIG.; TOPON.; MIDIAN.; INTERTEXT
1.34	Abraham; the sons of Isaac: Esau and Israel	
1.35-37	The descendants of Esau	
1 Chron. 1.36	36 *The sons of Eliphaz: Teman, Omar, Zephi, Gatam, Kenaz, Timna and Amalek.*	תִּמְנָע Timna I GEN.-AMBIG.; TOPON.; INTERTEXT

Reference	Text	Names
1.38-42	The descendants of Seir	
1 Chron. 1.39	*39 The sons of Lotan: Hori and Homam; and Lotan's sister was Timna.*	תמנע Timna II GEN.-AMBIG.; TOPON.; INTERTEXT
1.43-50	The Edomite Kings	
1 Chron. 1.50	*50 When Baal-hanan died, Hadad succeeded him; the name of his city was Pai and his wife's name Mehetabel daughter of Matred, daughter of Me-zahab.*	מהיטבאל Mehetabel GEN.-AMBIG.; ARAM.; N. EMPH.; INTERTEXT מטרד Matred GEN.-AMBIG.; INTERTEXT מי זהב GEN.-AMBIG.; INTERTEXT
1.51-54	The Edomite chieftains	
1 Chron. 1.51-54	*[51 And Hadad died.] The clans of Edom were: clans Timna, Aliah, Jetheth, 52 Oholibamah, Elah, Pinon, 53 Kenaz, Teman, Mibzar, 54 Magdiel and Iram; these are the clans of Edom.*	תמנע Timna III GEN.-AMBIG.; TOPON.; INTERTEXT אהליבמה Oholibamah GEN.-AMBIG.; TOPON.; INTERTEXT
2.1-2	The sons of Israel: Reuben, Simeon, Levi, Judah, Issachar, Zebulon, Dan, Joseph, Benjamin, Naphtali, Gad, Asher	
1 Chron. 2.3-55	**The genealogies of Judah I**	
2.3-4	The sons of Judah	
1 Chron. 2.3-4	*3 The sons of Judah: Er, Onan and Shelah; these three the Canaanite woman Bath-shua bore to him. Now Er, Judah's firstborn, was wicked in the sight of the LORD and he put him to death. 4 His daughter-in-law Tamar also bore him Perez and Zerah. Judah had five sons in all.*	בת־שוע Bath-shua I ETHN.; INTERTEXT תמר Tamar I TOPON.; INTERTEXT
2.5	The sons of Perez	
2.6-8	The descendants of Zerah	
2.9	The descendants of Hezron	
2.10-17	The descendants of Ram (family of David)	
1 Chron. 2.16-17	*[13 Jesse became the father of Eliab his firstborn, Abinadab the second, Shimea the third, 14 Nethanel the fourth, Raddai the fifth, 15 Ozem the sixth, David the seventh;] 16 and their sisters were Zeruiah and Abigail. The sons of Zeruiah: Abishai, Joab and Asahel, three. 17 Abigail bore Amasa and the father of Amasa was Jether the Ishmaelite.*	צרויה Zeruiah INTERTEXT אביגיל Abigail I INTERTEXT
2.18-20	The descendants of Caleb	

Reference	Text	Names
1 Chron. 2.18-19	18 Caleb son of Hezron had children by his wife *Azubah* and by *Jerioth*; these were her sons: Jesher, Shobab and Ardon. 19 When *Azubah* died, Caleb married *Ephrath*, who bore him Hur. [20 Hur became the father of Uri and Uri became the father of Bezalel.]	עזובה Azubah ONLY 1 CHR 1–9 יריעות Jerioth ONLY 1 CHR 1–9 אפרת(ה) Ephrath(ah) TOPON.; ONLY 1 CHR 1–9
2.21-24	Additional descendants of Hezron	
1 Chron. 2.21-24	21 Afterward Hezron went in to the *daughter of Machir father of Gilead*, whom he married when he was sixty years old; and *she* bore him Segub; [22 and Segub became the father of Jair, who had twenty-three towns in the land of Gilead. 23 But Geshur and Aram took from them Havvoth-jair, Kenath and *its villages (daughters)*, sixty towns. All these were descendants of Machir, father of Gilead.] 24 After the death of Hezron, in Caleb-ephrathah, *Abijah* wife of Hezron bore him Ashhur, father of Tekoa.	The daughter of Machir, father of Gilead GEO.; NAMELESS; ONLY 1 CHR 1–9 ואת־בנתיה Daughter villages (Töchterstädte) אביה Abijah I GEN.-AMBIG.; ONLY 1 CHR 1–9
2.25-33	The descendants of Jerahmeel	
1 Chron. 2.26-30	[25 The sons of Jerahmeel, the firstborn of Hezron: Ram his firstborn, Bunah, Oren, Ozem and Ahijah.] 26 Jerahmeel also had another wife, whose name was *Atarah*; *she* was the mother of Onam. [27 The sons of Ram, the firstborn of Jerahmeel: Maaz, Jamin and Eker. 28 The sons of Onam: Shammai and Jada. The sons of Shammai: Nadab and Abishur.] 29 The name of Abishur's wife was *Abihail* and *she* bore him Ahban and Molid. [30 The sons of Nadab: Seled and Appaim; and Seled died childless. 31 The son of Appaim: Ishi. The son of Ishi: Sheshan. The son of Sheshan: Ahlai. 32 The sons of Jada, Shammai's brother: Jether and Jonathan; and Jether died childless. 33 The sons of Jonathan: Peleth and Zaza. These were the descendants of Jerahmeel.]	עטרה Atarah N. EMPH.; ONLY 1 CHR 1–9 אביהיל Abihail GEN.-AMBIG.; N. EMPH.; ONLY 1 CHR 1–9
2.34-41	The descendants of Sheshan	
1 Chron. 2.34-35	34 Now Sheshan had no sons, *only daughters*; but Sheshan had an Egyptian slave, whose name was Jarha. 35 So Sheshan gave his *daughter* in marriage to his slave Jarha; and *she* bore him Attai.	Daughters of Sheshan NAMELESS GROUP; ONLY 1 CHR 1–9 Daughter of Sheshan NAMELESS; ONLY 1 CHR 1–9
2.42-50a	Additional descendants of Caleb	
1 Chron. 2.46-50a	46 *Ephah* also, Caleb's concubine, bore Haran, Moza and Gazez; and Haran became the father of Gazez. 47 The sons of Jahdai: Regem, Jotham, Geshan, Pelet, *Ephah* and Shaaph. 48 *Maacah*, Caleb's concubine, bore Sheber and Tirhanah. 49 She also bore Shaaph father of Madmannah, Sheva father of Machbenah and father of Gibea; and the daughter of Caleb was *Achsah*. 50a These were the descendants of Caleb.	עיפה Ephah II GEN.-AMBIG.; TOPON.; MIDIAN.; ONLY 1 CHR 1–9 עיפה Ephah III GEN.-AMBIG.; TOPON.; MIDIAN.; ONLY 1 CHR 1–9

Reference	Text	Names
		מעכה Maacah I GEN.-AMBIG.; TOPON.; ARAM.; ONLY 1 CHR 1–9 עכסה Achsah INTERTEXT
2.50b-55	The descendants of Hur	
1 Chron. 2.50b-51	*50b The sons of Hur the firstborn of Ephrathah: Shobal father of Kiriath-jearim, 51 Salma father of Bethlehem and Hareph father of Beth-gader.*	אפרתה Ephrathah TOPON.; ONLY 1 CHR 1–9
1 Chron. 3.1-24	**The house of David**	
3.1-9	The children of David	
1 Chron. 3.1-9	*1 These are the sons of David who were born to him in Hebron: the firstborn Amnon, by Ahinoam the Jezreelite; the second Daniel, by Abigail the Carmelite; 2 the third Absalom, son of Maacah, daughter of King Talmai of Geshur; the fourth Adonijah, son of Haggith; 3 the fifth Shephatiah, by Abital; the sixth Ithream, by his wife Eglah; 4 six were born to him in Hebron, where he reigned for seven years and six months. And he reigned thirty-three years in Jerusalem. 5 These were born to him in Jerusalem: Shimea, Shobab, Nathan and Solomon, four by Bath-shua, daughter of Ammiel; 6 then Ibhar, Elishama, Eliphelet, 7 Nogah, Nepheg, Japhia, 8 Elishama, Eliada and Eliphelet, nine. 9 All these were David's sons, besides the sons of the concubines; and Tamar was their sister.*	אחינעם Ahinoam the Jezreelite GEN.-AMBIG.; GEO.; INTERTEXT אביגיל Abigail II the Carmelite GEO.; INTERTEXT מעכה Maacah II daughter of King Talmai of Geshur GEN.-AMBIG.; TOPON.; ARAM.; INTERTEXT חגית Haggith INTERTEXT אביטל Abital INTERTEXT עגלה Eglah INTERTEXT בת־שוע Bath-shua II daughter of Ammiel INTERTEXT (Bathsheba) David's secondary wives NAMELESS GROUP; ONLY 1 CHR 1–9 תמר Tamar II TOPON.; INTERTEXT
3.10-14	The descendants of Solomon	
3.15-19a	The sons of Josiah, Jehoiaqim, Jeconiah and Pedaiah	
3.19b-24	The descendants of Zerrubbabel	

Reference	Text	Names
1 Chron. 3.19-20	*[19 The sons of Pedaiah: Zerubbabel and Shimei;] and the sons of Zerubbabel: Meshullam and Hananiah and <u>Shelomith</u> was their sister; [20 and Hashubah, Ohel, Berechiah, Hasadiah and Jushab-hesed, five.]*	שְׁלֹמִית Shelomith GEN.-AMBIG.; ONLY 1 CHR 1–9
1 Chron. 4.1-23	**The genealogies of Judah II**	
4.1	The descendants of Judah	
4.2	The descendants of Reaiah	
4.3	The children of Etam	
1 Chron. 4.3	*3 These were the sons of Etam: Jezreel, Ishma and Idbash; and the name of their sister was <u>Hazzelelponi</u>,*	הַצְלֶלְפּוֹנִי Hazzelelponi ONLY 1 CHR 1–9
4.4	The descendants of Hur	
1 Chron. 4.4	*4 and Penuel was the father of Gedor and Ezer the father of Hushah. These were the sons of Hur, the firstborn of <u>Ephrathah</u>, the father of Bethlehem.*	אֶפְרָתָה Ephrathah TOPON.; ONLY 1 CHR 1–9
4.5-7	The descendants of Ashhur, Helah and Naarah	
1 Chron. 4.5-7	*5 Ashhur father of Tekoa had two wives, <u>Helah</u> and <u>Naarah</u>; 6 <u>Naarah</u> bore him Ahuzzam, Hepher, Temeni and Haahashtari. These were the sons of <u>Naarah</u>. 7 The sons of <u>Helah</u>: Zereth, Izhar and Ethnan.*	חֶלְאָה Helah ONLY 1 CHR 1–9 נַעֲרָה Naarah TOPON.; ONLY 1 CHR 1–9
4.8	The descendants of Qoz	
4.9-10	Jabez	
1 Chron. 4.9	*9 Jabez was honored more than his brothers; and <u>his mother</u> named him Jabez, saying, 'Because I bore him in pain'. [10 Jabez called on the God of Israel, saying, 'Oh that you would bless me and enlarge my border and that your hand might be with me and that you would keep me from hurt and harm!' And God granted what he asked.]*	Mother of Jabez NAMELESS; ONLY 1 CHR 1–9
4.11-12	The Men of Recah	
4.13-14	The descendants of Qenaz	
4.15	The descendants of Caleb	
4.16	The descendants of Jehallelel	
4.17-19	The descendants of Ezrah and his Egyptian and Judahite wives	
1 Chron. 4.17-19	*17 The sons of Ezrah: Jether, Mered, Epher and Jalon. These are the sons of <u>Bithiah, daughter of Pharaoh</u>, whom Mered married; and <u>she</u> conceived and bore <u>Miriam</u>, Shammai and Ishbah father of Eshtemoa. 18 And his <u>Judean wife</u> bore Jered father of Gedor, Heber father of Soco and Jekuthiel father of Zanoah. 19 The sons of <u>the wife of Hodiah, the sister of Naham</u>, were the fathers of Keilah the Garmite and Eshtemoa the Maacathite.*	מִרְיָם Miriam I GEN.-AMBIG.; ONLY 1 CHR 1–9 The Judean wife ETHN.; NAMELESS ; ONLY 1 CHR 1–9 בִּתְיָה Bithiah daughter of Pharaoh (ETHN.); ONLY 1 CHR 1–9 The wife of Hodiah, the sister of Naham NAMELESS; ONLY 1 CHR 1–9

Reference	Text	Names
4.20a	The sons of Shimon	
4.20b	The descendants of Ishi	
4.21-23	The descendants of Shelah	
1 Chron. 4.24-43	**The genealogies of Simeon**	
4.24-27	Introduction	
1 Chron. 4.27	*27 Shimei had sixteen sons and <u>six daughters</u>; but his brothers did not have many children, nor did all their family multiply like the Judeans.*	Six daughters NAMELESS GROUP; ONLY 1 CHR 1–9
4.28-33a	The Simeonite settlements	
1 Chron. 4.28-31	*28 They lived in Beer-sheba, Moladah, Hazar-shual, 29 <u>Bilhah</u>, Ezem, Tolad, 30 Bethuel, Hormah, Ziklag, 31 Beth-marcaboth, Hazar-susim, Beth-biri and Shaaraim. These were their towns until David became king.*	בלהה Bilhah I GEN.-AMBIG.; TOPON.
4.33b-38a	Genealogical registration	
4.38b-41	Simeonite expansion to the West	
4.42-43	Simeonite expansion to Seir	
1 Chron. 5.1-26	**The genealogies of the Transjordanian Tribes**	
5.1-2	Reuben, Judah and Joseph	
5.3-10	The sons of Reuben	
5.11-17	The sons of Gad	
5.18-22	Reuben, Gad and East Manasseh at war	
5.23-24	The half-tribe of East Manasseh	
5.25-26	Assyrian Exile	
1 Chron. 5.27–6.38	**The genealogies of Levi** [NRSV ≅ 1 Chron. 6.1-53]	
1 Chron. 5.27-30	*[27 The sons of Levi: Gershom, Kohath and Merari. 28 The sons of Kohath: Amram, Izhar, Hebron and Uzziel.] 29 The children of Amram: Aaron, Moses and <u>Miriam</u>. [The sons of Aaron: Nadab, Abihu, Eleazar and Ithamar. 30 Eleazar became the father of Phinehas, Phinehas of Abishua.]*	מרים Miriam II GEN.-AMBIG.; INTERTEXT
1 Chron. 6.39-66	**The settlements of Levi** [NRSV ≅ 1 Chron. 6.54-81]	
1 Chron. 7.1-5	**The genealogies of Issachar**	
1 Chron. 7.3-5	*[3 The son of Uzzi: Izrahiah. And the sons of Izrahiah: Michael, Obadiah, Joel and Isshiah, five, all of them chiefs;] 4 and along with them, by their generations, according to their ancestral houses, were units of the fighting force, thirty-six thousand, for they had <u>many wives</u> and sons. [5 Their kindred belonging to all the families of Issachar were in all eighty-seven thousand mighty warriors, enrolled by genealogy.]*	Many wives NAMELESS GROUP; ONLY 1 CHR 1–9
1 Chron. 7.6-11	**The genealogies of Benjamin I**	
1 Chron. 7.8-9	*8 The sons of Becher: Zemirah, Joash, Eliezer, Elioenai, Omri, Jeremoth, <u>Abijah</u>, Anathoth and Alemeth. All these were the sons of Becher. 9 And their enrollment by genealogies, according to their generations, as heads of their fathers' houses, mighty warriors, was 20,200.*	אביה Abijah II GEN.-AMBIG.
1 Chron. 7.12-13	**The genealogies of Dan and Naphtali**	

Reference	Text	Names
1 Chron. 7.13	13 The descendants of Naphtali: Jahziel, Guni, Jezer and Shallum, the descendants of _Bilhah_.	בלהה Bilhah II GEN.-AMBIG.; TOPON.; INTERTEXT
1 Chron. 7.14-19	**The genealogies of Manasseh**	
1 Chron. 7.14-19	14 The sons of Manasseh: Asriel, whom _his Aramean concubine_ bore; _she_ bore Machir the father of Gilead. 15 And Machir took a _wife for Huppim and for Shuppim_. The name of his sister was _Maacah_. And the name of the second was Zelophehad; and Zelophehad had _daughters_. 16 _Maacah_ the wife of Machir bore a son and _she_ named him Peresh; the name of his brother was Sheresh; and his sons were Ulam and Rekem. 17 The son of Ulam: Bedan. These were the sons of Gilead son of Machir, son of Manasseh. 18 And his sister _Hammolecheth_ bore Ishhod, Abiezer and _Mahlah_. 19 The sons of Shemida were Ahian, Shechem, Likhi and Aniam.	The Aramean secondary wife of Manasseh ETHN.; NAMELESS A wife for Huppim and for Shuppim NAMELESS; ONLY 1 CHR 1–9 מעכה Maacah III sister of Machir GEN.-AMBIG.; TOPON.; ARAM.; N. EMPH.; ONLY 1 CHR 1–9 Zelophehad's daughters NAMELESS GROUP; INTERTEXT (Mahlah, Noa, Hoglah, Milcah and Tirzah) מעכה Maacah IV wife of Machir GEN.-AMBIG.; TOPON.; ARAM.; ONLY 1 CHR 1–9 המלכת Hammolecheth (ARAM.); ONLY 1 CHR 1–9 מחלה Mahlah II GEN.-AMBIG.; ARAM.; ONLY 1 CHR 1–9
1 Chron. 7.20-27	**The genealogies of Ephraim**	
1 Chron. 7.20-27	[20 The sons of Ephraim: Shuthelah and Bered his son, Tahath his son, Eleadah his son, Tahath his son, 21 Zabad his son, Shuthelah his son and Ezer and Elead. Now the people of Gath, who were born in the land, killed them, because they came down to raid their cattle. 22 And their father Ephraim mourned many days and his brothers came to comfort him.] 23 Ephraim went in to _his wife_ and _she_ conceived and bore a son; and he named him Beriah, because disaster had befallen his house. 24 His daughter was _Sheerah_, who built both Lower and Upper Beth-horon and Uzzen-sheerah. [25 Repah was his son, Resheph his son, Telah his son, Tahan his son, 26 Ladan his son, Ammihud his son, Elishama his son, 27 Nun his son, Joshua his son.]	The wife of Ephraim NAMELESS; ONLY 1 CHR 1–9 שארה Sheerah TOPON.; ONLY 1 CHR 1–9
1 Chron. 7.28-29	**The settlements of Manasseh and Ephraim**	
1 Chron. 7.30-40	**The genealogies of Asher**	
1 Chron. 7.30-33	30 The sons of Asher: Imnah, Ishvah, Ishvi, Beriah and their sister _Serah_. [31 The sons of Beriah: Heber and Malchiel, who was the father of Birzaith.] 32 Heber became the father of Japhlet, Shomer, Hotham and their sister _Shua_. [33 The sons of Japhlet: Pasach, Bimhal and Ashvath. These are the sons of Japhlet.]	שרח Serah INTERTEXT שועא Shua GEN.-AMBIG.; ONLY 1 CHR 1–9

Reference	Text	Names
1 Chron. 8.1-40	**The genealogies of Benjamin II**	
8.1-7	Benjamin, Bela and Ehud	
8.8-12	Shaharaim's wives and descendants	
1 Chron. 8.8-11	*8 And Shaharaim had sons in the country of Moab after he had sent away his wives <u>Hushim</u> and <u>Baara</u>. 9 He had sons by his wife <u>Hodesh</u>: Jobab, Zibia, Mesha, Malcam, 10 Jeuz, Sachia and Mirmah. These were his sons, heads of ancestral houses. 11 He also had sons by <u>Hushim</u>: Abitub and Elpaal.*	ח(ו)שׁים Hushim <small>GEN.-AMBIG.; ONLY 1 CHR 1–9</small> בערא Baara <small>ONLY 1 CHR 1–9</small> חדשׁ Hodesh <small>ONLY 1 CHR 1–9</small>
8.13-28	Beriah, Shema, Elpaal and Jeremoth	
8.29-40	The Jeielite genealogy	
1 Chron. 8.29-32	*29 Jeiel the father of Gibeon lived in Gibeon and the name of his wife was <u>Maacah</u>. [30 His firstborn son: Abdon, then Zur, Kish, Baal, Nadab, 31 Gedor, Ahio, Zecher, 32 and Mikloth, who became the father of Shimeah. Now these also lived opposite their kindred in Jerusalem, with their kindred.]*	מעכה Maacah V <small>GEN.-AMBIG.; TOPON.; NON ARAM.; N. EMPH.; INTERTEXT</small>
1 Chron. 9.1-2	**Conclusion of the genealogies of the tribes**	
1 Chron. 9.3-34	**The inhabitants of Jerusalem**	
9.2	Repatriation	
9.3-9	Judah and Benjamin	
9.10-16	Priests and Levites	
9.17-22	Gatekeepers	
9.23-34	Their duties at tent and temple	
1 Chron. 9.35-44	**Appendix of the genealogies of the house of Saul (Benjamin III)**	
1 Chron. 9.35	*35 In Gibeon lived the father of Gibeon, Jeiel and the name of his wife was <u>Maacah</u>.*	מעכה Maacah V <small>GEN.-AMBIG.; TOPON.; ARAM.; N. EMPH.; INTERTEXT</small>

Appendix 2

Scene Protocol *My Life Part 2*

Sequence 1: Opening [time: 1990s]

1 -	00:00:00	Ursula's legacy to her daughter Angelika
2 -	00:00:39	The power of the name Levi
3 -	00:01:42	Memory objects of Angelika's mother
4 -	00:02:40	Title
5 -	00:02:58	Mother–daughter mirror (Ursula and Angelika)
6 -	00:03:24	Aim of the film

Sequence 2: Setting out the genealogy: family lines, bodily inscriptions and political demarcations [time: pre-war until end of fascism]

7 -	00:04:30	The 'who is who' of the family line
8 -	00:05:18	Embodied lineages: anti-Semitic ascriptions and Jewish self-perception
8a	00:05:18	Anti-Semitic discrimination in the 1930s
8b	00:06:18	Identity, difference and discrimination as teenagers in the 1930s
8c	00:06:41	Inherited self-perception as Jewish/non-Jewish
8d	00:07:14	The yellow sifter as sign of distorted significance
9 -	00:07:50	The Neustadt Goblet
9a	00:07:50	Ursula Levi recounts the suicide of her grandmother
9b	00:10:11	The goblet in Angelika's childhood memories
9c	00:10:44	The goblet back in Neustadt
9d	00:11:57	Political continuity of racism and anti-Semitism in Neustadt
9e	00:12:49	History of anti-Semitism in Neustadt in the 1930s

Sequence 3: Nazi Germany: exile, murder and persecution [time: fascism in Germany]

10 - 00:17:19		Angelika's grandfather emigrates to Chile
11 - 00:18:40		Angelika recalls her murdered relatives: the memorial album

12 -	00:19:29	Ursula recounts the deportation of uncle Rudi
13 -	00:20:28	Karla, Ursula and Jürgen living through the 1940s in Germany
14 -	00:23:16	The Becker-Levi family in beach chairs in the 1980s and 1990s
15 -	00:23:45	Silence about how Karla, Ursula and Jürgen survived the war
16 -	00:24:06	Name changes
16a	00:24:06	Karla changes her name Levi back to her maiden name Heins
16b	00:25:16	Name changes of uncle Jürgen
16c	00:26:13	Angelika assumes her mother's maiden name Levi as artistic pseudonym
16d	00:26:33	Ursula's names and passport

Sequence 4: Emigration to Chile and return to Germany [time: 1947–1959]

17 -	00:27:11	Arrival in Chile
17a	00:27:11	'Deutschland Ade!' and reunion with Ursula's father
17b	00:28:14	Close bond between mother and daughter; jealousy of the father
17c	00:29:09	Ursula's reflection on her difficult status between the lines
17d	00:30:49	'Rascal and the Pesky Airplane'
18 -	00:31:34	Ursula as young ecologist in Chile
18a	00:31:34	Ursula's passion, plans and professional prospects
18b	00:32:09	Ursula's work as first female ecologist in Chile
18c	00:33:27	Congruence between Ursula's profession and biography
18d	00:33:54	Excursions with Ursula as only woman, sustaining the male colleagues with grape sugar
19 -	00:35:22	Death and trauma intrude again; return to Germany
19a	00:35:22	The death of uncle Jürgen
19b	00:36:17	Daughter–mother mirror (Ursula and Karla); joint return to Germany
19c	00:37:45	Cut Polylepis trees—'the picture that brought Ursula Levi back to Germany'
19d	00:38:30	Ursula meets her husband Johannes Becker
19e	00:39:01	Ursula marries in Germany against the advice of her teacher

Sequence 5: Starting a family: introduction of a second line and perspective [time: 1960s–1970s]

20 -	00:39:19	The Protestant perspective
20a	00:39:19	Perspectives of Johannes Becker
20b	00:40:57	Ursula transforms from Jewish immigrant and scholar to a clergyman's wife
20c	00:41:15	The church perspective: 'a sort of reconciliation'
21 -	00:42:26	The parents as a young couple
22 -	00:43:00	Ursula's political engagement and spirituality
23 -	00:43:41	Intrusion of the past
24 -	00:45:10	Daily life in the manse, former Jewish property

Sequence 6: Illness, traumatic recall and loss of/grasp for control [time: late 1960s–1970s]

25 -	00:45:28	Cancer and the ascription of being hysterical
26 -	00:46:10	The fact of cancer and reflections on dying
27 -	00:47:06	Grandfather visit/visit of the past
28 -	00:47:38	Return of cancer, chemotherapy, self-observation and documentation
29 -	00:50:33	Certainty of death, hospital stays, depression
30 -	00:51:33	Stay in a psychiatric clinic and psychiatric counseling before Ursula comes home
31 -	00:53:43	Back in the family: isolation and traumatic recall

Sequence 7: Recalling, forgetting, re-enacting and debating the past: political and personal positions [time: 1970s–1990s]

32 -	00:56:52	Home movies and Angelika's first film: The Red Banister
33 -	00:58:08	Public debates in the 1970s: Margarete Mitscherlich pleads for recall and discussion
34 -	00:59:03	Position of the father: let healing grass grow over 'the thing'
35 -	01:00:55	Public debates in the 1990s: Martin Walser's plea for a culture of looking away
36 -	01:01:23	Public debates in the 1990s
37 -	01: 01:43	Again Walser
38 -	01:02:09	The past in the present: Angelika recalls scenes at the beach overshadowed by her mother's illness
39 -	01:05:11	The past in the present: as a Christmas gift for her children, Ursula gives them documents and money for a possible flight to Chile

Sequence 8: Responses to traumatic histories [time: 1990s]

40 -	01:07:25	Heterosexual reproduction/building a new future
41 -	01:08:07	Search for non-biological answers & clownery
42 -	01:08:46	Letting the line go
43 -	01:09:24	Reflections on being Jewish
44 -	01:11:36	*Chaim*/life as another answer: lesbian subculture

Sequence 9: Revisiting Chile [time: retrospective from the 1960s–1990s]

45 -	01:13:15	Why not Chile?
46 -	01:13:50	Unexpected difference

Sequence 10: Closing circles [time: 1990s]

47 -	01:19:09	Closing circles: the sifter is back as a bread basket
48 -	01:19:31	Closing circles: the family beach is back as a trip to the coast with woman friends
49 -	01:20:33	Closing circles: the mother is back with her strength, originality and humor in her stories old and new
50 -	01:21:27	Closing circles: Spirituality and revisiting biblical Levi

Sequence 11: Retrospective and Closing

51 -	01:23:54	Revisiting the legacy with Angelika's response to it
52 -	01:25:03	Revisiting names and word plays
53 -	01:26:05	Revisiting winter
54 -	01:27:15	Closing

Credits

55 -	01:27:28	Credits

BIBLIOGRAPHY

Aichele, George, 'The Possibility of Error: Minority Report and the Gospel of Mark', in *The Bible in Film-The Bible and Film* (ed. J. Cheryl Exum; Leiden: E.J. Brill, 2006), pp. 144-57.

Aichele, George, and Richard Walsh, 'Introduction: Scripture as Precursor', in *Screening Scripture: Intertextual Connections between Scripture and Film* (ed. George Aichele and Richard Walsh; Harrisburg, PA: Trinity Press International, 2002), pp. vii-xvi.

Aichele, George, and Gary A. Phillips (eds.), *Intertextuality and the Bible* (Semeia, 69/70; Atlanta, GA: Scholars Press, 1995).

Aichele, George, and Richard Walsh (eds.), *Screening Scripture: Intertextual Connections between Scripture and Film* (Harrisburg, PA: Trinity Press International, 2002).

Albertz, Rainer, *Israel in Exile: The History and Literature of the Sixth Century B.C.E.* (Studies in Biblical Literature, 3; trans. David Green; Atlanta, GA: Society of Biblical Literature, 2003).

Allan, Graham, *Intertextuality: The New Critical Idiom* (London: Routledge, 2000).

Allen, Leslie C., *The Greek Chronicles: The Relation of the Septuagint of I and II Chronicles to the Masoretic Text, Part 2: Textual Criticism* (VTSup, 25.2; Leiden: E.J. Brill, 1974).

Alphen, Ernst J. van, 'Second Generation Testimony, the Transmission of Trauma, and Postmemory', *Psychoanalyse im Widerspruch* 33 (2005), pp. 87-102.

—'Towards a New Historiography: Péter Forgács and the Aesthetics of Temporality', in *Resonant Bodies, Voices, Memories* (ed. Anke Bangma *et al.*; Rotterdam: Piet Zwart Institute, 2008), pp. 90-113.

Amit, Yairah, 'Araunah's Threshing-floor: A Lesson in Shaping Historical Memory', in *Performing Memory in Biblical Narrative and Beyond* (ed. Athalya Brenner and Frank H. Polak; Sheffield: Sheffield Phoenix Press, 2009), pp. 13-23.

Anderson, Benedict, *Imagined Communities: Reflections on the Origin and Spread of Nationalism* (Verso: New York, 2nd edn, 1991).

Assmann, Aleida, *Erinnerungsräume: Formen und Wandlungen des kulturellen Gedächtnisses* (Munich: Beck, 1999).

—'Gedächtnis als Leitbegriff der Kulturwissenschaft', in *Kulturwissenschaften: Forschung-Praxis-Positionen* (ed. Lutz Musner *et al.*; Freiburg: Rombach, 2003), pp. 27-47.

—'Memory', *BDR* III, pp. 1212-18, section 6.

—'Canon and Archive', in *Cultural Memory Studies: An International and Interdisciplinary Handbook* (ed. Astrid Erll and Ansgar Nünning; Berlin: W. de Gruyter, 2008), pp. 97-107.

Assmann, Jan, *Das kulturelle Gedächtnis: Schrift, Erinnerung und politische Identität der frühen Hochkulturen* (Munich: Beck, 1999).

—'Communicative and Cultural Memory', in *Cultural Memory Studies: An Inter-*

national and Interdisciplinary Handbook (ed. Astrid Erll and Ansgar Nünning; Berlin: W. de Gruyter, 2008), pp. 109-18.

Austin, J.L., *How to Do Things with Words: The William James Lectures delivered in Harvard University in 1955* (ed. J.O. Urmson and Marina Sbisà; Oxford: Oxford University Press, 2nd edn, 1975).

Bakhtin, Mikhail M., 'Discourse in the Novel', in *The Dialogic Imagination: Four Essays by M.M. Bakhtin* (ed. Michael Holquist; Austin, TX: University of Texas Press, 1981), pp. 259-422.

Bakker, Freek L., *Jezus in beeld: Een studie naar zijn verschijnen op het witte doek* (Utrecht: Uitgeverij Van Gruting, 2011).

Bal, Mieke, 'Introduction', in *Acts of Memory: Cultural Recall in the Present* (ed. Mieke Bal, Jonathan Crewe and Leo Spitzer; Hanover: University Press of New England, 1999), pp. vii-xvii.

Bal, Mieke, Fokkelien van Dijk-Hemmes and Grietje van Ginneken, *Und Sara lachte: Patriarchat und Widerstand in biblischen Geschichten* (Münster: Morgana-Frauenbuchverlag, 1988).

Bal, Mieke, Jonathan Crewe and Leo Spitzer (eds.), *Acts of Memory: Cultural Recall in the Present* (Hanover: University Press of New England, 1999).

Bark, Franziska, 'The God Who Will Be and the Generations of Men: Time and the Torah', in *Judaism* 49.3 (2000), pp. 259-68.

Barnouw, Erik, *Documentary: A History of the Non-Fiction Film* (Oxford: Oxford University Press, 2nd edn, 1993).

Barr, James, 'The Symbolism of Names in the Old Testament', *BJRL* 52 (1969/70), pp. 11-29.

Barthes, Roland, *S/Z* (trans. Jürgen Hoch; Frankfurt: Suhrkamp, 1976).

—'The Death of the Author', in *The Rustle of Language* (trans. Richard Howard; Berkeley, CA: California Press, 1989), pp. 49-55.

—'From Work to Text', in *The Rustle of Language* (trans. Richard Howard; Berkeley, CA: California Press, 1989), pp. 56-64.

Bartlett, John R., *Edom and the Edomites* (JSOTSup, 77; Sheffield: Sheffield Academic Press, 1989).

Barton, John, *Reading the Old Testament: Method in Biblical Study* (Louisville, KY: Westminster/John Knox Press, 2nd edn, 1996).

Baudry, Jean-Louis, 'Le Dispositif: approches métapsychologiques de l'impression de réalité', in *Communications* 23 (1975), pp. 56-72.

Baumann, Gerd, and Andre Gingrich, 'Foreword', in *Grammars of Identity/Alterity: A Structural Approach* (ed. Gerd Baumann and Andre Gingrich; Oxford: Berghan Books, 2004), pp. ix-xiv.

Baumann, Gerd and Andre Gingrich (eds.), *Grammars of Identity/Alterity: A Structural Approach* (Oxford: Berghahn Books, 2004).

Becking, Bob, 'In Babylon: The Exile in Historical (Re)construction', in *From Babylon to Eternity: The Exile Remembered and Constructed in Text and Tradition* (ed. Bob Becking, Alex Cannegieter, Wilfred van de Poll and Anne-Mareike Wetter; London: Equinox, 2009), pp. 4-33.

—'Exilische identiteit als post-exilische ideologie: Psalm 137 opnieuw gelezen', *Nederlands theologisch tijdschrift* 64.4 (2010), pp. 269-83.

—'David between Evidence and Ideology', in *History of Israel between Evidence and Ideology* (ed. Bob Becking and Lester L. Grabbe; *OTS*, 59; Leiden: E.J. Brill, 2011), pp. 1-30.

—*Ezra, Nehemiah, and the Construction of Early Jewish Identity* (FAT, 80; Tübingen: Mohr Siebeck, 2011).

—'Zedekiah, Josephus and the Dating of Chronicles', *SJOT* 25.2 (2011), pp. 217-33.

Beentjes, Pancratius C., *1 Kronieken* (Verklaring van de Hebreeuwse Bijbel; Kampen: Kook, 2002).

—*'Die Freude war groß in Jerusalem' (2Chr 30,26): Eine Einführung in die Chronikbücher* (SEThV, 3; Münster: LIT Verlag, 2008).

—*Tradition and Transformation in the Book of Chronicles* (SSN, 52; Leiden: E.J. Brill, 2008).

Ben Zvi, Ehud, 'The Book of Chronicles: Another Look', *SR* 31 (2002), pp. 261-81.

—'A Sense of Proportion: An Aspect of the Theology of the Chronicler', in *History, Literature and Theology in the Book of Chronicles* (London: Equinox, 2006), pp. 160-73.

—*History, Literature and Theology in the Book of Chronicles* (London: Equinox, 2006).

Benjamin, Walter, *Zur Kritik der Gewalt und andere Aufsätze* (Edition Suhrkamp, 103; Frankfurt: Suhrkamp, 1965).

Bernstorff, Madeleine, 'MEIN LEBEN TEIL 2 von Angelika Levi, D 2003' (download available at http://www.madeleinebernstorff.de/seiten/leben_tx.html; accessed June 8, 2013).

Berquist, Jon L., and Claudia V. Camp (eds.), *Constructions of Space I: Theory, Geography, Narrative* (LHBOTS, 481; New York: T. & T. Clark, 2007).

Bhabha, Homi, *The Location of Culture* (London: Routledge, 1994).

Bial, Henry, 'Performativity', in *The Performance Studies Reader* (ed. Henry Bial; London: Routledge, 2007), pp. 175-76.

—'What is Performance?', in *The Performance Studies Reader* (ed. Henry Bial; London: Routledge, 2007), pp. 59-60.

—'Play', in *The Performance Studies Reader* (ed. Henry Bial; London: Routledge, 2007), pp. 135-36.

Bial, Henry (ed.), *The Performance Studies Reader* (London: Routledge, 2007).

Bible & Culture Collective (eds.), *The Postmodern Bible* (New Haven, CT: Yale University Press, 1997).

Blenkinsopp, Joseph, *Creation, Un-creation, Re-creation: A Discursive Commentary on Genesis 1–11* (Edinburgh: T. & T. Clark, 2011).

Boer, Roland, 'No Road: On the Absence of Feminist Criticism of Ezra-Nehemiah', in *Her Master's Tools?: Feminist and Postcolonial Engagements of Historical-Critical Discourse* (ed. Caroline Vander Stichele and Todd Penner; Global Perspectives on Biblical Literature, 9; Atlanta, GA: Society of Biblical Literature, 2005), pp. 233-52.

Bohmbach, Karla G., 'Names and Naming in the Biblical World', in *WiS*, pp. 33-40.

Bouquet, Mary, 'Family Trees and their Affinities: The Visual Imperative of the Genealogical Diagram', in *The Journal of the Royal Anthropological Institute* 2.1 (1996), pp. 43-66.

Braun, Christina von, and Inge Stephan, 'Einleitung', in *Gender-Studies: Eine Einführung* (ed. Christina von Braun and Inge Stephan; Stuttgart: Metzler, 2nd edn, 2006), pp. 3-9.

Breitmaier, Isa, 'Angestaute Gegenwart: Zur Zeitkonstruktion in Genealogien (Gen 5)', in *Zeit wahrnehmen: Feministisch-Theologische Perspektiven auf das Erste Testament* (ed. Hedwig-Jahnow-Forschungsprojekt; SBS, 222; Stuttgart: Katholisches Bibelwerk, 2010), pp. 66-99.

Brenner, Athalya, 'Foreword', in *Culture, Entertainment and the Bible* (ed. George Aichele; Sheffield: Sheffield Academic Press, 2000), pp. 7-12.

—*I am...Biblical Women Tell Their Own Stories* (Minneapolis, MN: Fortress Press, 2005).

—'Alternative Families: From the Hebrew Bible to Early Judaisms', essay based on the paper of the same name delivered at the ISBL in Tartu, Estonia, in July 2010 (download available at http://www.uva.nl/over-de-uva/organisatie/medewerkers/content/b/r/a.brenner/a.brenner.html; accessed June 8, 2013).

Bronner, Leila Lea, 'The Invisible Relationship Made Visible: Biblical Mothers and Daughters', in *Ruth and Esther: A Feminist Companion to the Bible (Second Series 3)* (ed. Athalya Brenner; Sheffield: Sheffield Academic Press, 1999), pp. 172-91.

Brueggemann, Walter, *Theology of the Old Testament: Testimony, Dispute, Advocacy* (Minneapolis, MN: Fortress Press, 1997).

Bruzzi, Stella, *New Documentary: A Critical Introduction* (London: Routledge, 2000).

Buikema, Rosemarie, and Iris van der Tuin, 'Introduction', in *Doing Gender in Media, Arts and Culture* (ed. Rosemarie Buikema and Iris van der Tuin; New York: Routledge, 2009), pp. 1-4.

Burlein, Ann, 'Countermemory on the Right', in *Acts of Memory: Cultural Recall in the Present* (ed. Mieke Bal, Jonathan Crewe and Leo Spitzer; Hanover: University Press of New England, 1999), pp. 209-17.

Butler, Judith, 'Performative Acts and Gender Constitution: An Essay in Phenomenology and Feminist Theory (1988)', in *The Performance Studies Reader* (ed. Henry Bial; London: Routledge, 2007), pp. 187-99.

Butting, Klara, *Die Buchstaben werden sich noch wundern: Innerbiblische Kritik als Wegweisung feministischer Hermeneutik* (Wittingen: Erev Rav, 2nd edn, 1998).

Camp, Claudia V., *Wise, Strange and Holy: The Strange Woman and the Making of the Bible* (JSOTSup, 320; Sheffield: Sheffield Academic Press, 2000).

—'The Problem with Sisters: Anthropological Perspectives on Priestly Kinship Ideology in Numbers', in *Embroidered Garments: Priests and Gender in Biblical Israel* (ed. Deborah W. Rooke; Sheffield: Sheffield Phoenix Press, 2009), pp. 119-30.

Carroll, Robert, 'Exile! What Exile?: Deportation and the Discourse of Diaspora (In Memoriam Ferdinand Deist)', in *Leading Captivity Captive: 'The Exile' as History and Ideology* (ed. Lester L. Grabbe, JSOTSup, 278; Sheffield: Sheffield Academic Press, 1998), pp. 62-79.

Carsten, Janet, *After Kinship* (Cambridge: Cambridge University Press, 2004).

Caruth, Cathy, 'Introduction I', in *Trauma: Explorations in Memory, Part I: Trauma and Experience* (ed. Cathy Caruth; Baltimore, MD: Johns Hopkins University Press, 1995), pp. 3-12.

—'Introduction II', in *Trauma: Explorations in Memory, Part II: Recapturing the Past* (ed. Cathy Caruth; Baltimore, MD: Johns Hopkins University Press, 1995), pp. 151-57.

—*Unclaimed Experience: Trauma, Narrative, and History* (Baltimore, MD: Johns Hopkins University Press, 1996).

Caruth, Cathy (ed.), *Trauma: Explorations in Memory* (Baltimore, MD: Johns Hopkins University Press, 1995)

Caselli, Daniela C., *Beckett's Dantes: Intertextuality in the Fiction and Criticism* (Manchester: Manchester University Press, 2005).

Cassuto, U., *A Commentary on the Book of Genesis* (trans. Israel Abraham; Jerusalem: Magnes Press, 1944).

Childs, Brevard, *Introduction to the Old Testament as Scripture* (Philadelphia, PA: Fortress Press, 1979).

Connerton, Paul, *How Societies Remember* (Cambridge: Cambridge University Press, 1989).

Crüsemann, Frank, 'Human Solidarity and Ethnic Identity: Israel's Self-Definition in the Genealogical System of Genesis', in *Ethnicity and the Bible* (ed. Mark G. Brett; BIS, 19; Leiden: E.J. Brill, 1996), pp. 57-76.

Curtis, Edward Lewis, and Albert Alonzo Madsen, *A Critical and Exegetical Commentary on the Books of Chronicles* (ICC, 11; Edinburgh: T. & T. Clark, 1952).

Davies, Philip, 'Exile? What Exile? Whose Exile?', in *Leading Captivity Captive: 'The Exile' as History and Ideology* (ed. Lester L. Grabbe; JSOTSup, 278; Sheffield: Sheffield Academic Press, 1998), pp. 128-38.

Davis, M. Stephen, 'Sheerah (*Person*)', *ABD* V, pp. 1190-91.

De Regt, L.J., *Participants in Old Testament Texts and the Translator: Reference Devices and their Rhetorical Impact* (Assen: Van Gorcum, 1999).

Deacy, Christopher, and Ulrike Vollmer (eds.), *Blick über den Tod hinaus/Seeing Beyond Death: Bilder vom Leben nach dem Tod in Theologie und Film/Images of Afterlife in Theology and Film* (Film und Theologie, 18; Marburg: Schüren-Verlag, 2011).

Deleuze, Gilles, and Félix Guattari, *A Thousand Plateaus* (trans. Brian Massumi; London: Continuum, 2004).

Demsky, Aaron, 'The Clans of Ephrath: Their Territory and History', *Journal of the Institute of Archaeology of Tel Aviv University* 1 (1986), pp. 46-59.

Derrida, Jacques, *Archive Fever: A Freudian Impression* (trans. E. Prenowitz; Chicago, IL: University of Chicago Press, 1996).

—'Archive Fever (A Seminar by Jacques Derrida, University of Witwatersrand, August 1998, transcribed by Verne Harris)', in *Refiguring the Archive* (ed. Carolyn Hamilton *et al.*; Dordrecht: Kluwer Academic Publishers, 2002), pp. 38-80/even pages.

Dijk-Hemmes, Fokkelien van, 'Tamar and the Limits of Patriarchy: Between Rape and Seduction', in *Anti-Covenant: Counter-Reading Women's Lives in the Hebrew Bible* (ed. Mieke Bal; Sheffield: Sheffield Academic Press and the Almond Press, 1989), pp. 135-56.

Dorman, N., and D.C. Bourne, 'Canids and Ursids in Mixed-species Exhibits', *Int. Zoo Yb.* 44 (2010), pp. 75-86.

Du Toit, Jaqueline S., *Textual Memory: Ancient Archives, Libraries and the Hebrew Bible* (The Social World of Biblical Antiquity, Second Series, 6; Sheffield: Sheffield Phoenix Press, 2011).

Dyck, Jonathan E., *The Theocratic Ideology of the Chronicler* (Leiden: E.J. Brill, 1998).

Ebach, Jürgen, *Genesis 37–50* (HThKAT; Freiburg: Herder, 2007).

Ehrenreich, Eric, *The Nazi Ancestral Proof: Genealogy, Racial Science, and the Final Solution* (Bloomington, IN: Indiana University Press, 2007).

Elsaesser, Thomas, 'Subject Positions, Speaking Positions: From *Holocaust, Our Hitler*, and *Heimat* to *Shoah* and *Schindler's List*', in *The Persistence of History: Cinema, Television and the Modern Event* (ed. Vivian Sobchack; New York: Routledge, 1996), pp. 145-81.

Engar, Ann W., 'Old Testament Women as Tricksters', in *Mappings of the Biblical Terrain: The Bible as Text* (ed. Vincent T. Tollers and John Maier; Lewisburg, PA: Bucknell University Press, 1990), pp. 143-57.

Erll, Astrid, 'Cultural Memory Studies: An Introduction', in *Cultural Memory Studies:*

An International and Interdisciplinary Handbook (ed. Astrid Erll and Ansgar Nünning; Berlin: W. de Gruyter, 2008), pp. 1-15.

Erll, Astrid, and Ann Rigney, 'Introduction: Cultural Memory and its Dynamic', in
Mediation, Remediation, and the Dynamics of Cultural Memory (ed. Astrid Erll
and Ann Rigney; Berlin: W. de Gruyter, 2009), pp. 1-11.

Eskenazi, Tamara C., *In an Age of Prose: A Literary Approach to Ezra-Nehemiah*
(Atlanta, GA: Scholars Press, 1988).

—'Out from the Shadows: Biblical Women in the Post-Exilic Era', in *A Feminist Companion to Samuel and Kings* (ed. Athalya Brenner; Sheffield: Sheffield Academic
Press, 1994), pp. 252-71.

Exum, J. Cheryl, 'Raped by the Pen', in *Fragmented Women: Feminist (Sub)Versions of
Biblical Narratives* (JSOTSup, 163; Sheffield: Sheffield Academic Press, 1993),
pp. 170-201.

—*Plotted, Shot, and Painted: Cultural Representations of Biblical Women* (JSOTSup,
215; Gender, Culture, Theory, 3; Sheffield: Sheffield Academic Press, 1996).

—'Judges: Encoded Messages to Women', in *Feminist Biblical Interpretation: A Compendium of Critical Commentary on the Books of the Bible and Related Literature*
(ed. Luise Schottroff, Marie-Theres Wacker and Hans Martin Rumscheidt; trans.
Lisa E. Dahill; Grand Rapids, MI: Eerdmans, 2012), pp. 112-27.

Exum, J. Cheryl (ed.), *The Bible in Film–The Bible and Film* (Leiden: E.J. Brill, 2006).

Finkelstein, Israel, 'The Historical Reality behind the Genealogical Lists in 1 Chronicles', in *JBL* 131.1 (2012), pp. 65-83.

Fischer, Irmtraud, *Die Erzeltern Israels: Feministisch-theologische Studien zu Genesis*
(BZAW, 222; Berlin: W. de Gruyter, 1994).

Fishbane, Michael, *Text and Texture: Close Readings of Selected Biblical Texts* (New
York: Schocken Books, 1979).

—*Biblical Interpretation in Ancient Israel* (Oxford: Clarendon Press, 1985).

—'Types of Biblical Intertextuality', in *Congress Volume: Oslo 1998* (ed. André Lemaire
and Magne Sæbø; VTSup, 80; Leiden: E.J. Brill, 2000), pp. 39-44.

Foucault, Michel, 'Nietzsche, Genealogy, History', in *Language, Counter-Memory,
Practice: Selected Essays and Interviews* (ed. Donald F. Bouchard; New York:
Cornell University Press, 1977), pp. 139-64.

Gerstenberger, Erhard S., *Israel in der Perserzeit: 5. und 4. Jahrhundert v. Chr.* (BE, 8;
Stuttgart: Kohlhammer, 2005).

Geyer, Paul, 'Das Paradox: Historisch Systematische Grundlegung', in *Das Paradox:
Eine Herausforderung des abendländischen Denkens* (ed. Paul Geyer and Roland
Hagenbüchle; Tübingen: Stauffenburg, 1992), pp. 11-24.

Gingrich, Andre, 'Conceptualising Identities: Anthropological Alternatives to Essential-
ising Difference and Moralizing about Othering', in *Grammars of Identity/Alterity:
A Structural Approach* (ed. Gerd Baumann and Andre Gingrich; Oxford: Berghahn
Books, 2004), pp. 3-17.

Grabbe, Lester L., 'Introduction', in *Leading Captivity Captive: 'The Exile' as History
and Ideology* (ed. Lester L. Grabbe; JSOTSup, 278; Sheffield: Sheffield Academic
Press, 1998), pp. 11-19.

—'Reflections on the Discussion', in *Leading Captivity Captive: 'The Exile' as History
and Ideology* (ed. Lester L. Grabbe; JSOTSup, 278; Sheffield: Sheffield Academic
Press, 1998), pp. 146-56.

Grabbe, Lester L. (ed.), *Leading Captivity Captive: 'The Exile' as History and Ideology*
(JSOTSup, 278; Sheffield: Sheffield Academic Press, 1998).

Greenspahn, Frederick E., *When Brothers Dwell Together: The Preeminence of Younger Siblings in the Hebrew Bible* (Oxford: Oxford University Press, 1994).

Hachlili, Rachel, 'Hebrew Names, Personal Names, Family Names and Nicknames of Jews in the Second Temple Period', in *Families and Family Relations as Represented in Early Judaism and Early Christianities: Texts and Fictions* (ed. Jan Willem van Henten and Athalya Brenner; Leiden: Deo Publishing, 2000), pp. 83-115.

Halbwachs, Maurice, *Das Gedächtnis und seine sozialen Bedingungen* (ed. Heinz Maus and Friedrich Fürstenberg; trans. Lutz Geldsetzer; Berlin: Luchterhand, 1966).

—*On Collective Memory* (ed. and trans. Lewis A. Coser; Chicago, IL: University of Chicago Press, 1992).

Hallo, William W., 'Compare and Contrast: the Contextual Approach to Biblical Literature', in *The Bible in the Light of Cuneiform Literature* (ed. William W. Hallo, Bruce William Jones and Gerald L. Mattingly; New York: The Edwin Mellen Press, 1990), pp. 1-30.

Henten, Jan Willem van, 'Judith as an Alternative Leader: A Rereading of Judith 7–13', in *Esther, Judith and Susanna: A Feminist Companion to the Bible* (ed. Athalya Brenner; Sheffield: Sheffield Academic Press, 1995), pp. 224-52.

Herman, Judith L., *Trauma and Recovery* (New York: Basic Books, 1992).

Hieke, Thomas, *Die Genealogien der Genesis* (HBS, 39; Freiburg: Herder, 2003).

—'Genealogie als Mittel der Geschichtsdarstellung in der Tora und die Rolle der Frauen im genealogischen System', in *Hebräische Bibel—Altes Testament: Tora* (ed. Irmtraud Fischer, Mercedes Puerto Navarra and Andrea Taschl-Erber; Die Bibel und die Frauen, 1.1; Stuttgart: W. Kohlhammer, 2009), pp. 149-85.

Hirsch, Marianne, 'Projected Memory: Holocaust Photographs in Personal and Public Fantasy', in *Acts of Memory: Cultural Recall in the Present* (ed. Mieke Bal, Jonathan Crewe and Leo Spitzer; Hanover: University Press of New England, 1999), pp. 3-23.

Hirsch, Marianne, and Valerie Smith, 'Feminism and Cultural Memory: An Introduction', *Signs* 28, no. 1: Gender and Cultural Memory (2002), pp. 1-19.

Hirsch, Marianne, and Leo Spitzer, 'Testimonial Objects: Memory, Gender, Transmission', *Poetics Today* 27.2 (2006), pp. 137-63.

Hobsbawm, Eric, and Terence Ranger (eds.), *The Invention of Tradition* (Cambridge: Cambridge University Press, 1983).

Hoffmann, Hilde, '*Mein Leben Teil 2—My Life Part 2* (2003): Reflections about Recent Autobiographical Documentaries', in *Gendered Memories: Transgressions in German and Israeli Film and Theatre* (ed. Vera Apfelthaler and Julia B. Köhne; Vienna: Turia & Kant, 2007), pp. 128-43.

Hübner, Ulrich, 'Oholibamah (*Person*)', *ABD* V, p. 10.

Ilan, Tal, *Lexicon of Jewish Names in Late Antiquity Part I: Palestine 330 BCE-200 CE* (Texte und Studien zum Antiken Judentum, 91; Tübingen: J.C.B. Mohr, 2002).

Ishizuka, Karen L., and Patricia R. Zimmermann (eds.), *Mining the Home Movie: Excavations in Histories and Memories* (London: University of California Press, 2008).

Jackson, Melissa, 'Lot's Daughters and Tamar as Tricksters and the Patriarchal Narratives as Feminist Theology', in *JSOT* 98 (2002), pp. 29-46.

Japhet, Sara, 'Conquest and Settlement in Chronicles', *JBL* 98.2 (1979), pp. 205-18.

—*I&II Chronicles: A Commentary* (London: SCM Press, 1993).

—*The Ideology of the Book of Chronicles and its Place in Biblical Thought* (BEATAJ, 9; Frankfurt: Peter Lang, 1997).

—'Exile and Restoration in the Book of Chronicles', in *The Crisis of Israelite Religion: Transformation of Religious Tradition in Exilic and Post-Exilic Times* (ed. Bob Becking and Marjo C.A. Korpel; *OTS*, 42; Leiden: E.J. Brill, 1999), pp. 33-44.

Johnson, Marshall D., *The Purpose of the Biblical Genealogies with Special Reference to the Setting of the Genealogies of Jesus* (SNTSMS, 8; Cambridge: Cambridge University Press, 1969).

Kalimi, Isaac, 'Was the Chronicler a Historian?', in *The Chronicler as Historian* (ed. M. Patrick Graham, Kenneth G. Hoglund and Steven L. McKenzie; JSOTSup, 238; Sheffield: Sheffield Academic Press, 1997), pp. 73-89.

—*The Reshaping of Israelite History in Chronicles* (Winona Lake, IN: Eisenbrauns, 2005).

Kartveit, Magnar, *Motive und Schichten der Landtheologie in I Chronik 1–9* (CBOTS, 28; Stockholm: Almqvist & Wiksell, 1989).

Kelso, Julie, *Oh Mother, Where Art Thou?: An Irigarayan Reading of the Book of Chronicles* (London: Equinox, 2007).

Kessler, Frank, 'The Cinema of Attractions as *Dispositif*', in *The Cinema of Attractions Reloaded* (ed. Wanda Strauven; Amsterdam: Amsterdam University Press, 2006), pp. 57-69.

Kessler, Rainer, *Sozialgeschichte des alten Israel: Eine Einführung* (Darmstadt: Wissenschaftliche Buchgesellschaft, 2008).

Ketelaar, Eric, 'Tacit Narratives: The Meaning of Archives', *Archival Science* 1 (2001), pp. 131-41.

Kiesow, Anna, *Löwinnen von Juda: Frauen als Subjekte politischer Macht in der judäischen Königszeit* (Münster: LIT Verlag, 2000).

Kirk-Duggan, Cheryl A., 'Black Mother Women and Daughters: Signifying Female-Divine Relationships in the Hebrew Bible and African-American Mother-Daughter Short Stories', in *Ruth and Esther: A Feminist Companion to the Bible (Second Series)* (ed. Athalya Brenner; Sheffield: Sheffield Academic Press, 1999), pp. 192-210.

Klein, Lillian R., 'Achsah: What Price this Prize?', in *Judges: A Feminist Companion to the Bible (Second Series 4)* (ed. Athalya Brenner, Sheffield: Sheffield Press, 1999), pp. 18-26.

Knoppers, Gary N., '"Great among His Brothers", But Who Is He?: Heterogeneity in the Composition of Judah', *JHS* 3, article 4 (2001), no pages.

—'Intermarriage, Social Complexity, and Ethnic Diversity in the Genealogy of Judah', *JBL* 120.1 (2001), pp. 15-30.

—*I Chronicles 1–9: A New Translation with Introduction and Commentary* (AB, 12; New York: Doubleday, 2003).

—'Shem, Ham and Japheth: The Universal and the Particular in the Genealogy of Nations', in *The Chronicler as Theologian: Essays in Honour of Ralph W. Klein* (ed. M. Patrick Graham, Steven L. McKenzie and Garry N. Knoppers; London: T. & T. Clark, 2003), pp. 13-31.

—'Comments', in *Chronicles and the Chronicler: A Response to I. Kalimi, An Ancient Israelite Historian: Studies in the Chronicler, His Time, Place and Writing* (ed. Gary N. Knoppers; *JHS* 6.2 [2006]), pp. 26-35.

Kraemer, Phyllis Silverman, 'Biblical Women that Come in Pairs: The Use of Female Pairs as Literary Device in the Hebrew Bible', in *Genesis: A Feminist Companion to the Bible (Second Series)* (ed. Athalya Brenner; Sheffield: Sheffield Academic Press, 1998), pp. 218-32.

Kreitzer, Larry J., *The Old Testament in Fiction and Film: On Reversing the Hermeneutical Flow* (Sheffield: Sheffield Academic Press, 1994).

Kristeva, Julia, *Desire in Language: A Semiotic Approach to Literature and Art* (ed. Leon S. Roudiez; trans. Thomas Gora, Alice Jardine and Leon S. Roudiez; Blackwell: Columbia University Press, 1980).

—'The Bounded Text', in *Desire in Language: A Semiotic Approach to Literature and Art* (ed. Leon S. Roudiez; trans. Thomas Gora, Alice Jardine and Leon S. Roudiez; Blackwell: Columbia University Press, 1980), pp. 36-63.

—'Word, Dialogue and Novel', in *Desire in Language: A Semiotic Approach to Literature and Art* (ed. Leon S. Roudiez; trans. Thomas Gora, Alice Jardine and Leon S. Roudiez; Blackwell: Columbia University Press, 1980), pp. 64-91.

Labahn, Antje, and Ehud Ben Zvi, 'Observations on Women in the Genealogies of 1 Chronicles 1–9', *Biblica* 84 (2003), pp. 457-78.

Laffey, Alice L., '1 and 2 Chronicles', in *The Women's Bible Commentary: Expanded Edition with Apocrypha* (ed. Carol Ann Newsom and Sharon H. Ringe; Louisville, KY: Westminster/John Knox Press, 1998), pp. 110-15.

Landsberg, Alison, *Prosthetic Memory: The Transformation of American Remembrance in the Age of Mass Culture* (Columbia: Columbia University Press, 2004).

Levin, Yigal, 'Who was the Chronicler's Audience?: A Hint from His Genealogies', in *JBL* 122.2 (2003), pp. 229-45.

Lévi-Strauss, Claude, *The Elementary Structures of Kinship* (ed. Rodney Needham; trans. J.H. Bell, J.R. von Sturmer and Rodney Needham; Boston, MA: Beacon Press, 1969).

Löwisch, Ingeborg, 'Frauengenealogien in Film und Hebräischer Bibel: Erinnerungsformen und politische Akte', *Schlangenbrut* 23 (2005), pp. 14-18.

—'Genealogies, Gender, and the Politics of Memory: 1 Chronicles 1–9 and the Documentary Film "Mein Leben Teil 2"', in *Memory in Biblical Narrative and Beyond* (ed. Athalya Brenner and Frank Polak; Sheffield: Sheffield Phoenix Press, 2009), pp. 228-56.

Luker, Lamonette M., 'Ephrathah (Person)', *ABD* II, p. 557.

—'Ephrathah (Place)', *ABD* II, pp. 557-58.

Lux, Rüdiger, 'Die Genealogie als Strukturprinzip des Pluralismus im Alten Testament', in *Pluralismus und Identität* (ed. J. Mehlhausen; VWGT, 8; Gütersloh: Gütersloher Verlagshaus, 1995), pp. 242-58.

Marsh, Clive, and Gaye Ortiz (eds.), *Explorations in Theology and Film: Movies and Meaning* (Oxford: Blackwell, 1998).

Marsman, Hennie M., *Women in Ugarit and Israel: Their Social and Religious Position in the Context of the Ancient Near East* (Leiden: E.J. Brill, 2003).

McClaurin, Irma (ed.), *Black Feminist Anthropology: Theory, Politics, Praxis, and Poetics* (New Brunswick, NJ: Rutgers University Press: 2001).

McKinlay, Judith, 'Meeting Achsah on Achsah's Land', *The Bible and Critical Theory* 5.3 (2009), pp. 39.1-39.11.

Meyers, Carol, *Discovering Eve: Ancient Israelite Women in Context* (Oxford: Oxford University Press, 1988).

—'"Women of the Neighborhood" (Ruth 4.17): Informal Female Networks in Ancient Israel', in *Ruth and Esther: A Feminist Companion to the Bible (Second Series)* (ed. Athalya Brenner; Sheffield: Sheffield Academic Press, 1999), pp. 110-27.

—'Naamah', *WiS*, p. 129.

—*Exodus* (NCamBC; Cambridge: Cambridge University Press, 2005).

Meyers, Eric M., 'The Shelomith Seal and the Judean Restoration: Some Additional Considerations', *Eretz Israel* 18 (1985), pp. 33-38.

Mirguet, Francoise, 'Implicit Biblical Motifs in Almodovar's *Hable Con Ella* and *Volver*: The Bible as Intertext', *Journal of Religion and Popular Culture* 23.1 (2011), pp. 27-39.

Misztal, Barbara A., *Theories of Social Remembering* (Theorizing Society Series, 2; Maidenhead: Open University Press, 2003).

Morin, Peter J., *Community Ecology* (Malden, MA: Blackwell Science, 1999).

Myers O'Brian, Julia, 'Hammolecheth', *WiS*, p. 89.

Myers, Jacob M., *I Chronicles* (AB, 12; New York: Doubleday, 1965).

Nichols, Bill, *Introduction to Documentary* (Bloomington, IN: Indiana University Press, 2001).

Niditch, Susan, 'The Wronged Woman Righted: An Analysis of Genesis 38', *HTR* 72 (1979), pp. 143-49.

—'Genesis', in *The Women's Bible Commentary: Expanded Edition with Apocrypha* (ed. Carol Ann Newsom and Sharon H. Ringe; Louisville, KY: Westminster/John Knox Press, 1998), pp. 13-29.

—*A Prelude to Biblical Folklore: Underdogs and Tricksters* (Urbana, IL: University of Illinois Press, 2000).

Nielsen, Kirsten, 'Intertextuality and Hebrew Bible', in *Congress Volume: Oslo 1998* (ed. André Lemaire and Magne Sæbø; VTSup, 80; Leiden: E.J. Brill, 2000), pp. 17-31.

Nietzsche, Friedrich, *Zur Genealogie der Moral: Eine Streitschrift* (Leipzig: Verlag von C.G. Naumann, 1887).

Nolan Fewell, Danna, 'Deconstructive Criticism: Achsah and the (E)razed City of Writing', in *Judges & Method: New Approaches in Biblical Studies* (ed. Gale A. Yee; Minneapolis, MN: Augsburg–Fortress, 2nd edn, 2007), pp. 115-37.

Noordegraaf, Julia, 'Iterating Archival Footage and the Memory of War', in *The Archive: XVIII International Film Studies Conference* (ed. Alessandro Bordina, Sonia Campanini and Andrea Mariani; Udine: Forum, 2012), pp. 265-72.

—*Performing the Archive: Tracing Audiovisual Heritage in the Digital Age* (forthcoming).

Noth, Martin, *Die israelitischen Personennamen im Rahmen der gemeinsemitischen Namengebung* (Stuttgart: Kohlhammer, 1928).

—'Eine siedlungsgeographische Liste in 1. Chr 2 und 4', *ZDPV* 55 (1932), pp. 97-124.

—*Überlieferungsgeschichtliche Studien 1: Die sammelnden und bearbeitenden Geschichtswerke im Alten Testament* (SKG.G, 18.2; Halle: Niemeyer, 2nd edn, 1943).

O'Connor, Kathleen M., *Jeremiah: Pain and Promise* (Minneapolis, MN: Fortress Press, 2012).

Oeming, Manfred, *Das wahre Israel: Die 'genealogische Vorhalle' 1 Chronik 1–9* (Stuttgart: Kohlhammer, 1990).

Olick, Jeffrey K., 'From Collective Memory to the Sociology of Mnemonic Practices and Products', in *Cultural Memory Studies: An International and Interdisciplinary Handbook* (ed. Astrid Erll and Ansgar Nünning; Berlin: W. de Gruyter, 2008), pp. 151-61.

Perdue, Leo G., Joseph Blenkinsopp, John J. Collins and Carol Meyers (eds.), *Families in Ancient Israel* (The Family, Religion and Culture Series, 7; Louisville, KY: Westminster/John Knox Press, 1997).

Pfister, Manfred, and Ulrich Broich, *Intertextualität: Formen, Funktionen, Anglistische Fallstudien* (Tübingen: Max Niemeyer, 1985).

Pisters, Patricia, and Wim Staat (eds.), *Shooting the Family: Transnational Media and Intercultural Values* (Amsterdam: Amsterdam University Press, 2005).

Polliack, Meira, 'Joseph's Trauma: Memory and Resolutions', in *Performing Memory in Biblical Narrative and Beyond* (ed. Athalya Brenner and Frank H. Polak; Sheffield: Sheffield Phoenix Press, 2009), pp. 73-105.

Poser, Ruth, *Das Ezechielbuch als Trauma-Literatur* (Leiden: E.J. Brill, 2012).

Prewitt, Terry J., 'Kinship Structures and the Genesis Genealogies', *Journal of Near Eastern Studies* 40.2 (1981), pp. 87-98.

Rehm, Merlin D., 'Levites and Priests', *ABD* IV, pp. 297-310.

Reinhartz, Adele, *Scripture on the Silver Screen* (Louisville, KY: Westminster/John Knox Press, 2003).

Ricoeur, Paul, 'Gedächtnis–Vergessen–Geschichte', in *Historische Sinnbildung: Problemstellungen, Zeitkonzepte, Wahrnehmungshorizonte, Darstellungsstrategien* (ed. Klaus E. Müller and Jörn Rüsen; Reinbek: Rowohlt, 1997), pp. 433-54.

Rindge, Matthew S., Erin Runions and Richard S. Ascough, 'Teaching the Bible and Film: Pedagogical Promises, Pitfalls, and Proposals', in *Teaching Theology & Religion* 13.2 (2010), pp. 140-55.

Rothstein, J. Wilhelm and Johannes Hänel, *Das erste Buch der Chronik übersetzt und erklärt* (KAT, 18.2; Leipzig: Deichert, 1927).

Rudolph, Wilhelm, *Chronikbücher* (HAT, 21; Tübingen: Mohr Siebeck, 1955).

Runions, Erin, *How Hysterical: Identification and Resistance in the Bible and Film* (New York: Macmillan, 2003).

Schechner, Richard, *Performance Studies: An Introduction* (London: Routledge, 2002).

Schley, D.G., 'Maacah (Place)', *ABD* IV, p. 430.

Schmid, Konrad, *Literaturgeschichte des Alten Testaments: Eine Einführung* (Darmstadt: Wissenschaftliche Buchgesellschaft, 2008).

Schmidt, Uta, *Zentrale Randfiguren: Strukturen der Darstellung von Frauen in den Erzählungen der Königsbücher* (Gütersloh: Chr. Kaiser Verlag, 2003).

Smith, Jonathan Z., 'In Comparison a Magic Dwells', in *Imagining Religion: From Babylon to Jonestown* (ed. Jonathan Z. Smith; Chicago Studies in the History of Judaism; Chicago, IL: The University of Chicago Press, 1982), pp. 19-35.

Söderbergh Widding, Astrid, 'From Grammar to Graphics: The Concept of Text in Cinema Studies', in *Travelling Concepts: Text, Subjectivity, Hybridity* (ed. Joyce Goggin and Sonja Neef; Amsterdam: ASCA Press, 2001), pp. 67-77.

Southwood, Katherine, 'Die ‚heilige Nachkommenschaft' und die ‚fremden Frauen': ‚Mischehen' als inner-jüdische Angelegenheit', in *Zwischen Integration und Ausgrenzung: Migration, religiöse Identität(en) und Bildung—theologisch reflektiert* (ed. Johanna Rahner and Miriam Schambeck; Bamberger Theologisches Forum, 13; Münster: LIT Verlag, 2011), pp. 61-82.

—*Ethnicity and the Mixed Marriage Crisis in Ezra 9-10: An Anthropological Approach* (Oxford Theological Monograph Series; Oxford: Oxford University Press, 2012).

Sparks, James T., *The Chronicler's Genealogies: Towards an Understanding of 1 Chronicles 1–9* (Academia Biblica, 28; Atlanta, GA: Society of Biblical Literature, 2008).

Spencer, John R., 'Levitical Cities', *ABD* IV, pp. 310-11.

Stamm, J.J., 'Hebräische Frauennamen', in *Hebräische Wortforschung: Festschrift zum 80. Geburtstag von Walter Baumgartner* (ed. G.W. Anderson *et al.*; VTSup, 16; Leiden, E.J. Brill, 1967), pp. 301-39.

Steins, Georg, *Die Chronik als kanonisches Abschlußphänomen: Studien zur Entstehung und Theologie von 1/2 Chronik* (BBB, 93; Weinheim: Beltz Athenäum, 1995).

Sternberg, Meir, *The Poetics of Biblical Narrative: Ideological Literature and the Drama of Reading* (Indiana Studies in Biblical Literature; Bloomington, IN: Indiana University Press, 1987).

Sterring, Ankie, 'The Will of the Daughters', in *A Feminist Companion to Exodus and Deuteronomy* (ed. Athalya Brenner; Sheffield: Sheffield Academic Press, 1994), pp. 88-99.

Stoler, Ann L., 'Colonial Archives and the Arts of Governance', *Archival Science* 2 (2002), pp. 87-109.

—*Along the Archival Grain: Epistemic Anxieties and Colonial Common Sense* (Princeton, NJ: Princeton University Press, 2009).

Strathern, Marilyn, *After Nature: English Kinship in the Late Twentieth Century* (Cambridge: Cambridge University Press, 1992).

Talstra, Eep, *Oude en Nieuwe Lezers: Een inleiding in de methoden van uitleg van het Oude Testament* (Kampen: Kok, 2002).

Taylor, Diana, *The Archive and the Repertoire: Reforming Cultural Memory in the Americas* (Durham, NC: Duke University Press, 2003).

Vollmer, Ulrike, 'Sprechen, Hören, und dann? Film und Theologie im Dialog', *Medienheft* (2003), pp. 1-10.

—*Seeing Film and Reading Feminist Theology: A Dialogue* (Yew York: Palgrave Macmillan, 2007).

Wacker, Marie-Theres, 'Die Bücher der Chronik: Im Vorhof der Frauen', in *Kompendium Feministische Bibelauslegung* (ed. Marie-Theres Wacker and Luise Schottroff; Gütersloher Verlagshaus: Gütersloh, 3rd edn, 2007), pp. 146-55.

Wahlberg, Malin, *Documentary Time: Film and Phenomenology* (Minneapolis, MN: University of Minnesota Press, 2008).

Wareham, David C., *Elsevier's Dictionary of Herpetological and related Terminology* (Amsterdam: Elsevier, 2005).

Waterton, Claire, 'Experimenting with the Archive: STS-ers As Analysts and Co-constructors of Databases and Other Archival Forms', in *STHV* 35.5 (2010), pp. 645-76.

Weber, Max, *Die protestantische Ethik und der Geist des Kapitalismus* (Tübingen: J.C.B. Mohr, 1934).

Weigel, Sigrid, '"Generation" as a Symbolic Form: On the Genealogical Discourse of Memory since 1945', in *The Germanic Review* 77 (2002), pp. 264-77.

Wellhausen, Julius, *Prolegomena zur Geschichte Israels* (Berlin: W. de Gruyter, 6th edn, repr. 1927).

Westermann, Claus, *Genesis 37–50* (BKAT, I/3; Neukirchen–Vluyn: Neukirchener Verlag, 1982).

Wetter, Anne-Mareike, 'Verschuivende Visies: De Kronist over de rol van de vrouw', in *Nederlands theologisch tijdschrift* 65.3 (2011), pp. 227-41.

Wieringen, Willien van, 'Why Some Women Were Included in the Genealogies of 1 Chronicles 1–9', in *Rewriting Biblical History: Essays on Chronicles and Ben Sira in Honour of Pancratius C. Beentjes* (ed. Jeremy Corley and Harm van Grol; DCLSt, 7; Berlin: W. de Gruyter, 2011), pp. 291-300.

Willi, Thomas, 'Late Persian Judaism and its Conception of an Integral Israel according to Chronicles: Some Observations on Form and Function of the Genealogy of Judah in 1 Chronicles 2.3–4.23', in *Second Temple Studies: 2. Temple Community in the Persian Period* (ed. Tamara C. Eskenazi and Kent H. Richards; Sheffield: Sheffield Academic Press, 1994), pp. 146-62.

—*1 Chr 1–10* (BKAT, XXIV/1; Neukirchen–Vluyn: Neukirchener Verlag, 2009).

Williamson, H.G.M., *1 and 2 Chronicles* (NCB, 20; Grand Rapids, MI: Eerdmans, 1982).

Wilson, Robert R., *Genealogies and History in the Biblical World* (New Haven, CT: Yale University Press, 1977).

Wolde, Ellen van, 'Trendy Intertextuality?', in *Intertextuality in Biblical Writings: Essays in Honour of Bas van Iersel* (ed. Sipke Draisma; Kampen: Kok, 1989), pp. 43-49.

—'Intertextuality: Ruth in Dialogue with Tamar', in *A Feminist Companion to the Bible: Approaches, Methods and Strategies* (ed. Athalya Brenner and Carole Fontaine; Sheffield: Sheffield Academic Press, 2nd edn, 1997), pp. 426-51.

Wright, C.J.H., 'Family', *ABD* II, p. 762.

Wright, Melanie J., *Moses in America: The Cultural Uses of Biblical Narrative* (Oxford: Oxford University Press, 2002).

Zakovitch, Yair, 'Inner-Biblical Interpretation', in *Reading Genesis: Ten Methods* (ed. Ronald Hendel; Cambridge: Cambridge University Press, 2010), pp. 92-118.

Online Resources

Filmography of Angelika Levi, http://www.german-films.de/app/filmarchive/film_view.php?film_id=975 (accessed June 8, 2013).

Trailer of *My Life Part 2* on YouTube, http://www.youtube.com/watch?v=IMarqtWIowY (accessed June 8, 2013).

Information about *My Life Part 2* on the *Berlinale* Website, http://www.berlinale.de/external/de/filmarchiv/doku_pdf/20031008.pdf (accessed June 8, 2013).

Information about *My Life Part 2* and an interview with the filmmaker by Stefanie Schulte Strathaus, http://www.arsenal-berlin.de/forumarchiv/forum2003/katalog/mein_leben_teil_2.pdf (accessed June 8, 2013).

Interview with the filmmaker Angelika Levi on YouTube, http://www.youtube.com/watch?v=0neLtUTdJ3o (accessed June 8, 2013).

Motivation of the reward from the *Duisburger Filmwoche*, http://www.duisburger-filmwoche.de/festival03/ (accessed June 8, 2013).

Advertisement of the film-series *Divided History: The Meaning of the Shoah in the Life of the Descendents of Persecutors and Survivors* in Vienna in 2004, http://www.kinoki.at/mikrokino/pro/p112.htm (accessed June 8, 2013).

Excerpt from the program of the *San Francisco Jewish Film Festival*, http://www.sfjff.org/film/detail?id=2074 (accessed June 8, 2013).

Festival advertisement of the *6th Annual Barcelona Jewish Film Festival*, http://www.accesomedia.com/display_release.html?id=16885 (accessed November 17, 2010).

International research group *Film and Theology*, http://www.film-und-theologie.de/ (accessed June 8, 2013).

Exposé of *Literaturtage 2008*: 'Am Nullpunkt der Familie: Generationen und Genealogien in der Gegenwartsliteratur' at Zentrum für Literatur- und Kulturforschung Berlin, http://www.zfl-berlin.org/veranstaltungen-detail/items/am-nullpunkt-der-familie-generationen-und-genealogien-in-der-geg.html (accessed June 8, 2013).

Leo Englisch-Deutsch Wörterbuch, Forum, 'vergesellschaften', 26.04.2004, 20:49, http://dict.leo.org/forum/viewUnsolvedquery.php?idThread=176430&idForum=1&lp=en de&lang=de (accessed June 8, 2013).

Photograph of the altar windows of the church of the Apostles in Hamburg Eimsbüt-
tel, http://www.kirche.eimsbuettel.de/kg.root/kg.1123301410.22/kg.1123301410.
22.2/index.html (accessed June 8, 2013).

INDEX OF AUTHORS

Super clear writing style
Strong counter argument antithesis
No access to the film - a negative

memory vs. archive: how do these interplay?
when does she see one; &
when the other?

Performance Studies] drops these w/o much
Archive Theory $ context & or clarity in
how they're useful]

Does the film predispose what she sees in
the text?

↓

Mieke Bal - Jello chapter
intention vs. performance

What is the effect of reading/viewing
trauma lit? Does it reinscrib trauma?
Perpetrate it?
↳ who decides what qualifies as
trauma?
↳ Are two traumas comparable, or are
the experiences too complex & individual.

Appropriate Traumatic Legacy - pg 161
- who does trauma belong to?
- is it healthy to appropriate it
- traumatic legacy — why pass this
on?

Who writes these things? For whom?
Who reads? Does readerly position matter?

"Rediscovering Eve - Does Meyers already
make the point   p 183-4

What is the trauma?

w film fills in gaps to make Chr a
narrative- Chr. fills gaps to make film a genealogy